RED SCARE!

RED SCARE!

Right-wing Hysteria
Fifties Fanaticism
and Their Legacy
in Texas

BY DON E. CARLETON

★

TexasMonthlyPress

Texas Monthly Press, Inc.
P.O. Box 1569
Austin, Texas 78767

A B C D E F G H

Library of Congress Cataloging in Publication Data

Carleton, Don E., 1947–
   Red scare!

   Bibliography: p.
   Includes index.
   1. Subversive activities—Texas—Houston—History—
20th century. 2. Houston (Tex.)—History. 3. Internal
security—Texas—Houston—History—20th century.
I. Title.
F394.H857C37   1985   976.4′1411063   84-24007
ISBN 0-932012-90-6

To the memory of
 Genvieve Marie Carleton
 Ernest G. Young
 and Louis J. Kestenberg

CONTENTS

FOREWORD
BY JOHN HENRY FAULK

It was a dreadful time in the land. Some called it Scoundrel Time. Others called it the Time of the Toad. Historians call it the McCarthy Era. It was a time when intimidation and repression overwhelmed orderly political processes, a time when denigrating epithets and vicious labels were substituted for rational political dialogue, a time when mindless fear and hysteria swept away common sense and resulted in a terror whose repercussions were felt in all branches of our government and in the minds and conduct of the people of the United States. Above all, it was a time when vigilantism took over our national life.

A vigilante, by definition, is one who believes (or claims to believe) that the laws of the land and the institutions that enact, administer, and enforce those laws are not capable of protecting society from some real or imagined danger that the vigilante perceives to be imminent. The vigilante joins with like-minded neighbors, and the group appoints itself the judge, the jury, the prosecuting attorney, and the executioner of those believed to constitute the danger. The danger takes on the attributes of the Antichrist; thus anyone who does not publicly condemn it becomes suspected of supporting it.

Vigilantism creates and orchestrates an atmosphere of suspicion and fear, the sine qua non for the exercising of vigilante "justice." Such "justice" is the very antithesis of our traditional Anglo-American system of justice. In fact, established legal processes are often viewed with deep distrust. Vigilante justice upends the judicial maxim that an accused person is presumed innocent until proven guilty by due process of law. In the world of the vigilante, the accused is presumed guilty until proven innocent to the satisfaction of the vigilante. Usually this is achieved by the accused's embracing the opinions of the vigilante. Don Carleton's masterful dissection of the Houston Red Scare of three decades ago is what makes his brilliant study such an important work. He has delineated every wrinkle and seamy furrow in the grim visage of vigilantism.

Of course, Houston is not the only community in which such Red Scares flourished. Dozens of communities had fully orchestrated variations on the Houston Red Scare theme going on at that time. For instance, the Red Scare that was sweeping through the entertainment world from Hollywood to New York left a trail of destroyed reputations, blasted careers, and destitute victims in its wake.

I managed to get a ringside seat for that Red Scare. I got caught up in one of its insidious manifestations—blacklisting. I can't think of anything that educates a person on vigilantism as effectively as the experience of being one of its victims does. I considered myself qualified for a Ph.D. on the subject before I was finished with it.

There are several important conclusions that Carleton reaches about the Red Scare. They correspond with the conclusions I reached on the subject. These conclusions are rather startling when one first confronts them. Then they become so obvious that one wonders why they were not understood from the very first.

These are some of the most important:

1. In spite of the great hue and cry about traitors and a Communist conspiracy raised by Senator McCarthy and his imitators during the Red Scares, they never produced a single Communist spy whose guilt was proved in court. Nor was a single person ever indicted for treason, let alone tried for the crime. In other words, the whole Red Scare business, from beginning to end, stands condemned by history as a colossal fraud on the American public. Even today, thirty years later, few people admit this truth.

2. In Houston, and in other communities where Red Scares flourished, some of the most affluent and respected citizens often actively engaged in vigilantism or gave their approval. They did so, shamefully enough, not because they believed that the community was threatened by subversion but because they saw an opportunity to strengthen their political advantages.

3. That "bulwark of liberty," our free press, behaved most slavishly in the midst of Red Scares. The media not only aided and abetted the vigilantism but also often instigated and orchestrated the witch-hunt, hiring experts on subversion to write the inflammatory pieces on the peril threatening the community.

4. The tactics and attitudes of the vigilantes took on the character and qualities of the totalitarians that the vigilantes claimed to oppose and despise.

5. The main victims of the vigilantism of that period were the ideals and principles upon which this republic is founded. Perhaps one of the greatest tributes to the founding fathers' vision and wisdom is that the republic they founded survived that terrible period.

PREFACE

In the fall semester of 1968 I was a student teacher assigned as part of my formal training to observe the American history classroom of a veteran Houston Independent School District teacher. That year was one of the most tumultuous in recent American history, and I was eager to hear some of the issues of the day discussed and debated by the teacher and students under my observation.

Although the school hallways buzzed with talk about such topics as the Vietnam war, the recent assassinations of Dr. Martin Luther King and Senator Robert F. Kennedy, and the Nixon-Humphrey presidential contest, that talk was not allowed in the classroom. Instead, my teaching supervisor refused to mention anything that had occurred after World War II. Discussion and debate were vigorously discouraged. Aware of the students' discontent and boredom and full of my own brand of youthful impatience, I eventually confronted my assigned mentor about the situation. He looked at me with weary eyes, smiled, put his hand on my shoulder, and said, "Son, have you ever heard of McCarthyism?" I replied, "Yes, but so what?"

Over the course of the next few weeks, during his "off-period," my supervising teacher explained the relevancy of that comment and the source of his timidity and caution. He talked about the Minute Women, George Ebey, John Rogge, the Committee for Sound American Education, and other personalities and events of the Red Scare that were etched in his memory. Although it was 1968 and the Red Scare was seemingly a dead issue, at least one Houston public school teacher acted as though it could return at any moment. As a result of his experiences in Houston during the 1950s, this teacher had decided to adhere rigidly to educational conformity and never to discuss anything in the classroom that anyone might perceive as controversial.

This book is rooted in the curiosity created sixteen years ago by my discussions with that Red Scare–scarred teacher. That curiosity was subsequently converted into a systematic research project as a result of the influence of the late Louis J. Kestenberg, a professor of history at the University of Houston. My personal and professional debts to Dr. Kestenberg go well beyond this book.

John O. King, Richard Younger, George T. Morgan, and James M. Poteet read early drafts of this manuscript and made invaluable suggestions for improvement. Harold M. Hyman, Deborah Bauer, and Robert

Haynes critiqued an early version of chapter six, a portion of which first appeared in the *Houston Review* (Spring, 1981). L. Tuffly Ellis and his editorial staff likewise improved an early draft of chapter seven that appeared in a slightly different form in the *Southwestern Historical Quarterly* (October, 1976). I owe a special editorial debt to Tom Kreneck, Kate Adams, and John Henry Faulk. They not only suffered through patchwork-quilt copies of a book in progress but they also helped with my research, gave up their own free time to discuss and argue ideas, and generally provided crucial moral support. Scott Lubeck of Texas Monthly Press encouraged me to finish this project when I had doubts. His strong interest has meant much to me.

This book could not have been written without the cooperation of the many individuals who agreed to share with me their memories and, in some cases, their papers. Most of these individuals are listed in the oral history references in the endnotes. I am grateful to them all.

My special thanks go to Mrs. Ralph S. O'Leary and George W. Ebey. I also benefited from the help of archivists and librarians at the Lyndon B. Johnson Library, the Dwight D. Eisenhower Library, the Texas State Archives, the Library of Congress, the Labor Archives at the University of Texas at Arlington, the Sheridan County Public Library in Wyoming, the Sam Houston Research Center, the Houston Metropolitan Research Center, and the Humanities Research Center and Barker Texas History Center of the University of Texas at Austin. Other individuals who have helped in different ways include Vickie Vogel, Harold Billings, Michael Gillette, Mimi Crossley, Carol Williams, Norman Spellman, Beverly Garrett, Sherri Richardson, Beth Cotner, Denise Miller, Mary Hill, Louis Marchiafava, and Maury Maverick, Jr. Most of the final draft of this book was written in splendid seclusion in Big Horn, Wyoming. This was made possible through the generous hospitality of Christy Love and John Kings. The O'Connor Foundation and Parten Foundation provided crucial research grants through the Texas State Historical Association. For this financial aid I especially thank Louise O'Connor, Major Jubal R. Parten, John Henry Faulk, and L. Tuffly Ellis.

Finally, because so much of this book was researched and written during weekends and on "vacations," my wife, Suzanne, probably deserves credit as a coauthor simply from having had to endure it all. Suzanne did more than endure, however; she provided inspiration and motivation and I am profoundly grateful to her.

                                                    DON E. CARLETON
                                                    November, 1984

PROLOGUE

In a nation in which every man is supposed to be on the make, there is an overriding fear of being taken in.

—David Brion Davis[1]

Doctor George Ebey carefully unfolded his handkerchief and wiped beads of perspiration from his forehead. The heat and humidity of a typical August night in Houston made the forty-five-year-old educator long for the relief of the cool air of his native northern California. Ebey quickly pushed such distractions from his mind, however, as he entered the meeting room of the Houston school board. This was only Ebey's second night in Houston and he could adjust to the uncomfortable Gulf Coast climate. Besides, he was too excited about his new job as deputy superintendent of the Houston public schools to let anything as mundane as the weather bother him.[2]

A descendant of Danish-American pioneers, George Ebey was a large man—well over six feet tall—with a rapidly receding hairline and a full and kind face that expressed a self-confidence others sometimes perceived as arrogance. Bright, gregarious, and ambitious, Ebey was delighted to be in Texas' largest city. As a fast rising "star" in the educational world, Ebey planned to use Houston as the final step up the career ladder to his ultimate professional goal: the superintendency of a large school district.

Bill Moreland, superintendent of Houston schools and Ebey's boss, met Ebey at the board room entrance and escorted him to his chair. Moreland was a soft-spoken native Texan in his mid fifties whose demeanor radiated competency and decency. But Moreland's eyes revealed an inner sadness that troubled Ebey. It occurred to the veteran educator from California that here was an administrator under much pressure. As Moreland's new second in command, Ebey resolved to do what he could to relieve that pressure.

After Ebey took his seat, several school trustees came by to welcome him to his first board meeting. As the trustees went to their places in front, Ebey glanced around the austere, unornamented room. He was pleasantly surprised to see the large converted former high school classroom half-filled with spectators. Such a turnout on a hot night during summer vacation impressed Ebey. He had heard of a few controversies related to the city's school system and was aware that someone had produced a pamphlet protesting his own employment, but he remained unconcerned. Controversies were a fact of life for public school administrators; they came with the job. In the seven years following the end of the Second World War, public education had endured a host of new problems, usually related to crowded classrooms and a shortage of teachers. Ebey preferred to deal with situations caused by parents interested in their children's schools rather than problems resulting from parental apathy.

As Ebey continued to look around the room he noticed a group of about twenty-five stern-looking women staring at him in what he interpreted as a rather unfriendly manner. His smiles in their direction went unreciprocated. He noted that they seemed to know one another. A mere curiosity, Ebey told himself as he focused attention on the opening of the board meeting.

Holger Jeppeson, chairman of the board, introduced Dr. Ebey as the school district's new deputy superintendent and officially welcomed him to Houston. Ebey acknowledged the introduction with a smile and a nod. His smile disappeared, however, when three women sitting among the group he had noticed earlier asked for permission to address the board and present information about Ebey's "background." The board chairman frowned but reluctantly agreed.[3]

The first to speak, Norma Louise Barnett, was a stout woman in her late forties with beefy arms and sharp facial features similar to those of a predatory bird. Barnett stood and faced the school board, charging that while in Portland, Oregon, Ebey had recommended to the city's teachers a film, *The House I Live In*, that, she alleged, had been written by Albert Maltz. Maltz, one of the "Hollywood Ten," had been sent to prison in 1947 by the House Committee on Un-American Activities (HCUA) for contempt of Congress. The second accuser was Barnett's good friend Anne Harrison. Shorter than Norma Barnett, Anne Harrison had a plump, cherubic face and a simple mind. Ebey was not only a subversive who recommended films written by Communists, said Harrison, but he also encouraged race mixing. Harrison announced that she had evidence that indicated Ebey had allowed black teachers to teach white children in the Portland schools. Anne Harrison sat down and a young, attractive woman named Mary Drouin made the last accusation. Drouin told the board that Ebey had forced the Portland schools to use subversive literature written by Maxwell Stewart and H. L. Kilpatrick. According to Mary Drouin, Stewart belonged to no less than twenty Communist front organizations and Kilpatrick nine. Kilpatrick was also a "progressive" educator who favored an unstructured curriculum and opposed student report cards, Drouin declared, adding that such ideas would lead children "down the road to socialism and uniformity" by eliminating all incentives for individual achievement. Before sitting down, Mary Drouin turned toward Ebey and asked him if he planned to continue his subversive ways in Houston.[4]

Ebey, dismayed by this turn of events, nonetheless responded with a vigorous defense. He stood and asked the young woman if she really believed what she said. Mary Drouin replied, "You're trying to confuse me. We are here to ask questions, not to answer them." She then retreated to her chair. Ebey faced his accusers and declared his "violent" dislike of Communism and stated that he firmly opposed the employment of Communists in the public schools. Ebey, denying the women's charges, turned back to face the school board, declaring that he also opposed "witch burning and intimidating good American teachers."

The women's attack startled Ebey's boss, Bill Moreland, and angered some members of the school board. One board member, Jimmy Delmar, scolded the women and told them that they had acted "underhandedly and in an un-American way." Having given the women their hearing, the board proceeded to other business. The women remained, however, staring at Ebey and cooling themselves with their furiously flapping fans.

Ebey, outwardly self-assured and calm but inwardly anxious and confused, coveted one of those fans to alleviate the discomfort of what by now had become an unbearably hot room. The remainder of the board meeting echoed in Ebey's ears as though it were being conducted in a cave. He searched his mind for an explanation for this wearisome development. The brief meeting seemed interminably lengthy to Ebey.

After the meeting adjourned, Bill Moreland and others apologized to Ebey. The educator shrugged his shoulders and said he would forget it. Out of the corner of his eye, however, Ebey could see the women congregating by the exit, waiting to confront him. He excused himself, turned, and walked through the group, trying to avoid them. As he passed through the door, one matronly woman asked if he supported the United Nations. Believing that this was safe ground, Ebey turned and answered that Americans were fighting in Korea under the UN command and that he believed it to be a patriotic duty to support the organization. As Ebey walked away from his accusers he heard one of the women loudly exclaim, "They'd rather be dying under their own flag than under that dirty blue rag [of the UN]!"

Ebey hurriedly left the building and walked down the sidewalk. The Houston school administration building was on the edge of the city's rapidly expanding central business district. Ebey gazed at the light streaming from the windows of skyscrapers rising from the flat Gulf Coast terrain. Questions ran through his head this night of August 18, 1952. What was happening to him? Who were those women? What kind of place is this? Ebey feared that he would know soon enough. He decided to return to his room in the Sam Houston Hotel and telephone his wife, Leonor, back in Portland. She and their two small children would soon be driving more than two thousand miles to join him in their new city.

Before Ebey could get away, however, Martin Dreyer, a reporter for the Houston *Chronicle* and a political liberal, asked Ebey to join him at the Houston Press Club to wash away thoughts of the women protesters with a cool beverage. Ebey was more than willing. The new deputy superintendent glanced down and noticed that his once carefully folded handkerchief was now carelessly wadded up in his hand and soaked with perspiration. He stuffed it in his pants pocket and walked away with Dreyer.[5]

George Ebey did not know on that August night in 1952 that he had come to a city convulsed by its own virulent version of what has become known as America's second Red Scare. A dominant facet of life during the post–World War II decade in the United States, the Red Scare was characterized by a widespread series of actions by individuals and groups whose intentions were to frighten Americans "with false and highly exaggerated charges of Communist subversion for the purpose of political, economic, and psychological profit." The usual tactic employed by those carrying out the Red Scare is known as "McCarthyism": the use of indiscriminate, often unfounded accusations, inquisitorial investigative methods, and sensationalism ostensibly in the suppression of Communism. English historian David Caute has written that the anti-Communist hysteria of the late 1940s through the 1950s was "perhaps the greatest crisis that America has ever suffered in terms of her liberal and democratic values." The Red Scare permeated nearly every aspect of American culture, but its most well known symbol was Joseph R. McCarthy, the Republican senator from Wisconsin whose own behavior provided a name for the principal Red Scare technique.[6]

George Ebey, of course, was well aware of the national Red Scare. He and millions of other Americans had followed the frightening national and international events of the postwar era that included the development of the atomic bomb by the Soviet Union, the Communist victory in China, the Soviet occupation of Eastern Europe, the Berlin crisis, the Alger Hiss affair, and the seemingly never-ending disclosures about alleged subversives and "Red" spies ensconced in the federal government. Ebey had watched the activities of Senator McCarthy and the House Committee on Un-American Activities with disgust as they hurled unsubstantiated charges and compiled lists to use against their fellow citizens. Ebey had already dealt with incidents in his own career indirectly related to irrational anti-Communism and the Cold War, but he had never been a target of Red Scare groups. This would no longer be true. George Ebey was the wrong man coming to the wrong place at the wrong time. As a result, he would become a victim.[7]

His story, however, is but a part of a much larger one. The city of Houston after the Second World War was caught up in rapid growth and change, unsettling enough to encourage fear among those unable to adjust. An economic and industrial transformation was occurring that helped spawn new labor unions and attract persons to the city espousing political views more liberal than the norm. A power elite existed in the city, one whose members wished, among other things, to return the Republican party to power in Washington, purge the federal government of its New Deal–Fair Deal inheritance, and keep the Russians, blacks, and labor unions in their respective places. This power elite was willing to Red-bait and print scare stories in the newspapers it controlled to achieve its goals. Just as in other communities throughout the United States, there existed in postwar Houston a relatively small group of individuals who were politically extreme "true believers," anxious for recognition and credibility and eager to lead a local ideological crusade against fellow Houstonians with opinions and life-styles different from their own. Because the public school system represented an intellectual pathway into Houston for the beliefs and ideas of the outside world, these true believers focused much of their attention on it—a communal institution already coming under the severe strains of the "baby boom," educational reform, and dramatic racial change.

These and other factors, complex and diverse, intermingled with the influence of international, national, and state events to give Texas' largest city its own version of the Red Scare in the 1950s. What occurred and how and why it happened is the story that follows. To better understand it, one must know something about Houston and its past.

ONE

A NERVOUS NEW CIVILIZATION

*"Was Houston here last year?" asked a visitor. . . . "Of course,"
said her friend, the local. "Why?" "Because," said the newcomer,
"it looks like they built everything last week."*

—*Thomas Thompson*

*. . . when there's rapid change there are just a lot of usable,
intense human dramas that will develop.*

—*Larry McMurtry*[1]

Two rather unimpressive streams, White Oak Bayou and Buffalo Bayou,
merge at a point on the flat Texas Gulf coastal plain approximately fifty
miles north of Galveston Island. It was near the confluence of those
bayous that Augustus Allen, a native of Brooklyn, New York, sat in 1836
and, using his top hat as a table, sketched the plat of a town he and his
brother John hoped to build. The Allen brothers, typical Americans of
the Jacksonian era, moved from New York to the then Mexican province
of Texas in 1832. They were driven by the same urge that had motivated
many who had preceded them and many more who would follow in the
years to come: the desire to acquire wealth as rapidly as possible through
land speculation. In August of 1836, four months after the defeat of Santa
Anna's Mexican army at San Jacinto, the Allens purchased the south half
of the lower league of the John Austin grant situated at the head of tide
on Buffalo Bayou for $5,000. Almost at once, the Allens began selling lots
and promoting their new "city," shrewdly naming it after Sam Houston,
the hero of the newly established Republic of Texas. After much effort,
they persuaded the government of the Republic to make Houston
the capital.[2]

From the first, Houston became a speculative town whose communal
ethos would be the philosophy of liberated capitalism, the belief in
the superiority and sacredness of the individual's right to promote,
build, buy, and sell without outside restraint or control. The persistence
and continuity of this ethos has shaped nearly every aspect of Houston's
historical development. It created a city characterized by rapid growth,
boosterism, and the constant presence of people very much "on the
make."[3]

Houston's development paralleled that of the rest of Texas. The city lost its status as a capital in 1839 but it soon firmly established itself as a commercial center. It endured the Civil War without much effect. By the middle of the 1870s, Houston had evolved from a frontier society to a minor southern town as a result of the construction of a few railroads, the development of the cotton trade, and the virtual elimination of the dreaded yellow fever.[4]

Houston consolidated its position as an important Texas town during the last two decades of the nineteenth century. The growth of the lumber and cotton trades pushed the town forward economically and population continued to increase steadily. Yet, as late as the 1890s, Galveston reigned as the most important town of the Texas Gulf Coast. This pattern of steady growth would end as the new century began. The twentieth century roared into Houston with a mighty hurricane and the surge of a monumental oil discovery. These events began a process that would transform Houston into the largest city in Texas and an important southern urban center.[5]

On September 8, 1900, a catastrophic hurricane almost obliterated Galveston, killing over six thousand people. From that point on, Galveston would never again challenge Houston for commercial supremacy. As a direct result of the storm's devastation, important merchants and bankers on the island began to realize that they had to move their businesses inland, to Houston, for protection from the ravages of the unpredictable Gulf of Mexico. This movement accelerated in 1915 after another costly storm. A second event of even greater significance for Houston's growth occurred on January 19, 1901, with the discovery of oil at Spindletop near Beaumont. Other important oil discoveries near Houston made the city the logical location for a burgeoning new petroleum empire.[6]

Intimately related to the development of the oil industry in Houston was the completion of a long-dreamed-of deep water ship channel in 1914. The completion of the channel equaled the discovery of oil as a significant factor in Houston's growth from 1900 to 1920. Once Houston became a true seaport its growth potential became unlimited. By 1919, Houston's railroad system, ship channel, lumber and cotton trades, and oil industry had all received an enormous boost from the requirements of a war economy. World War I provided the final surge for Houston to join the ranks of the South's most important cities. Not only did new wealth come to Houston, but the enormous changes of the era from 1900 to 1920 also brought new people. In 1900, approximately 44,000 people lived in Houston. By 1920 that number had increased to nearly 140,000, a staggering 214 percent increase in population.[7]

Other aspects of Houston's development reflected its maturation as a city in this era. As in other sections of the United States, when many towns were becoming cities, urbanism was partly defined as a process of providing cultural amenities. Nineteenth-century civil leaders recognized that in "true" cities one could find theaters, libraries, museums, universities, and music appreciation societies. Houston followed this pattern. After 1900, the city slowly acquired a few of the cultural and educational institutions indicative of its new growth. As a result of a gift from Andrew Carnegie, a public library opened in 1904. Rice Institute opened its doors in 1912. A symphony society was formed in 1913 that later created and supported a symphony orchestra. The Houston Art League, founded in 1900, eventually opened a fine arts museum in 1924.[8]

Houston also expanded in geographic size as real estate speculators promoted new suburbs and land developments. Probably the most significant of all the new subdivisions during this period was River Oaks. Planned, built, and promoted by Will Hogg, Mike Hogg, and Hugh Potter, River Oaks symbolized another aspect of Houston's new position of power. From the very beginning this new land development was planned as a community where Houston's new entrepreneurial elite could live in an ordered, protective environment separated from the chaotic growth it had helped to create. The need for such a community reflected the existence of a new entrepreneurial leadership group in the city.[9]

Typically American, Houston's history has always been greatly determined by the decisions and actions of entrepreneurial elites. But with the discovery of oil and the subsequent expansion of business, Houston's entrepreneurial elite possessed a degree of wealth and power unheard-of in its precity stage. Oil money and the wealth produced by its various "spin-offs" created an informal group whose power now transcended the community and went beyond the city limits. Such men as Will Hogg, oil man and land developer; John Henry Kirby, lumber baron; Ross Sterling, a founder of the Humble Oil Company; Joseph S. Cullinan, founder of the Texas Company (Texaco); and Jesse H. Jones, banker, builder, and commercial real estate developer were generally acknowledged to be among the city's unofficial decision-making group. The actions and inactions of this group would be a factor in determining the societal repercussions of Houston's future growth explosion after World War I. In the 1920s, the building of River Oaks and other exclusive subdivisions symbolized the new wealth and power of this group and its perceived need to separate physically and geographically from ordinary Houstonians.[10]

Another indication of Houston's new wealth and rapid growth as a result of the changes of the period from 1900 to 1920 was an expansive building program. A construction boom swept the central business district from 1921 to 1928, creating a skyline appropriate to Houston's new prestige. During the same period, Jesse H. Jones became the most important developer of commercial buildings in the city, constructing nearly thirty important business structures by 1929.[11]

By 1928, Jesse Jones had become the most prominent individual in the city. His influence was especially evident when the Texas Democratic party cast its votes for Jones as favorite son candidate for the presidential nomination at the 1928 national convention held in Houston. This convention, attracted to Houston by Jones' financial enticements, was further evidence of Houston's new status. Newspaper reporters from all areas of the United States, bored with the inevitable first ballot nomination of Al Smith, focused attention on Houston as a "newly discovered" Texas city. The national press produced a multitude of stories announcing that Houston had taken its place among the major cities of the South and Southwest.[12]

While Houston possessed the population and economy to qualify as a full-fledged city, the transition from town to city was not easy for everyone. The rapidity of change was not only exciting, it was also, to some Houstonians, a frightening experience. All of the symbols of city maturation existed, but many residents had not yet accepted or adjusted to the inevitable disruptions resulting from rapid urbanization.

Former governor William P. Hobby would later recall, "World War I brought a change to the atmosphere of Houston." Rapid urbanization created diversity. It also brought an increase of crime and, to a degree, some social deterioration. A rapidly urbanizing society must inevitably contend with what many of its members perceive to be its most undesirable feature: a lack of moral or social conformity. "Lawlessness and looseness," the handmaidens of urban diverseness, frightened white Protestant Texans who had been recently transplanted into a strange environment and removed from the security of the rural community. Novelist and essayist William Goyen, who in 1923 at the age of eight moved with his family to Houston, later recalled the feelings of alienation among his newly arrived neighbors. Goyen remembered that "Houston in those early days seemed to me a place of the half-lost and the estranged, even the persecuted."[13]

Texas politicians, elite spokesmen, and newspapers excitedly denounced the "lawless epidemic" and disordered social conditions. At the same time, on the national level, a postwar hysteria had broken out, aimed at anything that did not conform to a rigid concept of Americanism. A product of wartime hostility and rabid nativism, the national Red Scare that immediately followed the end of World War I contributed to Houston's "change of atmosphere" during this crucial transition period. Rapid urbanization and its resultant dislocations, combined with elite rhetoric and the nation's first Red Scare, legitimated the efforts of those shrewd enough to understand and manipulate the new fears.[14]

In the early 1920s in Texas, many of those most affected by the problems of the town to city transition turned to the Ku Klux Klan. The white-hooded order promised to preserve the rural-minded Texan's conception of true morality. Scholars such as Kenneth Jackson and S. M. Lipset have demonstrated a correlation between the rapid growth of southwestern cities and the presence of the Klan chapters. Jackson found that although the Klan had strength in many southern small towns, its greatest strength could be found in the "growing cities of the region. . . ." Lipset concluded that the "most significant statistic is the one which indicates that Klan strength correlated with rate of population increase" and that this tended to validate the assumption that the Klan's strength "reflected the social strains imposed by rapid community growth."[15]

Accordingly, booming Houston was the first Texas city to have a Ku Klux Klan chapter. In 1920 the "secret society" formed the Sam Houston Klan Number One. The national Klan leadership appointed former Harris County deputy sheriff George B. Kimbro to be "Kleagle" for Texas with authority to organize chapters throughout the state. Houston thus became the base of operations for the Texas Klan. By the end of 1921, the Texas organization had acquired a degree of power and influence unsurpassed in any other state.[16]

In Houston and Dallas, the Klan was particularly active and membership steadily grew. Many members turned to the Klan as a means to enforce law and order. Klansmen in Houston became communications monitors, tapping telephone wires, intercepting messages at telegraph offices, and placing spies in the post office. The city's Klan chapter seems to have been particularly adept at spying on its fellow citizens. Spying was used for such diverse purposes as locating vice operations to determining the eligibility of the needy for the Klan's Christmas baskets.[17]

At first, Houston's power elite either supported or ignored the Klan. Mayor Oscar Holcombe joined the organization for a brief period. As Houston adjusted to its new status as an important southern city, however, disenchantment with the Klan quickly set in. Members of the civic and entrepreneurial power elite, such as Joseph S. Cullinan, John Henry Kirby, Ross Sterling, Will Hogg, and Jesse Jones, eventually perceived that the Klan was bad for business and that it encouraged rather than controlled disorder.[18] The city's "establishment," including the disillusioned Oscar Holcombe, withdrew its tacit approval and attacked the Klan. The opposition of Houston's elite, coupled with a quickly adjusting populace and a stabilizing national and local environment, eventually resulted in the Klan's decline. With the onset of the Great Depression of the 1930s, the Ku Klux Klan's power dwindled to impotence. Only scattered handfuls of hard-core extremist faithful remained to sustain the organization.[19]

The nationally disastrous stock market crash of 1929, followed by the Great Depression decade of the 1930s, did nothing to threaten Houston's status as an important city. Unlike the nation as a whole, the economic crisis of the early 1930s brought stabilization rather than stagnation. A less frenzied pattern of gradual and controlled growth marked the decade. For example, Houston's population increased from 138,000 in 1920 to 292,000 in 1930, an increase of 111.4 percent. The city increased in population from 1930 to 1940 by only 31.5 percent. Nevertheless, because of such influential leaders as Jesse Jones, who served as chairman of the Reconstruction Finance Corporation under President Franklin D. Roosevelt, and the city's petroleum-based economy, Houston remained financially healthy.[20]

As the 1930s drew to a close, contemporary observers believed that Houston had at last reached the ultimate stage of American urban evolution. Houston, with its population of approximately 385,000 in 1940, had seemingly ceased to be just a city. A worker for the Writers' Program of the Work Projects Administration earnestly boasted at the end of the 1930s that "at some unmarked time after 1919, Houston had ceased to be merely another large city and assumed the aspect of a modern metropolis." Another bragged that Houston's "cosmopolitan character" could be seen "on any busy downtown street corner."[21]

Boastful rhetoric about Houston's cosmopolitan status, however, failed to match reality. Even though it had grown rapidly since 1900, Houston remained a provincial city. In 1940, Houston ranked only twenty-first in size among United States cities. "Cosmopolitan" bragging ignored the fact that Houston was one of the largest cities in the nation with official racial segregation. It ignored the fact that a rural-oriented gubernatorial candidate, W. Lee ("Pappy") O'Daniel, could carry the city offering little more than the Ten Commandments as his basic political philosophy. Houston before World War II was still only a few years removed from the "hell fire faiths of the frontier." It was still small enough to be politically and economically controlled by a handful of powerful entrepreneurial civic elites whose informal decision making usually occurred over poker games in hotel suites and at race track clubs during group excursions out of state. The city's power structure was still close to being monolithic. In short, Houston was not a metropolis, ". . . that giant complex . . . swallowing the hinterland with its clusters of suburban communities and satellite cities." *Fortune* magazine, viewing the city from afar in 1939, simply concluded that "without oil Houston would be just another cotton town."[22]

Houston, however, stood at the threshold of an era of rapid change that would once again ignite a frenzy of growth and commence a new period of transition. World War II would begin the transition from city to true metropolis, a transition of rapid change that would produce, in conjunction with other factors, a new symbol of societal malaise comparable to the Ku Klux Klan of the 1920s. The Klan had disappeared, but its spirit and example remained, sustenance for new crusades for "100 percent" Americanism. The symbol of societal costs accompanying Houston's transition from city to metropolis would be the Red Scare of the early 1950s. The changes of World War II would come first.

Richard Polenberg has written that "Pearl Harbor marked more than the passing of a decade, it signified the end of an old era and the beginning of a new." World War II altered the character of American society, since the United States was more technological, industrial, and urban at the end of the war than it was when the war began. The overall national effects of World War II were especially noticeable within the South and Southwest. Certain American cities were microcosms for observing the rapid changes flowing out of the war. Houston was among the cities most affected by those changes.[23]

World War II provided the momentum that ultimately propelled Houston into the metropolitan stage of development. George Fuermann, a columnist for the Houston *Post* and a student of Houston's history, concluded that no period in the city's history approached the importance of World War II and the decade immediately following. "Before the war," Fuermann asserts, "Houston was an ambitious small city. A few years afterward . . . the city was altered in character, aspirations, and appearance."[24]

The needs of a modern war rapidly expanded the area's petroleum production and spawned completely new regional industries in chemicals and metals. The Texas Gulf Coast, with its cheap fuel and varied resources, proved to be a natural location for the new petrochemical industry. By the end of the war, Houston led the United States in value of industrial construction with over $850 million of petrochemical plant construction completed during the 1940s.[25]

The extent of war-spurred growth was as staggering as its rapidity. In ten short years between 1939 and 1949, Houston's industrial employment trebled, the annual value of its industrial products increased by 600 percent, and its consumption of natural gas increased by 400 percent. In 1940 there were 180 chemical employees in Houston; nine years later there were 20,000. Industrial payrolls increased from $194,000 in 1940 to $60 million in 1949. In 1948, the Association of State Planning and Development Agencies concluded that Houston was the center of the fastest expanding industrial section in America. Author John Gunther, visiting the area in 1947, observed that the "entire region between Houston and Beaumont seems, in fact, to be a single throbbing factory. . . ."[26] This boom in chemical and related industry growth was paralleled by an explosion of growth in all facets of Houston's urban development. Statistical indices for the period, such as telephone, electric, water, and gas connections, together with building permits and bank clearings, reveal the pace of Houston's rapid urbanization.[27]

More visible and publicized indicators of the city's rapid expansion confronted Houstonians following the war's end. On March 28, 1948, the Houston *Post* proclaimed in a front-page headline "The Great Deluge of Dollars," which announced the economic boom. A retail firm sold a downtown lot for $2,000 a front inch. The city council embarked on a $200 million public works project. Houston Lighting and Power completed a $30 million expansion of services to keep up with the city's growth. Work began in 1946 on the Texas Medical Center, which at that time consisted of one small hospital located in a forest within the city. After ten years and $50 million the project had become one of the nation's leading medical research, educational, and hospital centers.[28]

The sound of major construction echoed through the city. An editorial in the Houston *Post* noted that "there is the visual evidence of huge construction projects which confront the eye in all directions, and streets congested with an ever-increasing volume of traffic." One writer claimed that since the end of the war there had been no single time when Houston's downtown streets had been completely clear of carpenters' scaffolding. The writer, a newspaper columnist, complained that "one is almost afraid to park one's car in a vacant lot for fear of returning to find it on top of a thirty story building which has sprung up in the afternoon."[29]

One of the most significant changes wrought by World War II was the immense increase in population. George Fuermann noted that "Houston is a city of working people. They came in mass during the Second World War . . . and most remained." Theodore White, sent to Houston to report on postwar Texas, wrote that "most of the new city people are . . . farmers or ranchers from the Southwest . . . many are distant arrivals from New York or California . . . all have come here for the same reason: to seek their fortune."[30]

Whether they came from outside of Texas or from within the state's borders, people came in large numbers. A comparison of population increase in the 1930s with the 1940s reveals the effect World War II had on the area's population. From 1930 to 1940, Houston's population grew from 300,000 to 410,000, for a net gain of 110,000. By 1950, however, Houston's population had grown to over 726,000, a gain of over 315,000 people.[31]

Just as Theodore White observed the influx of newcomers and outsiders, so did the prewar residents. In an editorial, the Houston *Post* declared that Houston "is growing so fast it can't keep up with itself . . . outsiders have been—and are—pouring in on every train, bus, and airplane. . . ." When a population increases as rapidly as Houston's, those who arrived before the increase suddenly consider themselves to be natives, particularly when they compare themselves with those who came from out of state. While this perception never seemed to mean much to the vast majority of Houstonians, a fear of "outsiders" would surface later as one of the operative fears in Houston's Red Scare.[32]

While cultural maturity and urban cosmopolitanism does not develop overnight, the changes caused by World War II cast Houston into a transition period wherein the city acquired new symbols of culture and sophistication. The Museum of Fine Arts opened in 1924, but it remained a small and relatively insignificant musuem with a part-time director until after 1945. After the war, the museum grew in popularity, helped considerably by the city's new atmosphere. In 1953 the museum hired a full-time director and added a three thousand–square–foot wing.[33]

The Alley Theatre, destined to become one of the Southwest's most successful centers for the dramatic arts, opened in Houston shortly after the war. The Alley's opening was accompanied and followed by several "little theaters" and art galleries. George Fuermann noted at the time that only the symphony and one art museum predated World War II and concluded that "slowly, perceptibly, Houston is becoming cosmopolitan." John De Menil, a cultured Frenchman of wealth who adopted Houston as his home and was as responsible as anyone for the city's growing cultural awareness, declined to be as cautious as Fuermann. De Menil, commenting on how Houston had changed after the war, argued, ". . . you must not go to London, Paris, or New York to be cosmopolitan. Just open your ears and your eyes and here you have it, right in Houston."[34]

The change in Houston's economy, population, culture, and cosmopolitanism soon received its own symbolic monument in 1949 with the opening of the Shamrock Hotel. Built and operated by "wildcat" oil man Glenn McCarthy at a cost of $21 million, the hotel became an instant sensation. Its opening day symbolized perfectly the growing pains and confusion Houston experienced in its transition from city to metropolis. McCarthy, who allegedly served as Edna Ferber's inspiration for the character Jett Rink in her novel *Giant*, chartered a special sixteen-car private train and several airplanes to bring dozens of radio and movie stars from Hollywood to the opening. The National Broadcasting Company (NBC) carried the opening festivities over its radio network. An estimated 50,000 people turned out for the celebration, which quickly degenerated into total chaos. NBC cancelled the radio program while in progress because inebriated members of the audience reportedly seized the main microphone to yell and hoot salutations from Texas to the rest of the nation. The noise level from the unruly crowd made it impossible for the radio network's celebrities to be heard. One participant, who paid the $42 charge for the dinner served at the opening, complained that it was like "trying to eat dinner in the Notre Dame backfield."[35]

The Shamrock, located on extremely flat land five miles from downtown, seemed more massive and taller than it was in reality. McCarthy had its interior painted in sixty-seven shades of green to reflect his Irish heritage. Trying to evaluate the building's interior after a visit, famed architect Frank Lloyd Wright remarked, "I always wondered what the inside of a juke box looked like." Whether viewed from a negative or positive perspective, the Shamrock became a universally accepted symbol of Houston during the postwar decade. Writing in the Houston Chamber of Commerce magazine, Glenn McCarthy said he believed that his hotel marked the opening of a "new and more exhilarating era" in Houston. Others shared McCarthy's perception. Marguerite Johnston reflected that the hotel "[is] a bubble which seems to top and epitomize the turmoil of present day Houston. . . ." The *New York Times* declared simply that the Shamrock "[is] symbolic of . . . Houston."[36]

Not only did the Shamrock project an image of the city to the outside, it also gave some Houstonians a new self-image. George Fuermann observed that "if a specific combination of steel and brick could be said to have an influence on a city, then the Shamrock Hotel is a mighty . . . force in Houston, circa 1951." Tommy Thompson, a reporter for the Houston *Press* at the time, later recalled that Houston newspapers, "eager to establish a sophistication for the city, encouraged their gossip columnists to fabricate a racy dream world of beautiful people afloat on flying carpets of gold." Thus, like most cultural symbols, the Shamrock was larger than life and to some extent it symbolized the aspirations of Houston rather than the actual state of reality. As one pretty young socialite admitted while lounging by the hotel pool, "I like it here, its like you were somewhere else — not in Houston at all."[37]

Just as the Shamrock Hotel symbolized national prestige to many Houstonians, to others it symbolized the evils of cosmopolitanism, the embodiment of the wickedness of the new urbanism. *Time* magazine observed that the Shamrock was less a hotel than "a kind of Versailles."

Another observer believed that "it is to Houston roughly what Hollywood is to the world." George Fuermann wrote that "the Shamrock is the site of some of the most un-Texan scenes possible." The hotel's swimming pool was the daytime setting for a peculiar new sophisticated level in Houston. Fuermann labeled it the "Shamrock super-*haute monde*" and concluded that "Houston . . . never before had anything like it."[38]

Houston's almost instant transition from city to metropolis, while exciting and welcome to most of its citizens and civic leaders, nevertheless had its negative aspects. Eric Hoffer in *The Ordeal of Change* writes, "It is my impression that no one really likes the new. We are afraid of it . . . even in slight things the experience of the new is rarely without some stirring of foreboding." Contemporary observers of the new, postwar Houston could sense, underneath the general and surface excitement, an undercurrent of foreboding.[39]

One writer, when contemplating the changes in postwar Houston, concluded that they had affected the "people's collective nervous system." Theodore White observed that it seemed to him that the people were all strangers, "rootless in place or time." He too perceived a "nervous new civilization" in Texas' booming cities. George Fuermann noted that urban life is difficult enough, but to have it created so suddenly placed extra burdens on the "mass psyche." There are several cities that are "incomparably" larger than Houston, Fuermann wrote, but they experienced a gradual population expansion. He believed that "this sudden surge in population . . . puts the face of Houston a little on edge." Marguerite Johnston, writing in 1949 about Houston, concluded that "with the suddenness of the growth . . . has come the scars of growing pain." These scars were physical as well as mental. One former Houston reporter remembered the impact of the new petrochemical industry on the area in the late 1940s: "The air . . . noxious with fumes from a cauldron—sulphur, oil, petrochemicals, and gas fires—that burned every minute of the day and night, spewing excess into the skies."[40]

As the postwar decade wore on, collective restlessness and insecurity became more obvious. Marguerite Johnston reported that more and more Houstonians were vocally mourning "the loss of the small Southern city which Houston was before the war . . . their dismay is an understandable sentiment." In 1950, the Houston *Post* claimed that "the feeling of insecurity is running rampant."[41]

Houstonians, of course, had no monopoly on psychological insecurity in the postwar decade. Americans throughout the nation were caught up in the growing feeling of fear, confusion, and alienation. The war experience itself contributed much to the national mood, especially in terms of depersonalization. Hundreds of thousands of Americans experienced a type of forced regimentation for the first time in their lives during their service in the military. The tactical necessities of war further enhanced depersonalization by transforming the individual into a faceless number, moved and shifted from one locale to another as strategy demanded. This massive militarization had a decisive psychological impact. The regimentation of life continued after the war, as returning soldiers discovered a society increasingly dominated by the great corporate entities of business, labor, government, and the peacetime military. Most Americans found employment in one of these corporate organizations and quickly learned that the nature of these enterprises demanded conformity and a surrendering of individualism. One student of the period has called this mass process a "ubiquitous assault upon the self."[42]

While subordination of the self to the larger realities of organized American life had its negative results in terms of alienation, it also produced unprecedented economic rewards that created a massive middle class and some nouveaux riches. Many of these additions to the middle class found themselves ill at ease in their new status. They desperately desired peace and stability in society so that they could protect their new economic position. They were joined in this desire by those of sudden wealth, especially in Texas and such boom areas as southern California, who feared the expansion of government and organized labor. Richard Hofstadter, Daniel Bell, and others have argued that these groups suffered from status anxiety, a resentment against those in the established "old" elite who refused to accept them, and a fear of ill-defined forces that might take away their newly acquired place in society.[43]

Perhaps too much emphasis can and has been placed on such impressionistic statements about what was going on in the collective and individual minds of Houstonians and other Americans immediately after World War II. But there remains the fact that widespread fear and frustrations were identifiable facets of postwar American life, and this included Houston. The strains created by the altered structure of the nation's economic and social existence in the late 1940s and early 1950s produced an insecurity among ordinary Americans that provided fertile ground for anyone perceptive and willing enough to exploit it. In Houston, the cultural and social changes associated with rapid urban growth served to heighten the already widespread sense of alienation and insecurity prevalent throughout the United States.

Looming over all, of course, was the so-called Cold War between the United States and the Soviet Union. This postwar conflict between two superpowers with opposite world views provided a frightening overlay in a time of new and incomprehensibly destructive nuclear weapons.

Overseas, from Berlin to China, the Russians were pressing and pushing and apparently winning. At home in the United States, Russia's spies—fellow Americans unrecognizable from you and me—seemed to be everywhere, subverting government, the entertainment industry, churches, schools, and libraries. To some Americans, including too many Texans, the confusion of postwar rapid change or, as Theodore White calls it, the "Anguish of Modernization" flowed from or was somehow related to Communism and its related ideologies. One such citizen articulated the concerns of many others when he wrote a letter to the Houston *Post* attacking the city's new "metropolitan cafe society who condone immorality, drunkenness, plural marriage, divorce, and worse among themselves. . . ." The letter's author announced that he and others of like mind supported Senator Joe McCarthy's anti-Communist activities against "these traitors and their ilk. . . ." Such statements were repeated by other Houstonians who turned to Red Scare groups as a means of grappling with the perplexing and confusing changes of the postwar era.[44]

World War II thus brought important changes to Houston. The war began the transformation process whereby Houston would become a metropolis. But, as Richard Polenberg has written, "in the long run the legacy of World War II would not be confidence but uncertainty." To certain elements of the community, the postwar decade of transition only brought confusion and fear. Some ordinary Houstonians disliked the changes in their community and perceived a variety of evils that needed to be expunged. A tiny contingent of these Houstonians, mostly members of the extremist fringe, was willing to organize and lead a crusade to exorcise the radical demons from their midst and protect their city and nation from further insidious incursions. Many of these people had warned their fellow citizens of the dangers around them for years, only to be ignored. Their accusations and unsubstantiated charges went largely unheard. With the onset of the Cold War, however, their time had come. Events at home and abroad were making the charges of the extreme anti-Communists seem plausible. In Houston, moreover, two series of events beginning in the 1930s played a crucial role in giving legitimation and credibility to the city's Red Scare activists of the 1950s. One was the flurry of leftist activism in the Houston area during the late 1930s and 1940s. The other was the anti-Communist rhetoric of individual elites and groups with a high degree of community visibility and access to influential mass media. The former consisted of an actual series of events, while the latter was more of a process. To better understand Houston in the Red Scare, one must know about both.[45]

TWO

VOICES FROM THE LEFT

Communists in Houston? Why, my goodness yes! They've been around here since those labor union racketeers came to Texas before [World War II]. We had people running around openly admitting they were commies. They got smart and hid later on—but we knew they were still around.
—Adria Allen (former Minute Woman)[1]

Contemporary Houston has a justly earned reputation as one of the last strongholds for the philosophy of unrestrained capitalism. In the recent past, the city has been among those American communities least hospitable to anyone with an outlook on the left end of the political spectrum. While the Bayou City has never been a hotbed of left-wing activism, for fifteen years prior to the Red Scare Houston did experience a series of highly publicized incidents resulting from the actions of a handful of admitted Communists, socialists, leftist sympathizers, and labor radicals. Throughout those years the Communist party of the U.S.A. (CPUSA) operated openly and legally in the Houston-Galveston area, sustained by its close affiliation with colleagues in the locals of the Congress of Industrial Organizations (CIO). These voices on the left attracted public attention from the mid 1930s until the onset of the Red Scare in 1950. Their activities and the response by the press and local and state governments throughout this period helped give credibility to the charges of Red Scare activists that Houston was crawling with subversives. In turn, this Red-baiting served the interests of the powerful antilabor elements in Texas who were fearful of the growing strength of the labor union movement, especially as represented by the CIO.

Founded nationally in 1935 by John L. Lewis and other labor leaders recently expelled from the American Federation of Labor over a dispute about the need to organize by industries rather than by crafts, the CIO became a vigorous force in the push to organize American workers. After the formation of the CIO, the Communist party played an active role in organizing affiliate unions at the local level. By 1940, Communists had openly obtained complete or partial control of about 40 percent of the CIO unions nationally. Since most Communist and leftist support was at the grassroots level, they exerted great influence within the CIO's local and

regional councils. The Communists were weaker in the Houston CIO
affiliates than in many other regions; one knowledgeable source estimated
a total of no more than one dozen actual members. Nevertheless, they
did hold important posts in the local chapters of the CIO's National
Maritime Union.[2]

Because of constant police harassment despite their lawful activities,
Texas Gulf Coast Communists and their associates maintained a close
relationship with the Houston law firm of Mandell and Wright. The connection between leftists and Herman Wright and Arthur J. Mandell, the
senior partners of the firm, stemmed from their status as the CIO lawyers on the Texas Gulf Coast. Because of the scarcity of liberal, much less
radical, lawyers in the area, Wright and Mandell were close to many of
the left-wing activists in Houston during the 1930s and 1940s. Their
association with a few ineffective radicals, however, did not concern legal
authorities and the business elite nearly as much as the fact that these
two lawyers were the legal bulwark behind the CIO's effort to organize
labor along the Texas Gulf Coast. As a result, local law enforcement
agencies, lawyers, politicians, and the press as well as the United States
House of Representatives' Committee on Un-American Activities (HCUA)
perceived the Mandell and Wright law firm as a beehive of anti-
establishment, radical, and Communist activism. HCUA, for example,
maintained a file on Arthur Mandell. (The notorious committee, of course,
maintained a file on thousands of Americans, including such "subversives" as Eleanor Roosevelt.) Other than his CIO connection, HCUA
noted Mandell's association with the National Lawyers' Guild and the
National Federation for Constitutional Liberties, two left-leaning organizations involved in civil liberties work. Arthur Mandell and Herman
Wright always denied being members of the Communist party. Wright
later insisted that he and Mandell were "New Deal Liberal Democrats"
and all evidence tends to substantiate that claim, although Mandell had
strong sympathies for the CPUSA throughout the 1930s and 1940s.[3]

Born in Rumania in 1903, Arthur Josephus Mandell immigrated to the
United States at the age of nineteen, attended the Cumberland University Law School in Tennessee, and began the practice of law in 1929.
When Mandell moved to Houston in 1930, he faced a difficult professional
situation. He was a handsome man, blessed with a brilliant mind, who
had worked hard to become a skillful attorney. But Mandell, a Jewish
rabbi's son, spoke with a heavy Eastern European accent. This, coupled
with a political and economic viewpoint decidedly to the left of Houston's
business and legal establishment, barred Arthur Mandell from the city's
mainstream. He understood and supported the American workers' struggle to organize labor unions, however, and this provided his opportunity. Mandell cast his lot with an element of the working class that would

ignore foreign accents, one that was also not in the establishment main-stream yet was vital to the Gulf Coast economy—the men who toiled on Houston's docks and sailed on the freighters and oil tankers streaming through the ship channel. He became a specialist in maritime law and began to represent rank and file longshoremen and seamen in personal injury suits.[4]

In some ways, Mandell seemed out of place among his burly clients. A cultured man, a lover of classical music and fine literature, Mandell radiated genuine charm. The wife of one of his law partners observed that when in Mandell's presence she always felt as though he had just kissed her hand. Yet Arthur Mandell's cultivation sprang from his deeply felt sensitivity toward others, not from any desire to be aristocratic or elite. His working-class clients felt his sensitivity and trusted him because of it.[5]

Mandell seldom charged for his services, choosing instead to share in whatever settlement he could win from defendants. This contingency fee policy, along with the mere fact that he would associate with poorly edu-cated men who had a reputation for radical and sometimes violent union activities, earned Mandell a reputation among the dock workers as a man who "had a feeling for the underdog." This work led to Mandell's becoming in 1936 one of the CIO's chief lawyers on the Texas Gulf Coast. He was particularly active in the CIO's National Maritime Union (NMU) after its formation in the mid 1930s and became identified with the NMU's Communist and leftist faction. During the "Popular Front" period, Com-munists operated openly in the NMU and were welcomed by its leftist but largely non-Communist leadership.[6]

The year 1936 was a time of great ferment in labor relations and, to help with the growing case load, Mandell formed a partnership with William Arthur Combs, a studious, almost scholarly thirty-nine-year-old prolabor attorney and liberal Democrat. Combs and Mandell, representing CIO unions from Port Arthur to Corpus Christi, played a significant role in the promotion of labor union growth along the Texas coast. With the addition of the Carpenters and Teamsters unions, among others, they soon found business increasing beyond their ability to keep up. In 1937, the attorneys decided to add some young lawyers to the firm. Due to the intense hostility to labor unions by business leaders in the Houston-Galveston area, young lawyers usually sought the safety of less "radi-cal" clients. After a frustrating search, Combs and Mandell went to Austin to seek recommendations from some friends in the economics department of the University of Texas.[7]

The University of Texas was experiencing a rare liberal era during the late 1930s, partly as a result of a politically moderate board of regents appointed by Texas' New Deal governor, James V. Allred. Its Department of Economics in particular had a reputation for radicalism. In his memoirs, Harvard economist John Kenneth Galbraith states, with some exaggeration, that during this period the university had "the most radical of the major economic departments in the United States . . . even active Marxists were tolerated."[8]

Although not a Marxist but a fervent and crusading New Dealer, Professor Robert Montgomery was probably the department's most well known liberal political activist. The popular teacher, known on campus as "Dr. Bob," has been described by one of his former students as a ". . . bushy-haired, Scotch Presbyterian, Texas born . . . genie of the spoken word." A scourge of the Texas business establishment, especially the public utilities, Montgomery's fiery lectures on the evils of business monopoly and regressive taxation were campus legends. A student of Thorstein Veblen and Charles A. Beard, Montgomery's politics were firmly rooted in the progressive tradition. He was a primary influence in the lives of a generation of students who would later be among the leaders of the postwar liberal faction of the Democratic party in Texas, including political strategist Creekmore Fath and seven-term congressman Robert C. Eckhardt. Ronnie Dugger, himself a former student of Montgomery, has written that "the lords of Texas industry . . . knew him as their bedeviler in . . . those little classrooms in Garrison Hall, from which he was sending forth disrespectful young people who understood what they should not."[9]

In 1948, when asked by an investigatory committee of the Texas state legislature if he belonged to any radical organizations, Montgomery replied that, indeed, he belonged to the two most radical organizations in existence, "the Methodist Church and the Democratic Party." He explained to the puzzled legislators that "Christ's theory of brotherhood is the most radical theory ever created; and democracy is the most radical political idea man's ever had." When the committee asked if he favored private property, Montgomery smiled and retorted, "I do . . . and so strongly that I want everyone in Texas to have some."[10]

Arthur Combs and Robert Montgomery were old friends, so the Houston attorney asked Montgomery for the names of talented and politically compatible young lawyers. The economics professor knew several good candidates through his sponsorship of the university's Young Democrats club. He referred Combs to one named Chris Dixie, who had recently graduated, moved back to his hometown of Dallas, and run unsuccessfully for the Texas state legislature in the 1936 Democratic primary. Combs contacted the financially struggling Dixie and offered him a job with a salary of $100 a month. Dixie eagerly accepted and told Combs about two friends named Otto Mullinax and Herman Wright who were also recent graduates of the University of Texas. Mullinax lived in a small town in east Texas, while Wright and his wife resided in Amarillo. Both men, like Dixie, had lost legislative elections in 1936 and both were struggling. They too joined the law firm of Combs and Mandell.[11]

Of the three young new labor attorneys who moved to Houston in February 1938, Herman Wright was the most idealistic and closest in political outlook to Arthur Mandell. While at the university, Wright also "fell under the spell" of Dr. Montgomery, whose influence pushed Wright's politics to the left of center. The twenty-five-year-old attorney was having a tough time earning a living in the conservative political climate of Amarillo when the opportunity to go to Houston beckoned. Unlike his two college friends, Wright would soon become closely identified with Arthur J. Mandell and radical politics.

While close politically, Wright and Mandell were direct opposites in certain ways. Mandell was an idea man, comfortable with abstract concepts, philosophical discourse, and subtle nuance. In these early years of their association, however, Herman Wright was more of a true believer, an ideologue who tended to see issues in black and white with no shade of gray in between. This combination of differences, however, served each well and they remained partners for over forty years.[12]

The firm of Combs and Mandell prospered as Gulf Coast workers, protected by the federal Wagner Labor Relations Act, began to organize and negotiate with hostile employers. Arthur Combs worked with several American Federation of Labor (AFL) affiliates in the building trades and transportation industries, while Mandell, Wright, and Chris Dixie usually represented CIO locals. Due to the controversial nature of labor relations work, the adversarial role of the attorneys in opposition to management, and the propensity of labor disputes to result occasionally in violence, Mandell and Combs attracted substantial amounts of publicity in Houston-area newspapers.[13]

Throughout the late 1930s, whenever Houstonians read in their local newspapers about a strike, they saw the names of Arthur Mandell, Art Combs, and their young associates. Even before Mullinax, Wright, and Dixie joined them, the two senior attorneys played prominent and heavily publicized roles in a textile workers' dispute against a Houston manufacturer in August 1937. Their visibility increased in 1938 as they became involved in a variety of cases ranging from a longshoremen's quarrel in Galveston to an attention-getting strike by female "car hops" against a Houston hamburger chain.[14]

Until 1939 the Combs and Mandell firm remained free of any charges of subversive activities. They were disliked by the business establishment and viewed as labor agitators by some, but no one publicly accused them of being Communists. Art Mandell and Herman Wright looked more like establishment bankers than agitators. Enjoying considerable financial success through their near monopoly on labor union business, both men took to wearing expensive, well-fitted double-breasted suits. Herman Wright acquired and flew his own small airplane to help him tend to clients in Corpus Christi and Port Arthur. Most of the lawyers' cases were against major steamship and petroleum companies that, while lucrative, also won them the enmity of the Texas business elite.[15]

A strike lasting from April through June of 1939, however, brought the first public accusations of a link between the Combs and Mandell firm and the Communist party. The dispute pitted the National Maritime Union (NMU), which represented a significant portion of American seamen on the Gulf and Atlantic coasts, against Standard Oil of New Jersey (now Exxon), Socony-Vacuum Oil Company (now Mobil), and three other oil and shipping companies. The strike revolved around basic "bread and butter" issues as well as an effort to unionize more of the seamen operating the tankers. It effectively hampered the shipment of oil from Texas' port cities. NMU members not only picketed the oil tankers but also the retail gasoline service stations of the companies involved. Both sides played tough, bargaining broke down, and sporadic fighting erupted between some NMU strikers and employees of the companies. One veteran NMU leader later recalled that company goons (men such as former Texas Ranger Frank Hamer), who were hired by the companies to assault strike leaders, were a problem throughout the 1930s along the Texas waterfront. Hamer, famed for his role in the killing of Bonnie Parker and Clyde Barrow, was alleged to have participated in the beatings of several NMU strikers. NMU members, however, never shied away from responding in kind. The NMU veteran, recalling the 1939 strike and others, admitted that "one of the best ways to stop these [goons] was stop 'em from walkin'. We had three or four experts who knew how to lay that leg across that curb and slam right down on it and break hell out of it. And I mean we done a job on 'em! Same as they were doing on us."[16]

Houston newspapers, unfriendly to the CIO unions, eagerly reported each violent incident. The Houston Police Department also took a dim view of the seamen strikers and periodically swept through the wharf areas along the ship channel to haul NMU members to jail, usually without bothering to concoct charges. Chris Dixie would go to the city jail to bail out the incarcerated seamen, but the desk sergeant would refuse to reveal the names of his prisoners. Whenever Dixie persisted, the police would become irritated, threaten him with a charge of soliciting clients, and promptly escort him out of the building.[17]

The Harris County district attorney, Dan W. Jackson, took a more legal tack and created a special grand jury to investigate the violence. The grand jury ordered Harry Alexander, local NMU secretary and a dedicated Communist, to turn over the union's strike records so that the jury would have a list of NMU leaders. Alexander, strike chairman E. J. ("Jimmy") Cunningham, Art Mandell, and various other NMU members were subpoenaed to testify. When they entered the courthouse, a Houston *Chronicle* photographer took their picture, which the newspaper subsequently published. Mandell, looking especially dapper in his pinstripe suit and sporting a pencil-thin mustache, was prominently featured in the news article.[18]

Harry Alexander, a tough engine-room tender and veteran of years of waterfront battles, adamantly refused to give up the NMU records. He was thrown in jail for his recalcitrance. Mandell urged Alexander to comply with the jury's order but he continued to refuse and remained in the Harris County jail. A week later, fourteen ill-tempered NMU seamen caught an unlucky scab engineer in a Baytown cafe and beat him senseless. The following day, Mandell succeeded in convincing Alexander to give up the NMU records out of fear of an almost certain physical retaliation against the NMU secretary at the hands of his jailers. Despite acquisition of the NMU strike records, the jury's investigation proceeded slowly and with difficulty, largely due to Combs' and Mandell's legal stratagems.[19]

As the strike continued, Houston's business leaders began to issue public warnings about the danger posed by militant workers. A Chamber of Commerce official declared that "irresponsible labor agitators" were threatening Houston's economic future. Claiming that "big industrialists" were reconsidering plans to move to Houston because of "the labor situation," the official warned "a few more instances such as this and . . . this city is doomed."[20]

Finally, frustrated by the lengthy strike and Mandell's effective legal maneuvers, Houston city attorney Sewall Myer resorted to Red-baiting. Myer, a longtime crony of Mayor Oscar Holcombe and a former general counsel for the Texas Federation of Labor, appeared before the Houston Ministerial Alliance on June 5, 1939, to denounce the strike as a Communist plot. Myer, referring to Mandell and Combs, charged that "Communist lawyers and imported Communist agitators" were responsible for the labor crisis in Houston. In his speech, portions of which Houston's three major newspapers carried on their front page, Myer declared that the "eyes of the world are upon Houston for twenty-eight Communist agitators have been sent from Detroit for the express purpose" of creating violence. Myer warned that these "cunning and insidious" men were supported by a large fund of money from Russia and "Communist lawyers" who were maintained to obstruct the grand jury's investigation. One minister asked Myer if he could describe a typical Communist. Without hesitation Myer explained solemnly that a Communist was a "low creature with no respect for God, who does not believe in law, and is a cross between an anarchist and a fox."[21]

Myer's accusations about Russian money and Communist control of the NMU strike were provocative distortions of reality. The conservative former AFL lawyer, with over thirty years' experience working with the older skilled crafts unions, certainly knew that the NMU strike was no more subversive than any other. But he also knew that Arthur Mandell in particular was susceptible to such charges. The Communist party had been active, visible, and highly vocal in Texas and Houston throughout the late 1930s. Mandell, while apparently never a party member, had sympathies for the Communist cause and believed, with his partners, that American Communists had the same constitutional rights enjoyed by other American citizens. Mandell's feelings on this issue led to his becoming an unofficial legal adviser to individual CPUSA members in Houston, particularly Homer Brooks, state party chairman. His connection with CPUSA affairs in the 1930s may have also included advice on political strategy. Myer's knowledge of this (Mandell saw no reason to hide his association with Texas Communists) gave his accusations a patina of plausibility.[22]

The Communist party existed openly in Texas throughout the 1930s and 1940s. While the Lone Star State is known for its ethos of rigid conservatism and rugged individualism, it has also nurtured and sustained its own varieties of radicalism, especially the agrarian type. For example, the militant Texas Farmers' Alliance, a precursor of the People's Party (Populist), was formed in Lampasas County, Texas, in the early 1880s. Throughout the Populist era of the 1880s and 1890s, Texas had one of the most radical of the state parties. Likewise, Texas had a surprising number of socialists during the first two decades of the twentieth century. Socialist party candidate for president Eugene V. Debs received 8.5% of the total vote in Texas in the 1912 election. In an amazing act of tolerance that would be unthinkable forty years later, Houston mayor Baldwin Rice invited anarchist and feminist Emma Goldman to make a speech at City Hall when Goldman came to Houston in 1908. Goldman's disapproval of government did not allow her to accept the invitation, although she did thank Baldwin for his "astonishing courtesy."[23]

The suppression of dissent during World War I, followed by the first Red Scare and the dominance of the Ku Klux Klan in the early 1920s, overwhelmed Texas radicals as it did everywhere in the United States. The economic dislocations of the 1930s, however, produced a radical revival. The extreme hardships created by unemployment and foreclosures raised questions about the nature of capitalism. The new atmosphere allowed the existence of a state Communist party.

The CPUSA was founded in 1919 following the Bolshevik Revolution in Russia. Governmental suppression forced it underground in the 1920s, but it reemerged in 1929. At the height of its popularity during the Popular Front days of the 1930s and the American-Soviet alliance in World War II, the CPUSA could claim an estimated 60,000 to 80,000 members nationwide. In 1933, about the time the party made its appearance in Texas, the CPUSA had a total membership of 19,000. The actual date when the Communists formed a Texas party is unclear. Individuals professing to be CPUSA members could be found working openly in the state throughout the early 1930s, usually doing nothing more than distributing party literature.[24]

When the CIO began its efforts to organize unskilled workers in Texas in the mid 1930s, the Texas Communist party became a visible and formal organization. A handful of key CIO grassroots organizers were CPUSA members and they played a crucial role in providing an impetus to the creation of a state party. Such party activists as Emma Tenayuca, Ruth Koenig, Homer Brooks, Enoch Hardaway, and J. Lloyd Wright had strong ties to CIO labor unions. CPUSA general secretary Earl Browder later admitted that "the rise of the CIO trade unions . . . was the basis of the Communist advances in all other fields."[25]

Certainly by fall of 1935 the Texas Communist party was in business. Literature with that identification, urging support of worker demands, began to appear wherever strikes occurred along the Texas Gulf Coast. Gilbert Mers, a longshoreman and militant labor unionist in Corpus Christi, later recalled that ". . . it would have been about '35 before [the CPUSA would] have been throwing an influence that was very marked, I suppose. At the end of the '35 [longshoremen] strike, we began to see a little Communist sheet here and there." The party opened a state headquarters in Houston and designated its Houston-Galveston chapter District 23. A chairman, secretary, and a few field workers led the party and operated a local propaganda outlet called Progressive Book Distributors, which sold literature produced by the CPUSA's International Publishers and New Century Publishers. In the late 1940s the local chapter published an official newspaper, the *Texas Spur*.[26]

Nationally, the CPUSA was organized from the top down rather than from the bottom up and functioned bureaucratically more like a military organization than a political party. Each of the local branches or groups (the term "cell" was officially abandoned in the 1920s, although some members continued to use the term) were self-sustaining financially. The Texas CPUSA had to send money to party headquarters in New York City and had to pay its own way, surviving on what money it could raise locally. The most influential members were full-time professionals on the party payroll, earning their living as party functionaries. These professionals were usually poorly paid and suffered economic hardships, existing on the edge of poverty, particularly those working in states like Texas where the party was weak. In the late 1930s, however, the chief CPUSA organizer in Texas made as much as $25 per week plus expenses, which was considerably above poverty level. Texas had very few professional Communists, no more than a half-dozen in the entire state at any one time. The vast majority of actual dues-paying members of Texas' tiny Communist party were laborers scattered in CIO locals along the Gulf Coast; a few college students, mainly at the University of Texas; some ideologically committed lawyers, teachers, and other professionals isolated here and there; and some of the poverty-stricken unemployed, especially in San Antonio's Mexican-American barrios and Houston's black ghettos. In general, however, the CPUSA made little progress as a movement in the South, Texas included. One source claims that there were 409 members in Texas by 1937 and over 500 by 1938. While estimates differ, the Communist party of Texas certainly had no more than a thousand members at its strongest. The Houston local, which was the state's largest, never had more than two hundred members, according to the party's own estimate.[27]

Despite the party's inability to win a mass following, it nevertheless succeeded in establishing public visibility. The party encouraged news coverage of its activities and its positions on various issues of the day. During the 1930s, the Communist party of Texas followed the national leadership of the CPUSA's Earl Browder and his policy of uniting with other "progressive forces" in a Popular Front against facism. Accordingly, the state party's political platform in these years abandoned its revolutionary stance and advocated programs that dovetailed with basic reforms supported by the liberal wing of the Democratic party. For example, the Texas Communists proposed a minimum wage and eight-hour work day act, an "adequate" old age pension, low interest state loans to landless farmers and agricultural workers, application of the Wagner Labor Relations Act to farm workers, a state income tax, abolition of the poll tax and white primary, and civil rights for blacks and Mexican-Americans. Enjoying a degree of tolerance in the ten years before the end of World War II, the Communist party of Texas busily issued press releases and conducted news conferences whenever possible. To increase its visibility, the party offered a slate of candidates for public office in Texas in the biennial general elections from 1934 to 1940.[28]

The existence of an organized state Communist party became especially conspicuous to Houstonians in 1938 and 1939. A pecan shellers strike in San Antonio, led by the fiery Emma Tenayuca, known to San Antonio Mexican-Americans as "la Pasionaria de Texas," garnered much publicity in Houston's newspapers during 1938. The strike, which has become an important landmark in the history of the Mexican-American struggle for economic and social justice, originated in oppressive working conditions and had the support of persons of various political philosophies. Emma Tenayuca was a Communist, however, and this did not fail to get the attention of Houstonians interested in the strike.[29]

The Communist party of Texas held its state convention in Houston on August 9, 1938. This meeting, which further raised public awareness of the party, nominated Emma Tenayuca as a candidate for Congress from the San Antonio area. Other candidates included Enoch Hardaway, a west Texas oil field worker and union activist, for railroad commissioner; and Ben Lauderdale, a Breckenridge farmer and veteran of the old Populist party, for commissioner of agriculture. Of more interest to Houston's anti-Communists, however, were the nominations of three of the city's residents. Nathan ("Jeff") Kleban, a native of San Antonio but temporarily residing in Houston, was secretary of the Houston party local. He was nominated for the position of attorney general. A black man, Cecil B. Robinett, described by party literature as a "militant young Houston leader of the fight for Negro rights," stood for lieutenant governor. For governor, the state party nominated the twenty-seven-year-old Homer Lester Brooks, son of a railroad worker and a native of New Brighton, Pennsylvania.[30]

Brooks, whose real name was Bartchy, was a well-known figure in Texas leftist political circles and among radical labor unionists. An attractive man with a slender frame, blonde wavy hair, and large blue eyes, Brooks divided his time between San Antonio and Houston, working as a professional CPUSA functionary. He served as the party's state secretary throughout the late 1930s, had previously run for governor of Texas in 1936, and would be the nominee for senator in 1940. Brooks graduated from high school in Los Angeles, California, and briefly studied electrical engineering at Carnegie Tech in Pittsburgh. He was drawn into the radical labor movement while in college and left school to work for the CPUSA. His first assignments were in New York City, where he organized Puerto Ricans, and Florida. He was sent to Texas in the early 1930s to help organize CIO unions. He quickly won the attention of CIO militants along the Texas Gulf Coast who eventually gave him the nickname "Blue-eyed Boy." In 1937 Brooks married San Antonio's Emma Tenayuca and worked with her in support of the pecan shellers strike.

Also called the "Flying Dutchman" because of his constant traveling around the state, Brooks was always working and on the move. Those who knew Brooks well remember him as a "fanatical" supporter of the CPUSA who would sacrifice family and friends to achieve party goals.

Unlike the Texas rank and file, Brooks was well read in Marxist-Leninist writings. A persuasive person, Brooks was more effective in small groups than in large ones. One former party member remembers the "Blue-eyed Boy" as an "inspiring" individual who was personally responsible for much of the energy in Texas' small CPUSA.[31]

Brooks gave the keynote address at the party's 1938 convention in Houston. In his speech, Brooks emphasized the party's position of solidarity with the liberal-progressive movement. "We want to keep [Democratic candidate for governor W. Lee] O'Daniel from creating a machine like [Huey] Long's in Louisiana" and halt Texas' drift "toward fascism," the party secretary declared. The state convention adjourned without incident as most Houstonians ignored the proceedings.[32]

The fact that the party conducted its convention in Houston and maintained its state headquarters in the city without harassment, coupled with the growth of labor unions in the area, apparently convinced CPUSA leaders in New York City that the port city was ripe for a more serious organization effort in 1939. Accordingly, the national party sent the famous former "child genius," Elizabeth Benson, to Houston to serve as a full-time organizer and party education director. Elizabeth Benson was the daughter of Charles Benson, an editorial writer for the Fort Worth *Star-Telegram*, and Ann Austin, a novelist. Born in Waco in 1914 when her parents were students at Baylor University, Benson grew up in New York and California after her parents separated. When Benson was a precocious nine-year-old, psychologists determined that she had an IQ of 214, the highest ever recorded at that time. Educational psychologists and newspaper reporters dominated her adolescence as she graduated from high school at the age of twelve and Barnard College at age sixteen. She became a serious student of social conditions at age fifteen and eventually joined the CPUSA when she was twenty-two. The party leadership, recognizing her talent, selected Benson to attend their training school and become a professional party organizer.

Houston was Elizabeth Benson's first assignment. The young round-faced radical, appearing scholarly in wire-rimmed eyeglasses, arrived in the city in January 1939. She held a press conference and was treated like a celebrity by local newspapers. Benson proudly announced that she asked for the Houston assignment because of a homesickness for Texas. Although this was her initial visit to the city, she declared that Houston had more potential for Communist recruitment than any other city in the state because of its rapidly expanding industrialization. Announcing a "membership campaign," Benson stated that she wanted "to meet with groups who are interested in bettering conditions for the masses. . . ."

Indicative of the city's temporarily tolerant environment, the journalists portrayed Benson as an up-and-coming young professional person eager to do well on her first job. Jesse Jones' *Chronicle* prominently featured a lengthy interview with Benson complete with a photograph of the smiling young Communist. The *Chronicle*'s benign and flattering treatment of Benson was in sharp contrast to the newspaper's behavior six years later, when it served as the leading Red Scare organ in the city.[33]

Thus, by June 1939, when Houston city attorney Sewall Myer made newspaper headlines with his charges about Mandell, Combs, Wright, and Dixie being "Communist lawyers," the Texas district of the CPUSA had established a distinct presence in the city and state. Arthur Mandell had become a close friend of Homer Brooks, the "Blue-eyed Boy." This provided Myer and Mayor Oscar Holcombe with a weapon to use in their campaign to discredit the NMU and its legal counsel and deny the NMU public support.

The lawyers fought back. An irate Art Combs led a delegation of Houston labor leaders to Mayor Holcombe's office to protest Myer's charges. Holcombe, a shrewd politician known to many Houstonians as the "Old Gray Fox," told the group that he agreed with his city attorney and that he was conducting his own investigation of Communist infiltration in local unions. Holcombe turned to Combs and accused him and Mandell of being "largely responsible" for much of Houston's labor violence. The mayor told the union leaders to clean their own house and implied that they should quit working with Mandell and his partners. Combs angrily denied that he and his partners were Communists or were responsible for violence. Holcombe refused to retract his accusation.

After the meeting with Mayor Holcombe, Combs presented a detailed defense in a letter to the Houston Ministerial Alliance. Combs charged Myer and Holcombe with seeking to discredit organized labor by Red-baiting. Referring to Myer's former position as the chief legal counsel for most of the city's labor unions before the creation of the CIO, Combs declared that Myer resented losing his business to the Mandell firm. Combs told the ministers that Houston business firms had employed professional spies and strikebreakers to assault peaceful picketers. "If members of organized labor have been guilty of violence," Combs charged, "it has been in . . . defense of existing wrongs." Addressing the "Reds" issue, Combs stated that "progressive labor in Houston is not Communist led or Communist dominated. I am not a Communist . . . and neither is any member of my firm a Communist." Nevertheless, Combs argued that Communists were entitled to the right "to express freely" their opinions, and he pleaded, "Let those who . . . call upon the name of democracy practice a little of their own preachments." Combs invited the ministers to conduct their own investigation, but the alliance declined.[34]

A week later, on June 15, 1939, Nathan Kleban, secretary of the Houston local of the CPUSA, appeared before the Houston City Council and denied party responsibility for union violence. Kleban admitted that some local unions included Communists and that the Houston party had "about 125" members. "The Communist Party does not dictate policies to any trade union," Kleban told the council, and added that the CPUSA "rejects terrorism and violence." Kleban's unsolicited appearance before the city council and Mayor Holcombe and his candid statements about party membership reflected the Communist party's continuing and rather naive attempt to gain public respectability in Texas during the late 1930s. Brooks, Kleban, Benson, and their associates in the Texas party revealed an innocent optimism in their public statements and activities about the potential for CPUSA growth and acceptance. This illusion of respectability, created by the economic crisis that had allowed its flowering, was sustained by the national leadership of Earl Browder, who adopted Thomas Jefferson and Abraham Lincoln as party heroes and proclaimed that "Communism is the Americanism of the twentieth century." Except for the debacle of the Hitler-Stalin Pact of 1939–41, which created a temporary alliance between Germany and the Soviet Union, this optimism continued during World War II as a result of the Soviet-American military alliance. An indication of the future, however, occurred after Nathan Kleban's city council appearance.[35]

In a press conference held on June 16, 1939, Mayor Holcombe responded to Combs' and Kleban's protests by announcing a full-scale police investigation to discover who in Houston either belonged to the Communist party or had "communistic tendencies." The investigation, Holcombe added, would include all city employees. "Any city employee found to be a Communist," the mayor declared, "will be discharged immediately." Holcombe stated that he wanted a list of Houston's Communists to determine if they controlled the local labor unions. When asked if it was against state law to be a Communist (which it was not), Holcombe retorted, "As far as I am concerned, it is." At the end of the news conference Holcombe, using a technique that Senator Joseph R. McCarthy would make famous eleven years later, waved a three- or four-page document at the reporters and claimed it contained the names of approximately one hundred Houston Communists. Refusing to let the journalists read it, Holcombe grinned and explained, "I'm not through with it yet."[36]

The tensions of Houston's short-lived "little Red Scare" of 1939 were relieved in July by the end of the NMU strike and also by an unanticipated source: the Harris County grand jury. On July 12, the jury concluded that a minority of both labor and management shared the blame. "A few misguided labor leaders, using typical racketeering methods, succeeded . . . in terrorizing a community of 500,000 people," the jury charged. It added that "a minority of employers, some of whom exploited their workers . . . must share . . . responsibility." While complimenting Mayor Holcombe, the police, and the district attorney "for stamping out the terrorism," the grand jury refrained from blaming Communists and declared that "the vast majority of labor unions in Houston . . . are an asset to the city and county." The grand jury findings came close to repudiating Holcombe's and Sewall Myer's Red-baiting tactics.[37]

An event in San Antonio a month following the grand jury report, however, gave Holcombe a brief chance again to portray himself as the guardian of Houston's patriotism. The Communist party of Texas decided to hold its 1939 state convention in San Antonio and applied for a permit to meet in the municipal auditorium on August 25. Mayor Maury Maverick's decision to grant the permit unleashed a whirlwind of protest in the city from Catholic leaders, American Legion spokesmen, the Ku Klux Klan, and others. Maverick, himself a victim of Red-baiting when he was defeated for reelection to Congress in 1938, declared, "I am catching hell, but will stand firm." Tensions remained high in San Antonio as a result of the pecan shellers strike the year before. The strike was widely perceived as being caused by "Red" agitators such as Emma Tenayuca, who was organizing the party convention.

Despite threats of violence, the Texas Communists refused to cancel the meeting. On the night of August 25, with the city auditorium surrounded on the outside by a hostile mob of an estimated five thousand people and a contingent of 120 San Antonio policemen, Houston's Elizabeth Benson, serving as convention chair, attempted to convene the meeting. Sharing the stage with Benson were Homer Brooks and his wife, Emma Tenayuca. When Benson asked the party members to rise and sing "The Star-Spangled Banner," which opened all public party functions, the mob descended on the building, heaving bricks and swinging clubs. The San Antonio police later estimated that 75 percent of the rioters were between the ages of seventeen and twenty-five. The only person arrested was a fourteen-year-old boy, caught holding a brick. The police escorted Brooks, Benson, and Tenayuca out of the building, but twenty to twenty-five persons received injuries before the riot ended.[38]

The "Commie" riot in San Antonio received much national attention.

In Houston, Mayor Oscar Holcombe, seeing an opportunity to remind voters about his earlier warnings, held a press conference. The "Old Gray Fox," with an "I told you so" look on his face, grinned at reporters and announced that he had dispatched Houston police inspector Roy Floyd and a "secret investigator" to San Antonio to study the riot and to obtain the names of the Houstonians involved. After returning from San Antonio, the two policemen had submitted a "confidential report" detailing the participation of Brooks, Benson, and other Houstonians in the CPUSA meeting. Holcombe reminded his audience that he had directed an investigation of Communist activities in Houston for several months and warned that his city was prepared for any eventuality. He repeated his earlier performance of waving a list and charging that it was a file "on local communists and their sympathizers" and again refused to let the reporters read it.[39]

Nazi Germany's invasion of Poland in September 1939 soon dominated Houston's newspaper headlines and Holcombe abandoned his Red Scare tactics. As the war swept across Europe, fears of "Red" subversion diminished and Holcombe's list of Houston Communists disappeared. Inexplicably, Holcombe never returned to Red Scare tactics even though he again served as Houston's mayor from 1947 to 1953, the years that anti-Communist hysteria and McCarthyism rampaged across his city. In that period, Holcombe paid minor lip service to anti-Communism, but he basically stood aloof from the turmoil of the early 1950s.

Soon after Holcombe and Myer Red-baited their law firm, Art Combs severed his partnership with Arthur Mandell. Although Combs claimed the two events were unrelated, ideological differences contributed to the split. Combs was more conservative than his partner and had less empathy for the Communists. Combs later blamed the break on a dispute over internal business arrangements, but other members of the firm denied this. The available evidence indicated that Combs was trying to escape the taint of radicalism and that Holcombe's and Myer's tactics took their toll on him. Regardless of reasons, the split created bad feelings between Combs and Mandell that were increased when Dixie agreed to go with Combs. Dixie later admitted that he too may have wanted to get away from the "Red" accusations. Herman Wright stayed with Mandell.[40]

The new firm of Combs and Dixie added some AFL unions and lured several CIO affiliates away from Wright and Mandell, leaving them with the more radical NMU, the Oil Workers International Union, and two locals of the United Steel Workers. Eventually Combs and Dixie became identified more with mainstream Democratic party politics while Mandell and Wright retained their leftist reputation. The presidential election of 1948, for example, emphasized their political differences as Combs and Dixie supported and worked for the reelection of Harry S Truman, while Mandell and Wright campaigned for Henry A. Wallace and the Progressive party.[41]

Events in Europe had other repercussions for local radicals. One of the most important was a forced overhauling of CPUSA official policy. From August 1939 to June 1940, the CPUSA, following the line necessitated by the Hitler-Stalin Pact, became a "peace party," advocating strict U.S. neutrality. The national party's abrupt shift from antifascism to neutral pacifism cost the CPUSA dearly. The Texas Communist party suffered along with its national version. The Houston group became temporarily quiet, traumatized by the radical shift in ideological gospel. This new policy left the CPUSA in a vulnerable position. Strikes occurring in the 1939 to 1941 years were immediately branded as "Red" inspired, even by some former CPUSA allies in the New Deal. Police surveillance and harassment intensified due to a fear that the Communist peace position would hinder the expansion of national defense industries.[42]

An incident in Houston on the night of March 5, 1941, indicated the increase in government harassment of radicals. Two Houston policemen parked outside of Arthur Mandell's home evidently to determine the identity of individuals attending a meeting at the lawyer's house. What occurred after the police arrived is unclear, but supposedly those attending the meeting feared a raid. According to the two police officers, Mandell's house went dark and approximately twenty men ran out the front door, scattering in several directions. Three men jumped into a car and sped away with their lights off. The police chased the car for several blocks. When they eventually stopped the automobile, two of the men succeeded in escaping. They arrested the third man, who turned out to be the "Blue-eyed Boy," Homer Brooks. The policemen took Brooks to police headquarters where Federal Bureau of Investigation agents were waiting to interrogate him. According to the two arresting officers, Brooks confessed that he had been attending a CPUSA "cell" meeting at Mandell's house. He refused to give any other information and the police eventually released him without charges.

It is highly unlikely that the event occurred as the police described it, since at this time Brooks and his party associates still operated openly. It is difficult to believe that Brooks would think he could conduct a secret conspirational meeting at such a conspicuous location. Many years later, Herman Wright could not remember the incident but did recall that his partner often met with clients at his home and that it was no secret that Mandell did legal work for the Texas Communist party.

The alleged "Keystone Cop" comedy exit from Mandell's house, which the police claimed Brooks said was the way "they always left meetings," is too incredible to take seriously. It appears that the police were simply waiting for Brooks outside Mandell's house to pick him up for questioning and harassment and, possibly frightened by the reality of police brutality in Houston, Brooks ran.

No matter what the accurate version of the incident was, the incident reveals that federal authorities were watching Homer Brooks closely. The police "leaked" news about the episode to local reporters, who spread word that the city's Communists were plotting subversive activities in league with Mandell.[43]

In June 1940, the CPUSA had to reverse policies once again. The German invasion of Russia suddenly converted the CPUSA into a "super-patriotic" organization urging total American commitment to the war effort. The CPUSA quickly adopted a "no strike" pledge to avoid slow-downs in defense plant output. Earl Browder, taking a pragmatic approach, announced that "class divisions or political groupings had no significance now." This new stance ironically placed the CPUSA to the right of the CIO leadership, which continued to make demands for improved working conditions despite the war. As historian Bert Cochran points out, "Workers' concerns about . . . an extra dime an hour seemed . . . frivolous to Communist global strategists when the fate of mankind rested on the Russian battlefronts." The Texas Communist party followed this policy reversal. Its members in the Gulf Coast CIO unions vigorously opposed strike talk among the rank and file. Eventually the Japanese attack on Pearl Harbor in December 1941 gave party members the best of both worlds: they could now be Russian and American patriots simultaneously. American Communists threw themselves into the war effort.[44]

Once again, Homer Brooks typified CPUSA reactions. On February 11, 1942, anticipating a draft notice to report to the army, Brooks left Texas on board the ship *Pan Rhode Island*. He arrived in New York City and went to the NMU hiring hall, where he applied for sea duty with the foreign merchant marine service. Brooks' departure deprived the Texas party of its most aggressive and dedicated leader. But the "Blue-eyed Boy" had a hatred of fascism that came close to being an obsession. He seized the opportunity to become personally involved in the "anti-fascist war" and also serve the official policy of his party.

The federal government was less enthusiastic about Homer Brooks' war fervor. Brooks' move to New York provided a long-awaited opportunity. Declaring that he had failed to notify the Houston draft board about his change in residence, FBI agents arrested Brooks in New York City on

March 11, 1942, for draft evasion. Brooks was brought to trial in Houston on April 17, 1942, with conservative Republican Thomas M. Kennerly serving as judge.

Wishing to avoid a deepening of the prejudice already existing against him in the courtroom, Brooks decided against being represented by Arthur Mandell. Instead, he hired Bernard Golding, a non-Communist civil liberties lawyer. Eccentric and flamboyant (he would never appear in court without a freshly cut red rose pinned to his coat lapel), Golding was a specialist in constitutional law. Brooks' attorney claimed that his client had mailed a change of address notice to the Houston draft board. The NMU office in New York, Brooks' new address, mistakenly returned an induction notice to the Houston draft board, thinking Brooks had already shipped out. Brooks observed the spirit of the law, Golding argued, and was guilty of no more than the most minor of technicalities. Brooks testified that he wanted to fight in the "war against fascism" and believed he could contribute more as a seaman than as a soldier in the army. He pleaded for the court not to deny him the opportunity to "go after the Nazis." A procession of character witnesses, including local NMU port agent James ("Blackie") Merrill, testified on Brooks' behalf.

The government prosecutor, assistant federal district attorney William Eckhardt, almost ignored the technical charge in the case. Instead, Eckhardt stressed Brooks' unofficial crime: he was a Communist. This is no ordinary individual, the prosecutor warned Judge Kennerly. It was obvious, Eckhardt explained, that Brooks "thought he could do more for the party as a communist organizer aboard ship than he could in the army and for that reason evaded the draft."

Judge Kennerly acquitted Brooks of the more serious charge of willful draft evasion. Instead, the federal judge ruled that Brooks was guilty of failure "to keep his local board advised at all times of the addresses where mail will reach him." After lecturing Brooks about the educational potentialities of jail, Kennerly sentenced the Communist organizer to sixty days' imprisonment. Bernard Golding appealed the case and succeeded in freeing Brooks under bond for the duration of the appellate process. Homer Brooks proceeded to enlist in the merchant marine and went to sea.

On June 7, 1943, the United States Supreme Court voted 7 to 2 to reverse Judge Kennerly's decision. Justice Stanley Reed noted that the law required all registrants to "keep in close communication" with their draft boards. The justice concluded that if this vague suggestion is interpreted by the government as a rule of law that registrants must "at short intervals" inquire about their mail at every possible prior address, "we are of the view that the Government demands more than the regulation requires." The Court ruled that Bartchy (alias Brooks) had acted properly. Justices Harlan F. Stone and Owen J. Roberts dissented and argued that "uncontradicted evidence" supported Kennerly's decision that the "petitioner knowingly failed to keep his local Board advised at all times of the address where mail would reach him."

No longer under the threat of a jail sentence and by now divorced from Emma Tenayuca, Homer Lester Bartchy "Brooks," Houston's "Blue-eyed Boy," dropped out of the Texas district of the CPUSA and never again played a role in local affairs. Brooks, the hardworking revolutionary, was eventually expelled from the CPUSA because of the draft evasion incident. The party leaders in New York had ordered all professional workers to obey draft notices. They perceived Brooks' actions to be a violation of their orders. Brooks moved to Los Angeles after the war, remarried, and worked at Warner Brothers Studios in a nonacting job until his death from a heart attack in the early 1960s. Elizabeth Benson and Emma Tenayuca also moved to California, the former to Los Angeles in 1941 and the latter to San Francisco in 1948. Nevertheless, their shadows remained in Houston, radical specters to be used by extreme anti-Communists in the 1950s as evidence of what had been and, surely, they said, what still remained.[45]

The National Maritime Union's Texas lawyers, Arthur Mandell and Herman Wright, maintained their close association with radical labor and leftist politics throughout the war years. The firm prospered despite competition from its former associates, Combs and Dixie. The rapid growth of war industries along the Texas Gulf Coast, especially in Houston, meant more workers, larger unions, and increased business for labor attorneys. In addition, carelessness caused by the haste of the war effort resulted in a rash of personal injury suits that contributed large sums of money to the Mandell and Wright coffers.

Mandell and Wright also continued their personal political activism. They often persuaded their union clients to support particular candidates, even at the local level. Mandell and Wright did not limit their support to leftists. In the spring of 1943, for example, they convinced the Oil Workers International Union, the United Steel Workers, and the NMU to work and vote for Miss Ima Hogg and Dr. Ray K. Daily in their bids for positions on the Houston school board. At Mandell's and Wright's behest, the labor unions they represented printed leaflets urging workers to vote for Hogg and Daily and distributed them throughout Houston's blue-collar neighborhoods.[46]

No one could possibly accuse Ima Hogg, daughter of former Texas governor James S. Hogg and a wealthy patron of the local cultural scene, of radicalism or leftist sympathies. Dr. Daily, a well-known physician and liberal Democrat, was not so well protected. Foreign born and Jewish, she attracted some minor Red-baiting but easily won reelection. Daily would not do so well during the postwar Red Scare days, however. After the election, Arthur Mandell wrote Ima Hogg and told her about his clients' support. He emphasized that the unions did not expect special favors, they only wanted Hogg and Daily to "do your utmost to raise the teachers' pay . . . and provide for all Americans . . . equal educational opportunities. . . ."[47]

Art Mandell's letter to Ima Hogg described only one of many similar Popular Front–style campaigns led by the two lawyers during the war. The war years represented the peak of their influence as well as the zenith of Communist and leftist respectability. Many on the political left antici-pated—while some just hoped for—a postwar era of American-Soviet cooperation to sustain the development of their vision of a progressive society.[48] For the CPUSA and its various allies on the left, the heady days of American-Soviet cooperation abroad and the political Popular Front at home soon came to an end—a victim of the Cold War. Rather than being an era of peaceful accommodation and cooperation, the post-war domestic environment would be defined by fear and a demand for orthodoxy. The American left could not escape from either.

After the end of World War II, an intense power struggle erupted between the leftist and anti-Communist factions within the CIO as the onset of the Cold War renewed old animosities within the labor move-ment. The CIO found itself increasingly under attack from anti-union conservative politicians, newspapers, and industrialists as well as the American Federation of Labor for tolerating Communists and leftists in the union. "Middle grounders" and some leftists soon realized that the CIO had to make rapid adjustments to the realities of domestic anti-Communism or face the possibility of extinction. To save their unions as well as their individual power, CIO non-Communist leaders, led by Phillip Murray, CIO president, initiated a purge of their leftist member-ship. Because of their strength at the local levels, the leftists were able to put up a stout resistance that sometimes led to violence. In the Houston-Galveston area, the anti-Communist labor purge centered on the National Maritime Union (NMU).[49]

A cadre of militant seamen had organized the NMU in 1937 and elected Joseph Curran its first national president. During the union's early years, Curran allied himself with the NMU's leftist faction and used the Communist members to maintain personal control. After the United States entered World War II, the Communists elected 107 of 150 NMU officials, threatening Curran's iron-fisted rule. Curran nevertheless held on, looking for an opportunity to regain lost ground. In 1946, with the war over and tensions building between the United States and the Soviet Union, Curran, like some other "leftist" CIO union heads such as Walter Reuther of the United Auto Workers and Mike Quill of the Transport Workers, turned against his former allies and initiated a lengthy struggle to purge the Communists.[50] Curran began his attack in December 1946 by removing CPUSA member Joe Stack, an NMU vice-president, on trumped-up charges of "misfeasance" and neglect of duties. Stack's removal mobilized the leftist faction, including the Communists, to defend its power within the union.[51]

The NMU factional struggle at the national level spread to the locals as Curran's allies began to remove local officials associated with the left. One Texas CIO labor leader later recalled that after the war the NMU national office frequently changed its local port agents because it feared they were CPUSA members. The veteran labor leader remembered that the NMU was "probably the heaviest infiltrated because the communists were in the formative stages" of the NMU's creation. In Houston, the membership voted in April 1947 to remove James P. Boyle as NMU port agent because of his membership in the Communist party. Two leftist NMU national board members, Ferdinand Smith and Howard McKenzie, immediately ordered Chester Young, an NMU field investigator, to Houston to reinstate Boyle. When Young arrived, he met with Arthur Mandell and asked him to lead the reinstatement fight. The lawyer agreed and Young called a meeting to repeal Boyle's removal. Mandell rallied enough members of the leftist faction to assure Boyle's return to his post. At the meeting, Mandell warned the members that if they failed to rescind their action against Boyle the Houston local would be expelled from the NMU. Despite the protest of the anti-Communist faction's leader that the entire meeting was illegal because his group had not been properly notified, Boyle was reinstated by a 35 to 23 vote. The local press covered the incident and eagerly quoted Boyle proudly telling reporters, "I have been a Communist for seven years. All my officers know that I am a Communist."[52] Boyle's honesty only provided more evidence to be used later by Houston's Red Scare activists in convincing potential supporters that a local Communist threat existed. To NMU president Joseph Curran the Boyle incident also clearly demonstrated Arthur Mandell's strong support of the leftist faction.

Mandell provided more substance for his pro-Communist image a few months later when he joined the legal team defending Joe Stack at his NMU trial in New York City in the summer of 1947. The NMU jury found Stack guilty of aiding interests "harmful to the union" and barred him from office for five years. The left-wing faction issued a minority "pro-Stack" report to protest the NMU trial committee's decision. Anti-

Communist NMU members accused Mandell of writing the report. He later denied authorship, but his enemies remained unconvinced. After the Stack trial, an NMU member in Houston wrote Joe Curran that Gulf Coast NMU Communists were telling other members that "Mandell was the only attorney they could trust" because he was "sympathetic with the long-range Communist program in the NMU."[53]

Any doubts about the existence of a CIO anti-Communist campaign or the national leadership's commitment to it were quickly dispelled at the Texas state convention in October 1947. Meeting in San Antonio, the convention delegates heard CIO regional director A. R. Hardesty proclaim the new doctrine. Referring to CIO Communists, Hardesty declared, "We have defeated them again and again at their own game and will continue to beat them until they give up their subversive activities in our ranks." The CIO leader also claimed, possibly for the benefit of antilabor forces, that "the small influence which [Communists] might have once held in Texas is all but extinct." Such pronouncements were premature when applied to the Houston-Galveston NMU. For example, CPUSA member James Boyle, who had recently resisted a purge attempt, was a delegate to the 1947 state convention and a member of the executive board of the CIO's Texas State Industrial Union Council. Boyle refused to be cowed by Hardesty or anyone else. Undeterred, Boyle demanded that the CIO state convention pass a resolution calling for a federal antilynching bill and laws against racial discrimination "in all facets of American life." He also submitted a resolution denouncing and calling for the revocation of President Truman's Executive Order 9835, which established federal employee loyalty oaths. Boyle's resolutions went nowhere as the convention's legislative committee refused to submit them to the delegates.[54]

Despite the purge of Joe Stack at the national level, the attempted purge of James Boyle locally, and claims by CIO leaders, leftists and Communists retained influential positions in the Houston and Galveston NMU chapters throughout 1947 and most of 1948. Two NMU port agents for Houston, Jimmy Cunningham and James Boyle, and one for Galveston, H. K. Deuchare, were all admitted members of the Communist party and all continued in their positions. Another Communist, Clyde ("Tex") Drake, was an important CIO Houston port agent. James ("Blackie") Merrill, while apparently not a Communist, was a part of the leftist faction and was considered to be a "Red" by the local authorities. Some of these men were active and aggressive pro-Communist union members. For example, the young and forceful Jimmy Cunningham openly used the Houston NMU hall as a base to recruit new Communist party members and to collect party dues. There is no evidence that these men ever conducted any "subversive activities." All of them were long-time pro-union workers whose party memberships dated back to the early days of the Depression. None of them kept their party membership a secret.

It is doubtful that any of these individuals, unlike Homer Brooks or Elizabeth Benson, had ever read a line of Marx or Lenin. Their involvement in the radical faction of labor stemmed from years of struggle against wretched working conditions on board their ships, poor wages, and managerial tyranny. These factors created a radical tradition on the waterfront. The Communist party, at the height of the Depression, had demonstrated more concern for their plight than any other organization. In a major national study, CPUSA members were questioned about why they joined the party. A typical answer was the one given by an anonymous respondent: "I didn't worry through the thick books of Marx. I joined the party when it moved a widow's evicted furniture back into her house. I thought it was right. That's why I joined." A leftist but non-Communist longshoreman, Gilbert Mers, who worked on the Corpus Christi and Houston wharfs in the 1930s and 1940s, explained: ". . . the Communist Party seemed to have a pretty good deal. They were going to work this way and that way and the other way. I thought they could be as benevolent as anybody else." Even though some were ignorant of ideology, these men responded positively to the concern shown them by the party. One seaman who flirted with the Communist party during these years later stated that he and most of his colleagues were never "pro-Russian," they just wanted safe working conditions and a living wage. The NMU member argued, "I think we [the United States] have the best constitution in the world. We just don't live up to it." In the post–World War II decade, such innocent idealism made these men easy fodder for the Red Scare.[55]

At the same time that the NMU Communists were struggling to defend their positions in the Houston-Galveston ports, the Texas Communist party was returning to its prewar level of visibility. Gone, however, were Homer Brooks and Elizabeth Benson. They were replaced by new leadership. Ruth Koenig, a native of the Texas Rio Grande Valley and associated with the International Longshoremen's Union, now served as chairman. James J. Green worked as secretary of the state party. What evidence exists about Green indicates that he was a CPUSA professional. Koenig and Green would always identify themselves as Communist leaders when speaking at public gatherings and issued press releases in the name of the party.

Green and Koenig, along with William H. Crawford, also served as editors of the party's two-page newspaper, the *Texas Spur*. Produced monthly in the party's office in suite 305 of the Hermann Building, the *Spur* usually focused on one topic with each issue. For example, the March

1947 *Spur* was devoted to an attack on proposed anti-Communist bills pending in Congress, while the April issue focused on the Taft-Hartley labor union regulation bill.[56]

Several pamphlets were also published from the little office in the Hermann Building, including an eighteen-page booklet titled *What the People of Texas Need: The Communist Program for the Lone Star State*. The booklet presented a detailed discussion of the CPUSA's postwar political policy toward minority rights, veterans, farmers, labor unions, women, health, education, and housing. *What the People of Texas Need* featured a strong statement in favor of woman's rights, including a demand for "equal pay for equal work," government subsidized child care centers for working women, and an end to discrimination against women in professional education and employment. Other policies reflected the postwar demands of liberal and progressive Democrats, including a call for subsidized housing and an end to racial segregation. Copies of *What the People of Texas Need* eventually found their way into the hands of some American Legion and future Minute Women leaders. After the disintegration of the Texas CPUSA in 1950, Red Scare activists would wave the booklet in the faces of those doubting the existence of a local CPUSA threat.

James J. Green, Ruth Koenig, and their little band of associates in Houston were busy with their printing activities in the 1946 to 1949 period. They even managed to purchase a large block of space in the Houston *Post* on April 25, 1947, that demanded a "full-scale Congressional investigation of the conditions in Texas City" that had allowed the tragic explosions and disaster a few days earlier. The CPUSA called for immediate federal and state relief for victims "with no discrimination as to race, creed, or color."[57]

If Houstonians failed to notice local Communist activity before or during 1947, they would have had difficulty not noticing it in 1948. That year represented the peak of radical visibility, both for Communists and the non-Communist left, in Houston during the Cold War era. Former vice-president Henry Wallace's announcement on December 29, 1947, that he would be a candidate for president of the United States on a third-party ticket brought Houston's left together in a final pre–Red Scare coalition. Lawyers Herman Wright and Arthur Mandell, NMU leftists, the Texas Communist party, civil rights leaders such as Lulu B. White and Moses Leroy, anti–Cold War liberals, and others pooled their efforts for the last time in an attempt to elect Wallace to the presidency.[58]

The firm of Mandell and Wright had survived the war years in fine shape. Continuing to prosper financially with their lucrative workmen's compensation insurance and labor counseling business, the two faced the future with confidence. Both continued their commitment to progressive causes. Mandell joined the Civil Rights Congress (CRC) and attended its national conferences in Detroit in 1946 and Chicago in 1947. Joining the CRC plunged Mandell even deeper into the radical mainstream. The CRC was widely perceived as a front organization for the Communist party. Its main purpose was to provide legal services for the pro-Communist left.[59]

Mandell and Herman Wright both joined the National Association for the Advancement of Colored People (NAACP) and added the black civil rights struggle to their list of causes. Wright became a member of the Houston chapter's Committee on Legal Redress. This brought Wright into close contact with Houston's black leadership. The connection was strengthened further in February 1947 when Mandell and Wright brought Ben Ramey, a recent graduate of the University of Texas law school, into their firm. An articulate political leftist crippled by polio, Ramey was a dedicated champion of the black civil rights movement. Shortly after joining Mandell and Wright, the gifted young lawyer became a member of the team, headed by future Supreme Court justice Thurgood Marshall, that represented Heaman Sweatt in his fight to integrate the University of Texas law school.[60]

In keeping with their left-of-center political outlook, Mandell, Wright, and Ramey opposed the election of Harry S Truman for president in 1948. Henry A. Wallace provided them with a suitable progressive alternative. Wallace had emerged in the immediate postwar years as a vocal supporter of long-range Soviet-American cooperation. No Communist or socialist, the eccentric and idealistic Wallace often argued, "I wouldn't want Communism over here, but it makes more sense in Russia." The former vice-president and New Deal cabinet member called for a "Century of the Common Man" in which American society would be transformed into what one historian has described as "a curious blend of humanitarian reform and progressive capitalism." Many of the participants in the Popular Front of the 1935 to 1945 era looked to Wallace and the Progressive party for leadership to preserve and continue the coalition of the left.[61]

Wallace's presidential announcement was not unexpected. The CPUSA told its pro-Communist labor union activists at least two months prior to the announcement to anticipate such a development and begin plans for mounting a campaign. The CPUSA had quietly worked since 1945 for the creation of a third party to run a candidate for president in 1948. Their efforts had played a role in convincing Wallace to oppose Truman. Nevertheless, Wallace made his own decision and did so at the behest of many non-Communists. Communist and pro-Wallace non-Communist interests had coincided for separate reasons. As a result of the pre-announcement information, which was transmitted through CPUSA channels, Houston's left was ready to organize local support for the Progressive crusade.[62]

The day after Wallace's announcement, Herman Wright began creating an organization for the Texas campaign. Wright announced that "I am going to do what I can for [Wallace]. In due course we'll have meetings, organize and hold rallies." The Texas Communist party immediately followed with a pledge of its own support. Ruth Koenig and James Green held a press conference on January 3, 1948, in Houston and proclaimed they would work closely with the Wallace effort.[63]

Houston's pro-Wallace coalition anticipated support from the local NMU affiliate. Accordingly, port agent Jimmy Cunningham began enlisting NMU members as Wallace workers early in 1948. Unfortunately for the pro-Wallace movement, however, the CIO national leadership proclaimed in January that it expected every affiliate to work within the Democratic party, and that support for Henry Wallace would be interpreted as a deliberate attempt "to create confusion and division within the labor movement." At the same time the CIO was issuing its anti-Wallace policy, NMU president Joseph Curran escalated his efforts to expel Communists from every NMU office. General elections for all NMU officials, both local and national, were scheduled from April through June 1948. Curran decided to concentrate on defeating every Communist and leftist candidate for NMU office. The Immigration Service helped Curran in February 1948 by arresting Ferdinand Smith, the national secretary of the NMU and an opponent of Curran's anti-Communist policies. Federal authorities charged Smith with being a Communist alien and deported him to his native British West Indies. Meanwhile, Communist and leftist NMU members chose to ignore the CIO order to stay out of the Wallace campaign. This decision played into Curran's hands as he subsequently charged them with anti-union activity.[64]

Joe Curran used an anti-Communist official at each local to direct the purge of leftist members. In Houston, Joe Dunn, an NMU port agent allied with Curran's faction, succeeded in organizing a majority of the Houston membership to control the upcoming union elections. On March 12, 1948, Dunn maneuvered the Houston NMU into voting against supporting Wallace for president.[65] Meanwhile, the day after the Houston NMU decision, the city's Wallace supporters met at the Food, Tobacco, Agricultural, and Allied Workers of America (FTA) hall at 815½ Congress Avenue and created a formal organization, the Harris County Wallace for President Committee. The FTA union, led locally by Jack Frye, a self-proclaimed CPUSA member, was one of the more radical CIO affiliates and was also a Mandell and Wright client. It disregarded the CIO prohibition against helping the Wallace movement and allowed its office to become the state headquarters for the Progressive party. The CIO would eventually expel the entire union because of its refusal to purge its Communist leadership. Although the FTA had over 46,000 members nationally in 1948, the union had just begun to organize in Houston and Texas and had little influence in the region. Nevertheless, faced with hostility from other CIO locals, the Wallace supporters welcomed the FTA's help. This was especially the case in light of unanticipated problems with the NMU.[66]

The first statewide Wallace for President meeting occurred in Austin on March 21. The organizers included Lulu B. White of Houston, a prominent NAACP leader; Elvierto Bela of Laredo, secretary of the local Mine, Mill and Smelter Workers; Harriet Leary of San Antonio's Voters League; H. K. Deuchare of Galveston, NMU port agent; Pat Lunsford of Baytown, a member of the Brotherhood of Railroad Trainmen; and Herman Wright. Representatives from thirty Texas counties met at Green Pastures, a restaurant that had been the old family home of humorist John Henry Faulk. This site was selected because it was one of the few public places in Texas that would allow a racially integrated meeting. Herman Wright, presiding over the conference, was elected temporary state party chairman. The Wallace supporters created a formal organization to secure places on the state ballots for their candidates. The old mansion in south Austin echoed with enthusiastic resolve as the optimistic Texans vowed to spread the word about Wallace's progressive vision. The Wallacites cheered as Herman Wright read the keynote address written by Pat Lunsford, who was unable to attend. Lunsford's speech was a hell-raiser, even at the hands of Wright, not the most effective of speakers. Lunsford called for no less than a "life and death struggle with monopoly and its attendant evils, disease, poverty, discrimination, imperialism and war." The speech was a veritable litany of postwar evils as viewed from the left. Lunsford denounced the attack on organized labor, the "rising terror against minorities," police brutality, the draft, Truman's domestic and foreign policy aimed at supporting "reactionaries" at home and abroad, inflation, the "crisis" in medical care and housing, fascism in Spain and South America, and the "Republocrats" in Congress "working toward war instead of peace." Stating that the Austin meeting was a landmark in Texas history, Lunsford concluded that the conference would "unleash the pent-up progressive forces" of Texas. The participants would look back on the meeting "in the years of victory to come" as the start of a "new era."

While Lunsford's keynote address provided the necessary pep talk, the highlight of the day was a written message from the venerable Texas folklorist and author J. Frank Dobie. The former University of Texas professor declared, "The Truman Administration has left liberal democracy in the lurch. In this lurch, I and others turn to the Progressive Party headed by Mr. Wallace. Mr. Truman's mediocrity of both mind and character leaves us no other alternative. He may mean well. Hell is paved with good intentions. Henry Wallace . . . is in harmony with the inevitable evolution of society." The appreciative audience, buoyed by Dobie's message, proceeded to elect him in absentia honorary chairman of the Progressive party in Texas. The Progressives also voted to have the party's founding convention in Houston on April 25, 1948. After electing an eight-member executive committee that included Art Mandell and James P. Boyle, the conference adjourned.[67]

Herman Wright and Art Mandell returned to the harsh realities of Houston immediately following the exhilarating but unreasonably optimistic meeting in the state capital. As they made plans for the April 25 convention, the two lawyers got a bitter first taste of what to expect from the so-called pent-up progressive forces of Texas.

The pro-Wallace minority within the Houston NMU, led by E. J. ("Jimmy") Cunningham, tried to ignore the CIO decision not to support the Progressive party. Cunningham rented the NMU hall to the Wallace supporters so that they could meet on March 27, 1948, to plan for a state convention. When the anti-Communist NMU faction heard about Cunningham's action, they locked the NMU hall the night of the meeting and confronted the Wallace supporters as they attempted to enter. A burly spokesman for the anti-Wallace seamen announced to news reporters covering the incident that Wright and his associates could not enter because "we don't allow no Communists in here." The Wallace supporters wisely decided to retreat and hold their meeting in the tiny FTA hall. Houston's newspapers excitedly reported the episode as another "Communist" incident.[68]

Even though the CIO national leadership had declared its opposition to Wallace in January and the Houston NMU chapter had joined them in March, the Wallace forces in Texas held out a slight hope that the state CIO Council might not follow suit. Nearly three months had passed since the national decision but nothing had been heard from the Texas CIO leaders. On April 3, 1948, the executive board of the Texas State CIO Council met to discuss a letter received from John Brophy, a former socialist currently serving as the director of the CIO's Industrial Union councils. James P. Boyle, CPUSA member, NMU port agent, and Wallace activist, attended the board meeting as vice-president of the CIO Council. Brophy's letter ordered all Texas locals to oppose the third party and endorse the Marshall Plan for aid to Europe. Boyle argued that it was a violation of the CIO constitution for the national leadership to interfere with the political views of the local affiliates. His fellow board members disagreed and voted 9 to 2 to comply with Brophy's order. Boyle, seeing the handwriting on the wall, resigned from the executive board.

The CIO, the major source of strength for Texas' small but promising movement on the left, was now in full-scale retreat. National headquarters warned Mandell and Wright that the prohibition against working for the third-party movement also applied to them. The attorneys were told to quit leading the Wallace campaign. Both men refused, sending word back through the CIO hierarchy that the union had bought their legal skills, not their politics.[69]

On April 25, 1948, three hundred delegates from fourteen of Texas' thirty-one senatorial districts gathered in Houston's Music Hall to attend the state's Wallace for President convention. After hearing Herman Wright's keynote address on "Why We Need a Third Party in Texas," the delegates endorsed a party platform that included demands for a $1 per hour minimum wage, abolition of the state poll tax, the lowering of the voting age to eighteen years of age, state legislative redistricting, racial desegregation, repeal of the Taft-Hartley labor law, day care centers for working mothers, support for the United Nations, and opposition to the military draft. The convention nominated Herman Wright for governor of Texas, along with the Reverend Stacey Adams of Dallas for lieutenant governor and Houston attorney Morris Bogdanow for attorney general. The delegates raised a total of $8,513 to support a state campaign office in Houston.

For entertainment, the convention delegates heard humorist and progressive political activist John Henry Faulk perform his satirical imitation of a southern politician pleading for "Poor Old Truman." Herman Wright's young partner, Ben Ramey, followed Faulk with a fund-raising speech. A state fund quota was set at $50,000. O. John Rogge of New York gave the guest speech. Rogge, a former U.S. assistant attorney general, spoke over a state-wide radio network about the current threat to civil liberties and why he was for Wallace. The Progressive party's state convention adjourned without incident or any harassment from local police or newspapers.[70]

While the leftist-liberal coalition supporting Henry Wallace was organizing and working in Houston during the spring of 1948, the fight to destroy the power of the left within the NMU spread to Galveston. NMU president Joseph Curran had successfully retained control over the NMU in Houston but Galveston remained a leftist stronghold. H. K. Deuchare, a Communist NMU port agent and Wallace activist, was firmly in control. Curran transferred a twenty-five-year-old brawler named S. D. ("Tex") George from New York to Galveston to run against Deuchare as port agent in the upcoming union election and purge the leftists from the local union.

As soon as Tex George arrived in Galveston he set up an office and announced his candidacy for Deuchare's job. At the same time, George secretly met with Galveston police and fire commissioner Walter L. Johnston, who agreed to provide police support for George's activities. This secret alliance between the police and the pro-Curran faction proved crucial to George's eventual success. Encouraged by the knowledge that Galveston's police backed them up, Tex George and his NMU supporters went aboard every ship that docked, passed out leaflets, talked with the men, and organized an anti-Communist faction strong enough to control NMU meetings. NMU members were never known for their restraint. The union had an unusually turbulent membership. Seamen in Galveston began arming themselves with brass knuckles, clubs, and guns. The youthful but tough Tex George told one newsman, "You gotta play 'em at their own game. . . . you gotta hate 'em. When they get rough, you just get a little rougher." And both sides got rough. Years later, George recalled that "some of our boys who didn't agree with the Communists were really getting worked over . . . getting beat up bad. It was really a vicious thing." Some of the pro-Curran men were beaten by opponents with baseball bats and chains. Tex George himself pistol-whipped two men on a Galveston street with a .45-caliber handgun he always carried. George later claimed that the two men were "tailing" him and he just took preventive action.

Meanwhile, the Galveston police harassed NMU members opposing Tex George. Galveston's merchant marine population had increased noticeably after George began organizing his faction. Leftist seamen migrated from New Orleans and West Coast ports to vote for Deuchare and his associates in a bid to preserve their power. Galveston police responded with nightly arrests of dozens of the newly arrived seamen. Each was charged with vagrancy and if it was shown that he had been in port several weeks without a job he was heavily fined for staying in town without visible means of support. The police also set up a movie camera in an office overlooking the entrance to the NMU hiring hall and photographed everyone entering and leaving. Deuchare's supporters were identified and listed. Police then used the lists to periodically round up the men for interrogation and intimidation.

Eventually, the internal factional struggle in Galveston's NMU became a public spectacle when violence erupted at the union hall. On June 2, 1948, during a meeting to discuss a new contract with ship owners, a fight broke out between the embattled factions. When Tex George argued in favor of the new contract, Otto Von Schmitt, a member of the leftist faction, accused him of being a tool of the ship companies. Tex George responded by hitting Von Schmitt in the face and, with the help of another seaman, Sylvester Polosky, apparently tossed him out the second-floor window. (George later claimed that Von Schmitt jumped out of the window.) Von Schmitt managed to fall on a canvas canopy and avoid serious injury. A general melee erupted as H. K. Deuchare came to Von Schmitt's aid by attacking Polosky with a metal stapling machine. The union hall emptied and the fighting continued in the street. Von Schmitt began running toward the Galveston police station nearby. One of George's men saw him running, whipped a pistol out of his pants, and raced after Von Schmitt, chasing him into the police building. Galveston police quickly ended the brawl by arresting Deuchare, George, Von Schmitt, and Polosky. The police chief told George, "Look Tex, this is going too strong when your god damned goons come running up our steps with their pistols out."

Herman Wright, in the midst of the Wallace campaign, rushed from Houston to represent Deuchare at the hearing held the following day. No charges were filed against Von Schmitt but George was charged with assault. Wright refused to represent Tex George and Polosky, the anti-leftist opponents of Deuchare, arguing that neither George nor Polosky was a union official while Deuchare was an NMU port agent. As NMU lawyer, Wright reasoned, he had to defend Deuchare.

Because of his alliance with the Galveston police, however, George did not need a lawyer. At the request of the county prosecutor, the justice of the peace dismissed all charges. Nonetheless, the episode provided more evidence of the pro-leftist stance, duly noted by Curran's NMU leadership, taken by the Mandell and Wright law firm. The incident also received considerable radio news coverage and was reported as being instigated by "local Reds."

Meanwhile, negotiations between the NMU and shipping companies over a new national contract continued. When the old contract expired on June 15, 1948, a federal court issued an injunction against a strike called by the NMU. In Galveston, the NMU leadership, still controlled by H. K. Deuchare, rejected Joe Curran's order to obey the injunction and refused to open the hiring hall to service ships in port. Deuchare's action finally gave Tex George legal cause to ask for his removal as port agent. On June 17, Curran quickly approved the suspension of Deuchare, Von Schmitt, and two patrolmen.

Tex George's success at ousting the Communist leaders in Galveston's NMU resulted in further violence. On June 18, the two factions attacked each other on the Port of Galveston docks. The violent brawl spread from the 22nd Street Pier to the 26th Street Pier but was centered mainly on the SS *Robert S. Lovett*. The fight was marked by gunfire from both sides, but only one man was wounded. Galveston police riot squads eventually arrived and restored order, arresting eighteen men on charges of carrying concealed weapons and vagrancy. One man was charged with assault to murder. The riot, which the anti-Curran faction seemed to have instigated, represented a final cathartic response to its loss of control over the Galveston local. Herman Wright called for Deuchare's reinstatement and Deuchare opened a rival hiring hall, all to no avail. The anti-Communist, pro-Curran faction enjoyed total victory and Tex George became the youngest port agent in NMU history. Years later, George recalled the 1948 purge and said, "After that we had no trouble from the Communists around here. Everybody loves a winner. When the commies were winning, they had support. Now we are in the saddle . . . that's the way it is, padnuh. People are sheep."

Local Galveston-Houston radio stations eagerly pounced upon the NMU Galveston brawls, consistently referring to the anti-Curran faction, which consisted of non-Communist leftists as well as Communists, as a "Commie goon squad." Individual members were always called "Reds." One radio commentator, reporting on the vagrancy trials of several anti-Curran NMU members, declared to his listeners that "the shadow of communism loomed large" in the Galveston courtroom. Although the NMU leadership permanently expelled the few Communists involved in the episodes, the union's factional struggle and resulting publicity helped give credence to the accusations of Red Scare activists three years later that Communists were in the area.[71]

The end of Galveston's NMU problems in June 1948 did not stop the public activity of Houston-area leftists. The Henry Wallace presidential campaign continued to be conducted by the area's leftist coalition. All through the summer and early fall of 1948, Wallace leaders such as Herman Wright, Morris Bogdanow, and Ben Ramey attracted public attention in their efforts to get Wallace elected. As a result, Mandell and Wright received numerous telephone threats and hate mail. Their anonymous enemies painted the sidewalks outside the homes of both men with red hammer and sickle symbols. Schoolmates spat the term "nigger lover" at Wright's children. Ramey received hate mail when he organized an interracial Students for Wallace club at the racially segregated University of Houston. Bogdanow, Progressive party candidate for Texas attorney general, conducted meetings statewide as the party's chief fundraiser and attracted even more attention when the Beaumont police arrested him for allegedly violating an obscure city ordinance prohibiting sound truck operations on public streets.[72]

Awareness of the Progressive party campaign reached its peak in Houston when Henry Wallace made a swing through the South that eventually brought him to Texas' largest city. The Houston *Post* welcomed Wallace's visit with a belligerent editorial prophetically titled "Omelets for Wallace." The *Post* called Wallace a "radical candidate" and suggested the only motive behind his trip through the South was to "stir up more dissension and strife and chaos." The *Post* added that Wallace's troublemaking tour was the way "Commies" acted and "[the Communists] are all supporting Mr. Wallace."[73]

Henry Wallace and his entourage spent two highly publicized days in Houston, September 28–29, 1948. His hectic first-day schedule included a speech over radio station KPRC, a press conference, a speech at a Negro Businessmen's Club luncheon, and a reception at the Women for Wallace auxiliary. At each stop, Wallace was harassed by hecklers. The next day Wallace spoke at a rally that was one of the most sensational political events in Houston in the late 1940s. Approximately four thousand people attended the meeting. Wallace's southern campaign, in which he refused to speak before segregated audiences, seems to have been intended to gain Wallace votes in the North rather than in the South. Local newspapers pointedly noted that blacks constituted at least 65 percent of the crowd. They also observed that several people were going through the audience selling copies of the *Daily Worker*, the official organ of the American Communist party. Appearances by Ruth Koenig, chairman of the Texas Communist party, and Paul Robeson, the black actor and singer who was an admitted member of the Communist party, added considerably to the radical atmosphere. Robeson sang several work songs and gave a speech denouncing President Harry Truman's civil rights record.

Wallace concluded the evening with a campaign speech. Before Wallace could speak, however, an anti-Communist NMU seaman gave meaning to the *Post*'s editorial, "Omelets for Wallace," when he tossed eggs and tomatoes at the speaker's rostrum. The eggs splashed on Wallace as a large portion of the audience applauded. When the noise eventually subsided and the seaman was escorted out of the building, Wallace delivered a stinging denunciation of "Mr. Houston," Jesse H. Jones. Wallace, recalling his many fights with the former cabinet member, declared that Jones was really a Republican and had fought socially progressive legislation while a member of Franklin Roosevelt's New Deal.

After the rally, the Wallace entourage went to Herman Wright's home to spend the night. Wallace's party had reservations at the Rice Hotel, owned, ironically, by Jesse Jones. But they refused to stay when the hotel informed a Wallace aide that Edith Roberts, Wallace's black secretary, would have to go elsewhere. Herman Wright offered his house to the group and he stayed at a hotel. Wallace and his staff failed to get much sleep, however, as the house was barraged with telephone calls and telegrams threatening Wallace and Wright and demanding that they leave town before dawn. Curtis MacDougall, the official chronicler of the Wallace campaign, has written that many of the telephone calls were directed at Edith Roberts, with the typical message being "Get that nigger out of the house!" At about 2:00 A.M., according to MacDougall, a Western Union messenger rang the doorbell. Lewis Frank, Jr., Wallace's main speech writer, answered the door as a New York policeman who served as Wallace's bodyguard stood behind him with a drawn revolver. The startled delivery boy quickly handed the telegram to Frank and departed. The message simply read "Get out of town!"[74]

The Wallace coalition dissolved in Houston after November 2, 1948. On that day, Wallace managed to attract only 1,156,103 popular votes nationally, one-third of that total from New York alone, and failed to receive any electoral votes. Wallace polled a minuscule 3,764 votes in Texas while Herman Wright received only 3,747 votes in his token bid for governor.

Wallace had begun with considerable non-Communist support, but he lost hundreds of thousands of potential votes during the campaign. The major reason was the close association of the CPUSA and the Progressive party. By election day, many voters believed that Wallace was simply a Communist dupe. Undoubtedly, Wallace was also the victim of Truman's spirited campaign and his rhetorical veer to the left on domestic issues. J. Frank Dobie, the Texas Progressive party honorary chairman, symbolized Wallace's plight. The sagacious Texas Hill Country philosopher played a passive and unenthusiastic role in the Progressive campaign, eventually voting for the "mediocre Mr. Truman." After the election, Dobie wrote Herman Wright and demanded that his name be disassociated from any connection with Wallace or the Progressive party. Dobie nonetheless assured Wright that he would "always be for free minds and [I] appreciate your stand." Obviously Dobie, as well as an unknown number of other Americans, had been repelled by the ultimate direction and conduct of Henry Wallace's campaign.[75]

President Truman's reelection convinced NMU president Joseph Curran of the wisdom of his anti-Wallace stand and allowed him to complete his purge of the union. This led to the inevitable firing of Arthur Mandell and Herman Wright as NMU attorneys in Texas. As their former associate Chris Dixie recalled years later, "They both had a real devotion to the Wallace cause but they paid for it. After 1948, Herman Wright and Arthur Mandell were persona non grata among the leaders of the labor movement." An editorial in the *Pilot,* the NMU newspaper, announced Mandell's expulsion, charging that for years he had helped guide the union's Communist faction. The *Pilot* stated that "to this day he is still representing some of the disruptive elements that are harassing the peaceful operation of our union." The NMU was thoroughly purged and in 1949 passed a constitutional amendment barring "Communists, Nazis, and Fascists" from membership. After the Wallace debacle, other CIO unions also severed relations with the firm. Mandell and Wright lost every union client, but they continued to represent individuals from the rank and file in personal injury suits. Herman Wright, who later claimed that he had never intended to be so personally involved in the Wallace movement but had been pulled along by events, bitterly withdrew from the Progressive party and did not participate in politics "of any kind" for years after. Mandell, Wright, and Ben Ramey, severed from their CIO connections, concentrated on NAACP and civil liberties cases for the next several years. These new developments left the labor union field in Houston to Art Combs and Chris Dixie. (The latter left Combs in April 1949 to form his own firm.) Arthur Mandell's long association with the CIO was thus terminated, a victim of the emerging Cold War and the growing conservatism of organized labor.[76]

The year 1948 was a particularly bad one for the American Communist party. The federal government indicted and arrested the party's national leadership in July for violating the Smith Act of 1940 by "conspiring to advocate" the violent overthrow of the government. The CPUSA also paid a high price for the support of the Progressive party—it lost almost all influence in the labor movement. The Henry Wallace debacle indicated to the CIO's national leadership that the vast majority of CIO members identified with the Democratic party and rejected the pro-Soviet attitude of its left-wing faction. This combination of disasters began a process that would see the Communist party go underground in 1950 and eventually, in the mid 1950s, disintegrate almost completely. After 1948, a handful of Communist and pro-Communist activists still openly operated in Houston. Deprived of their labor union associations, however, their actions were usually confined to defensive responses to increasing governmental repression and public hysteria.[77]

One of the last attempts by local CPUSA activists to promote their program openly occurred in January 1949. At that time the party made a feeble effort to organize a Communist students' club at the University of Houston. The attempt was unsuccessful and the overreaction to the party's activity warned of much darker days ahead. The party announced the new club, called the Hewlett Johnson Club after the so-called Red Dean of Canterbury, by distributing literature at the university. The next day the Houston *Press* printed a front-page headline screaming "U of H 'Flooded' by Red Literature." The literature, which had been distributed several times throughout the 1940s without any special notice by the community, was a typical attack on Wall Street bankers and President Truman's foreign policy. But with the Truman administration's prosecution of Communist leaders, the growing tensions of the Cold War, and the increasing societal uneasiness in Houston, such "radical" activity could no longer be tolerated. What was in reality an extremely minor incident caused by a handful of party diehards was reported by the newspapers as if the Communists had attempted to seize the campus. The university's president, Dr. E. E. Oberholtzer, called a news conference to assure the community that the school did not approve of the literature. He also promised to appoint a special student-faculty committee to investigate and "get to the bottom of the situation." This satisfied the newspapers, since they then dropped the matter.[78]

The attempt to organize at the University of Houston in January 1949 was one of the last examples of the Communist party openly working in Houston. As the months passed, harassment from the federal government increased. By the end of the year, the principal concern for the city's few remaining party members was not to organize college students but simply to stay out of jail.

After the indictment of the national Communist hierarchy in the *Eugene Dennis et al.* case in July 1948, the federal government initiated a series of legal proceedings against selected, alleged Communists. The strategy was twofold: some individuals were indicted for violating the Smith Act while noncitizens were deported as aliens. The federal government used the latter tactic against alleged CPUSA members in Texas and elsewhere. In December 1949, as a part of a larger strategy that included 140 so-called political aliens in nineteen states, the United States Immigration Service initiated deportation proceedings against aliens in San Antonio, Dallas, and Houston for alleged membership in the Communist party. All of the cases were similar in that the government attempted to use the proceedings to subpoena United States citizens and force them to testify about their individual political beliefs and associations. For example, the government would single out an alien for alleged Communist party membership and initiate deportation hearings. Next, the defendant's friends and associates, who were citizens, would be forced into court to testify about their own political beliefs. The government argued that by knowing the politics of the alien's friends, the court could better determine the alien's beliefs. This would accomplish at least two goals. The government could deport the "radical" aliens, and their American citizen friends would be "exposed" and subjected to official and unofficial harassment. However, the government's strategy violated the spirit of the Fifth Amendment to the United States Constitution by its denial of a citizen's right to protection against self-incrimination. During this period, former Texas congressman Maury Maverick complained that the Immigration Service was so obsessed by the "Terror of Communism" that it "looks upon all aliens as wicked people. . . ."[79]

A German couple's attempt to return to their hometown in the Soviet-occupied zone of Germany gave the federal government an opportunity to employ the deportation tactics in Houston. In 1939, at the age of twenty, Kurt Wittenburg fled Nazi Germany and immigrated to Uruguay. While in South America, he became a member of the Communist party. In 1947, Wittenburg immigrated to Houston to work in a meat-packing plant owned by a family relative. The next year, having earned enough money, Wittenburg moved his wife to Houston and the couple applied for United States citizenship. During the several months of waiting for his application to be processed, Wittenburg became involved in an attempt to unionize his relative's meat company. As a result of his pro-union activity, Wittenburg was fired. Without a job or savings the Wittenburgs thought they had no future in the United States. In the midst of their problems they turned to the Texas Communist party and applied for membership. They found no help there either. Even though the couple had earlier contributed money to the party, James Green, party chairman, refused to accept their application because they were not citizens. The American Communist party discouraged aliens from joining because of the deportation situation. Removed from the comforts of job security, family support, and political association, the Wittenburgs decided to return to Germany.

The Immigration and Naturalization Service (INS) became aware of the Wittenburgs in August 1949 when they sought visas to travel to the Soviet sector of Germany. Their application started an investigation that led immigration officials to conclude that the couple presented an excellent opportunity for the government to harass Houston Communists. Accordingly, the Immigration Service rejected their visa applications on the grounds that the Wittenburgs were illegal aliens. The INS charged that Kurt Wittenburg had lied about his Uruguayan Communist party membership when he applied for citizenship. Immigration officials questioned the Wittenburgs about their associates but they refused to talk. They were subsequently ordered to appear in federal court for a deportation hearing. Before they appeared in court, the German couple admitted to federal agents that they had applied for Communist party membership through James J. Green. They promised to testify to this in a closed immigration hearing if the government would agree not to subject them to a deportation trial in federal court.

The deportation hearing occurred on December 15, 1949, in the chambers of federal judge Thomas Kennerly, who had presided in the Homer Brooks draft evasion case. The official reason for deportation had changed to the charge that the Wittenburgs were Communists. This violated no law, but the Immigration Service had ruled that party membership was grounds for deportation of aliens. The hearing's real purpose was to place James Green under oath to question him about the Texas Communist party. Judge Kennerly ordered Green to produce all records, books, and documents that he possessed that might provide information about the Wittenburgs. Green went to the offices of Herman Wright and Arthur Mandell to seek help from the battle-weary attorneys. Mandell advised Green to cooperate with the Immigration Service since the Wittenburgs were certain to be deported. Green rejected Mandell's advice and responded that the hearing was not actually for the Wittenburgs but in reality was a "fishing expedition" to obtain names of party members. Thus, neither Wright nor Mandell represented Green. Instead, he was represented by the Wittenburgs' lawyer, Morris Bogdanow.

When Green appeared in Judge Kennerly's chambers on December 16, 1949, he refused to answer any questions and invoked the Fifth Amendment. Kennerly ruled that the Fifth Amendment did not apply because they were in a closed hearing, not open court. Bogdanow argued that Green's testimony was not needed because the Wittenburgs wanted to leave the country anyway and deportation was unnecessary. Kennerly also overruled this objection. When Green again refused to testify, Judge Kennerly ordered him to appear in open federal court to show why he should not be jailed for contempt. As Green left the judge's office, he distributed a printed statement to newsmen waiting outside titled "Stop the Witch Hunt in Texas!" that denounced similar deportation hearings in Dallas and San Antonio. Green told reporters that the "so-called investigations of aliens are really aimed at jailing citizens who are Communists or Progressives." He then announced, "My name is James J. Green. The 'J' stands for Jack—not Judas."

Houston's newspapers reported the Wittenburg case in detail. Using headlines such as "Red Leader on Trial for Contempt," the newspapers impressed on their readers a vision of a city crawling with subversives. The Houston *Post*, considered by many Houstonians to be the epitomy of moderation and middle-of-the-road politics, responded to James

Green's case with emotional outrage. On December 19, 1949, the *Post* published an editorial that declared Green was a "home grown Communist" who had defied authority and insulted the dignity of a United States court by refusing to testify. The *Post* argued that the government needed his information to protect the nation's safety and welfare. The newspaper warned that Green's handbill, "Stop the Witch Hunt in Texas!," had all the appearances of being produced by "a central party authority," a dark hint that a powerful conspiracy was at work in Houston. As for the Wittenburgs, the *Post* declared that "the United States is waging a desperate Cold War with Communism" and that it was essential "to root out and block the infiltration of Red aliens who might join in a fifth column to destroy us." Finally, the *Post* editorial signaled the arrival of a new atmosphere of fear when it concluded that individuals who refused to give information about acquaintances who were Communists were disloyal themselves. The *Post* demanded that such people, including James Green and the Wittenburgs, "deserve to be dealt with accordingly."

Meanwhile, the day Green refused to testify, the United States Department of Justice also asked Judge Kennerly to compel Ruth Koenig, former Texas Communist party chairman, and Robert Brannan, a party worker, to testify in the Wittenburg hearing. With three Communist deportation hearings going on at once in Texas and party members and leaders being subpoenaed to testify, one of the most important Communist party lawyers in the United States arrived in Texas for the defense effort. Carol King of New York City, a veteran with over thirty years' experience in deportation and civil liberties cases, joined Morris Bogdanow for Green's, Koenig's, and Brannan's defense. King had served as defense counsel in the highly publicized deportation case of Gerhart Eisler, a self-confessed Soviet spy.

On December 21, Judge Kennerly held a hearing to determine if Ruth Koenig and Robert Brannan should be forced to testify in the Wittenburg matter. Prior to the hearing, Carol King engaged in a shouting match with reporters outside the judge's chambers. Beset by a barrage of questions from reporters in the hallway, King yelled, "This is nonsense — vicious nonsense." King told the newsmen that the Wittenburg case was an attempt "to terrorize aliens so that no one can stand up . . . and say what they think." The reporters asked King if she was a Communist. The lawyer replied that she was not, but added, "There's nothing sinister about Communism . . . it's not half as bad as the Immigration Service in this case."

In the hearing, King argued that the government was investigating the Wittenburgs only as an excuse to harass citizens because of their political beliefs. King contended that since the Wittenburgs were willing to be deported, the government had no right to compel witnesses to testify before the Immigration Service. She pointed out that no warrant of arrest had ever been issued in the matter and that no statute existed that would force anyone to testify before immigration agents. "There is no deportation case against the Wittenburgs," King asserted. "[They] are willing to leave this country anyhow." King concluded her argument by charging that the government's action was a "fishing expedition" against private citizens. Judge Kennerly took the case under advisement and adjourned the hearing.

The following day, Judge Kennerly began James Green's trial for contempt. Federal prosecutors argued that Green had no legal excuse for refusing to testify at the Immigration Service hearing and they asked that Green be jailed until he decided to provide answers. The government insisted it needed Green's testimony to determine the veracity of the Wittenburgs' statements. Carol King and Morris Bogdanow repeated the same arguments that they had used the day before on behalf of Ruth Koenig and Robert Brannan. Despite their efforts, however, Kennerly found Green guilty of contempt and ordered him to jail. Bogdanow immediately filed an appeal with the United States Fifth Circuit Court in New Orleans. Because another Communist leader, Fred Estes, had received a similar sentence in a Dallas court, the Communist party in New York City sent lawyer Emanuel Bloch to argue both cases. In August 1950, the Fifth Circuit Court in New Orleans disagreed with the lower courts in Dallas and Houston and ruled that witnesses could invoke the Fifth Amendment when applicable in such hearings. The federal court overturned the decisions. The appeals victory ended the entire episode as immigration authorities finally deported the Wittenburgs.[80]

The Wittenburg-Green affair in December 1949 marked the end of the Texas Communist party's ability to defend itself with any degree of effectiveness. In 1950 the local contingent of party members fled the city and ceased to exist as an openly active group. The departure of the Communists from Houston in 1950 was the result of the cumulative events that began in 1948, but the outbreak of the Korean War on June 25, 1950, proved to be the final act. The summer of 1950 marked the real beginning of Houston's Red Scare. Ironically, it also marked the end of Houston's pathetically small Communist party.

The last concerted activity of Houston's Communists in the 1950s was an effort to solicit signatures for the Stockholm Peace Petition, which called for the prohibition of the use of atomic bombs and strict international control of all nuclear weapons. The CPUSA had launched a national campaign in the spring of 1950 to get five million signatures on the petition for presentation to the United Nations on October 24, 1950. In

Texas, however, the petition drive was late in starting, possibly due to the crippled condition of the state's Communist party. The drive did not begin in Houston until June 26, a most unfortunate case of bad timing, as the Communist North Korean army had invaded South Korea the day before. Because of the increasingly hostile anti-Communist atmosphere, however, party members, including James Green, party chairman, began circulating the petitions under the auspices of the front organization known as the Texas Peace Committee. The weak attempt at subterfuge fooled no one. Local law enforcement agencies harassed the petition drive at every turn, picking up the petitioners "for questioning" whenever they appeared on Houston streets. Police arrested James Green on June 26 for circulating the literature and arrested his party colleagues, including Robert Brannan, George Johnson, and John Guss, on July 4 and again on July 9.[81]

The activity of James Green and his associates on behalf of the Stockholm Peace Petition drive was, depending on one's perspective, either very courageous or stupidly self-destructive, since the police and newspapers could now wage open war on such efforts and even violate basic civil liberties knowing they had total support from the community. Every attempt to exercise their constitutionally protected right to petition the government was met with police repression. After Guss and Johnson were arrested on July 4, they were held in jail for several hours without charge. Prisoners severely beat both men as jailers looked the other way. When their lawyer Morris Bogdanow publicly protested the brutality, the Houston *Press* responded that it was typical of "Reds" to "squall" about their rights when patriotic policemen did their duty. The *Press* reported that the petitioners were actually "busily working to undermine support for American resistance to communist aggression" and were obeying an order from Soviet premier Joseph Stalin.[82]

The peace petition drive by James Green and his associates and a statement by Morris Bogdanow that they had succeeded in having "over one thousand" citizens sign their documents frightened the Houston Police Department. On July 15 the police combed the city looking for James Green's "subversive" allies. The frantic search netted one eighty-year-old "hobo," four Jehovah's Witnesses, and Morris Bogdanow. The police arrested the eighty-year-old man for distributing leaflets they believed might be Communistic. The old man, who was barefoot and shirtless, was discovered with a few handbills crudely handwritten by himself with a crayon. The Houston *Post* reported that the "literature," much of which was illegible, was full of grammatical and spelling errors. The police admitted uncertainty about what the handbills actually said, but one officer insisted they seemed to make a statement about wars being fought for profit. When questioned by reporters as he left the police station, the old man said he did not know any Communists but that he had read the *Daily Worker* once to find out how they "transacted business in Russia." When asked if he was being represented by one of the "Red" attorneys in town, the old bum pulled at his hair, tangled and matted with filth accumulated from what appeared to be years of living on the streets, and said that he did not have a lawyer because "I was just passing out handbills, if we haven't got that right, then what the hell?" Houston police arrested the four Jehovah's Witnesses because their literature, published by the Watchtower Society, advocated pacifism and opposed nationalism. Their arrest card stated that they were picked up on suspicion of having "Communist tendencies."

The Houston police also arrested Morris Bogdanow while he attended a watermelon party at the Negro Elks' Lodge. The police charged Bogdanow with violating Texas' segregation laws by "mingling with Negroes," but his hold card at the police station stated, "This white man . . . has been with several persons . . . known to belong or have something to do with the Communist party. . . ." The "Red" arrests of July 1950 generated publicity for the police department that fostered an image of efficiency in removing dangerous "subversives" from the community. It also supported the growing feeling that the city was infested with Communist agents. Meanwhile, not so well publicized, the police quietly released without charges all those arrested. Despite the blatant violation of basic constitutional rights in the affair, no apologies were given by the police nor were any protests issued from within the community. Instead, the day after the arrests, a gang of youths stoned James Green's house while he and his family were out of town. His address had been published earlier by Houston's newspapers. The youth gang left a note tacked to his front door, saying, "To the Commies: Warning . . . Veterans and Mothers and Fathers of sons who gave their lives in WW II." When the Greens returned, they also found an eviction notice from their landlord.[83]

If there had been any protest against the police "round-ups" of alleged subversives in July 1950, it would probably have been buried under the news of more arrests. Amazingly, the men the police arrested earlier for circulating the Stockholm Peace Petition continued their efforts. One of the petitioners gave the police grounds for further arrests when he twisted the arm of a woman who tried to tear up his petition. The woman notified the police and a manhunt was initiated. Perceiving that political gains could be obtained from the affair, Harris County sheriff Buster Kern, involved in a heated contest for reelection, called a news conference and announced solemnly that he was temporarily dropping his reelection campaign so that he could "take over personal direction of the Communist investigation."

On July 17, Kern's deputies arrested a forty-five-year-old labor organizer named Jack Van Raalte at a seedy Houston motel and charged him with vagrancy. The deputies discovered an address book and a correspondence file relating to the activities of the Texas Peace Committee's petition drive. Despite Van Raalte's protests that he was not a Communist, Sheriff Kern and Harris County district attorney A. C. Winborn told the newspapers that he would be questioned about Communist activities in Houston. The newspaper accounts of Van Raalte's arrest emphasized that he was an "outsider" from New York and that he had supported Henry Wallace. The Houston *Press* ran a story with the headline "Communist's Papers List 20 Houston Residents" and emphasized that Van Raalte was the key to the "Communist underground" in the city.

After three hours of intensive questioning and intimidation by Sheriff Kern, Van Raalte finally revealed that he had worked with the Communists. He also talked about Communist involvement in the petition drive and admitted that the Texas Peace Committee was a Communist front. Meanwhile, Kern's deputies discovered Robert Brannan, George Johnson, and John Guss removing materials from James Green's house and arrested all three as suspects in the "arm twisting incident." The sheriff's department also seized James Green's Texas Communist party records, which included financial statements, file cards of names and addresses for subscriptions to the *Daily Worker*, notes concerning party dues and memberships, a notebook containing cryptic messages, and a letter from Green to the three men. The file cards for the *Daily Worker* provided little information about individuals but they did indicate that few had subscribed. The financial records revealed a number of payments for rent, office supplies, mimeograph services, and several checks to the "National Committee, Communist Party, USA." Other records indicated that 210 individuals in Texas paid dues in December 1949, the last month dues had been collected. Seventy-three of the dues-paying members lived in Houston, but to the disappointment of police, the list contained no names. James Green's letter gave instructions to his arrested colleagues about what final arrangements needed to be made to move party records and close headquarters in Houston. Green, who had moved his family to Brooklyn, New York, asked the men to sell his furniture and ship his personal items to Brooklyn. He urged Brannan, Johnson, and Guss to "engage in campaign around Mor Bog [Morris Bogdanow]" and get Herman Wright and Arthur Mandell to lead protests against the Houston police harassment of local radicals.

James Green's instructions to his colleagues were destined to go uncompleted. Sheriff Kern, obviously delighted by the possibilities for publicity in the case, immediately called a press conference to reveal how efficiently his department had uncovered Houston's core of Communist activists. The newspapers responded with sensational headlines. The Houston *Press*, for example, dominated its front page with the headline "Sheriff Kern Seizes Texas Commie Files" and published the photographs of the four arrested men. Coverage of the "Red arrests" by other local news media was also sensational. When the men were released shortly after their arrests, they quickly fled the city.[84]

A combination of the Henry Wallace debacle, the CIO Communist purge, the Korean War atmosphere, constant police harassment, sensationalist news reporting, and the onset of the Red Scare proved to be too formidable an opponent for Houston's tiny band of radicals. Even nonradical leftists Herman Wright and Arthur Mandell were forced to concentrate on less controversial legal problems. While Wright and Mandell were successful in achieving a lower profile, they quietly continued their activities on behalf of liberal social change, particularly in regard to the growing black civil rights movement.

By 1950, Houston was entering a new era of fear and suspicion known as the Red Scare. The great irony is that the Red Scare's most virulent phase developed in the absence of any actual Communist organization or activity; by the fall of 1950 Communism in Houston as well as the rest of the nation had lost whatever influence and momentum it once possessed. From a national total of approximately 80,000 members at its height in popularity, the CPUSA had declined to approximately 40,000 members in 1951, with half of that total living in New York City. When compared to the national population of over 150 million in the late 1940s, one has to agree with David Caute's judgment that the American establishment had taken "a sledgehammer to squash a gnat."[85]

This was unimportant to Houston's Red Scare activists. What was significant was that Houston did experience a period of open activity by members of the Communist and non-Communist left. No matter how unsuccessful their efforts had ultimately been, those efforts played a role in making the charges of Red Scare participants seem credible and plausible. As important, however, as this "radical" activity may have been in the complex formula producing the local Red Scare, more significant and crucial was the role played by the leaders of Houston's establishment. The fearful rhetoric of these respected civic elites would prove to be among the most important factors of all.

THREE

FEAR AND MONEY

The small voice of a person such as myself does not carry the influence that the roar and thunder of voices such as yours and Mr. [Hugh Roy] Cullen's can carry. Through you, and others like yourself and Mr. Cullen, the voices of small business men and patriotic American citizens can be heard. We depend on men such as you. Please don't let us down!
—Marvin Henry to Jesse Jones, July 1950

Many people, Texans as well as non-Texans, hate Jesse Jones; and hatred often snaps out of his own cold eyes.
—John Gunther, 1947

H. R. Cullen? That ignorant son of a bitch?
—Maury Maverick, 1954[1]

In the early 1950s, Ralph S. O'Leary, a reporter for the Houston *Post*, observed that the city's power elite had "been overcome by an insecurity psychosis. They fear the rest of us are going to take their money away from them." The changes in Houston caused by World War II deeply affected members of the city's "establishment." The insecurity psychosis that O'Leary perceived was primarily evident in a flood of shrill rhetoric aimed against big government, New Deal Democrats, labor unions, and alleged Communists in the federal bureaucracy. The sensational and sometimes frightening pronouncements by some of Houston's most respected and prominent citizens, coupled with the rhetoric and actions of other state leaders, gave crucial credibility to extremists in the community prepared to carry out a local anti-Communist witch-hunt.[2]

Theodore White, analyzing local power structures in Texas in the early 1950s, noted the existence of autonomous "self-winding" cliques in each community that he characterized as the "local aristocracy of enterprise and commercial achievement." He argued that these people ran the cities as if the cities were clubs in which they constituted the nominating committees and the electorate-at-large acted as "the herd." Noting that these power cliques were not monolithic, White nonetheless concluded that their common characteristic was "a ruthlessness that arrogates to them sole control of local political life." White called these leadership groups "local businessmen's machines." It would be more precise to refer to Houston's, however, as an entrepreneurial power elite because it was mainly comprised of individuals engaged in the management of large businesses that they owned and, in some cases, founded.[3]

Houston's most powerful leaders, contrary to widely prevalent myths, have not been oil men. Many had direct and indirect relationships with the oil economy, but there was no single stereotypical "wildcat" oil man among them. Some Texas "wildcatters" became nationally famous because of their outrageous social behavior and predilection for conspicuous consumption, but characters such as "Silver Dollar" Jim West, who would toss silver dollars around airports to watch the "rabble" scramble for them, and the Shamrock Hotel's Glenn McCarthy had little or no real influence with Houston's power brokers. As historian James Presley has observed, oil men such as McCarthy and West, with their "colorful qualities," "lack of inhibition," and "knack for doing things with a flourish . . . made more sedate men grimace." With one or two prominent exceptions, most of Houston's establishment shunned publicity of any sort.[4]

Who then were Houston's most influential individuals? Those who discussed the membership of Houston's postwar entrepreneurial power elite usually offered a list of from fifteen to twenty names. (What is crucial here are *perceptions* of power and influence. Because these people were perceived as powerful by many deferential Houstonians, their opinions carried greater authority than the views of persons of more ordinary status.)[5] Despite disagreements about individuals on the fringe, everyone agreed on the group's most important members: Jesse Holman Jones, George and Herman Brown, Judge James A. Elkins, Gus Wortham, William P. Hobby and his wife, Oveta Culp Hobby, Hugh Roy Cullen, and Mayor Oscar Holcombe.[6]

Four of these leaders acquired a reputation for being the "elite of the elites" in Houston. Foremost was Jesse Jones, a nationally prominent personality whom local newspapers and speechmakers referred to as "Mr. Houston" for over forty years. Jones, well over six feet in height, with a fine head of snow-white hair, was so distinguished looking that his appearance alone commanded respect. Jones took himself seriously and behaved accordingly, which often caused Franklin Roosevelt to refer to him in private as "Jesus H. Jones." Arthur M. Schlesinger, Jr., has described Jones as "a great monument of a man . . . profane and taciturn in the Texas manner, loved power, was indifferent to ideology, never read books, . . . and kept his word."[7]

Jesse Jones had played a crucial role in Houston's development since the building of the ship channel. Because of his giant real estate empire, his prosperous banking, insurance, and investment companies, and his newspaper, the Houston *Chronicle*, Jones became the most powerful of all Houstonians by the end of the 1920s. In 1932, at the request of President Herbert Hoover, Jones served as director of the federal government's Reconstruction Finance Corporation (RFC). In 1933 the newly inaugurated president Franklin Roosevelt made Jones chairman of the RFC. Even though he remained in Washington for thirteen years and eventually became Roosevelt's secretary of commerce, Jones continued to hold a tight grip on his financial empire back home. Jones' power in Houston increased as a result of his control of the federal government's major loan agency and his access to New Deal administrators, since they placed him in an influential position to divert federal money for construction projects back in Texas.[8]

Whether in Washington or at home, Jones maintained an intensely personal interest in Houston. His self-identification with the city was remarkable. Charles G. Dawes, who preceded him as RFC chairman, once observed that Jesse Jones was as much an empire builder as Cecil Rhodes, the English imperialist and African colonizer, but that Jones differed in that he preferred to have his empire where he could see it most of the time. Accordingly, when Jones built the seventeen-story Lamar Hotel, he located his own living quarters on the top floor, with floor to ceiling windows on all four sides. From that vantage point he could see most of his downtown buildings. Jones' wife, referring to his personal obsession with Houston and his stake in the city, once remarked that her husband wanted to live downtown so that he could be near his buildings. "He has great sentiment about all of them," Mrs. Jones stated. "Every time he passes one, he pats and pets it." Such a hobby would have been quite time consuming for Jones by the late 1940s, since he owned over thirty major buildings. Because of his transcendent stature in the community and his control over its most influential newspaper, the *Chronicle*, Jones would play a key role in legitimating and sustaining Houston's Red Scare.[9]

Comparable though not equal in power to Jones was a native of Huntsville, Texas, Judge James A. Elkins, who controlled Texas' largest law firm, Vinson, Elkins. Because of this powerful legal base, he became a director of dozens of banks, insurance corporations, railroads, and oil companies. In the early 1950s, Elkins successfully merged his own City National Bank with Houston First National to form First City National Bank, the largest financial institution in Houston at the time.

A large man with a craggy, intimidating appearance, Elkins exercised enormous power and influence as a result of his law firm and bank and his financial connections with state legislators. Although quiet and publicity shy, Elkins was never reticent in his use of power. One of his colleagues conceded that "there wasn't a man alive who could dominate anything Judge Elkins was in." His power over state and local politicians was so pervasive that he was often referred to as "the secret government of Texas." Former Texas governor James V. Allred once observed, "Elkins doesn't practice law, he practices influence." George Fuermann, writing in 1951, concluded that "few Texans at any time ever had such compelling power" as did the formidable Elkins.[10]

The only other members of Houston's establishment comparable to Jones and Elkins in extent of power and influence were George and Herman Brown. The two brothers owned Brown and Root, Inc., which ranked among the most active private construction firms in the world by the late 1940s. The Browns built ships, off-shore oil well platforms, industrial plants, dams, bridges, highways, and military bases. Having made most of their wealth through government contracts, the brothers were sometimes referred to as "socialistic millionaires." After World War II, they formed Texas Eastern Transmission Corporation and became the major distributor of natural gas to most of the eastern United States. The Browns also generously subsidized the political campaigns of their favorite congressmen and state legislators; one particular benefactor of their support was Lyndon B. Johnson. They derived much of their personal influence and power from their close relationship with politicians like Johnson.

Of the two brothers, Herman was the most active politically. Like Judge Elkins, Herman Brown exercised an inordinate influence over many key Texas legislators. Robert Caro, in his biography of Lyndon Johnson, has written that Herman Brown "was a businessman who wanted value for money spent. His relationships with politicians were measured by that criterion." Hart Stilwell alleged in 1951 that Herman Brown "is the most powerful man in Texas and close to bossing the entire state." Robert Caro has described Herman Brown as a "hater" who "hated Negroes and . . . unions." He hated both for the same reason, says Caro. "He believed that Negroes were lazy, and that unions encouraged laziness in white men. . . ." Besides, Brown, who perceived himself to be the embodiment of the self-made man, viewed the desire of labor to organize and collectively bargain as an unwarranted interference in his personal affairs. Accordingly, the Brown brothers became the most effective and persistent opponents of labor unions in postwar Texas. One study credits Herman Brown with almost singlehandedly forcing nine antilabor bills through the Texas legislature in the late 1940s, statutes judged by one observer to be "the most vicious anti-labor laws in America."[11]

The other members of Houston's entrepreneurial elite also wielded extensive power and influenced the city's development in significant ways. None of them, however, equaled Jones, Elkins, or the Browns. This group included Gus Wortham, a friend of Jesse Jones. Wortham founded American General, the largest insurance company in the South, and directed an important holding company with extensive real estate, oil, banking, manufacturing, transportation, and construction interests. Active in a variety of Houston civic and educational affairs, Wortham participated in numerous projects significant in the city's development. These included the expansion of Rice University and the creation and growth of the Texas Medical Center. He twice served as president of the Houston Chamber of Commerce.

Wortham also made generous financial donations to his favorite politicians. Like the Browns, Gus Wortham especially favored Lyndon B. Johnson and, also like the Browns, he expected Johnson's attention in return. In 1950, in a letter to Johnson, who was then in the U.S. Senate, Wortham explained what he expected for his political support. Wortham wrote that he had never helped a candidate in expectation of special privileges. "On the other hand," Wortham hinted, "I hoped that these men would have confidence in me and would give consideration to my views. . . ." Wortham wrote the letter in reaction to an apparent snub from Johnson. The senator's reply to Wortham is a revealing example of the Johnson style as well as an indication of his perceptions of the power wielded by Wortham and his associates. The senator, pleading that he was unaware of his transgression, wrote: ". . . if you feel as I am told you do, I made a grave error. I am sorry. I will try not to make it again." The senator insisted that he was not unmindful of the support Wortham and his Houston friends had provided over the years. "I am not ungrateful," LBJ emphasized.[12]

William P. Hobby and his wife, Oveta Culp, also belong on a list of Houston's power elite. Hobby, a former governor of Texas, and his wife owned and operated Houston's second largest newspaper, the *Post*. "The Governor," as he was called by his friends, had assumed the position of an elder statesman in postwar Houston. This was partially due to his having been the state's chief executive, but it was also the result of Hobby's sharp political acumen, bolstered by over five decades of experience. Politicians in Houston and throughout Texas made regular pilgrimages to the city, not just to win the *Post*'s support, but also to gather in some sage Hobby wisdom. Oveta Culp Hobby served as head of the Women's Army Corps (the WACs) in World War II. Much younger than "The Governor," Oveta was as ambitious as she was charming—the equal of any man in toughness and shrewdness. Like the others in this group, the Hobbys were power brokers in state and national politics. Their support and activities were crucial to Dwight Eisenhower's election to the presidency in 1952 and a grateful Eisenhower appointed Oveta to the newly created post of secretary of health, education, and welfare.[13]

Two other individuals, Hugh Roy Cullen and Oscar Holcombe, belonged to the power elite as far as public perceptions were concerned. They certainly ranked with the Hobbys and Jones in terms of popular influence, but neither man possessed the type of real power held by the others. An independent oil man and conservative Republican, Hugh Roy Cullen was possibly the wealthiest individual in Texas in the decade following World War II. Cullen's stubborn independence and propensity to "shoot from the hip" when it came to personal opinions kept him somewhat separate from Houston's other power brokers. Nevertheless, in the public mind, when Cullen spoke (which was often) he did so as an influential Houston leader.[14]

Oscar Holcombe was the only elected politician who could be considered to be among this group. Holcombe built his power base as mayor of Houston, a position he held off and on from 1921 to 1957. Initially kept out of the establishment's inner circle, Holcombe persevered and by the late 1940s was a close associate of the entrepreneurs who held power in the city. Although Holcombe's importance among Houston's powerful increased as a result of his business association with Howard Hughes, who made him a director of Trans World Airlines, he never ranked with Jones, Elkins, or the Browns.[15]

Finally, revolving around this small core of dominant power were a dozen or so men who were influential to varying degrees of importance within particular areas of the city's life. These men usually joined with Jones, Elkins, Wortham, and the other primary power brokers to choose political candidates, finance campaigns, and exert influence over a variety of local institutions and events. In the postwar decade, this satellite group included W. Alvis Parish of the Houston Lighting and Power Company; Warren S. Bellows, owner of a major construction firm; James S. Abercrombie, an independent oil man; Robert W. Henderson, owner of a cotton company; Hines Baker, president of Humble Oil Company; and Lamar Fleming and Harmon Whittington of the Anderson, Clayton Cotton Company.[16]

Despite the fact that Houston's power brokers subscribed to the tradition of rugged individualism and cultivated images of the "loner" and the self-made man, it is quite evident that they constructed a tangled web of interlocking business arrangements, consulted one another frequently about political, civic, and business matters, and enjoyed each other's company in both official and unofficial social gatherings. Judge Elkins was the crucial link in these elite interrelationships. He had both legal and financial connections with almost every member of the group. Elkins' law firm represented the Browns' Texas Eastern Corporation and he served as a director of Brown and Root. Elkins was also a major stockholder and director of Gus Wortham's American General. The Browns and Wortham, in turn, served on the board of directors of Elkins' bank.[17] Wortham was a director of the Browns' Texas Eastern Corporation. Jesse Jones and Judge Elkins each loaned $75,000 to Wortham to help found American General. Jesse Jones also made it possible for the Hobbys to own the Houston *Post*. Jones acquired the *Post* and made it available to the Hobbys in the 1930s for the remarkable terms of only a $5,000 down payment and no collateral. At that time, the Hobbys lacked the funds to purchase the newspaper. Jones' largess provided the Hobbys their opportunity to a secure position of wealth and influence. As long as Jones and Governor Hobby both lived, no two independently owned major newspapers ever had a friendlier competition.[18]

The Brown brothers, Jesse Jones, Judge Elkins, Governor Hobby, Gus Wortham, and a few of their associates often met in Jones' Lamar Hotel, where they would play poker and discuss business. Named the "8-F Crowd" after the number of the hotel suite rented by the Browns in which they held their meetings, this group constituted the establishment in Houston throughout the 1940s and 1950s. One writer has referred to the meeting place as "one of the secret capitals of Texas." George Green lamented in his study of the Texas establishment that the 8-F Crowd may have been "very powerful, but it did not leave much of a trail for the historian to follow." Nevertheless, stories about their meetings are plentiful.[19]

Probably the most well documented episode about the 8-F Crowd related to their decision to support Roy Hofheinz instead of Oscar Holcombe for mayor in 1952. The group, including George and Herman Brown, William P. Hobby, Judge Elkins, Gus Wortham, and Emmet Walter of the Houston *Chronicle* substituting for Jesse Jones, invited former county judge Roy Hofheinz to join them and Holcombe in a closed meeting. At the meeting they indicated that the "Old Gray Fox" was perhaps a little too old and gray to be reelected. Herman Brown is alleged to have told Holcombe that it was time for him to quit. After questioning Hofheinz, they decided to make him the next mayor of Houston. Holcombe had already printed campaign literature, but that did not matter. He announced his retirement and Hofheinz, with 8-F help, proceeded to win the election against his main opponent, Louie Welch.

Referring to the Hofheinz-Holcombe episode and other similar incidents, Watergate prosecutor and prominent Houston attorney Leon Jaworski, who was also close to this inner circle, later recalled that "there was a time when Jesse Jones, for instance, would meet with Gus Wortham, Herman Brown and maybe one or two others and pretty well determine what the course of events would be in Houston. . . ." Glenn McCarthy got more to the point when remembering Houston in the late 1940s: "Jesse Jones was the politics [sic] in Houston. He run [sic] the mayor, he told the mayor just what to do and how to do it."[20]

Glenn McCarthy's simple statement is incorrect in its implication that Jones acted alone, but it captures the essence of the power elite's influence. Normally, the power elite would form a General Committee of from twelve to twenty persons among the inner and outer circle of power that would focus on a particular election of special interest to those constituting the committee. The composition of the General Committee would differ slightly with each election since some members of the group were not interested in school board elections while others might not care about municipal elections. In the postwar decade, Herman Brown led the General Committee concerned with state legislative elections while Robert W. Henderson usually chaired the committee on school board races. The General Committee would form two subcommittees, one to nominate candidates and another to raise money. Each committee member was expected to do all he could to help elect the chosen candidates. Elite solidarity was essential to a maintenance of power and control. For example, during the legislative campaign of 1952, Herman Brown told the group that "if this Committee is to survive and make its influence felt, every member must buckle down and give [their candidates] all possible support." Although a consensus was usually maintained, Houston's entrepreneurial leaders did occasionally disagree about specific issues. A clash over zoning in 1948 between Jesse Jones and Hugh Roy Cullen was an example of such intragroup conflict.[21]

Houston is the largest city in the United States without municipal land use zoning regulations. The question of zoning has been raised several times, always to be rejected. Essentially, in the 1948 dispute, Jesse Jones advocated zoning while Cullen vigorously opposed it as a danger to "free enterprise." Jones and his allies, including the Hobbys, favored zoning because it would rationalize the city's uncontrolled growth. That it would also stymie the decentralization of Houston's downtown business district also appealed to Jones, who owned a considerable portion of it. Cullen, on the other hand, simply and sincerely believed zoning to be socialistic and "foreign."[22]

Jones and Cullen personally disliked each other, which exacerbated the dispute. Two years prior to the zoning battle, Cullen wrote Jones, "I am sure Jesse, you wish me to be frank, and I am going to be. Our philosophies of life are so different. You build houses of mortar, stone and steel, while I build Man." During the debate leading to a popular referendum, Cullen complained about biased coverage in Jones' *Chronicle*. Cullen resentfully declared that it had been "a pleasure to help build this city up to now, but Jesse Jones has been away . . . for the last twenty-five to thirty years and has . . . decided, with the influence of the press here, and the assistance of a bunch of New York Jews, to run our city. . . ."[23]

Cullen and his antizoning position won. It was an unusual defeat for Jones, unaccustomed to losing in civic disputes. Jones never forgave Cullen. Years later, after Cullen sent Jones a copy of his authorized biography, Jones drafted a reply that revealed his opinion of Cullen. Jones wrote, "I have glanced through [the biography] and congratulate you on your great success and also upon always being on the winning side." Referring to the zoning battle, Jones claimed, incorrectly, that he had no property interests that would have been affected by the land use controls. He informed Cullen that because of a lack of zoning, many homes had become less desirable "with a filling station, a beer saloon, or other business along side of them." Jones reminded Cullen that he had built a home in River Oaks, the most tightly controlled land in the city. The main problem with Roy Cullen, Jones argued, was that he lacked humility. The letter not only reflects Jones' view of Cullen, it serves as an example of their differences in style. If Cullen had written the letter, he probably would have sent copies to the newspapers. Jones, on the other hand, never even mailed his letter to Cullen. Instead, he buried it in his files. The Jones-Cullen feud, however, was an exception to the usual pattern of power relationships.[24]

After World War II, Houston's establishment began to perceive a threat to its wealth and power from the growing labor movement in Texas and an ever-expanding federal government. Houston's leaders faced a federal government they believed to be controlled by socialists and left-wingers. They saw Washington attempting to make further incursions into sacred areas such as the oil depletion allowance, labor relations, corporate tax reform, medicine, education, and race relations. While the more clever and sophisticated among them (the Browns, for example) used the federal government as a major source of new business, most viewed the nation's capital with great distrust and fear.[25]

Houston's leaders saw the presidency as a significant part of the problem. At the hands of Franklin D. Roosevelt, the executive branch of government had accumulated unprecedented power in domestic and foreign affairs. Even Herman Brown, who benefited financially from Roosevelt's relationship with Lyndon Johnson, hated FDR. Robert Caro argues that although the Browns financed FDR's 1940 campaign in Texas, they held their noses while doing it. To Herman, "that Man in the White House" was responsible for policies that were helping those "unions and

Negroes." To some, like Jesse Jones and the Hobbys, FDR was acceptable as long as Jones himself played a role in the administration. Once Jones had been pushed out, the New Deal and the national Democratic party became anathema. To others like H. R. Cullen, FDR had always been a dangerous demagogue and collectivist. To them all, Harry S Truman, that "little man" from Missouri, was just an extension of the New Deal and even more dangerous than FDR because, they believed, he was more susceptible to control and influence by the labor unionists, "fellow travelers," and "one-worlders," whom FDR had merely used for his own purposes. Houston Lighting and Power's W. Alvis Parish reflected the view of his elite associates when he declared in 1949 that "there is no longer a Democratic Party. Those now controlling the Democratic Party . . . have formed . . . an unholy alliance with the . . . union racketeers in order to get the votes." By the late 1940s, most of Houston's business leaders agreed that Truman and the Democratic majority in Congress had to be defeated.[26]

Added to all of the other frightening developments in the power elite's world was the fearful specter of international Communism. The postwar decade confronted the elite with such shocking events as the victory of the Communists in China, the successful development of the atom bomb by the Soviet Union, and Communist domination of Eastern Europe.

Although the power elite could enjoy great material comfort and financial success in postwar Houston, for some it was a comfort and satisfaction tempered by anxiety. Theodore S. White, after interviewing some Texans of power and wealth during the immediate postwar years, observed that "a sense of menace, of unease, runs through their conversation as if the great wheel of fortune might turn and suddenly deprive them of the wealth they have so lately won. And the menace may be anywhere—in a neighbor's home, around the corner . . . certainly in Washington and New York." When interviewed by *Fortune* magazine, one wealthy Texan admitted, "We all made money fast. We were interested in nothing else. Then this communist business suddenly burst upon us. Were we going to lose what we had suddenly gained?" Such a visible combination of fear and money can transmit some strong communal images. John Gunther, after visiting and studying most of the large cities in the country in the late 1940s, formed a vivid impression of Texas' largest city. "Houston," Gunther wrote in his *Inside USA*, ". . . is, with the possible exception of Tulsa, Oklahoma, the most reactionary community in the United States. It is a city where few people think of anything but money. . . ."[27]

Thus, the power elite's problems, both real and imagined, sprang from a variety of sources. Nevertheless, taking their cue from a rising crescendo of voices across the nation, Houston's leaders, as well as other Texans, dispensed with complex explanations. Instead, they accepted a simplistic answer. Their problems were obviously the result of the Communist "conspiracy." Reds and Red sympathizers were taking their world away from them. Even if some of them did not really believe it in the literal sense (Jesse Jones, the Hobbys, the Browns, and Judge Elkins clearly did not), that was unimportant. The New Dealers, liberal Democrats, and their labor friends had to go anyway. If, after fifteen years, traditional issue-related campaigns could not root these people out, why not make use of something more effective? Houston's entrepreneurial leaders and other Texans jumped upon the Red Scare bandwagon, a transport already crowded with such national figures as Richard Nixon, Robert Taft, Tom Clark, J. Edgar Hoover, Francis Cardinal Spellman, John Wayne, Walter Winchell, and Hedda Hopper. It should be emphasized that neither Judge Elkins nor the Browns openly participated in Red Scare activities. Their silence, however, did not mean they opposed the actions of their colleagues—there can be little doubt of the existence of an 8-F Crowd consensus on this matter. These three men simply preferred to avoid the public limelight.[28]

With the exception of Hugh Roy Cullen, Houston's power elite contented itself with scaring the folks close to home. The entrepreneurial leaders had effective public mechanisms to manipulate the anti-Communist campaign. Judging from testimony provided by persons who enlisted in Red Scare pressure groups, these manipulations had their desired effects.

The Houston Chamber of Commerce provided one means of attack. The chamber was the forum for the 8-F Crowd and acted as its unofficial spokesman. While they all belonged to the chamber, the power elite's chief activist in the organization was Gus Wortham. Not only did Wortham serve two terms as the Houston chamber's president, he was also prominent in the affairs of the U.S. Chamber of Commerce, winning election to the national board of directors in 1953. The use of local chambers of commerce for local anti-Communist agitation was encouraged by the national chamber, which had waged since 1945 an intense national anti-Communist propaganda campaign with its Committee on Socialism and Communism. The U.S. chamber published a series of influential booklets, including *Communist Infiltration of the United States* (1946), *Communists within the Labor Movement* (1947), and *A Program for Community Anti-Communist Action* (1948). All were widely circulated, but the latter title proved especially popular with local Red Scare groups. A "how to do it" manual for witch-hunting, the 1948 publication explained the techniques for compiling a file system on local "Red" suspects. Houston's Chamber of Commerce distributed *A Program for Community Anti-*

Communist Action widely and it subsequently appeared on the recommended reading lists of such local groups as the Minute Women of the U.S.A., Inc.[29]

Displeased with the drift of postwar America, especially in regard to organized labor, the Houston Chamber of Commerce in 1946 launched a campaign to "awaken" citizens to the threats posed by strong labor unions and a continuation of the New Deal, which the chamber simply equated with Communism. It constantly harped at local businessmen that danger lurked in Houston as well as in Washington.

In its magazine, *Houston*, the Chamber of Commerce issued a warning with an editorial, "Has America's Campaign for Tolerance Backfired?" The chamber asked, ". . . will patriots continue to sleep?" It warned that Houston itself was in imminent danger and quoted Federal Bureau of Investigation director J. Edgar Hoover as saying that the Communist influence had infiltrated "newspapers, magazines, books, radio, . . . churches, schools, colleges, and even fraternal orders. . . ."[30]

More editorials urging Houstonians to organize and take action to protect their community soon followed. For example, in the January 1948 issue of *Houston*, the chamber declared, "Americans, patriots, stand up and be counted. Assert yourselves loyal men and women, now, or soon . . . you may find it too late." The editorial argued that Americans, by their "passiveness," were aiding the Communist takeover in the United States. The chamber dedicated its entire June 1949 issue to "What Can Americans Do to Stop the Spread of the ISMS?" and published several pages of statistics that argued that America was "fast becoming socialistic."[31]

While the chamber's magazine had slight influence over the vast majority of Houstonians, it did attract an avid readership among many small businessmen. This group, perhaps more than any other, felt threatened by progressive social legislation and the rise of labor unions. Small businessmen are usually "men on the make" with strong desires for upward economic mobility who tend to acquire the values or imagined values of business elites. Historian David Caute observed that "businessmen in general, particularly self-made entrepreneurs, were highly susceptible to alarm calls of collective paranoia." This group provided part of the membership and financial support for the Red Scare activist organizations. The editorial campaign of the chamber played a role in mobilizing members of the small business community by convincing them that Red Scare activity was an acceptable mode of behavior, approved by successful business leaders.[32]

While the Chamber of Commerce gave the establishment one voice to help shape public opinion, some individual members had much more effective ways to manipulate and foster the Red Scare. Jesse Jones and the Hobbys used their newspapers and Red Scare rhetoric as premeditated political weapons to elect General Dwight D. Eisenhower to the presidency. While the *Post* tended to be more moderate than the *Chronicle*, the editorial anti-Communism of both newspapers helped to create the atmosphere in which Houston's Red Scare thrived.

As others have written, it would require another book altogether to describe in adequate terms the role of the press in popularizing the Red Scare. Historian David Caute has emphasized that "without the assistance of the right-wing press, Red baiting would have yielded much lower dividends" for its adherents. Contemporary observers such as Richard Rovere and Alan Barth stressed the primacy of the press in creating Joe McCarthy, the most notorious practitioner of the Red smear. An article appearing in the *Journalism Quarterly* in the fall of 1952 warned that "without the press, the professional witch-hunters would wither and die away." Edwin R. Bayley, in his study of the press and Joe McCarthy, later observed that "it was no wonder that so many people were convinced that McCarthy was exposing Communists. The newspapers said so." David Caute found hundreds of local newspapers in the late 1940s and 1950s "clutching at circulation by feeding their dazed readers ever stronger doses of panic and hatred. . . ." In one example among many, during the last three months of 1947, Seattle, Washington's two major daily newspapers printed an average of one story every other day just about *local* Communists.[33]

Sociologist Kai Erickson has observed that the confrontations between "deviant offenders" and the agents of public order have always attracted public attention. Whereas deviants were once publicly hanged in the town square, in modern society newspapers, radio, and television perform that function. A significant amount of "news" is devoted not only to announcements about incidents of deviance but also about its consequences. Erickson admits that this might appeal to "a number of psychological perversities among the mass audience" and thus qualify as a type of entertainment, resulting, for example, in the sale of more newspapers. But "news" serves another purpose, Erickson concludes. It constitutes "one of our main sources of information about the normative outlines of society."

Erickson's hypothesis resulted from a study of the Puritan Witch Trials in seventeenth-century New England. But it also helps explain the role of the news media in the second Red Scare. The "agents of control," in this case congressional committees, politicians, police, and respected conservative elites, confronted the "deviant offenders"; that is, anyone even faintly associated with interests determined to be a threat to the American economic system. The newspapers devoted an inordinate amount of attention to this confrontation for at least two conscious or unconscious reasons: to sell newspapers and to educate their readers about the new boundaries of acceptable ideological belief and behavior. This process served to spread fear through exposure and thus enforced conformity. It was especially effective because of the near unanimity among established information brokers, even more so when those brokers were themselves the "agents of control," such as Jesse Jones and the Hobbys. This is not to say that the press conspired in some overt or covert plot to spread the Red Scare. It is, as Erickson believes, just the way a society disseminates information about itself. This process played a critical role in creating and sustaining the second Red Scare among ordinary Americans.[34]

In Houston, the local press performed the same function. It transmitted news about the newly drawn boundaries of acceptable political behavior. That these boundaries had shifted there could be no doubt. As discussed in the previous chapter, in the 1930s even the *Chronicle* could publish a neutral story about the arrival in the city of an official CPUSA organizer. In an editorial in the mid 1930s, the *Chronicle*'s only reaction to a speech by a self-admitted Communist at the Houston Public Library's "Houston Open Forum" was to lament that a speaker with a contrary view was not present to correct the Communist's "misinformation." Ten years later, the arrival of a CPUSA organizer or the appearance at the public library of a Communist speaker would have made front-page headlines, followed later by virulent editorials demanding arrests and dismissals.[35] Through its scare stories the press also seemed to verify the charges and claims of the right-wing extremist fringe. It conferred respectability and credibility on people who, in other periods, would have been either scorned or laughed at or both. It allowed these people on the fringe of the political process to assume an authority they eagerly seized. Finally, and most significantly to Houston's power elite, the press was a useful tool for achieving a very traditional goal. The press' manipulations of the Red Scare served the pragmatic needs of conservative politics—to restore the Republican party to national power.[36]

In 1945 President Roosevelt asked Jesse Jones to step aside as secretary of commerce to allow Roosevelt's former vice-president, Henry A. Wallace, to assume the post. Although the president offered Jones an ambassadorship to France or Italy, the Texan rejected it, resigned from the cabinet, and left the administration entirely. As Jones later wrote, "To be dismissed in such a manner . . . I could no longer have respected him or worked with him." Jones had been one of the leading conservatives in FDR's presidency, but his loyalty had become suspect after his nephew-in-law, George A. Butler, led the anti-Roosevelt Texas Regulars movement in 1944. Actually, FDR had begun to bypass Jones on Texas political matters and federal contracts as early as 1940, when Congressman Lyndon B. Johnson became the president's unofficial adviser on Texas. Jones was especially humiliated to be pushed aside in favor of Wallace, a liberal with whom Jones had fought bitterly over several issues during the Houstonian's thirteen years in the New Deal.[37]

Jesse Jones had been an active lifelong Democrat who had wielded power in the party since the Woodrow Wilson presidency. Now, however, Jones was ready to burn some political bridges. All vestiges of progressive New Deal programs, the liberal wing of the party, and the Roosevelt influence had to be expunged from the federal government. FDR's death in April 1945 and Harry S Truman's succession to the presidency made little difference to Jones. John Gunther once observed that Jesse Jones "carried a stronger note of the implacable than anybody else I have ever talked to in American public life." Implacable opposition to Truman's continuation of Roosevelt policies now consumed "Uncle Jesse."[38]

Actually, Jesse Jones seems to have had ambivalent feelings about Harry Truman. The president's feisty and candid style appealed to the Texan on a personal level. The private correspondence between the two men reflects a cordial and, occasionally, even a warm friendliness. Jones, a firm believer in noting anniversaries, conveyed enthusiastic birthday greetings to Truman throughout his presidency and in the years beyond. In correspondence and in conversations with friends, Jones frequently emphasized his personal feelings of friendship toward Truman—feelings Jones reiterated in his memoirs.

Truman's letters to Jones were also cordial, but privately the president admitted his dislike of the Houstonian and often repeated Roosevelt's "Jesus H. Jones" characterization. Truman's daughter, Margaret, no doubt reflecting her father's views, has written that Jones was "an arrogant man . . . not used to having his decisions questioned" who "sometimes sounded like a one-man government."[39]

Although Jesse Jones appears to have liked Truman as an individual (despite Truman's failure to reciprocate), Jones openly disliked his presidency. In 1948, for the first time in his life, Jones publicly advocated a Republican victory in a national election. Jones returned to Houston and told his old friends among the city's power elite that the national Democrats had been in power "entirely too long . . . maybe it's time we buried the Democratic Party."[40]

Jones had an excellent vehicle for the expression of his views. His newspaper, the Houston *Chronicle,* had the largest circulation in Texas. While it probably had less editorial power in the state than the older, ultraconservative *Dallas Morning News,* the *Chronicle* exerted great influence in the Houston area. Its readers usually assumed the newspaper's opinions to be no less than those of the city's power elite. When the *Chronicle* spoke, it did so as the voice of "the powers that be." Bascom Timmons, Jones' official biographer and a long-time *Chronicle* employee, wrote that Jones "loved his newspaper and the freedom it gave him to express his views. . . ." Accordingly, after his exit from Washington, Jones, although now living in New York, assumed control of the *Chronicle*'s editorials on national politics, personally writing its stinging denunciations of Truman, the Fair Deal, and the liberal wing of the Democratic party. After James F. Byrnes, Jones' friend from South Carolina, resigned as secretary of state in 1946, the *Chronicle* added Truman's foreign policy to its hate list.[41]

Operating out of his New York City apartment, Jones would consult with opponents of the Truman administration for ideas about future editorials. These included George E. Sokolsky, a right-wing newspaper columnist, who would discuss potential subjects over the telephone with Jones. Sokolsky was among those who encouraged Jones to have the *Chronicle* endorse the Republican presidential ticket in 1948. Jones, who needed little persuasion on this matter, subsequently made the endorsement by placing an unsigned editorial on the front page of his newspaper on September 17, 1948. The editorial was a compilation of generalities about "swollen bureaucracies" and a government grown too large during "sixteen years of unchanged control." Excusing his own participation in the creation of Big Government, Jones explained that it had been necessary because of economic depression and a world war, but both crises were past history. "Surgery must be executed by new leadership," Jones proclaimed, to dismantle the plethora of unnecessary agencies, bureaus, and programs. It was time for retrenchment, "time for change in philosophy of government and of our top leadership in Washington." To his fellow Democrats, Jones argued that "patriotism should tell us to forget party labels this year." Using a justification offered by the southern Democrats, who had formed the Dixiecrat party a few weeks earlier, Jones charged "this will not be a case of leaving our party[,] rather, our party . . . has left us." Jones concluded with a call for Texans to vote for the national Republican ticket of Thomas R. Dewey for president and Earl Warren for vice-president.[42]

The *Chronicle*'s editorial attracted national attention since no one could mistake its author's identity. Pro-Dewey newspaper publishers eagerly reprinted the endorsement and emphasized Jones' former New Deal connections. Jones told Sokolsky that he had purposely left the editorial unsigned, "but it might as well have been [signed], the way it has been taken by the press, which is all right."[43]

Despite Jones' best efforts and to the utter surprise of nearly everyone, Harry Truman defeated Thomas Dewey in 1948. This unforeseen development only served to push the Republican party and its conservative southern Democrat allies to new heights of frustration and despair. The 1948 election marks the point when, fueled by Republican desires for power in the White House, the anti-Communist campaign began to escalate and truly dominate national affairs. Aided, ironically, by Truman's own militant Cold War rhetoric and federal loyalty programs as well as by international events that seemed to indicate an extreme Soviet threat to the security of the United States, the Republicans and their associates beat the Red Scare drum loudly and frequently. Jones and the *Chronicle,* sharing in this conservative frustration and fueled by Jones' personal vendetta, eagerly adopted Red-baiting tactics and an extreme right-wing editorial policy.[44]

Jesse Jones was no political true believer; he had the pragmatic world view of a successful banker and was much more interested in the financial "bottom line" than in ideology. Nor was Jones a provincial bumpkin. He was worldly-wise, fond of reminding his friends that he had warmed his stocking-clad feet at the hearth of King George V when he accompanied President Woodrow Wilson to Buckingham Palace. While as a cabinet member he was certainly uncomfortable with many programs and tried to sabotage some of them, it is clear that Jesse Jones' behavior after his New Deal years had more to do with FDR's rejection than with political philosophy. A vain man with an enormous ego, Jones was deeply offended by the way Roosevelt dismissed him.[45]

That much of Jones' motivation against the Roosevelt-Truman administration was intensely personal is evident by his ambivalent behavior during the 1952 presidential campaign. He was eager for a Republican victory but he also wanted to preserve whatever influence he still had with conservative Democrats. Now that both FDR and Truman were out of the picture, Jones feigned neutrality. He sent a $2,500 donation to the national Democratic party and wrote chairman Stephen Mitchell a rather deceptive note that he would not take a position for either Adlai Stevenson or Dwight Eisenhower. "I am a friend of both men," Jones explained. "Either is entirely capable of making a good President." Later, he wrote to former secretary of state Cordell Hull that he still felt the country needed a change, "but I am inclined to the belief that Stevenson would bring integrity to our national government."[46]

While Jones struck a neutral pose for his Democratic friends, he was telling Dwight Eisenhower in personal correspondence that "more than ever I want you to be President of the United States." Before the Republican convention, Jones privately admitted to a banking associate that he supported Eisenhower "very much . . . but, of course, I cannot show an active interest." Thus, while Jones protected his statesmanlike image of neutrality, his newspaper carried out his actual political objectives. And it did so in a Red Scare voice that Jones himself would never use publicly.[47]

Another key factor in the *Chronicle*'s Red Scare response was its editor. After 1948, the seventy-four-year-old Jones, making a concession to age, returned the daily editorial burden to Martin Emmet ("Soapy Joe") Walter. Jones' editor was more conservative than the old man. One associate later recalled that Walter's politics owed more to Calvin Coolidge than to Jesse Jones. Walter, a Catholic and rock-ribbed Republican from Illinois, saw action in France during the First World War and received the prestigious croix de guerre for heroism. Walter joined the *Chronicle* in 1922 as a city hall reporter. Armed with three degrees from Notre Dame University and hardened by war, the aggressive Walter soon attracted Jones' attention. He made a rapid ascent within the newspaper's management. Beginning in the 1930s, Walter acquired his nickname from his popular column "Soapy Joe," which was a running commentary on local affairs written in a folksy, "old sage" style.[48]

Serving on the Houston Planning Commission and active in other civic affairs, M. E. Walter's knowledge of the city's day-to-day economic and political activities as well as his personal contacts both with established and "up and coming" civic leaders made him an invaluable resource for Jesse Jones. Walter's value to his boss increased after Jones moved to Washington to assume the directorship of the Reconstruction Finance Corporation. Walter became Jones' eyes and ears in Houston and, earning the boss' confidence, he eventually assumed editorial responsibility for the *Chronicle*. Except for a brief period immediately following Jones' bitter departure from government service, Walter had nearly a free hand in *Chronicle* policy, especially in regard to local issues.

An almost stereotypical, hard-nosed, old-time editor, Walter ran Jones' newspaper with an iron hand. His verbal brawls with *Chronicle* writers and reporters were legendary. He would warn his staff not to engage in any "lace-panty writing." A right-wing conservative in political outlook, Walter was a formidable opponent whenever he perceived a threat to establishment orthodoxy. Explaining his view of the *Chronicle*'s mission in Texas' largest city, Walter once said, "When we take up a fight, we've decided we're doing what is right for the people. From then on it's gloves off." As the United States moved deeper into the post–World War II era, Walter's "gloves off" editorial tactics became more frequent. Soapy Joe disliked what he perceived as "one-world" international trends and social- istic developments in the federal government. He especially opposed the United Nations and its sister agency in Paris, the United Nations Educa- tional, Scientific, and Cultural Organization (UNESCO). He was deter- mined to make the *Chronicle* Houston's watchdog, constantly alert to any sign of intrusions from the dangers of the outside world.[49]

If any one man could be said to have had the most responsibility for encouraging and stirring up the Red Scare activists in Houston, Emmet Walter comes close to being that man. While Jesse Jones was responsible for allowing Walter's excesses, there is evidence that during the Red Scare Walter led the aging and increasingly disinterested Jones more than he followed him. In the 1950s, Jones frequently relied on Walter's judgment about contemporary Red Scare issues. Jones often received letters from local right-wing advocates, pleading with "Mr. Houston" to do something about everything from "Red" school teachers to U.S. membership in the UN. Jones' secretary would refer these letters to Walter to draft suitable replies in Jones' name. One letter, questioning Jones about his view of the UN, was sent to Walter with a note, saying, "Mr. Jones would like for you to prepare an answer to this letter [on the UN] and if he is to do anything tell him what it is." Usually, Walter would receive Jones' issue- related mail with a simple "Emmet" scrawled in Jones' handwriting across the page.[50]

During the Red Scare, Jones found Walter particularly useful. Jones played his "Mr. Houston" role, the distinguished statesman and philan- thropist, one day receiving internationally famous personalities in his downtown office, the next day awarding college scholarships to worthy students. At the same time, his newspaper editor would be screaming "Communism" every time organized labor moved a finger or if anything seemed to threaten the sacred rights of property.[51]

While Soapy Joe sometimes went beyond Jones in some of his more intemperate and venomous editorials, he nevertheless reflected his boss' ideas in the abstract, if not always in the specific. For example, in 1952 Lyndon Johnson, rapidly becoming a Senate leader, complained to Jones about one of Walter's Red Scare articles that accused the Congress of sub- versive tendencies. "Uncle Jesse" candidly admitted that perhaps the article was to be regretted, but he reassured the junior senator from Texas that "I . . . do not think it will do you any real harm. You . . . know that the *Chronicle* is on your side. . . ." The implication was that John- son should understand that the *Chronicle*'s editorial positions were for public consumption to effect general purposes. If Johnson caught an occasional stray pellet from Emmet Walter's shotgun blasts at the "Communist" threat he should shake it off and not take it personally; Jesse still liked him. After all, as Jones advised Eisenhower during the 1952 campaign, "politics are not unlike war. Sometimes it is necessary to shoot from the hip."[52]

Although Jones apparently never expressed any personal opinions publicly about the Red Scare, he did tell *Fortune* magazine during the height of Joe McCarthy's visibility that he thought the senator from Wisconsin was "a vigorous fellow, doing a fine job in a vigorous way." Otherwise, Jones' newspaper and its editor did his talking for him.[53]

The *Chronicle* favored sensational headlines for Cold War news stories and specialized in a variety of syndicated, serialized, "official" reports on Communist influence in the nation's educational, religious, and governmental institutions. Prominent right-wing columnists such as Fulton Lewis, Jr., and Jones' friend George E. Sokolsky dominated the editorial page. The newspaper's daily editorial cartoons consistently reflected a Red Scare world view, often in frightening caricature.[54]

Under Walter's direction the *Chronicle* incessantly recited the warnings of the Republican party's right wing about the imminent Communist danger and called upon Houstonians to take an active role against subversion. "The conspiracy to undermine the United States government," warned the *Chronicle*, "will continue to be furthered by the Kremlin at every opportunity. We must, therefore, be constantly on guard." In another editorial, the *Chronicle* argued, "If we are to protect ourselves against Communists and their subversive activities, we must do so on every count. We cannot be tough in Korea and soft at home."[55]

In one of its more outrageous editorials, the *Chronicle* urged Houstonians to support the newspaper's demand that the federal government make a mass arrest of at least twenty-five thousand citizens alleged by the FBI to be members of the Communist party. "We have abandoned army and navy installations that could be used for places of detention." The *Chronicle* told its readers not to worry about the expense of such an operation because the "few millions" that concentration camps would cost would be devoted to a "worthwhile" purpose. Later, the *Chronicle* ran a series of articles about Communist fugitives from the FBI. The articles, which included "mug shot" photographs, exhorted Houstonians to search the community for these dangerous subversives.[56]

The *Chronicle*'s aggressive anti-Communist editorials and pro–Federal Bureau of Investigation articles attracted the attention of FBI director J. Edgar Hoover. Hoover's agents regularly clipped local newspaper stories mentioning the bureau and sent them to headquarters in Washington. When a story particularly pleased "The Director," he would dash off a personal letter of thanks to the lucky newspaper publisher. Jones received several of these communications. For example, after one of Emmet Walter's paeans to the FBI in an editorial titled "Deadly Atomic Espionage," Hoover wrote Jesse Jones of his appreciation for "underscoring for your readers the gravity of the problem presented by those forces whose subversive objectives threaten . . . our nation." Hoover assured Jones that he had been encouraged by the *Chronicle*'s "expressions of confidence . . . with respect to the manner in which we are discharging our responsibilities."[57]

Jesse Jones' and Emmet Walter's anti-Communist views were self-evident by just glancing at the *Chronicle*'s editorial page. Both men had their limits, however, when anti-Communism infringed on the company pocketbook. The right-wing Dallas millionaire H. L. Hunt frequently pestered Jones with requests to have articles, written by members of his organization, Facts Forum, published in the *Chronicle* and copies of *Facts Forum News* placed in Jones' hotels next to the Gideon Bibles. Typically, Jones sent Hunt's first request in December 1951 to Walter for advice. Soapy Joe explained to his boss that Sears, Roebuck was already running excerpts of Facts Forum articles in the *Chronicle* in paid advertisements. Why run Hunt's articles for free when Sears was paying for the privilege? As for the hotel offer, Walter emphasized that *Facts Forum News* would cost Jones 12¢ per copy or approximately $900 a month. Jones later wrote Hunt that he was "favorably impressed" with the Facts Forum articles, but he would have to decline the opportunity to publish them in the *Chronicle*. Referring to the 12¢ per copy *Facts Forum News*, Jones wrote, "I would not say a great deal of good would come from their distribution."[58]

While the *Chronicle* preached the Red Scare in the afternoon, its friendly competitor, the *Post,* taught it in the morning. The *Post*'s Red Scare editorial rhetoric was as inflammatory as the *Chronicle*'s, although the Hobbys enjoyed a public image of responsible moderation. These contradictory images stemmed from the fact that the *Post* was a newspaper with a dual personality during the postwar decade. Frequently, readers would be warned on one page by the editorial editor that "alien Red spies" were subverting every aspect of American life, while on another page a *Post* columnist would be extolling the virtues of the United Nations and international brotherhood. This contradictory tone was partially the result of slight differences between Will Hobby and his wife in political attitudes and world views. The elderly ex-governor was more provincial and conservative than Oveta, who was a dedicated Eisenhower Republican and internationalist. Will's views were generally articulated in the *Post*'s editorial columns by Ed Kilman, an old crony of Governor Hobby who had served as editorial editor since 1942. Oveta Hobby's attitude was more typically represented by staff writers Marguerite Johnston and George Fuermann, both of whom leaned toward a more liberal point of view.[59]

This dual image, however, was not a balanced one. Throughout the 1940s and early 1950s, Ed Kilman's right-wing extremism dominated the overall tone of the *Post*. Kilman, who considered the New Deal to be outright socialism, was an admirer and friend of Hugh Roy Cullen and shared Cullen's reactionary political views. As editorial editor, Kilman specialized in sensational anti-Communist diatribes and shares partial responsibility with his opposite at the *Chronicle*, Emmet Walter, in helping to create the city's Red Scare.[60]

Kilman's editorial style was to shoot first and ask questions later. For example, in the winter of 1947 the *Post*, under Kilman's guidance, created an unnecessary controversy when it denounced a "left-wing" meeting at the University of Texas' student union in Austin. The meeting, a "coffeorium" sponsored by the Student-Faculty Relations Committee of the Texas Union, featured a graduate student and two faculty members in a staged debate. The topic, "What Should We Do about the American Communist Party?," was discussed by each debator from a predetermined point of view. The student argued for outlawing the CPUSA, a government professor argued for a CPUSA registration law only, and an economics professor presented the Henry Wallace–Progressive party view. The university's student newspaper, the *Daily Texan*, reported the "debate" but failed to state that the entire program was "staged." The economics professor, Ernest Patterson, announced prior to his talk that although he would be giving the CPUSA position so that the audience would have all points of view, he did not necessarily agree with what he would be saying. The *Daily Texan* also left Patterson's caveat out of the story.[61]

What should have been an unnoticed and trivial event was seized by Kilman and made the subject of an outraged editorial. On December 24, 1947, relying on the unreliable *Daily Texan* version, the *Post* printed the editorial "Economics at Texas U." The *Post* mistakenly accused Patterson of teaching subversive economics and announced that the "Left-Wingers at the University of Texas" are "merrily" flapping their "wings." Kilman placed the editorial next to another that protested there were "too many Russkies" in the United States.[62]

Kilman was probably less concerned with the facts and more interested in taking the opportunity to attack the university's economics department. This was a favorite pastime among Texas' conservatives because of the presence of "Dr. Bob" Montgomery and his liberal colleague, Dr. Clarence E. Ayres. The mere fact that the Houston *Post* would overreact to such an insignificant episode is evidence of nerves frayed by the postwar climate.

The *Post's* handling of the affair created a furor among some right-wing Houstonians. Having only recently passed through several political crises swirling around the 1944 dismissal of university president Homer Rainey, the university now found itself under siege by Houstonians stirred up by the Houston *Post*. E. M. Biggers, a Houston printer whose son and daughter-in-law would later be leaders among Houston's Red Scare pressure groups, wrote the University board of regents and asked why it lacked the courage to fire instructors who teach Communism. Biggers' letter was joined by several others asking the same question.[63]

The besieged regents and university president T. S. Painter were able eventually to explain the "misunderstanding." The *Daily Texan* editor expressed regrets and admitted a case of poor reporting. Unfortunately, some of the "coffeorium" participants suffered severe criticisms from the university administration and the already fragile spirit of free discussion on campus received one more beating. Kilman, however, went on to bigger fish, never pausing to apologize for a totally unnecessary controversy.[64]

After the surprise of Harry Truman's reelection in November 1948 (an unwelcome development to Kilman as well as the Hobbys), the Houston *Post* embarked on the same course as the *Chronicle* and escalated its anti-Communist rhetoric. Like its competitor, the *Post* began to see Reds under every bush. Under Kilman's editorship the newspaper repeatedly informed its readers that ordinary citizens should help root out the subversive elements supposedly pervading not only the federal government but their own community. In one widely circulated editorial in 1950 titled "Citizens Can Aid FBI," the *Post* announced that the "home front" was just as much an area of conflict as Korea. The *Post* joined with the *Chronicle* and asked Houstonians to watch for "spies" and to notify the FBI if they saw any. Acknowledging that the task would not be easy, as "communists have been trained in deceit and are not always easy to identify," the *Post* advised Houstonians to "watch for anyone who can see no virtue in the American Way of Life. . . ."[65]

Although supportive of his anti-Truman editorials, Oveta Hobby was uncomfortable with Kilman's increasingly irresponsible anti-Communism. In February 1950, as keynote speaker before the Alabama Press Association, Hobby revealed her feelings about the type of editorials Kilman, Walter, and others across the nation were writing. She denounced the domestic Red Scare and the role played by the local press in sustaining it. "When sensational charges are made . . . by vacant-minded or hysterical people," Hobby stated, ". . . the charges are broadcast from coast to coast; and the public instinct is to accept charges as proof." Hobby denounced this as "a frightening tendency, to which the American press is contributing." She pleaded for her newspaper colleagues to "incessantly ask, 'What is your proof?' " Hobby also denounced the press' "fuzzy-minded habit of labeling all Communists, socialists and liberals together as 'left wing.' " Mrs. Hobby was proud of her Alabama speech, delivered in the very same month that Senator Joseph McCarthy first startled the nation with his outrageous charges of subversion in the United States Department of State.[66] Unfortunately, Oveta Hobby had also left herself open to a charge of hypocrisy, for her own newspaper—through Ed Kilman's editorials—was guilty of practices she had denounced in her speech. It appeared that her words failed to meet her actions. Kilman, for instance, was notorious for his editorial insistence that liberals were the same as Communists, a practice specifically denounced by Oveta.

What was little known at the time, however, was that Oveta had tried to move Kilman to another position, but her husband protected his old right-wing colleague. Despite Oveta's pleadings, "The Governor" refused to do anything about Kilman, who was much more reactionary than his mentor. After one of the *Post's* liberal reporters complained to Oveta about Kilman, she shrugged her shoulders in frustration, smiled, and said, "There comes a time in every marriage when a wife knows she has said all she can say about a particular matter." Nevertheless, under Oveta's patronage, the *Post* published Marguerite Johnston's editorial columns, which frequently presented a political view diametrically opposed to the one Kilman was presenting in the newspaper's "official" editorial section.[67]

Kilman unleashed a barrage of Red Scare editorials in 1951 guaranteed to encourage unwarranted local hysteria. In April an editorial titled "Red Fifth Column" called for the passage of federal and state anti-communist laws. Again the newspaper urged Houstonians to look for subversives in the city and to report all suspects to the FBI. The *Post* now warned that because the Communists had gone "underground" it would be even more difficult to expose them. Nevertheless, the *Post* assured Houstonians that "whoever helps to expose Red treason now helps to remove menace to his own safety."[68]

More Red Scare editorials followed in rapid fashion. Editorials with such titles as "Death for Spies," "A Dangerous Conspiracy," and "French Red Raps at Door of US" warned Houstonians of the insidious and immediate Communist menace. In July 1951, under the title "Those Who Play with Red Fire in US Do So at Their Peril," the *Post* declared that the

CPUSA was a "malign movement" and demanded that it be "suppressed" to prevent "the poisonous growth" from flourishing "at home." In August, Kilman reacted to Senator Pat McCarran's sensational and unsubstantiated charge that there were three to five million illegal "Red" aliens in the United States by writing an editorial titled "Alien Infiltration by Millions Raises Grave National Peril." Instead of following Mrs. Hobby's dictum of asking "What is your proof?," Kilman took McCarran at his word. Solemnly telling Houstonians that these aliens, including "wetbacks from across the Rio Grande River," were a peril to the nation, Kilman demanded that the "government crack down with all its might in every possible way on the hordes of subversives swarming over the country and coming in by the thousands daily." Such vivid imagery contributed much to Houston's Red Scare environment.[69]

The Scripps-Howard national news syndicate owned Houston's third major daily, the *Press*, so it was less reflective of the views of the city's power elite. George Carmack, the editor of the *Press*, although generally steering an independent course, often agreed with the Houston establishment's positions on anti-Communist issues. The *Press* had somewhat different reasons for indulging in Red Scare rhetoric and printing alarming stories about "subversive activity." It ranked third in circulation among Houston's newspapers and, to attract readers, often relied on sensationalism.[70]

The *Press*, just as the *Chronicle* and the *Post*, also tried to bring the Communist threat home. For example, in an editorial titled "Communism at Work," the *Press* told Houstonians that "we must recognize that we are at war . . . the battlefield today is everywhere – in the home, the school and the church. . . ." The *Press* urged Houston's citizens to support Senator Joseph McCarthy in his national campaign against Communism. "To those who are disturbed about McCarthyism," argued the *Press*, "we would suggest that once the communist threat is removed McCarthyism will not be a problem." The *Press* also featured the Communist exposé of Scripps-Howard writer Frederick Woltman, a reporter on the news chain's flagship paper, the *New York World-Telegram*.[71]

These declarations from Houston's influential newspapers were tantamount to official invitations from Houston's leaders for citizens to join in a Red Scare witch hunt. They certainly helped give credibility to the charges of extremists on the political fringe who accused their fellow citizens of harboring dangerous ideas.

In addition to editorials, all three of Houston's daily newspapers reported the activities of the city's small group of leftists in attention-grabbing front-page stories. The Henry Wallace campaign, the Wittenburg-Green trials, and the "Red" arrests of 1950 were given extensive and sensational coverage. Houstonians who took the editorials and scare stories seriously—and many did—could not help but react with fear and anxiety about the "radical" menace to their community.

Newspaper editorials in this period were an important part of the information process, more important than they are today. "The editorial page," journalist Edwin Bayley argues, "was the place where most readers sought help in trying to make sense of the puzzling, sometimes contradictory news reports." Bayley concludes that the press failed to fulfill its function properly during the Red Scare. Former University of Texas president Homer P. Rainey, later recalling his own experience in postwar Texas, claimed that the state's urban newspapers "played a big role in determining the way people in Texas think." Theodore White, after visiting Houston and other Texas cities during this period, observed that Texans found "all the papers and radio screaming at them to conform."[72]

Although Hugh Roy Cullen did not own a newspaper, he nevertheless contributed substantial public rhetoric and money, which helped create and sustain the Red Scare at the national and local levels. Cullen differed from his fellow elites. The oil man tended to wear his emotions on his coat sleeve and was much less politically discreet than Jesse Jones or the Hobbys. Compared to Judge Elkins, Gus Wortham, and the Browns, Cullen was a veritable wind tunnel of verbosity. He was stubbornly independent whenever questions of political or economic philosophy arose. A simple man who earnestly believed in the traditional moral values of home, family, and thrift, Cullen interpreted the possession of wealth as a sign of wisdom. Contrary to his own firm opinion, however, Cullen had much of the former and little of the latter.[73]

While one of the motives behind Cullen's political activities was probably the protection of his own wealth and its related prerogatives, his sincere belief in the creed of the self-made man also underpinned his actions. He believed that self-help and hard work could solve any problem better than government. Cullen also adhered to a version of the philosophy of the gospel of wealth. Like the Rockefellers, whom he despised as "liberals," Cullen felt that great wealth brought great social responsibility. This was manifested in his political work, his constant public exhortations on every possible subject pertaining to living a responsible life, and his extremely generous philanthropic endeavors. Although generous to his large family, Cullen distrusted inherited wealth. Cullen's interest in the University of Houston reflected his simple philosophy that hard work, education, and equality of opportunity were all anyone needed to carve out a respectable niche in society. He viewed the University of Houston as an institution that would allow everyone (blacks excluded) an equal opportunity, and he supported his views with money. Cullen donated

$269,000 to the university for a building in the 1930s and followed this with many other gifts, including one of $4.6 million in 1945. At one point, Cullen's investment in the university grew so large that some people suggested that the school be renamed "Cullen University." Instead, the city renamed a major street running past the campus "Cullen Boulevard."[74]

Cullen's generosity did not stop with the University of Houston. One estimate is that Cullen gave away approximately $175 million, amounting to nearly 93 percent of his total wealth, to various medical and educational agencies. Cullen left behind a foundation that has extended his gifts even further.[75]

Despite, or maybe because, he was a self-educated man with only a fifth-grade level of formal education, Cullen was always willing to share his views on every subject in which he felt the people of Houston needed tutoring. As one writer observed in 1947, "Cullen's generosity with his dollars is obvious, but it ought to be clear that a lot of advice goes with them, too." Because of the publicity his philanthropic activities generated, Cullen himself became a public figure whose opinions were guaranteed a prominent forum in the local press.[76]

An ultraconservative Republican, Cullen was an outspoken critic of the New Deal–Fair Deal of Roosevelt and Truman. He despised liberals as much as he hated Communists. Cullen believed the federal government was rotten with socialists and fellow travelers. On more than one occasion he demanded that President Truman and Secretary of State Dean Acheson be arrested and tried for treason. Even some conservative Republicans became objects of Cullen's spleen. Cullen once referred to John Foster Dulles, Eisenhower's secretary of state, as a "rat and . . . a crook" because he favored international alliances. Cullen was an isolationist who equated internationalism with "one-world" Communism. This view extended to the United Nations, which Cullen believed was "gradually usurping our national sovereignty." His idea of a foreign policy was to obliterate with nuclear weapons any nation foolish enough to oppose the United States with military arms. Alliances were "un-American."[77]

The Supreme Court's 1954 ruling against racial segregation in public schools also drew Cullen's wrath. In one of his numerous letters to President Eisenhower, Cullen declared that the Court's decision had "done more to destroy individual freedom than any government action since the founding of this nation."[78]

In a stream of public rhetoric, Cullen proclaimed his unhappiness with postwar changes in American society and government. Referring to developments in Washington, Cullen declared in a 1948 speech at the San Jacinto Monument, "I wonder if our grandfathers wouldn't decide it was time for another Texas Declaration of Independence." Addressing the

1950 graduating class of Baylor University Medical College in Houston, Cullen announced that "we are losing the Cold War. Both Socialism and Communism are gaining on us." Cullen's Baylor Medical College speech, which he reprinted and distributed across the United States, contained a typical Red Scare theme. The speech charged that "Joe Stalin has a great fifth column in this country, which is being trained in the underground for future use." The only way America could be saved would be for "men and women of all religious faiths" to join in a crusade against those seeking the destruction of the free enterprise system. "If we lose the struggle," Cullen warned, "our pulpits will be taken over by the most cruel pagan of our time. . . ."[79]

Hugh Roy Cullen's money also went to politicians. For example, Cullen contributed $10,000 in a futile attempt to defeat the reelection of Texas congressman Sam Rayburn in 1944. In that same year, the Houston oil man gave money to the equally futile anti-Roosevelt campaign of the so-called Texas Regulars. In 1948, Cullen "loaned" $60,000—almost their entire budget—to the Texas Dixiecrats in another doomed effort to throw Democrats out of Washington. Cullen's money was not always spent on the state's losing causes, as he contributed substantially to such conservatives as Price Daniel, Beauford Jester, and Allan Shivers.[80]

Cullen's financial support transcended state borders. As the Red Scare intensified in the early 1950s, Joe McCarthy earned Cullen's admiration. Hugh Roy Cullen's enormous wealth and obvious willingness to share it in turn attracted Joe McCarthy's attention. The two men struck up a friendly political partnership as Cullen opened his checkbook to the Wisconsin Republican. In 1952, for example, Cullen was the single largest contributor to McCarthy's Senate reelection campaign. At one point, Cullen announced at a press conference that "McCarthy is the greatest man in America." Despite his public pronouncements, Cullen privately had ambiguous feelings about McCarthy. When discussing the Republican senator with his official biographer Ed Kilman in 1952, Cullen admitted, "I admire McCarthy . . . he's an excellent man, but I think he has a method that's not good." Cullen's statement revealed McCarthy's ultimate weakness. His excesses and abuses eventually destroyed much of his base of support. Even Cullen disliked his style, although he never publicly admitted it and stood behind McCarthy to the bitter end. Kilman chose not to repeat the remark in the biography.[81]

Not only did Wisconsin's McCarthy benefit from the multimillionaire's wealth, so did conservative candidates from Florida to California. In 1950 he teamed with another Texas oil man, Jack Porter, in a "grassroots campaign" to disburse money and literature to help elect over two dozen conservative congressional candidates. Cullen money contributed to the defeat of senators Claude Pepper in Florida, Millard Tydings in Maryland, and Elbert Thomas in Utah and to the senatorial victory of Richard Nixon in California. During the 1950 campaigns, Cullen purchased and mailed over two million copies of right-wing author John T. Flynn's anti–New Deal tract *The Road Ahead* to several states. In addition, he distributed several hundred thousand copies of his Baylor Medical College speech, "Patriots Must Rally to Save Our Nation from Socialism!," to schools, churches, and political groups throughout the nation.[82]

In an indirect way, Cullen also had a radio voice. Early in 1951, John Flynn telephoned Cullen from New York and told him about a national radio network owned by a young man in Dallas named Gordon McLendon. The network, which was called the Liberty Broadcasting System, had supported itself by broadcasting simulated play-by-play renditions of major league baseball games. Flynn told Cullen that despite the popularity of the baseball games, McLendon was "in over his head" financially. McLendon was a good conservative, Flynn assured the oil man, and his network was a wonderful vehicle for transmitting right-wing viewpoints. Unfortunately, Flynn warned, if McLendon went under, some "radical element" would buy the network. Cullen subsequently had McLendon come to Houston to discuss options. McLendon told Cullen that he needed $1 million as soon as possible and he was willing to give Cullen a 51 percent share of the network in return. Cullen agreed to invest $400,000 and loan McLendon $600,000, but he wanted only a 50 percent share. Cullen told McLendon that he wanted the network to "further the principles of free enterprise" by featuring radio commentaries by such people as his good friend John T. Flynn.

Renewed by Cullen's money, McLendon returned to Dallas and continued the network. He ran the daily operations but consulted with Cullen over the telephone about policy. Despite Cullen's help the Liberty Broadcasting System went bankrupt in May 1952 and ceased operations. Nevertheless, Cullen's money made it possible for a wide range of right-wing, anti-Truman voices to be heard on a national radio system for a crucial year prior to the November 1952 general election.[83]

Among Houston's power brokers, no one equaled Hugh Roy Cullen's rhetorical and financial effort on behalf of anti-Communist causes. His efforts contributed materially to the Red Scare atmosphere in Houston and across the United States. In his home city, Cullen sponsored the public visits of such Red-baiters as his friend John T. Flynn and political extremist George W. Robnett, director of the right-wing Church League of America, as well as those of Joe McCarthy. Cullen's own virulently anti-Communist opinions were widely disseminated in Houston. One observer noted in the late 1940s that "no half diligent reader of Houston's newspapers . . . can have escaped some impression of Cullen. [He] has strong opinions . . . that are well known because they are printed frequently in Houston."[84]

In Texas, outside of Houston, Cullen's only rivals in this regard were Clint W. Murchison, Sr., and Harold Lafayette Hunt, both Dallas oil men. Murchison placed a generous portion of his estimated $281 million at the disposal of politicians throughout the United States who opposed internal subversion caused, according to Murchison, by "commies," the liberal Americans for Democratic Action, the CIO, and all "egg heads" and "long hairs." Senator Joseph R. McCarthy eventually became a principal benefactor of Murchison's gifts. Murchison also knew better. He and other Texas oil men admitted that Red-baiting anti-Communism was useful in keeping "the albatross hung about the neck of the New and Fair Deals."[85]

The eccentric H. L. Hunt, destined to become the richest of all Texans, was a different matter. Although he too promoted the Red Scare, Senator McCarthy, and other Red-baiters, his motives were far more complex. Hunt espoused a mélange of unusual beliefs and ideas, so his anti-Communism was probably much more sincere and less calculating than the others'. A close friend once described Hunt's political philosophy as being "to the right of [former President William] McKinley. He thinks that communism began in this country when the government took over the distribution of mail." Hunt's anti-Communist campaign would far surpass any other Texan's, including Houston's H. R. Cullen. His Facts Forum, a tax-exempt organization founded in 1951, produced a radio program that was broadcast at its peak on 222 stations. A television presentation appeared on fifty-eight outlets. In addition, Facts Forum published a magazine, *Facts Forum News,* with a circulation of sixty thousand and a newspaper column that was carried in 1,800 newspapers. Hunt's Facts Forum became a key source of information for Red Scare activists and witch-hunters at the local level and was especially popular among Houston's right-wing conservatives.[86]

The anti-Communist rhetoric and actions of prominent state politicians also contributed to Houston's Red Scare environment. Elected officials repeated the warning that "Reds" and "Commies" had moved surreptitiously into Houston and other areas of Texas and passed laws to help ferret them out. These politicians urged Texans to take direct action against the alleged threat posed by these local "radicals."

Extreme anti-Communist rhetoric and even Red-baiting by Texas politicians was not an entirely new development in the late 1940s. Texas politics produced Martin Dies, the man who pioneered the techniques that would later be adopted by Joe McCarthy. Dies, a congressman from east Texas, became the first chairman of the House Committee on Un-American Activities (HCUA) in 1938. Under Dies' chairmanship, HCUA began its practice of compiling lists of citizens suspected of subversive affiliations, a practice that would develop into a full-blown industry by the 1950s. Dies, who chaired the committee until 1944, bears chief responsibility for creating the impression that the federal government was saturated with Communists and their dupes in the 1930s. Eventually, Dies turned his attention toward his home state and created a temporary controversy at the University of Texas at Austin in January 1941. The east Texas congressman announced that he had evidence of the existence of a CPUSA cell at the university and that he would release this evidence in the near future. After Dies made his charge the Texas legislature created a "little Dies" committee to investigate. The Red Scare was still a few years in the future, however, and World War II loomed on the horizon. Most Texans paid little attention to Dies' wild charges and the chairman of the university's board of regents, Major Jubal R. Parten, called his bluff. Parten, an independent oil man and ardent New Dealer, demanded that Dies give his information to the regents. Dies vacillated as Parten continued to pressure the congressman with public demands for proof. Apparently having none, Dies quickly retreated under Parten's persistence and declared mysteriously that he had "cleared" the university of subversion. The legislative committee folded and the matter was dropped.[87]

A few months after the University of Texas debacle, Martin Dies was soundly defeated by Governor W. Lee O'Daniel in a bid for the United States Senate. In 1944, the pioneering Red-baiter retired from Congress when it became apparent that he could not win reelection. After another abortive attempt to become a senator in 1948, Dies' political career seemed to be over. The Red Scare, however, gave the east Texan new political life. He suddenly became a popular luncheon and dinner speaker for clubs and organizations throughout Texas, especially in Dallas and Houston.[88]

Dies, relishing his new status as an unheeded prophet, made frequent appearances in Houston, adding his voice to the growing chorus warning of evil subversives lurking on every street corner. In a speech at the Rice Hotel, Dies explained to a crowd of Lions Club members that Reds were not necessarily from poverty-stricken backgrounds: "I have known many Communists who were wealthy." Patriotic Houstonians could not even eliminate the rich as suspects. With the financial backing of Hugh Roy Cullen and others, Dies eventually returned to Congress, winning election in 1952 as Texas' congressman-at-large.[89]

Other prominent state politicians joined Dies in frightening Houston-ians and other Texans about their fellow citizens. A political speech was incomplete without some Red Scare oratory. Remarks about homegrown subversives were as necessary and common as kissing babies and posing in funny hats. For example, Governor Beauford Jester visited Houston in 1947 and exhorted the city's inhabitants to take personal action against "Reds" in the community. Jester was far surpassed in Red-baiting, how-ever, by his successor, Allan Shivers. In July 1950, Shivers publicly urged Houston's "patriotic" citizens to "keep an eye on all local communists." That same month, Texas attorney general Price Daniel came to Houston, warned of a "pink trend" on the local level, and called for a halt to "Com-munist tendencies at home."[90] Several months earlier, the Houston *Chronicle* had printed the Texas attorney general's warnings about "the infiltration of Communism into business and everyday life." Daniel warned his fellow Texans that "while we sleep, the Communists work day and night."

The Texas state legislature also joined the parade. Leading the way was an unctuous, soft-spoken, and gentlemanly representative from San Antonio by the name of Marshall O. Bell. A staunchly conservative Dem-ocrat, Bell was a tireless opponent of labor unions and taxation of any type. Beginning with the Fiftieth Legislature in 1947, Bell became the loudest and most aggressive anti-Communist in the House, regularly attracting newspaper headlines and stories throughout the state with his demagoguery. Bell found anti-Communism especially useful in his at-tempts to cripple the growing Texas labor union movement. "Commu-nists thrive on strikes," Bell would argue. "We . . . must be aware of the fact that the Reds will become more numerous as Texas grows industri-ally." In a speech in January 1948 to the Texas Society of Engineers meet-ing in San Antonio, Bell declared that "Texas has its share of Communists working insidiously to tear down the well-being of the nation." Refer-ring to the activities of Homer Brooks, Emma Tenayuca, and the small band of Texas CPUSA members, Bell warned that "we are fooling our-selves if we do not think they are working in Texas."[91]

Bell decided in January 1949 to translate his anti-Communist views into state law. In a dramatic news conference Bell declared that agents of the Soviet Union "are even now infiltrating" Texas' state government and schools. "The gravity of the dangers . . . creates an imperative public necessity for emergency legislation," the San Antonio representative stated. Accordingly, he announced his intention to submit a "Texas Loyalty Act of 1949," which would create a state loyalty board with broad powers to produce an official blacklist and purge state and local government and public schools of all alleged subversives. Bell also proposed an "American Education Act," which would ban from public schools any textbooks or teaching methods that might "breed disrespect for . . . the American way of life."[92]

Bell's loyalty board proposal became House Bill 19 when it was submitted with much media fanfare on February 7, 1949. His education proposal somehow never surfaced. Meanwhile, representatives Sam Hanna of Dallas and Preston Smith (a future Texas governor) of Lubbock sponsored a loyalty oath for college students and John Crosthwait of Dallas proposed a compulsory affidavit to be signed by college students and faculty members. This document would verify that the signer was not a member of the CPUSA. These two oath proposals were subsequently merged and passed into law. Bell's bill, however, died in the Senate. Senate Bill 228, proposed by John Bell of Cuero, banned from the official ballot in the general election any party "advocating or believing" in the tenets of Communism. This bill passed without opposition. Having passed a loyalty oath and an electoral ban against Communists, the Texas legislature, led by Marshall O. Bell, proceeded on May 2, 1949, to pass a resolution that officially declared a "Communist Threat to the United States." The resolution, essentially a reaction to the Russian blockade of West Berlin, warned that the American people "have not been alerted to our present peril" and concluded that the "Communist" threat to the United States was "far more dangerous" than any formerly posed by Nazi Germany or Imperial Japan.[93]

When the Fifty-second Legislature convened in January 1951, six months after the virtual disintegration of Texas' CPUSA, Marshall O. Bell again garnered headlines with Red Scare bombast. Making a pointed reference to the activities of the now purged NMU and other CIO unions, Bell announced that the state needed a law to deal with "agitators" in the Houston and Gulf Coast industrial areas. "There seems to be a steady stream" of radicals coming through the Houston-Beaumont region, Marshall concluded, warning that these "agitators" might somehow help "Russian submarines to lob guided missiles" into the "billion dollars of industry" between Beaumont and Brownsville. Bell's solution was to introduce a Texas Communist control bill. In House Bill 20, Bell proposed to require Communists and members of Communist front organizations to register with the Texas Department of Public Safety. The bill would also prohibit the names of Communists from appearing on party primary election ballots (they were already barred from the general election) and outlaw "probable Communists" from holding nonelective positions. Bell's definition of the Communist party included "any organization . . . which in any manner advocates, or acts to further, the world communist movement." The registration provision of the law compelled the registrant to list his or her sources of income, places of former residence, all organizations to which he or she belonged, the names of other persons known to be Communists, "and any other information requested by the Department of Public Safety . . . relevant to the purposes of this statute." Members of "Communist fronts" were compelled to register their organization, the names of all members living in Texas, the name of any person who had attended any meeting, and the names of all financial contributors. The law stated that if "reasonable grounds" existed for an employer or supervisor to believe a person holding a public job was a Communist or a member of a Communist front, the employer was required to remove that person from his or her job. "Reasonable evidence" went undefined and no provision was included that would require a hearing or allow an appeal for any person removed from his or her job. The act acquired a prison sentence of not less than two or more than ten years and/or a fine of from $1,000 to $10,000 for violation of the law. Homer Garrison, Department of Public Safety director, simply testified that the bill would give "the state control over people who ought to be controlled."[94]

The Texas House of Representatives passed Bell's anti-Communist bill by a 136 to 0 vote. John Barnhart, a twenty-five-year-old legislator from the conservative community of Beeville, asked to be placed on record as "present but not voting." Barnhart told his colleagues that he could not vote for the bill because he believed that it violated the Fifth Amendment of the United States Constitution. The Texas Senate nevertheless proceeded to pass a final version into law on February 21, 1951. When Governor Shivers signed the bill six days later, he told reporters that he hoped the law would provide the means for apprehending "those who would overthrow the government by force." Texas thus joined eleven other states in passing its own state registration act, despite the fact that the Federal Internal Security Act of 1950 extended the registration requirement of the 1939 federal law to the states.[95]

In March 1951, with visions of subversives resting heavily on their minds, the legislators decided to take another one of their periodic swipes at the University of Texas' economics department by passing a resolution denouncing professor Clarence Ayres. The economics professor had angered Marshall Bell and Sam Hanna by testifying against Bell's loyalty board proposal (HB 19) during committee hearings. Ayres' published views in favor of progressive taxation of income likewise drew Bell's hostility. Representative Hanna, who had earlier announced that only "punks, riff-raff, dirty skunks, and screwballs" opposed anti-Communist legislation, declared that Ayres was "the kind who should be run out of the University and out of the state." The resolution charged that Ayres had appeared at the committee hearing "in company with one self-acknowledged Communist named Wendell G. Addington [a University of Texas student]." It also repeated an old charge made in 1944 that Ayres had given a lecture at the university that denounced capitalism and private property. Bell, however, conveniently moved the date of the lecture up to 1951, seven years after Ayres allegedly made it. Bell's resolution denounced Ayres for allegedly advocating the "destruction of free enterprise and the adoption of a socialistic . . . system of government" and requested the university's board of regents to investigate the professor as a possible candidate for dismissal. The resolution carried by a 130 to 1 vote, with John Barnhart in opposition. University chancellor James P. Hart defended Ayres. Hart pointed out that Ayres did not accompany the alleged Communist student to the hearing; he merely testified against the loyalty board bill on the same day as Addington. The chancellor also corrected the date of Ayres' alleged subversive speech from 1951 back to 1944 and reminded the legislators that they had investigated Ayres at that time and found him completely innocent. Chancellor Hart's defense successfully thwarted Bell's attack, although the attack itself succeeded in the further discouragement of free speech and debate on campus and helped create resentment among the members of the board of regents toward faculty members responsible for attracting the attention of Red-baiters such as Marshall Bell.[96]

Three months after the Ayres incident, Dudley K. Woodward of Dallas, chairman of the board of regents, complained to Chancellor Hart that the university suffered from the fact that "a great many people feel that men and women of communist leanings . . . are . . . on the faculty . . ." and that many "responsible former students" often admitted that "instruction was definitely slanted toward the ultra liberal principles." Woodward declared that "the Ayres incident has done . . . untold harm" to the university because "the opinion is widespread that he was whitewashed by the Board." The regent complained that "the predominant political and economic views on the campus coincided with the left-wing element . . . identified . . . with Henry Wallace. . . ." Woodward warned that "these charges and suspicions . . . will remain to embarrass the University until the faculty and officers at Austin succeed in removing them." Woodward told Hart, "There must be some way to correct this situation. I hope you can find it." Under intense political pressure from the legislature and the regents, Chancellor Hart visited his friend Maury Maverick, Jr., and, with tears in his eyes, declared, "Maury, the lamps of liberty are going out one by one." Nevertheless, Hart refused to bow to these pressures and Ayres remained on the faculty.[97]

The passage of the Texas Communist Control Law and Marshall Bell's antics received widespread publicity in Houston newspapers. Much noted by Red Scare adherents was the act's preamble, which declared that "Texas . . . is in imminent danger of Communist espionage and sabotage." The Houston *Post* reported that the Department of Public Safety had a "carefully guarded list of suspects that they have been compiling ever since the Henry Wallace campaign." The Houston *Chronicle* featured the headline "Garrison Ready to Crack Down on Texas Reds," and referred to the control law as a "civil defense" measure. To help uncover Texas' nefarious Communists, the DPS' resident expert on Communism, N. K. Dixon, also head of the DPS' subversive intelligence division, explained to the press how average Texans could recognize a CPUSA worker. Dixon stated that "a good Communist is likely to lose respect for family ties and friends. He may become extremely critical of community service organizations and churches." Patriotic citizens should be especially alert to anyone prone to "lying, stealing, [or] murdering" since "anything for the good of the party . . . is all right" to a Communist. When asked by a University of Texas *Daily Texan* reporter where Communists were located in the state, Dixon said the Gulf Coast industrial areas. "I urge every citizen to be alert for these potential saboteurs," Dixon pleaded.[98]

After passage of the control law, the Houston Police Department and the Harris County Sheriff's Department announced that they were each sending three men to Austin to be trained for their departments' subversive, or "Red," squads. The police declared that "known communists" in Houston were being watched and their movements noted and that the newly formed subversive squad would arrest them if they failed to register. The *Chronicle* also applauded this action, stating that the local Red squads were needed to guard Houston against "those in our midst who would destroy the American rights which they so loudly proclaim for themselves when they get in trouble." These announcements, however, soon produced an unintended result. The Houston *Post* reported that the Houston Police Department's telephone lines were being jammed by a deluge of calls from frightened citizens who, one officer complained, "see a Red behind every tree." Houstonians were turning each other in faster than the telephone system could handle their calls. Despite the panic-stricken telephone calls and rhetoric from Homer Garrison and the police about surveillance of subversives, no one registered under the Communist Control Law and no arrests were made for failing to do so. According to David Caute, "Not a single organization registered anywhere in the United States."[99]

Thus, by 1951, as a result of the combination of shocking national and international events such as the Alger Hiss affair, the Korean War, and the fall of China to the Communists, the anti-Communist scare rhetoric of local and state elites, the sensationally publicized activities of a small band of local leftists, and the general state of societal confusion caused by rapid growth, Houstonians lived in a city ripe for an intolerant campaign for conformity. Theodore S. White observed the situation and concluded, "This emotional climate would be no more than a matter of morbid or humorous interest to other Americans as they watch a growing community fumble its way to maturity were it not for another set of facts: . . . millions of Texans are convinced that their primary enemies are other Americans. . . ."[100]

Instead of contending with a multitude of domestic and international postwar developments as individual and separate issues and events, many Houstonians and their fellow Texans and Americans accepted a simple explanation to deal with everything. As Houston Harte, a moderate Texas newspaper publisher, noted during this era, "The word Communist, at least in Texas usage, has come to mean practically anybody the rest of us don't like—a regrettable perversion of the old-fashioned son-of-a-bitch."[101]

FOUR

RED SCARE ACTIVISTS ORGANIZE

It is probable that every society contains certain personality types who are inclined to blame disrupting change on secret, diabolical forces and who gain hearers at times of particular stress.
—David Brion Davis

Brother, these reactionaries . . . lighted on Houston like corpuscles to a wound.
—Methodist Bishop W. Kenneth Pope[1]

In the spring of 1951, during the darkest days of the Korean War, the Houston *Post* received a letter from a man beset by fear. Intimidated by Red Scare rhetoric and bewildering events at home and abroad, the writer declared, "I'm just a boy from Mobile, Alabama who has come to Houston to make a living. I know I don't want any ugly Red kicking my front door down and taking the only beans I have. How about you? Somebody better do something and do it quickly."[2]

Unbeknown to the transplanted Alabamian, some Houstonians had already decided to join together and "do something and do it quickly." In the midst of the growing crisis of rapid change stood a small minority prepared to accept the challenge to action repeatedly hurled at them by the media and community elites. Houston's small group of hard-core intolerants from the extremist fringe who had always warned of alien and dangerous conspiratorial threats to the "American way of life" but who had usually been ignored now seemed to have a credible explanation for the problems of postwar society.

These heirs of the Ku Klux Klan and the Know-Nothing party tradition, sanctioned and encouraged by respected community leaders, took advantage of their newly acquired legitimacy and began to organize into new groups under an anti-Communist banner to deal systematically with communal fears. Most of these political extremists were white, upper-middle-class Republicans and conservative Democrats who attracted allies among some of the city's previously politically inactive professional and white-collar workers. These people used an existing organization, the American Legion, and created two new groups, the Committee for the Preservation of Methodism and a local chapter of the Minute Women of the U.S.A., Inc., to lead Houston's Red Scare.

For decades the national American Legion had campaigned to arouse the nation to the perils of Communism. Led by a special Americanism Committee active at both the state and federal levels, the Legion played an important role in molding public opinion about alleged subversive elements in American life. Its actions at the national level encouraged the creation of the House Committee on Un-American Activities.[3]

In Houston, the American Legion's Americanism Committee served as the main organization for small businessmen to participate in the effort to purge their community and nation of unwholesome elements and dangerous ideas. The Legion embodied the free enterprise vision that the average, ordinary, middle-class man should be able to operate a small business in any manner he might choose—the federal government, labor unions, and the United Nations to the contrary.

The leaders of Houston's Americanism Committee included John P. Rogge, an independent attorney who resided in Crosby, Texas, a small town near Houston; Loren Stark, the owner of an insurance agency; and Willard O. Hedrick, an oil well supply salesman. Their world was the world of the *American Legion Magazine* and its "smiling, pink-skinned family, one son, one daughter, a house, a garden, a car, a flag. No blacks in sight." The Legion's Americanism Committee had preached a Red Scare–style gospel in Houston for several years prior to 1950. Its basic forum had been anti-Communist advertisements in Houston's newspapers that added to the drone of fear pouring from the editorial pages.[4]

The Legion's newspaper campaign was in response to the activities of Houston's small band of Communists and leftists who operated openly in the city during the late 1940s. In a full-page, attention-grabbing advertisement that appeared in the Houston *Post* in March 1948, the Legion charged that the Communist party was "fully active—not just in Texas— right here at home, right here in Houston. . . ." The Legion warned that the Communists would spread propaganda into "every home and office in Texas" and that it was "up to Houstonians to drive them out." Another full-page advertisement charged that "there are 1,000 card carrying communists in Texas" and an unknown, larger number of fellow travelers. While the Legion's claim about the existence of a CPUSA group in Houston was correct, it greatly exaggerated the local CPUSA's influence. Nevertheless, the Legion, as in its other ads, urged Houstonians to do something about the local "Communist menace."[5]

The Americanism Committee relied on the newspaper ads as its chief means of protest until 1950. At that time, its activities increased as the group embraced such pressure tactics as picketing, public rallies, and boycotts. Later, the Legion, led by John P. Rogge, served as the public front group for a coalition of newly created Red Scare organizations, including the Committee for the Preservation of Methodism and the Minute Women of the U.S.A., Inc.

A group of laymen from Houston's Methodist churches created the city's first Red Scare–era anti-Communist organization: the Committee for the Preservation of Methodism. That these activists operated as Methodists was an important factor in raising community awareness about the Red Scare, since the Methodist church was the largest Protestant denomination in the United States and was second in size only to the Baptists in Houston. Methodists had played a prominent role in the city ever since the building of their first church in 1844. One traveler passing through Houston during the antebellum era disparagingly observed that the town was crawling with "Methodists and ants." In the late 1940s, some of Houston's most prominent civic and entrepreneurial leaders belonged to the Methodist church. A list of Houston Methodists would include not only such powers as Jesse H. Jones and Judge James A. Elkins, but also such influential persons as oil man R. E. ("Bob") Smith; Anderson Clayton Company directors Will Clayton and Lamar Fleming; Humble Oil president Hines Baker; Houston school board trustee Ewing Werlein; Harris County clerk J. W. Mills and his brother, school district business manager H. L. Mills; attorney R. A. Shepherd, a partner in the prestigious law firm Baker, Botts; and financier David C. Bintliff. Thus, any sustained dissension within Houston's Methodist churches would tend to attract the attention of the larger community. Likewise, communal social and political tensions external to the church were often reflected by internal conflicts within the institution. This cross-fertilization was highly evident during the Red Scare.[6]

While Houston's Committee for the Preservation of Methodism was a legitimate child of the postwar anti-Communist hysteria, it was created in specific response to the activities of a church-affiliated national organization, the Methodist Federation for Social Action (MFSA), which in 1950 had four thousand members and a headquarters in the Methodist Building in New York City.[7] Founded in 1907, the MFSA supported and directed welfare programs and fostered social awareness in church literature. The federation largely reflected the tenets of the urban social gospel movement of the late nineteenth and early twentieth centuries with its emphasis on industrial and economic reform, world peace, and social justice for all. Rising out of the slums and sweat shops of urban America, the social gospel stressed that concern for humanity's worldly secular life was as important as theological concerns about the hereafter. A vocal group of Methodist ministers was strongly influenced by the Christian idealism of the social gospel. As was the case with other Protestants, however, the Methodist social reformers were institutionally weak and had to function as an unofficial organization, unable to capture the official church. Nevertheless, in 1908 the MFSA enjoyed enough support within the General Conference (the national governing body of the Methodist church) to receive an official endorsement of its activities. It continued to receive the unqualified blessings of the national church until the 1930s. The most influential person in the MFSA in the 1920s and 1930s was Union Theological Seminary professor and Methodist minister Harry F. Ward, who served as its executive secretary and who had long sympathized with socialism. Ward also admired the programs of the Soviet Union and what he perceived as its social and economic democracy. The federation therefore often reflected a viewpoint decidedly to the left of the political spectrum, which made it vulnerable to criticisms from conservatives.[8]

In 1934, Elizabeth Dilling, in her book *The Red Network,* accused the MFSA of being a radical organization with close ties to the Communist party. Within Methodism itself, a politically right-wing extremist minister, Rembert Gilman Smith of Oklahoma, in 1936 published two anti-MFSA tracts: *Methodist Reds* and *Moscow over Methodism.* He continued his attacks in 1937 by founding the Methodist League against Communism, Fascism, and Unpatriotic Pacifism. Headquartered in Chicago, Smith's organization opposed the New Deal as much as the MFSA, but it attracted few followers. Nevertheless, enough laymen were aroused by these attacks that in 1936 the General Conference asked the MFSA to feature the word "unofficial" on its letterhead. Despite the accusations the MFSA continued to maintain its highly respected reputation among the church leadership. Although Harry Ward was interrogated by Martin Dies' special congressional committee in 1939, the MFSA generally continued its programs unfettered throughout the late 1930s and the war years of the 1940s.[9]

Neither the MFSA nor the social gospel doctrine had much visibility or influence in Texas before World War II. The MFSA did not have a chapter in Houston and many of the city's Methodist lay leaders were even unaware of its existence. This ended, however, in October 1947, when the national Scripps-Howard newspaper chain published a series of three articles by Rabbi Benjamin Schultz that charged that Communists had infiltrated the nation's religious organizations. Rabbi Schultz singled out the MFSA for what he charged was its cooperation with a "pro-Soviet network" and named the now-retired Harry F. Ward and his successor Jack McMichael as "fellow travelers." The Scripps-Howard newspapers, which included the Houston *Press,* followed these articles with another series of three stories in December 1947 aimed solely at the MFSA. This second series attracted a much larger audience within the Methodist church.[10]

Arthur J. Mandell, Houston labor union attorney. (Houston *Press* photo, HMRC.)

Herman Wright (1947), Houston attorney and partner of Arthur Mandell. Wright led the campaign in Texas to elect Henry Wallace to the presidency in 1948. (Houston *Press* photo, HMRC.)

The "Blue-eyed Boy," Homer (Bartchy) Brooks (1936), secretary of the Texas district, CPUSA during the 1930s. (Houston *Press* photo, HMRC.)

James J. Green and family (1949). Green was the CPUSA's Texas state secretary after World War II. (Houston *Press* Photo, HMRC.)

Houston's newspaper establishment during the Red Scare. (*left to right*) Jesse H. Jones, M. E. Walter, Oveta Culp Hobby, George Carmack, and former governor William P. Hobby. (Jesse H. Jones Papers, Barker Texas History Center.)

Sheriff Kern Seizes Texas Commie Files

Three Party Workers Picked Up With Car Containing Key Papers

By MARGARET DAVIS
Press Staff Writer

Sheriff Kern last night seized what he said was much of the headquarters records of the Communist party in Texas.

In the sheriff's possession today was what appeared to be a partial party membership list.

Records of the Communist party's financial transactions, including bank accounts and cancelled checks dated back several years to the time when Ruth Koenig held the office of state chairman, also were in the sheriff's hands.

JACK VAN RAALTE
He squealed.

GEORGE CARROLL JOHNSON
Lived with Commie boss.

ROBERT JOHN GUSS
'Peace' petitioner.

ROBERT L. BANNON
Caught with propaganda.

Propaganda, Too

Seized with the records was a quantity of Red propaganda showing on its face that it was issued by the Communist party and 900 of the "peace petitions" now being circulated by the Texas Peace Committee.

All the material was picked up last night in a car belonging to three men, two of them known workers in Communist headquarters, and all three recently picked up by police circulating the petitions.

Three Jailed

The three men are being held in the county jail for questioning. They are:

George Carroll Johnson, 22-year-old roomer in the home of State Communist Secretary Jack J. Green and his wife, Mrs. Billie Green, at 2918 Hamilton, until the building was stoned last weekend and the Greens

Sheriff Kern and Dist. Atty. Winborn to be prosecuted for assault.

Sheriff Kern yesterday dropped his political campaign for re-election to take over personal direction of the Communist investigation. The sheriff and Mr. Winborn yesterday questioned for almost three hours a man who admitted he was "a fellow traveler" but declined to say he was a Communist.

He is Jack Van Raalte, 45-year-old ex-regional organizer for the left-wing Food, Tobacco and Agricultural Union, Local 75, and also an organizer here for the Civil Rights Congress.

Turns Informer

Van Raalte, who was arrested Monday afternoon and who is still in jail—willingly, he told reporters—gave the sheriff and the district attorney a wealth of information about personalities involved in the interlocking left wing organizations in Houston.

Several "little black books" and a file of correspondence, picked up when his tourist court home on the Humble road was searched, gave officers a long list of names now under investigation.

A startling announcement in the Houston *Press* (July 19, 1950). Houston's daily newspapers reported the activities of the city's tiny group of radicals in attention-grabbing front-page stories.

(*left to right*) Hugh Roy Cullen, Dr. Walter W. Kemmerer, and General
Dwight D. Eisenhower prior to Ike's speech at the University of Houston in
November 1950. (Houston *Post* photo, HMRC.)

Dr. W. Kenneth Pope, minister of Houston's First Methodist Church (ca. 1952). (Houston *Press* photo, HMRC.)

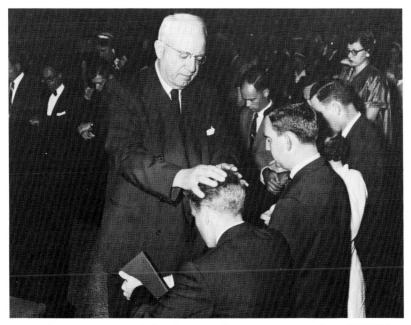

Methodist bishop A. Frank Smith (ca. 1953). (Houston *Post* photo, HMRC.)

Suzanne Silvercruys Stevenson, founder and national leader of the Minute Women of the U.S.A., Inc. (1951). (Houston *Press* photo, HMRC.)

John P. Rogge, spokesman for Houston's Red Scare coalition (1953). Rogge's dramatic appearance before the Houston school board on May 11, 1953, initiated the board's investigation of Dr. George Ebey. (Houston *Press* photo, HMRC.)

Dr. George W. Ebey (May 1953). "I find it a bit ironic . . . that probably my most significant contribution to education came from being lynched professionally by savages in a community where I was relatively a stranger." (Houston *Press* photo, HMRC.)

Dr. William E. Moreland (ca. 1953). "Moreland, a decent and sensitive man, was a sheep among wolves in his position as head of Houston's public schools." (Houston *Press* photo, HMRC.)

Ewing Werlein, Houston attorney, school board member, and a leader of the Committee for the Preservation of Methodism (1954). (Houston *Post* photo, HMRC.)

Dallas Dyer, Minute Woman and Houston school board member (1959). (Houston *Post* photo, HMRC.)

Dr. Henry A. Peterson, Houston physician and school board member (1953). (Houston *Press* photo, HMRC.)

Two stalwarts of the conservative faction of the Houston school board: (*left*) Stone ("Red") Wells and (*right*) James ("Jimmy") Delmar (1956). (Houston *Post* photo, HMRC.)

The Minute Women of Houston pack the front rows of the school board meeting room on the night of Ebey's defeat, July 15, 1953 (*left to right*) Virginia Hedrick, Mrs. H. W. Cullen, Norma Louise Barnett, Anne L. Harrison. (Houston *Post* photo, HMRC.)

Ralph S. O'Leary, Houston *Post* investigative reporter (1953). O'Leary told his readers that right-wing extremists had created a "reign of terror" in Houston. (Houston *Post* photo, HMRC.)

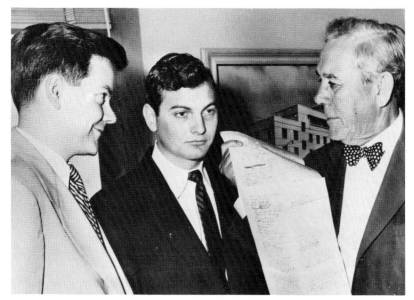

(*left to right*) Ronnie Dugger, Bob Kenney, and Hugh Roy Cullen (1954). Dugger and Kenney were delivering a petition signed by their fellow UT students protesting Joe McCarthy's planned speech at the San Jacinto Monument on April 21, 1954. (Houston *Post* photo, HMRC.)

Senator Joseph R. McCarthy in 1954.   *AP/Wide World*

Bertie Maughmer displays textbooks that she succeeded in banning from Houston's classrooms (March 1957). (Houston *Press* photo, HMRC.)

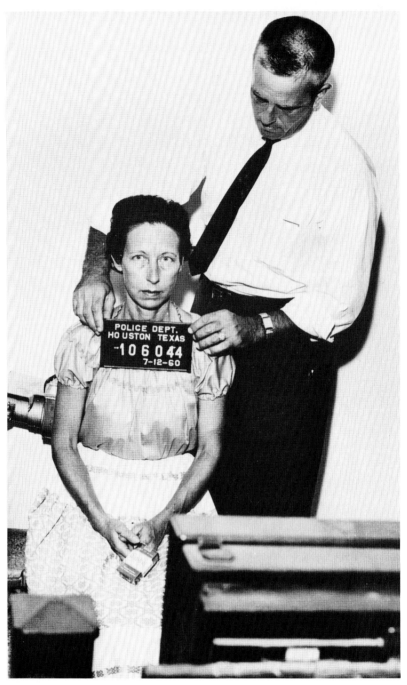

Bertie Maughmer is booked for attempted murder, July 12, 1960. (Houston *Press* photo, HMRC.)

Frederick Woltman, Scripps-Howard's resident "expert" on Communism, who had recently won the Pulitzer Prize for his exposé of subversive infiltration of other organizations, wrote the exposé on the MFSA. Scripps-Howard liked to advertise Woltman as "the premier Red baiter" among American newspaper reporters. Woltman, ostensibly reporting on the MFSA's annual membership meeting in Kansas City, wrote that the federation had attacked American foreign policy while praising both the domestic and foreign affairs of the Soviet Union. The series went on to portray the federation as a radical organization riddled with Communists and Red dupes.[11]

Houston Methodist lay leaders were shocked by Woltman's series, which they read in the Houston *Press*. Methodist bishop A. Frank Smith noted in his diary that "another article in the *Press* has set the local people wild. Laymen . . . want a statement from the Bishops." Smith, who abhorred such internal conflicts, decided to issue a personal statement about the MFSA that he intended for local consumption only. The bishop declared, in a release to the *Press*, that the federation was not an official Methodist agency and that its members spoke only as private individuals. "Any group calling themselves 'Methodist' . . . ," Smith stated, "that might discredit American democracy and exalt atheistic communism, or any other totalitarian philosophy is to be deplored, and has my unreserved condemnation." While Bishop Smith's statement avoided any direct criticism of the MFSA, its effect was to imply his personal condemnation of the organization. The Houston *Press* duly carried Smith's statement and it calmed Houston's Methodists. Unfortunately for Smith, however, the *Press'* parent syndicate, Scripps-Howard, blared his local statement across the United States with headlines such as "Methodist Bishop Disowns Group which Praised Reds." As a result, Bishop Smith became the target of severe criticism from national supporters of the MFSA.[12]

Despite the national uproar, Bishop Smith's action kept Houston's politically conservative Methodists relatively quiet for another two years. Nevertheless, local pressure continued to mount as national events seemingly revealed "Red" subversion within the Methodist church. In 1948, the House Committee on Un-American Activities denounced the MFSA as "a tool of the Communist Party." In its 1948 pamphlet, *100 Things You Should Know about Communism and Religion*, HCUA focused even more attention on MFSA. Crammed with unsubstantiated charges and innuendos, the pamphlet was organized in a "question and answer" format. It included instructions on how to uncover subversives who had succeeded in penetrating church groups. The publication explained: "To show up a fellow traveler, ask him to name ten things wrong with the

United States . . . and two things wrong with Russia. He will be on Russia's side every time." It was similar to thrusting a crucifix in front of a vampire; the little devils would always be unable to hide. The Methodist Council of Bishops meeting in December 1948 condemned the pamphlet.[13]

In 1949, John Flynn in his *The Road Ahead* added to the growing controversy by accusing Methodist bishop G. Bromley Oxnam of Washington, D.C., among others, of promoting a socialist revolution under the guise of religion. Although unproven, Flynn's charges had an impact on members of Houston's right wing because of his popularity among them. Flynn's chapter on religion was much discussed among Methodist conservatives in the city.[14]

In February 1950, the same month Senator Joseph McCarthy became a national anti-Communist celebrity, an article appeared in the *Reader's Digest* that sent shock waves throughout Methodism. Stanley High, an editor of the enormously popular *Digest*, attacked the MFSA in an essay called "Methodism's Pink Fringe." High, a Presbyterian, claimed that the federation's goals were to "discredit America at home and abroad, to condemn the American economic system as unchristian, and to . . . give aid and comfort to the Communists." To those who had argued that the MFSA was not an official Methodist agency, High asked why "the Federation's national offices are housed in the official Methodist building in New York City." High declared "for those of [the Methodist Church] to fail to reassert their faith against this growing, aggressive minority will be to fail both America and the church." The article also charged that MFSA executive secretary Jack McMichael belonged to thirty-six Communist front groups and that former secretary Harry F. Ward had no fewer than seventy such associations.[15]

Not only was the timing of High's article crucial because of current national developments such as the conviction of Alger Hiss for perjury and the sudden notoriety of Joe McCarthy, but its publication in the *Reader's Digest* guaranteed it a mass audience. Methodists throughout the United States were either afraid High might be correct or outraged because they believed him wrong. In Houston they were mostly frightened. In reaction to the High article, an informal coalition of conservative laymen—already disturbed by what they perceived to be socialistic propaganda in Methodist Sunday school literature, youth conferences, and the sermons of some local clergy—asked Bishop A. Frank Smith to meet with them to discuss a course of action. W. Kenneth Pope, minister of Houston's First Methodist Church and an anti–Red Scare moderate, offered his auditorium for the meeting. The Methodist laymen who assembled at Pope's church demanded that "someone do something" about "these Red traitors" in the MFSA. Bishop Smith, who was held in high esteem by most of the group, succeeded in easing tensions, at least for the day, by his calm and reassuring pastoral manner. Smith later recalled that "some of the best men we had in Houston were greatly agitated over this article in the *Reader's Digest*. I knew that . . . the charges . . . were too preposterous. But these men read that stuff, and they thought their church had sold them down the river. That Stanley High did more harm than you could even imagine." Although Smith eased the tension at the meeting, the laymen decided to continue their informal group and work to sever the MFSA from the Methodist church. Bishop Smith may have been able to prevent further action, but his own position was weakened by his statement about the MFSA two years earlier.[16]

It is clear that Smith, who had baptized many of Houston's Methodist Red Scare leaders and who was close to the city's power elite, was in an uncomfortable position during these years. A man of influence among Houston's powerful Methodists, perhaps Smith could have played a more vigorous role in moderating the extremists among his flock. He abhorred their excesses and generally disagreed with their views. As one of Smith's associates later observed, their actions "cut him to the bone." But these were his friends and when others urged Bishop Smith to assert himself and confront Houston's Red Scare Methodists, the bishop replied, "No, I will not denounce them. These are good men who love the church, and we are going to save them for the church." The bishop was not wholly inactive, but his basic response, like so many others, was to wait for things "to blow over." Thus, as Michael Paul Rogin has observed, the inactions of elites sustained the Red Scare as much as their actions.[17]

During February of 1950, Methodists in churches throughout Houston debated the *Reader's Digest* article. One minister, Grady Hardin, pastor of Chapelwood Methodist Church in the Spring Branch suburb of the city, went on the offensive and presented a special lecture one Sunday evening titled "Stanley High Hitting Low." Hardin, a liberal clergyman, succeeded in diffusing tensions within his congregation by analyzing High's allegations and demonstrating their lack of documentation. He was unexpectedly helped by a conservative church member who stood up after Hardin's lecture and revealed that he had been a schoolmate of Stanley High's. The layman turned to his fellow religionists and dismissed the *Digest* editor as a crass opportunist, saying, "Stanley will do anything for a dollar." This placated Hardin's congregation to the extent that his church was never represented in Houston's formal Methodist Red Scare organization.[18]

Not everyone remained calm, however. During his meeting with Methodist laymen in February, Bishop Smith agreed to appoint a committee to draft a "conciliatory" resolution in regard to the MFSA that would be submitted to the next Texas Annual Methodist Conference for consideration as the conference's official position toward the federation. In May 1950 Bishop Smith kept his promise and selected six laymen and four ministers for the committee. Hines H. Baker, president of Humble Oil Company, agreed to serve as chairman. After Smith created the committee he refrained from exerting any influence over its deliberations. The committee produced a draft that another special committee subsequently edited and then submitted as a Memorial to the Annual Conference on June 2, 1950.[19]

The Houston anti-MFSA memorial, which the Texas Annual Methodist Conference accepted by a near unanimous vote, called for the federation to drop the word "Methodist" from its title. It also "condemned" anyone who would "seek to use The Methodist Church . . . for the promotion of socialism or communism." While conceding that the New Testament "offers no blueprint of any economic, political, or social system of any kind," the memorial declared that the "private enterprise system . . . has proved to be the best system for the promotion of human welfare and happiness yet devised." Capitalism thus deserved the blessings of the church. Communism and socialism, however, "are basically contrary to Methodist thought and purpose." The memorial urged Methodists "to be vigilant" and to search "the background and beliefs of writers, speakers, teachers, and Church leaders in order . . . to make our Church literature and all teachings conform to the views and beliefs of Methodism. . . ."[20]

The Methodist Federation for Social Action leadership ignored these protests. They continued to use the title "Methodist" and to publish literature that took far more liberal positions on theological and secular issues than the Houston laity could accept. As the conservative Houston Methodists chafed in the summer and fall of 1950 at their inability to effect change within the national church and the MFSA, their world seemed to be falling apart. The Korean War erupted on June 25, a few weeks following the Annual Texas Conference. Joe McCarthy's sensational charges competed for headlines with the Asian war. In Houston, the *Post* and *Chronicle* featured stories in July about the arrests of local "communists," while in the autumn, as American casualties mounted in Korea, the local newspapers engaged in some of their most extreme Red Scare editorials as they warned Houstonians to watch for domestic traitors.

Led by men such as Ewing Werlein, J. O. Webb, Mercer Parks, Paul Wise, and Dr. John K. Glen, who were already swept up in the heightened passions of the Red Scare, forty-two of the anti-MFSA Houston laymen decided to make their group formal. On December 19, 1950, they created the Committee for the Preservation of Methodism (CFPM). Most of the members of the committee belonged to St. Paul's, Houston's wealthiest Methodist church, but also represented were First Methodist, St. Luke's, West University Place, Riverside, and Bering Memorial.[21]

The newly formed CFPM adopted three primary goals. First, it would promote and support the teaching of "the gospel of Christ in the world," which, it declared, was the primary function of the Methodist church. The conservative laymen pledged to support bishops and other Methodist leaders who opposed "the spread of Socialistic and Communistic theories in our church." Finally, the organization announced that it would do whatever was necessary to force the Methodist Federation for Social Action to drop the word "Methodist" from its name, move its office out of the Methodist Headquarters Building in New York City, and end its influence over the church. CFPM members hoped to persuade the governing Methodist conferences of the United States to condemn the Methodist Federation for Social Action and any other organization that would use the church for spreading socialist or Communist teachings.[22]

While the CFPM was determined to purify the Methodist church at the national level, it was equally determined to maintain orthodoxy and root out radicalism in Houston's churches. The CFPM warned local Methodist churches that it intended to carry out the earlier memorial's demand to "exercise renewed vigilance in searching the background and beliefs of writers, speakers, teachers, and church leaders" to ensure "Christian conformity."

For its first significant project, the CFPM published in the spring of 1951 a thirty-five-page booklet, *Is There a Pink Fringe in the Methodist Church?*, which borrowed High's "Pink Fringe" label. The booklet attacked the MFSA and charged it with seeking to use the Methodist church as a propaganda vehicle for spreading Communistic ideas. Excerpts from the *Social Questions Bulletin,* a journal published by the MFSA, were reprinted as evidence of the federation's radicalism. The booklet also contained portions of the HCUA's *100 Things You Should Know about Communism and Religion.* Another section of the pamphlet listed officers and committee members of the MFSA and its alleged membership in organizations cited by HCUA as Communist fronts.[23]

The CFPM eventually published and distributed nationally fifty thousand copies of *Is There a Pink Fringe in the Methodist Church?* As the publication circulated during 1951, the Houston-based CFPM succeeded in winning the attention of Methodist leaders in other states. In California, Robert P. ("Bob") Schuller, editor of the conservative evangelical magazine *The Methodist Challenge,* praised Houston's Red Scare Methodists in an editorial. "If every Methodist Community were aroused as is Houston,

Texas, concerning the dangers that beset the Methodist Church," Shuler wrote, "we would have a reformation . . . speedily." The *Christian Century,* published in Chicago, noted the *Pink Fringe* pamphlet and concluded that it signaled a coming effort to induce the Methodist General Conference to sever all connections with the MFSA. The *Christian Century* charged that the CFPM was composed of a group of Texas laymen who were attempting to gain control of the denomination. Calling them "self-styled 'circuit riders' whose calluses if any come from riding Cadillacs," the *Christian Century* accused the CFPM of using "the intimidative techniques of the Red hunt."[24]

The CFPM's *Is There a Pink Fringe in the Methodist Church?* played a key role in mobilizing Methodist conservatives, as well as many moderates, to force the Methodist General Conference to take action against the MFSA. The CFPM served as an inspiration and model for the creation of a national Methodist Red Scare organization. Thirty-three prominent conservative Methodists from several states met in Chicago in October 1951 to form the Circuit Riders, Inc., to combat radicalism within the church. CFPM activist Clarence Lohman, a Houston attorney and a member of St. Luke's Methodist Church, became vice-president of the Circuit Riders. This national group, which established headquarters in Cincinnati, Ohio, also attacked the MFSA. Many moderate and liberal Methodists, while rejecting the extreme accusations of Houston's CFPM and the Circuit Riders, were nevertheless unhappy with the Methodist Federation for Social Action. They argued that the church would avoid controversy if it could conduct its social gospel work through regular channels instead of through an unofficial organization. This view eventually prevailed and dominated the Methodist General Conference meeting in San Francisco in May 1952. The conference agreed with Houston's conservative laymen and officially demanded that the MFSA drop the word "Methodist" from its title and vacate its offices in the Methodist Building in New York.[25]

Unhappy with conditions back in their own city, the CFPM initiated a systematic Red Scare literature campaign by circulating copies of *Is There a Pink Fringe in the Methodist Church?* and, in 1953, reprints of Herbert Philbrick's article in the *Christian Herald,* "The Communists Are after Your Church!" Quoting Philbrick, the CFPM distributed handbills in Houston's Methodist churches that warned, "Subversion in the sanctuary is no scare cry — it's happening! Ruthless Communists — in clerical garb and out — are 'using' unsuspecting church members in a vicious assault on . . . religion." Circulars appeared on the bulletin boards and office doors of Houston's Methodist churches, charging that several unnamed local clergymen were actually Communist agents and that church youth groups had been infiltrated by subversives. One circular declared that the "bishops and ministers should be leading this crusade, not the laymen. Too many of them rise in protest when such is presented to them."[26]

The continued growth of the local anti-Communist reaction caused Bishop A. Frank Smith much personal distress. "These were good men," Smith later lamented, "men who were young with me, and we had grown old together here, and I had looked forward to the time when they would be our leaders in the church—and they had gotten led off by this 'Pink Fringe' business." Smith continued, however, to do little but wring his hands during the period. The organized anti-Communist crusade thus had begun in Houston with the formal creation of the CFPM in December 1950, two months before Senator Joseph McCarthy launched his anti-Communist campaign within the federal government.[27]

While conservative Methodists were the first to organize a new group to combat their collective fears, non-Methodist anti-Communists soon followed their lead. The CFPM was focusing on the narrow issue of Communist subversion in the Methodist church. Red Scare advocates needed another organization to spearhead anti-Communist purges within other components of the city such as the public schools and to protect Houstonians from "un-American" propaganda. A group of conservative, mostly Republican affiliated women filled this role in 1951 when they organized a local chapter of the Minute Women of the U.S.A., Inc.

The national Minute Women organization had been founded two years earlier in Connecticut by Suzanne Silvercruys Stevenson, a Belgian-born artist who had become an American citizen in 1922. Daughter of Baron Silvercruys, a former president of the Supreme Court of Belgium, she immigrated to America when the German army overran her native country. She eventually married a colonel in the United States Army Reserve, Edward Ford Stevenson, and settled on a farm in Connecticut. A graduate of the Yale School of Fine Arts, Suzanne Stevenson became well known for her sculptures and she traveled the country exhibiting her work, using the name Baroness Silvercruys. Greatly influenced by her aristocratic family upbringing and devout Catholicism, Suzanne Stevenson developed an intense hostility for Communism and anything that she believed remotely resembled or related to it.[28]

In the late 1940s Suzanne Stevenson became concerned about what she perceived to be the drift of American institutions toward socialism. A confident and independent woman, Stevenson advocated a type of political feminism made famous years later by Phyllis Schlafly. She believed that conservative women could be united and activated to become a potent pressure group in the fight to preserve traditional political, economic, and moral values. Some of her followers admitted that Stevenson appealed to their latent feminist feelings, which encouraged them to speak out and "be somebody."[29]

Suzanne Stevenson decided that "the world cannot be safe without good women." She proclaimed that "women must mobilize all . . . efforts" to defend the "traditional" American way of life in a national crusade that she would personally lead. To advance this goal Stevenson formed the Minute Women of the U.S.A., Inc. For her new organization, Stevenson composed a vague doctrine of twelve principles, elaborated some general goals, and prescribed strategy and tactics appropriate for pressure group activists.

Stevenson's basic Minute Women principles were:

1. Belief in God and Country
2. Principles Embodied in the Constitution
3. States' Rights
4. Clean Politics
5. Economy and Efficiency in Government
6. Fairer Taxes
7. A Sound Dollar
8. Free Enterprise
9. Right to Work
10. Courageous and Enlightened Foreign Policy
11. Free Press and the Truth
12. Patriotic Teaching in Schools and Colleges

Minute Women literature clarified these principles. For example, "States' Rights" meant continued racial segregation and support for the states in the tidelands oil issue. "Fairer Taxes" referred to the group's battle to repeal the income tax laws, while "Right to Work" referred to the Minute Women's opposition to labor unionism and support of the open shop concept. Stevenson's "Courageous and Enlightened Foreign Policy" generally reflected the standard right-wing Republican view of supporting the Nationalist Chinese, pushing the Russians out of Eastern Europe, providing military aid to Spain and Fascist general Francisco Franco, brandishing the atom bomb in place of "effete, striped-pants diplomacy," and withdrawal from the United Nations.[30]

Suzanne Stevenson also proclaimed a set of "major objectives" to complement the twelve principles. With one exception, they were as vaguely stated as the principles. They called for the teaching of "American heri-

tage" at all levels of education, "efficiency and strict economy" in government, a "stabilized" currency, and a "strong" national defense. The only
objective specifically defined was one demanding passage of a constitutional amendment to limit the tenure of office of the president of the
United States to two four-year terms. It subsequently became the twenty-
second amendment to the Constitution. The women later added to their
objectives a demand for passage of a constitutional amendment sponsored by Senator John Bricker, an ultraconservative Republican from
Ohio, to severely restrict the president's ability to conduct foreign policy.
This so-called Bricker Amendment would eventually become a major
Minute Women cause célèbre.[31]

Viewed as a composite, Minute Women principles and major objectives
reflected positions generally associated with such Republican party stalwarts as senators Robert Taft, Everett Dirkson, Karl Mundt, and William
Jenner. While officially nonpartisan, the Minute Women's goals meant
that they functioned nationally as an unofficial pressure group in support of the right wing of the Republican party. They were less concerned
with international affairs; their concern was at home.

Despite Suzanne Stevenson's claim that the organization had "a definite
ideology," the Minute Women never offered a specific plan of legislation
or action and seldom lined up behind any one political proposal. Their
"ideology," if it can be called that, seems to have been purposefully vague
and nonspecific, a phantom platform concocted to chase phantoms.
"Guarding the Land We Love," the Minute Women proclaimed—guarding it against Communists, socialists, and New Dealers; "one-worlders"
and progressive educators; labor unions and the Internal Revenue Service; anything and anybody threatening the "Traditional American Way
of Life." How this was to be done and to whom was never specifically
explained. This vagueness attracted those persons basically at war with
modern life and inevitable change. It also simply gave some conservative upper-middle-class women something to do. These women, vic-
timized by a sexist culture, were not supposed to work for pay, as it
reflected badly upon their husbands' ability to support them. Many were
in their late thirties to fifties in age. Their children were either no longer
at home or too old to need constant attention. Some of these women were
affluent enough not to have to worry much about household chores, yet
not wealthy enough to emulate Miss Ima Hogg and employ secretaries
to help with a variety of projects and spend the summers in Europe.
While not especially well informed, most of the Minute Women were not
unintelligent. They needed an outlet. For some women, an organization
that called itself a "Woman's Crusade" led by a dynamic, suave, attractive,

and "well-bred" woman espousing a "cause" matching their husbands' politics was too good to be true. It offered a way for certain individuals to channel deep frustrations and combat a host of personal fears. "This is THE answer to prayer," one woman wrote Stevenson. Another wrote, "For a long time I have hoped for something like this." And yet another said, "I wondered what a woman could do—perhaps this is the answer for me."[32]

Accordingly, after a woman pledged to vote in every election, promised to support an undefined traditional American way of life, and documented her American citizenship, she could pay her $2 dues and become a Minute Woman. She would, in return, be kept busy in a flurry of activity. Each member received a monthly newsletter (compiled and written by Suzanne Stevenson) and a bronze lapel pin in red, white, and blue with gold trim. The slogan "Guarding the Land We Love" appeared at the top of the pin. "Minute Women U.S.A." appeared at the bottom with an eagle covering a capital M and W in the center. The women attended group meetings and discussions, heard speeches by anti-Communist "authorities," and wrote protest letters in concert with fellow members. They relied on Stevenson's monthly newsletter to provide information that was "independent" of the local newspapers, although in Houston the Minute Women felt less of a need for "independent" news as they trusted the version provided by the Houston *Chronicle*.[33]

Suzanne Stevenson devised a telephone chain system by which the organization could quickly send announcements of meetings and other news to members. Using a pyramid type of structure, the national leadership gave messages to the chapter chair, who then passed them down to five previously designated members. These five members possessed a list of five other members to be called and so on. Because the plan often did not work perfectly, each person had an additional five members to call to prevent a breakdown in the chain. This technique allowed individual members to retain a degree of anonymity as the process often dispensed with regular meetings.

The Minute Women usually held meetings without public notice. Members assembled in the local American Legion or Veterans of Foreign Wars hall, or in a member's home. The crusaders warmed up for the evening's battle against subversion by singing the Minute Women song (to the tune of "America the Beautiful"):

As Minute Women now we pledge
Unitedly we stand
And strive with loyal hearts to guard
Our most beloved land.

America, we hear thy call—
America, for thee—
We pray for might to keep alight
The torch of Liberty.

Since the Minute Women had no constitution, bylaws, or parliamen-
tary procedure to guide the conduct of meetings, the local chapter chair
held complete control over the proceedings. As one Houston Minute
Women member recalled, "The meetings were social, but they didn't play
around. Everything was well organized." The leadership did not allow
motions from the floor and the agenda of the meeting was decided before-
hand by the policy committee. Suzanne Stevenson explained that such
procedures were necessary to prevent Communist infiltration. They also
preserved Stevenson's control of the organization.

Stevenson ordered members to act as individuals and never officially
as a pressure group. The major tactic of the group soon became the
telephone calls and letters to public officials by hundreds of individual
citizens supposedly not representing any organization. In this way,
Stevenson hoped to make their protests seem spontaneous and unorga-
nized. Suzanne Stevenson often told the members that next to their votes
their individual pens and voices were their best weapons.

Besides holding study groups, hearing speakers, and pressuring public officials, the Minute Women became self-appointed anti-Communist
watchdogs in communities throughout the United States. They specialized in harassing visiting speakers whom they thought sympathized
with Communism and therefore were "controversial." To aid them in
this task, they faithfully followed the suggestions made by the United
States Chamber of Commerce in its booklet *A Program for Community
Anti-Communist Action*. The Chamber of Commerce advised that a questionable speaker's positions should be publicized in advance by letters to local newspapers. "Trained listeners" should be present to ask
embarrassing questions after the speech. Letters should also be sent
to the newspapers after the speaker had left town to rebut the points
made in his or her speech. A summary of the entire incident should
be written and mailed, with news clippings, to anti-Communist organizations such as the HCUA. Finally, the chamber advised the local
patriots to write letters of protest to the booking agents responsible
for the appearance of the controversial speaker.

In a relatively short time, the Minute Women established chapters from
coast to coast. By 1952 the organization existed in at least twenty-seven
states. Caught in a moment of over-enthusiasm, a conservative magazine,
the *American Mercury*, predicted an eventual enrollment of approximately

two million members. Estimates of their peak strength, however, are varied. At one point in 1952, Stevenson announced that 500,000 members belonged to 104 chapters in forty-six states. Three months later, however, she declared that there were fifty thousand Minute Women members in "several" states. The latter figure was closer to the truth, although probably still much exaggerated. Despite the confusion about total membership, the Minute Women did flourish in California, West Virginia, Texas, Maryland, and Connecticut. Active chapters existed in Houston, Texas; Baltimore, Maryland; St. Petersburg, Florida; Charleston and Wheeling, West Virginia; Cincinnati, Ohio; and Detroit, Michigan. Membership rolls included such women as popular novelist Taylor Caldwell and the wife of conservative intellectual William F. Buckley. Three of the most prominent Minute Women leaders, other than Suzanne Stevenson, were Vivien Kellems and Hester McCullough, both from Connecticut, and Mary D. Crain of Mississippi.[34]

Kellems, owner of a small manufacturing company, drew national attention in February of 1948 when she refused to withhold federal income taxes from her employees' paychecks, stating that the tax law was "illegal, immoral, and unconstitutional." She later authored *Taxes, Toil, and Trouble*, which advocated the abolition of the federal income tax. In 1950, Kellems made an unsuccessful attempt to win the Republican nomination for the U.S. Senate in Connecticut.[35]

Mary D. Crain led the Memphis chapter of the Minute Women and made national news with her refusal to collect Social Security taxes from employees of her newspaper, the Summit (Mississippi) *Sun*. She announced in one speech that "Social Security is Communism!" A tireless supporter of racial segregation, Crain told one news conference that ". . . the federal government apparently knows more than God Himself [about] the races of mankind, although God created them as separate—not mongrel—races."[36]

Another fiery leader, Mrs. Hester McCullough, directed the Minute Women's Committee against Subversive Activities. She specialized in accusing liberal entertainers of being pro-Communist. McCullough was involved in the campaign directed against dancer Paul Draper and musician Larry Adler that led to their being blacklisted.[37]

Suzanne Stevenson held the position as the undisputed leader and driving power behind the Minute Women. Stevenson radiated evangelistic fervor in her crusade and often referred to herself as "Sizzling Sue" and the "Paul Revere of the Fair Sex." She and her husband, who served as publicity director, toured the nation in a house trailer emblazoned with the legend "M-W's Caravan of 1951" to organize Minute Women chapters in several states.[38]

In her public appearances, Stevenson often carried a giant copy of the United States Constitution as a theatrical prop to emphasize points in speeches. An effective orator, she stirred her audiences to a high pitch of excitement, often delighting her listeners by feverishly working on a piece of sculpture while she talked. One of Stevenson's favorite speeches hinted ominously that Communism "honey-combed" the public schools, including even the elementary grades. She also warned that Communist sympathizers had replaced many of "our true American textbooks" with new and dangerous ones hostile to American values.[39]

A variety of persons shaped general Minute Women positions. John T. Flynn was among the group's favorite writers. Flynn's basic world view was more sophisticated and complex than that of other Minute Women favorites. In 1948 he wrote *The Roosevelt Myth,* which accused President Roosevelt of "selling out" Eastern Europe to the Russians at the Yalta Conference in 1945. Flynn also charged that under FDR, federal agencies "became roosting places for droves of Communist termites who utilized their positions . . . to advance the interests of Soviet Russia. . . ." Flynn's prolific writings appeared throughout the late 1940s in such anti-Roosevelt publications as the *Reader's Digest,* the *Chicago Tribune,* and the Hearst newspaper syndicate. Many of his essays were on behalf of Chiang Kai-shek and his Nationalist Army during the Chinese civil war.[40]

In 1949, Flynn published his best-selling work, *The Road Ahead,* which sold 4.1 million copies. The sales were encouraged by a condensed version appearing in the February 1950 issue of the *Reader's Digest*—the same issue that featured Stanley High's attack on the MFSA. *The Road Ahead's* status as a "best-seller" was considerably aided by Hugh Roy Cullen, who purchased thousands of copies that he distributed free of charge during the 1950 congressional campaigns. *The Road Ahead* charged that the New Deal had created a bureaucratic machine that had established a "Welfare State" intent on subjecting "citizens to the serfdom" of the federal government through taxation and "handouts" to the poor. The ultimate and inevitable result of the New Deal–Fair Deal bureaucracy would be a totalitarian Communist state. *The Road Ahead* also included a chapter accusing Protestant clergymen and laymen of spreading socialist propaganda in their respective religious institutions.[41]

Flynn followed *The Road Ahead* in 1951 with the almost as successful work *While You Slept: Our Tragedy in Asia and Who Made It.* In this book, Flynn focused on the Communist takeover in China, alleging that "Reds" in the State Department gave China to Mao Tse-tung's Communists and tricked the United States into the Korean War to bleed the American army. Houston Minute Women so favored *While You Slept* that they and their associates persuaded the Houston Independent School District to use it in high school civics classes as a factual source for the study of American foreign policy in Asia. The schools used *While You Slept* as late as 1969.[42]

Flynn's personal friendship with Joseph McCarthy and his zealous support of McCarthy's activities solidified his popularity with the Minute Women. When the Wisconsin senator later became the object of withering attacks from his own party, Flynn published *McCarthy: His War on American Reds, and the Story of Those Who Oppose Him* (1954). This led to Flynn's achieving the status of being the nation's primary McCarthyite "intellectual." The Minute Women newsletter invariably contained high praise for Flynn's books and pamphlets. The group particularly relished a Flynn essay on public education entitled "Textbooks Are Perverted." Much of Suzanne Stevenson's writing reflected Flynn's influence and she urged her followers to purchase several copies of his publications to distribute to friends and neighbors in need of "enlightenment."[43]

The Minute Women read other right-wing authors. The name of Gerald L. K. Smith, head of the Christian Nationalist party, often appeared on Minute Women reading lists. A former minister and an impressive orator, Smith first came to prominence in the 1930s as an organizer for Senator Huey P. Long's Share Our Wealth program. Sociologist Seymour Martin Lipset has described Smith as the "dean of American anti-Semitism." Smith, who was also a white supremacist, earned this reputation through such public statements as "We believe in the complete . . . segregation of the black and white races in America" and "The danger to the white race comes from the aspirations of the Jewish race to dominate the world."[44]

Joseph P. Kamp, director of the Constitutional Educational League, spoke to Minute Women rallies and the organization also circulated his literature. Kamp, an anti-Semite in the Gerald L. K. Smith mold, had a well-known pro-Nazi record before World War II. He was a prolific pamphleteer, publishing such titles as *Behind the Lace Curtains of the YWCA, Vote CIO and Build a Soviet America,* and *We Must Abolish the United Nations.* Kamp led a smear campaign against Dwight D. Eisenhower after the war in an attempt to link him to the "communist conspiracy." When confronted at a public forum about his anti-Semitism, Kamp retorted, "I pull no punches in exposing the Jewish Gestapo or any Jew who happens to be a Communist."[45]

Dr. John O. Beaty, a professor of English at Southern Methodist University for thirty-four years and author of *The Iron Curtain over America,* was also on the Minute Women reading list. Beaty's book has been described by the Anti-Defamation League of B'Nai B'Rith as one of the most anti-Semitic books ever written in the United States. The SMU professor claimed that "Eastern European Jews" such as Felix Frankfurter, associate justice of the U.S. Supreme Court, and Samuel Rosenman, a speechwriter for Franklin Roosevelt, controlled the United States government. Beaty, who addressed several Minute Women rallies, called Jewish Americans "an undigested mass in the body politic, an ideologically hostile 'nation within the nation.' "[46]

The Minute Women also recommended the work of Allen Zoll, founder of the American Patriots, Inc. and an associate of Joseph P. Kamp and Gerald L. K. Smith. In his efforts to keep the public schools free of "socialistic progressive education," Zoll became executive vice-president of the National Council for American Education. His publications, eagerly read and promoted by Minute Women, included *Progressive Education Increases Delinquency, How Red Are the Schools?*, and *They Want Your Child!* An opponent of the United Nations, Zoll declared that the UN was a device to permit the "colored" races to rule the "white" races. Zoll gained a national reputation synonymous with the irrational criticism of public schools. In one speech, Zoll charged that UNESCO, "an alien conspiracy," had invaded the public school curriculum to teach sex delinquency to American school children. He advised his followers to ". . . form hell raising groups to find out what is being taught in schools, and then raise hell about it!"[47]

By far the most popular source of information and opinions for Houston's Minute Women was H. L. Hunt's Facts Forum. Created in June 1951, Hunt's *Facts Forum News* was required reading for the Houston women. Suzanne Stevenson also admired Hunt and his right-wing propaganda network, "which," she told her followers, "is making people think and voice their opinions."[48]

Starting out modestly, Hunt's program expanded in the fall of 1952 into three different radio broadcasts each week and added a half-hour television version of *Facts Forum News*. The radio and television programs featured Dan Smoot, a former FBI agent, and specialized in what Hunt called "public education" about the struggle between the "far-left" and "constructive conservatism." Hunt's constructive conservatism consisted of attacks on the welfare and regulatory states, the United Nations, liberal and moderate Democrats, and the usual list of right-wing enemies. One constant point preached by Smoot on his weekly broadcasts was that the United States was not a democracy but a "republic." Smoot argued that the founding fathers knew "that a democracy is the most evil kind of government possible." This position, although not a complete misrepresentation of the ideas of the writers of the Constitution, was an exaggeration and totally ignored 130 years of legislative reform to make the American political system more democratic. Smoot's argument reflected the strong strain of anti-democratic feeling in the anti-Communist right wing and a belief in an elite corporate state where access to power would be based on the amount of property one held. In 1960, Hunt himself articulated this view in the self-published and ghost-written utopian novel *Alpaca*.

While Hunt's extreme political ideas were distinctly his own, the anti-democratic bias as spread through *Facts Forum News* made an impression on many Red Scare activists in Houston and elsewhere. The idea that the United States was a republic and not a democracy was, of course, not original with Hunt, but it became a popular part of the ideology of such groups as the Minute Women and it appeared often in their Houston newsletter. Facts Forum provided a free circulating library that mailed out the writings of Joseph Kamp, John O. Beaty, Senator Joseph McCarthy, and other Hunt favorites. *Facts Forum News* disseminated reading lists, names and addresses of other right-wing organizations, and anti-Communist essays and included a "Letters to the Editor" column.[49]

A mere reading list does not, of course, mean that all Minute Women were anti-Semitic or as crazed as John O. Beaty. But the authors discussed above, producers of what one writer has called the "Subliterature of Hate," were aggressively promoted through Minute Women newsletters at the national and local levels. Minute Women reading lists did not include authors who contradicted the opinions of the Kamps, Zolls, and Flynns. These writers encouraged anti-Semitism and racism, advocated the abolition of public education, and preached dark conspiratorial theories of history. The Minute Women praised and distributed their writings on every possible occasion. Such enthusiastic approval and endorsement indicate that the ideas expressed in such literature represented the endorser's own world view. It should also be emphasized, however, that Minute Women membership did not necessarily mean total agreement with the opinions of the professional "hate" writers. Many women joined the group only out of a sincere fear of the Communist threat, completely divorced from any knowledge of such persons as Joseph Kamp or Gerald L. K. Smith. Some of these women were repelled by the anti-Semitic literature and resigned as a result. The significance of the Minute Women reading lists is that they accurately reflected the mind-set of the group's leadership, both nationally and in Houston.[50]

A chronicle of Minute Women protest campaigns throughout the United States is difficult because the organization usually kept its activities secret, acting only as "individuals." Several incidents, however, were known to be the work of the Minute Women. In Indianapolis, Indiana, the Minute Women prevented an American Civil Liberties Union meeting in the Indiana War Memorial Building. In 1950, led by Hester McCullough, the Minute Women objected to the casting of actress Jean Muir on "The Aldrich Family" television show because the Dies committee had cited her as belonging to subversive organizations. Despite Muir's denial, the National Broadcasting Company and the show's sponsor, General Foods, agreed to fire Miss Muir for being "controversial." The Minute Women disrupted a conference on foreign affairs in Cleveland, Ohio, sponsored by the Cleveland Foreign Policy Association in 1953. The conference featured speakers Kermit Eby of the University of Chicago and Ernest Gross, former United States delegate to the United Nations. The Minute Women attacked the conference and both speakers as Communist "tools." The group also led the attack against Anna Rosenberg's nomination as assistant secretary of defense in the Truman administration.[51]

Despite their semisecret tactics, Minute Women activities were overt enough to elicit some stinging editorial response from some of the nation's most respected newspapers. The *New York Times* declared that the Minute Women "display an inexcusable disregard for the principles of freedom of thought and freedom of expression." The Atlanta *Constitution* charged that the "Minute Women . . . inevitably attract a lot of neurotic fanatics . . . they are behind much, if not most, of the clamor against the public school system." The St. Louis *Post-Dispatch* said: "This is a free country and that gives the Minute Women a pretty wide franchise. We certainly do not want to revoke it. We have always felt that if you let the lunatic fringe talk, it will quickly expose its lunacy. But we are getting a little worried about the people who do not recognize lunacy when they hear it."[52]

The Minute Women were harmed more by internal factionalism than by criticism from hostile newspapers. Disagreements and internal strife erupted among the group's leaders. Vivien Kellems resigned in 1950 after accusations that she had attempted to use the group in her unsuccessful campaign to win election to the Senate. Kellems formed a rival but less successful organization, the Liberty Belles, Inc. Hester McCullough also left the Minute Women after charging them with following the Communist line because the organization purchased newspaper advertising in several cities to protest the war in Korea. The CPUSA shrewdly stole the Minute Women ads and ran them in the *Daily Worker*. Under more amicable conditions, the founder and guiding light of the organization, Suzanne Stevenson, left the group in 1952. She subsequently participated in the creation of the Constitution party of the United States, a third political party disgusted with the Republican presidential nomination of Dwight Eisenhower. Stevenson became national co-chair of the new party, but her association was short-lived. In a development tinged with irony, Stevenson unexpectedly resigned her position and left the party in February 1952. She complained that party members had treated her shabbily because of her foreign birth and Catholic religion. Stevenson also believed that the party was guilty of anti-Semitic prejudice. She did not return to Minute Women leadership, however. Dorothy B. Frankston became the new chair and the national headquarters moved to Wheeling, West Virginia.[53]

With the resignation of members Kellems, McCullough, and Stevenson the Minute Women lost much of their crusading zeal. Moreover, even before Suzanne Stevenson's departure, some local chapters had begun to eclipse the national organization in crusading fervor. This included the Houston group, which developed into one of the most active local branches in the United States and provided the central leadership role in the conduct of Houston's Red Scare.

Small gatherings of women at teas, country clubs, and at a meeting of physicians' wives at the Shamrock Hotel in the winter of 1950–51 promoted the founding of the Minute Women chapter in Houston. Suzanne Stevenson announced in her national newsletter of February 1951 that chapters would soon be formed in Texas and other states. Her March 1951 newsletter quoted from two letters received from women in Houston, Eleanor Watt and Helen D. Thomas. Watt's letter asked that a Minute Women chapter be formed in Texas, while Thomas' letter suggested that the Minute Women add a states' rights clause to their statement of beliefs. The Minute Women founder heartily endorsed the idea and announced the new addition to the platform.[54]

While Eleanor Watt and Helen Thomas proceeded to organize a Minute Women "cluster" in the early spring of 1951, Adria Allen, the wife of a supervisor for the Houston Transit Company, unaware of their activity, decided to form her own group. Allen was alarmed by Secretary of State Dean Acheson's foreign policy and "creeping socialism" at home. Wanting to do something about these problems, Allen went to the Houston *Chronicle* for advice on what she, as an individual, could do to stop subversion in the State Department and oppose "socialized education" in Houston schools. At the suggestion of *Chronicle* employees, Allen placed an ad in the newspaper asking for women as concerned as herself to telephone or write. Twenty-two women responded and agreed to attend meetings in the Allen home near Houston's Memorial Park. After a few sessions, the women noticed another ad in the *Chronicle* announcing the formation of a Minute Women chapter in Houston. The women contacted Suzanne Stevenson in Connecticut and she referred them to the Minute Women organizers in Houston, Eleanor Watt and Helen Thomas. The two groups combined and formed the Houston chapter of the Minute Women of the U.S.A., Inc.[55]

In June of 1951, weekly meetings began in the back yard of the Watt home. Jack Porter, a Houston oil man and Republican party activist, spoke at the first informal meeting. One month later, in July, the Minute Women held their first publicized meeting in Texas. Approximately two hundred men and women met at the Briar Club in Houston to hear national leader Stevenson speak. The sculptress declared that it was the duty of the Houston chapter to elect conservatives to office and to "fight socialistic trends in the federal and state governments." This was an unusual public admission, since the Minute Women always maintained that they endorsed no political candidates as an organization. The national leader entertained Houstonians with an emotional discussion of a women's movement in Gary, Indiana, that had inspired her to create the Minute Women. The Gary women organized in 1949 to combat a crime wave that had claimed the lives of eight citizens. When the Gary City Council proved unresponsive to their pleas, the women succeeded in voting them out of office and then disbanded. Stevenson told the Briar Club audience that she envisioned a similar women's crusade against the Truman administration and associated evils and this led to the birth of the Minute Women. She also outlined the structure of the national organization and discussed the twelve Minute Women principles. This first meeting attracted several new members and gave the group some momentum.[56]

After Stevenson's July visit, Eleanor Watt established the local Minute Women office in her home on tree-lined Rice Boulevard. An anonymous council of ten, appointed by the national leader, governed the local organization. Stevenson also established Minute Women chapters in other Texas cities; those in Dallas and San Antonio being the most active. The Dallas group would rival the Houston Minute Women in size of membership. Watt, founder of the Houston chapter, became chair of the statewide governing council.[57]

By the fall of 1951, the Houston Minute Women numbered at least three hundred members. A split occurred within the group in September 1951, however, that resulted in the resignation of approximately fifty women. A group of physicians' wives questioned the need for secrecy within the organization, especially in regard to financial records. Another small group objected to a pamphlet, *My American Credo,* written by Suzanne Stevenson, that demanded disfranchisement of citizens who failed to vote in elections. In October 1951, Stevenson hurried back to Texas to prevent the dissolution of her promising Houston chapter. She conducted a closed meeting of all Houston Minute Women members at San Jacinto High School. In a public speech following the closed session, Stevenson explained to her Houston followers that she wrote the credo prior to creation of the organization and it did not represent official Minute Women principles. Then, apparently feeling Eleanor Watt's leadership had contributed to the dissension, the national founder announced her removal as chair and appointed Virginia Biggers as the new leader. Stevenson

permitted no voting; only her arbitrary decision, taken silently and without objection by Eleanor Watt, prevailed. This action apparently ended
the local problems and the organization began a new period of growth.[58]

While Suzanne Stevenson was in Houston, she took the opportunity
to visit with Hugh Roy Cullen. Cullen obviously gave the Minute Women
leader a full hearing since Stevenson described her visit with him as a
"fairy tale." Meeting Cullen, according to Stevenson, was "an experience
in itself, for he is truly a very great American . . . who has amassed a
great fortune yet is . . . anxious to do public good with his money."
During the meeting, Stevenson tried to persuade the Houston millionaire
to give the Minute Women a radio program on the Liberty Broadcasting
System. Cullen refused to make any promises, but later did introduce
her to Gordon McLendon, who eventually agreed to give the Minute
Women their own program, "Minute Women Calling for Liberty," at
6:45 P.M. every Sunday. Stevenson, whose brother was the Belgian am-
bassador to the United States, also tried to convince Cullen to make oil
investments in the Belgian Congo.[59]

After the initial dissension in the early fall of 1951, the Houston Minute
Women chapter grew in strength with at least five hundred members by
the time of the presidential election in 1952. The affluent residential
areas in Houston provided a majority of the Minute Women membership. Many Houstonians thought of the Minute Women as a River
Oaks group, led by extremely wealthy women. Actually, River Oaks
merely provided a large percentage of the rank and file membership.
It did not provide the leadership. Minute Women leaders, with two
exceptions, lived in less exclusive but relatively affluent upper-middle-
class areas, including the neighborhoods surrounding Rice University
and the Tanglewood, Montrose, and Memorial Park sections. These
neighborhoods were populated by corporation technocrats, white-collar
workers, and successful small businessmen.[60]

Generally, the husbands of the most active Minute Women were
middle-class insurance and car salesmen, business managers, and city
employees at the management level who were economically and socially
aspiring. A tiny but militant portion came from less affluent circles, including elderly widows, boarding house operators, seamstresses, and
managers of small specialty shops. Many of these people depended on
the River Oaks trade for their livelihood.

Since Minute Women literature emphasized opposition to socialized
medicine, the group appealed strongly to the wives of physicians, with
at least sixty joining the organization. Minute Women support of the
states in the tidelands oil issue and vigorous approval of the oil depletion allowance appealed to women whose husbands worked in the oil

industry. A substantial number of members had husbands who were oil company executives, technicians, or professional personnel. Many Minute Women also belonged to older patriotic groups such as the Daughters of the American Revolution and Daughters of the Republic of Texas and had husbands belonging to the American Legion. Several Minute Women spouses helped to create the Committee for the Preservation of Methodism. Another source for membership came from those interested in education. Because of the Minute Women stand against "progressive education," some women joined the group because of a sincere concern about their children's schools. A few conservative leaders of parent-teacher associations, public school teachers, and Houston school administrators' wives also joined the Minute Women. The organization attracted many persons afraid of integration and race mixing. Many Houston Minute Women were imbued with the old white southern traditions and racism acquired its own unwritten but special niche in the group's ideology. For example, one prospective member alleged that she was recruited by a Minute Woman using racial scare tactics. The Minute Woman told the recruit, among other things, that the public school textbooks advocated white and black children intermarrying for a better race and this meant that "the schools are very bad."[61]

Thus, the Minute Women attracted members for a variety of individual reasons. One typical member, Mary Drouin, a devout Catholic, when relating her reasons for joining the organization, stated that the group attempted to keep "100 percent" American ideas and values from being lost. Drouin was very much the Catholic anti-Communist crusader whose actions were strongly influenced by church publications such as the Christophers' pamphlet *You Can Save the World,* which she felt offered "practical ideas on how we can change the dangerous trend our government has been taking." Drouin admitted that racism played an essential and important part in the Minute Women program because "members were interested in keeping a purity of the white race." Drouin, the wife of an engineer, stated that "I was concerned about socialism, concerned about big government, things were happening too fast. I could see a *Brave New World* coming." Houston Minute Women chair Virginia Biggers believed most of the nation had changed for the worse in the 1930s but that Houston and Texas had escaped. "After the war," she stated, "Houston seemed to change as well. I wanted to do what I could to save our town."[62]

By the beginning of 1952, the Houston chapter of the Minute Women had become the most militant Red Scare group in Houston. Most of this power and influence resulted from the dedicated work of a small core of approximately fifteen active women who exerted their leadership over the rest of the group. Most of the ordinary members accepted the charges made against individuals and issues and did not question the authority of their leaders. As one woman said, "We thought things were all black and white." The most active and visible Minute Women included Mrs. Ross (Virginia) Biggers, Mrs. Willard O. (Virginia) Hedrick, Mrs. James (Eleanor) Watt, Mrs. J. C. (Faye) Weitinger, Mrs. Rosser (Helen) Thomas, Mrs. Frank (Dallas) Dyer, and Mrs. Earl (Bertie) Maughmer.[63]

Virginia Biggers was the chair and unchallenged leader of the women. An intense right-wing conservative, Biggers ardently believed that socialists and Communist sympathizers had practically seized control of the government and had to be rooted out. Author of the Houston Minute Women's monthly newsletter, Virginia Biggers stated that Senator Joseph McCarthy was "living proof of what one man armed with knowledge, a clear conscience . . . and courage, can do in the face of intense . . . opposition from every Red, Pink, . . . and misguided 'liberal' in the United States." Her husband managed a large, nonunion printing plant in partnership with his father, E. M. Biggers, a well-to-do cattle rancher and dairy farmer. The Biggers Printing Company printed and distributed a significant amount of the most extreme right-wing literature produced in Texas and the Southwest during the 1940s and 1950s. E. M. Biggers wrote many of the pamphlets himself. Like his daughter-in-law, Biggers was a devoted follower of Joe McCarthy. His son, Ross, also shared Virginia Biggers' political views. They were both Taft Republicans and opponents of the UN, labor unions, and the New Deal. The entire family supported General Douglas MacArthur for president in 1952 after Dwight Eisenhower won the Republican nomination. Virginia Biggers joined the Minute Women soon after its founding in 1951. She lived on the same block of Rice Boulevard as Eleanor Watt, who invited her to attend political discussion groups in the Watt home. Prior to this, Biggers had not been personally involved in any political movement. But Biggers soon became one of the most active of Minute Women members. Once Suzanne Stevenson appointed her chair of the organization in 1951, she retained the position throughout the remainder of the group's existence.[64]

Virginia Hedrick, a resident of Tanglewood, an affluent Houston subdivision, exerted almost as much influence as Virginia Biggers in the Minute Women. The wife of American Legion leader Willard O. Hedrick, Virginia Hedrick participated in a variety of women's groups. Like the Biggers, the Hedricks were a team. Virginia, for example, served on the American Legion's Women's Auxiliary's Americanism Committee. Extremely aggressive, Hedrick was considered by some of her Minute

Women associates to be a bit too pushy. Hedrick was socially ambitious with strong pretensions of elitism and tended to maneuver herself into being the center of attention in whatever she did. Her energy and talents, especially as a speaker, made Hedrick a valuable member of the various groups to which she belonged. These included the Minute Women, which she served as national secretary, and an organization called Vigilant Women for the Bricker Amendment, in which she became Texas coordinator. A tireless worker on behalf of right-wing political causes, Hedrick became a familiar face in Houston as she manned petition drive tables in the downtown area, soliciting signatures for various protests. Hedrick, like her other Minute Women colleagues, depended on the Houston *Chronicle* for the proper conservative viewpoints. An unabashed fan of Jesse Jones, Hedrick wrote the *Chronicle* publisher, "I shall always remember your courageous fight against the socialistic tendencies of Mr. Henry A. Wallace. . . ." Hedrick recommended the *Chronicle*'s Red Scare editorials to her friends, calling the newspaper "a wonderful extension of the struggle against Socialism." Virginia Hedrick also served as one of the Minute Women's researchers, voraciously reading the *Congressional Record* and other government publications for resource material to be used in Minute Women activities.[65]

While Eleanor Watt founded the Minute Women chapter in Houston and served as its first chair, she lost influence after Suzanne Stevenson replaced her with Virginia Biggers. Watt and Biggers remained close friends and neighbors despite Stevenson's action. Eleanor Watt, the daughter of a long-time principal of Houston's San Jacinto High School, became involved in the Minute Women because of her intense opposition to the Truman administration. Like most of her Minute Women associates, Watt was a right-wing Republican. In her initial contact with Suzanne Stevenson, Watt emphasized how she believed the Minute Women could serve as a force to unite "Southern Democrats and true Republicans" for the 1952 national election. Watt's interest in the organization was probably more the result of her hopes for Republican political victories than anything else. This may have been one of the reasons for her removal as Houston chair since Suzanne Stevenson wanted the Minute Women to at least have the appearance of a "nonpartisan" organization. Eleanor Watt's husband, James, worked for the Humble Oil Company. He too shared his wife's political views. As with Biggers and Hedrick, Eleanor Watt got her political news straight from the Houston *Chronicle*. A "lifetime" reader of Jesse Jones' newspaper, Eleanor Watt frequently wrote *Chronicle* editor M. E. Walter to thank him for his "wonderful" editorials. She sometimes complained, however, that her "favorite newspaper" would be even better if it depended more on its own reporters and stopped printing the "lies and slantings" of the national wire services.[66]

The Minute Women's inner leadership circle also included Faye Weitinger, who served briefly on the national advisory council. Weitinger's husband worked as an executive of a major Houston convenience store chain. The Weitingers, unlike most of the Minute Women leaders, lived in elite River Oaks. Faye and her husband, J. C., worked together for ultra-right-wing causes. J. C. Weitinger, for example, headed a minor political group called the Conservative Citizens League, which seems to have had a short-lived and insignificant existence. Both of the Weitingers supported Robert Taft against Dwight Eisenhower in 1952, admired Joseph R. McCarthy, thought the Roosevelt-Truman administrations were "over twenty years" of betrayal, "perfidy," and "stupidity," and believed that "creeping socialism" endangered Houston's public schools. Faye Weitinger, like Virginia Hedrick and Helen Thomas, was a diligent researcher who could recite an impressive array of facts and figures in support of her right-wing arguments. She was a formidable opponent in such situations. A strong personality, Weitinger clashed with some of the other women and dropped out of the group after 1955.[67]

The fifth member of the Minute Women inner circle, Helen Darden Thomas, played a different role from the other leaders. Thomas, a 1928 graduate of the University of Texas, served as the unofficial "ideologist" and resident "intellectual" for the Minute Women. Most of the members deferred to this woman, who has been described by her associates as "very intelligent," "bright," and "perceptive." Unlike Biggers, Hedrick, Watt, and Weitinger, Helen Thomas was shy and retiring and preferred to work at home, avoiding the public spotlight. She spent much of her time poring over reams of *Congressional Reports,* government documents, and organizational membership lists. Helen Thomas was Houston's champion at compiling lengthy lists of persons she believed to be subversive. While Virginia Hedrick and a few other women also enjoyed list making, none compared to Thomas in terms of volume and persistence. The Minute Women relied on Thomas' information when making decisions about persons to attack, accuse, or generally harass. Thus, she played an especially significant role in Houston's Red Scare since many of the anti-Communist protests were based on Helen Thomas' research.[68]

Thomas gathered much of her information from the infamous and discredited files of the House Committee on Un-American Activities. These public records consisted of information gleaned from the press, letterheads, and other readily accessible sources. They were notoriously inaccurate and even HCUA members refused to vouch for their accuracy. Nevertheless, HCUA files became the single most important source used by Red Scare groups to discredit their enemies. HCUA files included lists of allegedly subversive organizations and the names of persons supposedly affiliated with them. HCUA published these lists in 1944 and 1948, followed by a supplement in 1951. In addition, HCUA and individual congressmen periodically published reprints of speeches and testimony containing even more allegedly subversive names and organizations.[69]

Helen Thomas collected as many HCUA publications as she could to create dossiers on her fellow Texans. She occasionally produced formal reports based on these dossiers and circulated them among the Minute Women. One particularly irresponsible report was a twenty-five-page list titled "Individuals from Texas Reported as Having Been Affiliated with Communist or Communist-Front Organizations—As Compiled from Official Government Reports, 1934–1954." In her report, Thomas informed the Minute Women of approximately two hundred Texans known to be "brazenly" associated with subversives. The report included educators, labor unionists, religious leaders, civil rights activists, politicians, journalists, lawyers, and students. Naturally, the names of self-admitted CPUSA members such as Homer Brooks, Emma Tenayuca, James J. Green, Ruth Koenig, and James Boyle were scattered throughout the list. The report, however, also included other Texans who had contributed to society in meaningful and positive ways and who were certainly not subversive in any sense of the word. These included University of Texas professors Clarence Ayres, Robert Montgomery, Carlos Castaneda, Harry Estill Moore, J. Frank Dobie, Wendell C. Gordon, and George I. Sanchez, as well as former UT president Homer P. Rainey and his wife. Thomas also listed the presidents of Texas Christian University, Texas Southern University, and Huston-Tillotson College. The Minute Women were told that religious leaders such as Houston's Rabbi Hyman Judah Schachtel and Presbyterian minister Donald Stewart, Catholic bishop Robert L. Lucey of San Antonio, and Presbyterian minister Thomas W. Curry of Austin were affiliated with organizations cited by HCUA as being "Communist fronts." Other alleged subversives, according to Thomas, included such names as John C. Granberry, a crusading San Antonio newspaper editor; Maury Maverick, the fiery former congressman and mayor of San Antonio; and Fredell Lack Eichorn, an internationally known violinist and music instructor at the University of Houston. Less surprising names on Helen Thomas' list included Herman Wright, Arthur J. Mandell, and W. A. Combs of Houston, and black civil rights leaders Juanita Craft, C. H. Richardson, Carter Wesley, and Lulu White, all prominent in NAACP work.[70]

Thomas obtained most of these names from a discredited document published by the HCUA in 1944 during Martin Dies' chairmanship. Consisting of seven volumes, Dies' list named some 22,000 Americans alleged to be "fellow travelers." This document, known as Appendix IX, was actually compiled by ex-radical J. B. Mathews, who served as the Dies committee's chief of research. Mathews attained national prominence as a "fallen-away" Communist who specialized as a paid witness at HCUA hearings, on one occasion stunning the nation with a suggestion that even child movie star Shirley Temple had once been a "Red" dupe.[71]

Helen Thomas also faithfully read the works of the right-wing authors recommended by Suzanne Stevenson and H. L. Hunt's *Facts Forum News.* She obtained multiple copies of *Facts Forum News* reprints, speeches by Martin Dies, and HCUA publications and mailed them to prominent Houston civic and educational leaders. She especially enjoyed Allen Zoll, personally distributing his anti–public education diatribes to whomever she felt needed educating. Sitting in her River Oaks home, the shy Minute Women "intellectual" also became one of Houston's most prolific letter writers, making her name a familiar one among dedicated readers of "Letters to the Editor" sections of newspapers. A Helen Thomas letter would often herald a Red Scare attack on a new victim.[72]

Helen Thomas, a Catholic and mother of two children, was married to Rosser Thomas, a manager for Houston Natural Gas Company. She had strong family influences shaping her ultraconservative Red Scare views. A native of Fort Worth, Thomas was the daughter of Ida Muse Darden, publisher of the right-wing monthly newspaper the *Southern Conservative,* which tirelessly attacked the New Deal, Harry Truman, organized labor, and nearly every progressive legislative reform passed since the Bill of Rights. Darden had an obsessive hatred for Eleanor Roosevelt and constantly called for the impeachment of President Truman. The *Southern Conservative* specialized in primitive comments about Jews and blacks punctuated with childish sexual innuendos. For example, in an article titled "Frustrated Females Should Fight Syphillis [sic] instead of Segregation," Darden claimed that nearly 70 percent of the black population in the South was afflicted with "syphilis, gonorrhea, and other venereal diseases." Darden wrote that white women such as Eleanor Roosevelt who were fighting racial segregation should focus on improving the morals of blacks instead of trying to force "the races . . . to sit, eat, work and sleep together."[73]

Suzanne Stevenson thought the *Southern Conservative* should be required reading for all Minute Women and called Ida Darden "brilliant." Darden reciprocated the Minute Women's adulation, especially since her only daughter was a key leader in Houston. In an article in her newspaper in March 1953 titled "If the Republic Is to Be Saved It Looks like Women Must Do It," Darden heaped praise on right-wing women's groups. Darden admitted that she had always believed woman suffrage to have been a terrible mistake since the majority of women had voted for Franklin Roosevelt. "Hordes of frantic, frustrated females . . . who had never used their heads for anything except to prop their ears apart," Darden wrote, "pitched in and did their bit . . . to wreck the American government" during the New Deal and Fair Deal. She had recently changed her mind, however, because "a new and responsible type of womanhood" had stepped forward after the war in an effort to restore "orderly government." Darden cited the Minute Women and members of similar organizations as examples of the new political woman engaged in the crusade to save the nation.[74]

Helen Thomas' uncle and Ida Darden's brother was Vance Muse, a former Fort Worth Chamber of Commerce public relations man and a long-time lobbyist for Houston lumberman John Henry Kirby. In the 1930s, Muse and Kirby organized the Southern Committee to Uphold the Constitution to oppose Franklin Roosevelt's 1936 reelection bid. Muse, who died in 1950, was also a racist and anti-Semite. He later created the Christian Americans, which evolved from an organization to fight "communism, atheism, Negroes, Jews, and unions" to one mainly concerned with destroying organized labor. Extremely close to her mother, Helen Thomas thus grew up in an environment defined by the heated passions of the extremist right. She sustained this political inheritance as an adult.[75]

Virginia Biggers, Virginia Hedrick, Eleanor Watt, Faye Weitinger, and Helen Thomas constituted Houston's Minute Women leadership. Another group of approximately twenty to thirty women provided the hard core of active followers. These women could be counted on to appear at every meeting, lick envelopes, make telephone calls, write letters, and generally do as they were told. Most of these women were "true believers" caught up in a confusing world of change beyond their understanding.

Elsie Daniel and Anne Harrison typified this energetic group. Both women lived in the West University area of Houston, a solidly middle-class neighborhood flanked by the affluent residences of physicians, architects, and upper-income business and professional people. This area provided a disproportionate number of the more vehement Minute Women members. Elsie's husband, John, sold insurance, while Anne's husband, E. M., sold cars. Both women took their political views straight from the Houston *Chronicle* and the Minute Women leaders. Elsie Daniel was a friend and admirer of Virginia Hedrick and often accompanied Hedrick to meetings. She and Anne Harrison could always be seen wherever the Minute Women decided to protest. Harrison, for example, appeared with two other Minute Women "foot soldiers" in the public confrontation with George W. Ebey in August 1952. Daniel and Harrison tended to profess their political beliefs with a vivid simplicity typical of the unthinking zealot. For example, Anne Harrison, whose chief obsession seemed to be the UN, owned an ink stamp that proclaimed "Get the US out of the UN and the UN out of the US." Anne would whip out letters arguing that anyone supporting the UN was guilty of treason and then blot the envelope and stationery with her instant political slogan. Harrison possessed another stamp that printed her poll tax number, which she placed on letters to elected officials. Elsie Daniel idolized Senator McCarthy. She owned a supply of stickers that announced, "ALL COMMUNISTS, REDS AND RADICALS HATE JOE McCARTHY. I AM FOR HIM!," which she would lick and place at the top of her correspondence. Like many of their fellow Minute Women, Elsie Daniel and Anne Harrison believed in taking firm positions unburdened by subtle arguments. "I am sick and tired of all this talk about Senator McCarthy doing this and that," Elsie Daniel said, "and not a word . . . about the harm the Socialists, Left-wingers, egg-heads, communists and fellow-travelers have done to our Country. Thank God for McCarthy. . . ." The Harrisons and the Daniels were the women who provided the steam to drive the Red Scare machine.[76]

The Minute Women included a third group of approximately seventy-five to one hundred persons who lived primarily in the upper-class River Oaks and Rice University sections of Houston and who, feeling somewhat superior to the middle-class hard core typified by Elsie Daniel and Anne Harrison, tended to avoid their public protests. These women, most of whom were physicians' wives, paid their dues and wrote letters but were less interested in such issues as the UN and other exotic topics. They focused on pocketbook causes, especially the progressive income tax, and the dangers of socialized medicine. For example, Mrs. J. D. Mabry, a physician's wife who generally typified this faction, consistently emphasized economics. Her special devil was the federal tax system. "We are taxed out of our souls . . . ," Mrs. Mabry would say. "The people are sick and tired of giving their . . . money" to the government. Instead of carrying picket signs or stamping her letters with vivid political statements, Mrs. Mabry chose other ways to protest. She and her husband, who was politically involved with a group of right-wing medical doctors, preferred to travel to the more fashionable Dallas to purchase clothing. During one trip, the Mabrys were leaving the Adolphus Hotel and stopped to ask

a boy at the newsstand which local newspaper carried the syndicated conservative writers such as Fulton Lewis, Jr., and George Sokolsky. The
young man answered (incorrectly) that neither Dallas paper did because
the city's merchants would not let them. This stunned the Mabrys to such
an extent that they turned on their heels, checked out of the Adolphus,
and returned to Houston. "We didn't buy any clothes in Dallas," Mrs.
Mabry said. "We decided we would spend our money in Houston where
FREEDOM was still more alive." Boycotting exclusive fashion stores in
another city was a form of protest unavailable to middle-class activists
such as Elsie Daniel and Anne Harrison. They had to stick to their ink
stamps and letter writing. This economic difference did create a type of
unstated internal schism in Houston's Minute Women chapter. When the
Mabrys would say, "What this country needs is not a car in every garage
but a Joe McCarthy in Washington," it emphasized the subtle differences
between a wealthy physician's views and those of a car salesman such
as E. M. Harrison.[77]

Two other important Minute Women leaders were Mrs. Frank (Dallas)
Dyer and Mrs. Earl (Bertie) Maughmer. Dyer, a native of Michigan who
grew up in Omaha, Nebraska, was not a typical member. A 1929 graduate of Rice University and a former elementary school teacher, Dallas Dyer
was neither a zany zealot nor an affluent woman with too much time on
her hands. Her lawyer husband, Frank Dyer, had been disabled in an
automobile accident, forcing Dallas into the work world where she became a successful insurance underwriter. Driven by a burning ambition
and fiercely independent, Dyer later recalled that she joined the Minute
Women because she thought the group would get women "interested in
government." Dyer never became a leader, however, because she had
ambitions for public office and was uninterested in running an organization such as the Minute Women. After all, Dyer later admitted, the
group did attract some "nuts." While she certainly shared much of their
world view, Minute Women membership was more important to her as
a way to build a political base.[78]

Bertie Maughmer was destined to become one of the most well known
of the Minute Women in Houston. Unlike the majority of her associates,
Maughmer lived in a blue-collar neighborhood in east Houston, an area
of low status when viewed from the affluent southwestern sections of
town. A product of a Baptist orphanage, Maughmer had a desperate
desire for recognition and attention. She joined and served as an officer
in a host of nonpolitical middle-class civic organizations. Bertie's husband,
Earl, was an ambitious patrolman with the Houston Police Department
and was active in rank and file policemen's efforts to organize for collective bargaining. A parentless childhood, a working-class environment,

the snobbery of her associates, and a certain emotional unbalance mixed with her simplistic, conservative, and racist political views produced in Bertie a most unpleasant personality. Although unpopular among the Minute Women leaders, her eagerness for approval and attention made Bertie Maughmer a useful tool for such women as Virginia Biggers and Virginia Hedrick. The one problem was that Bertie Maughmer would eventually break loose and become a sad public embarrassment to her mentors. Both Dallas Dyer and Bertie Maughmer were eventually elected to the Houston Independent School District school board and both, especially Bertie Maughmer, displayed a penchant for controversies often unrelated to Minute Women affairs.[79]

A nonmember who worked closely with the Minute Women probably did more to promote the causes of the group than did any official member. Mrs. W. J. Edwards supported the Red Scare by writing pamphlets attacking "controversial" persons in Houston, usually people associated with the public schools. Edwards' pamphlets became a regular source of information for Houston's newspapers and they played a particularly important role during the height of the Red Scare in 1952 and 1953.[80]

By the summer of 1951, all of the essential elements for Houston's Red Scare had coalesced to create a clear and distinct historical episode in the city's history. While some individuals and one or two established organizations such as the American Legion had employed Red Scare tactics for several years prior to 1950, they had failed to gain much attention or support. The creation of Red Scare groups such as the Committee for the Preservation of Methodism and the Minute Women of the U.S.A., Inc. revealed a new atmosphere in Houston. Extreme anti-Communism had become an acceptable cause with much appeal. Sustained by the confusion of the postwar era and encouraged by elite rhetoric, Houston's Red Scare advocates prepared to launch a campaign of community fear that would force some individuals out of their jobs, severely restrict freedom of speech, create contention in the churches, disrupt the public school system, and leave a legacy for the future.

FIVE

THE RED SCARE BEGINS

Men who fear witches soon find themselves surrounded by them.
— Kai Erickson

*Those were the days when the Communist obsession was like
Montezuma's Revenge to a tourist in Mexico. Everybody was
on the run.*
—Methodist bishop W. Kenneth Pope[1]

The Red Scare in Houston, just as with the nation as a whole, has no
specific beginning date. There is no single event that in hindsight can be
said to have announced the start of an era. This is because a "Red Scare"
has been simmering just beneath the thin skin of American tolerance since
the Bolsheviks seized power in Russia in 1917. After the first Red Scare
following World War I, however, it took the Cold War to bring extreme
anti-Communism back out into the open as a defining characteristic of
American society.

As noted in a previous chapter, Houston's conservative power elite
escalated its extreme anti-Communist rhetoric in the late 1940s. By that
time some Houstonians were beginning to perceive that the use of Red
Scare tactics might be the easiest way to ensure success in contests over
public issues. The controversy over zoning in 1947 is an example of this
new awareness. In previous years when the question of land use zoning became a subject of public debate, Houston's antizoning faction had
emphasized that governmental regulation of land development was func-
tionally unworkable and prone to corruption. Even in 1947 a "Report to
the Mayor by the Committee against Zoning" stressed that zoning would
slow urban growth and that automobiles and freeways would eventually decentralize the business district, making functional segregation
unnecessary. As one student of this movement has noted, the antizoning faction developed an "intelligent and rational critique" of zoning's
shortcomings. In presenting the issue to the public, however, antizoners
avoided this rational argument. Rather than attempting to explain a somewhat complicated position, the antizoners took advantage of the growing Red Scare and simply portrayed zoning as a "threat to the American
Way of Life." Advertisements, for example, argued that under zoning

physicians and dentists could not have home offices and that this was the "first step toward socialized medicine." An ironical aspect of this debate was that the antizoners, consisting mainly of small businessmen and real estate speculators, opposed the 8-F Crowd led by Jesse Jones. The Red Scare environment that Jones and the power elite had so actively cultivated was turned against them in this case. The city was entertained by the spectacle of Hugh Roy Cullen calling Jesse Jones' zoning plan "un-American." Houstonians soundly defeated the zoning proposal in an election on January 31, 1948, with 68 percent voting against and only 31 percent voting for land use planning.[2]

Despite the use of such tactics, the constant barrage of elite rhetoric, and the activities of the American Legion in the late 1940s, the organized Red Scare was not really in force in Houston until the fall of 1950. That autumn saw the formation of the Committee for the Preservation of Methodism and the increased visibility of the American Legion's Americanism Committee, which expanded operations beyond its newspaper advertisements. The Minute Women followed a few months later. The creation of formal anti-Communist groups provided the final link in the chain of events producing Houston's Red Scare. Before 1950, such factions as the antizoners had organized around specific single-issue controversies and had disbanded with the resolution of each issue. The Legion's Americanism Committee and the Minute Women, however, were organized to confront a multitude of problems symbolized by Communism. Due to their belief in the enormity of the threat, these groups saw their effort as a semipermanent one. The exposure of one subversive person, book, or idea—the defeat of one "un-American" proposal—would be insufficient. The threat would be continuous, the need for their services constant. The appearance of groups whose purpose was to transform rhetoric into action marks the general beginning of Houston's Red Scare.

While no single event officially opened Houston's Red Scare campaign, just as at the national level the appearance of Senator Joe McCarthy served as the symbolic beginning. Three months after the outbreak of the Korean War, the American Legion staged a public "Americanism" rally in the city's downtown Sam Houston Coliseum. The Legion chose as its speaker the Republican senator from Wisconsin who seven months earlier had become a national celebrity after delivering a speech in Wheeling, West Virginia. In that speech, Joe McCarthy contended that he had a list of 205 names "that were made known to the Secretary of State [Dean Acheson] as being members of the Communist Party and who nevertheless are still working and shaping policy in the State Department." Although McCarthy referred to an outdated and thoroughly misleading document written by former Secretary of State

James F. Byrnes (a document subsequently discredited by a Senate investigation), the daring accusation catapulted McCarthy into the national limelight. The Wisconsin Republican quickly assumed the symbolic leadership of the already ongoing national Red Scare. He was the man of the hour for all extreme anti-Communists and the perfect opening act for Houston's own Red Scare.[3]

The American Legion promoted McCarthy's appearance at its Americanism rally with great zeal. The city's three daily newspapers helped publicize the meeting with extensive pre-event coverage. The Legion easily persuaded Hugh Roy Cullen to introduce his new friend McCarthy at the rally. On the night of September 18, 1950, a crowd of several thousand gathered at Sam Houston Coliseum to hear the new hero of the Red Scare. Three local radio stations installed microphones to broadcast the speech. McCarthy, in his typically grinning and brutal manner, did not disappoint them. As he entered the hall, the senator assured reporters that he was not in Houston to deliver a political speech. "I'm just going to talk on Americanism," claimed McCarthy.[4]

Hugh Roy Cullen began the rally with a brief sketch of McCarthy's career. He pointed out that McCarthy had completed a four-year high school course in one year and had "worked his way through high school and college." The latter was a particularly important point to Cullen, an advocate of self-help. The Houston oil man announced that "Senator McCarthy has done more than anyone to throw the pinks and Reds out of the country." Calling McCarthy a man of courage, Cullen declared, "I hope Senator McCarthy keeps all the Communist spies running until they get to Moscow."[5]

McCarthy's appearance at the podium brought forth enthusiastic applause from the Legionnaires, their families, and other admirers. At home in his own element, the senator looked at the crowd and, to their delight, said, "It seems good to get out of Washington at least one day and get back here in the United States." McCarthy then ignored his "nonpolitical pledge" and proceeded to denounce the Truman administration and Secretary of State Dean Acheson. He called for Acheson's resignation "not tomorrow, not next week or next month, but tonight." McCarthy admitted to the Houston audience that some sincere people disliked his methods, but, he explained, "You can't fight Communism with a silk handkerchief, in a delicate fashion." The crowd erupted in approval when he declared, "If lumberjack tactics are all they can understand, then lumberjack tactics are what we will use." The senator then titillated his listeners with a discussion of widespread sexual perversion in the State Department and other federal offices, charging that the government was honeycombed with Reds and "3,750 homosexuals." McCarthy ended his performance with a plea for local Americans to join in the war against subversion and ferret out the traitors in their midst. He warned of the difficulty involved in identifying Communists. Nevertheless, there were ways to discover these people: they could be exposed by noting their associations. "There is certainly reason to suspect a man who is active in the affairs of 10 or 12 Communist front organizations," McCarthy advised his receptive audience. Houston's Red Scare had received its act of consecration.[6]

Eric Goldman has written that by 1951 "the fury against Communism [in the nation] was taking on . . . elements of a vendetta against . . . all departures from tradition . . . against the new, the adventurous, the questioning in any field." In Houston at the same time, the newly created Red Scare groups launched their own vendetta to protect the city from "un-American" influences.[7]

Even before the Minute Women organized, a little-noticed incident occurred that warned of the immediate future. In February 1951, India's representative to a special committee of the United Nations, Dr. Bharatan Kumarappa, visited several Texas cities as part of a lecture series. Dr. Kumarappa was a philosopher and academician imbued with a fervent anticolonial viewpoint nurtured during India's movement for independence. In a lecture at Highland Park Methodist Church in Dallas just prior to his scheduled visit to Houston, the Indian diplomat undiplomatically criticized the United States' support of European colonialism in the emerging Third World. Dr. Kumarappa also admitted to his Dallas audience that he believed the United States to be a violent nation. News of this heresy quickly spread to Houston. The reaction was immediate. The University of Houston and the Houston Settlement Association canceled lectures Kumarappa was slated to give on February 25 at each location. Dr. W. W. Kemmerer, at that time acting president of the University of Houston and a candidate for the permanent job, announced that Kumarappa's speech had been canceled because of his anti-American statements. This forthright action certainly pleased Kemmerer's boss, university board of regents chairman Hugh Roy Cullen. The YWCA, which had scheduled Kumarappa for a third lecture in the city, at first held fast. It too fell in line, however, after receiving a telephone call from Dr. Marshall T. Steel, pastor of Dallas' Highland Park Methodist Church. Steel informed the YWCA board of directors that Kumarappa had "expressed disdain for the United States" and, in Steel's opinion, the Indian was "definitely pro-Communist" because he had argued that the Chinese and Vietnamese Communists were nationalists and not subjects of the Soviet Union. Houstonians were thus saved from hearing such an obviously subversive opinion.[8]

In June 1951, the American Friends Service Committee, an organization supported by Quakers, decided to conduct annual Institutes of International Relations in Houston. The Quakers intended to bring nationally known experts representing a variety of viewpoints to Houston to speak on foreign affairs problems. The institutes encouraged audience participation and an open discussion of international issues. The American Friends Service had been presenting such institutes throughout the United States for twenty-seven years. Normally, the Friends would rent space in local religious institutions to house their sessions.

The Friends received permission from the Riverside Methodist Church, located near the University of Houston, to hold their four-day institute in Houston. At the start of the program their coordinators were shocked to learn that Helen Thomas had printed and distributed a circular accusing the Friends of "un-American activities." Fortunately for the Friends, they were able to conduct the institute in peace despite the ominous circular. They did not realize, however, that it would be the first and last time they would be able to work in Houston without harassment and disruption. The Friends had the distinction of being the first group attacked by the Houston Minute Women. The attack was ineffective because the Minute Women leaders were too involved with organizing their newly founded chapter. Nevertheless, Minute Women author Helen Thomas filed her anti–American Friends Service Committee material to be used with greater effectiveness at a later date.[9]

Once the Minute Women completed their organizing efforts and settled their internal leadership problems in the fall of 1951, they joined with their allies in the Committee for the Preservation of Methodism and the Americanism Committee of the American Legion to conduct Houston's Red Scare. Beginning late in 1951 and continuing through 1954, these Red Scare activists adopted the traditional techniques of political pressure groups. The Minute Women devised a telephone chain system to harass their enemies and initiated massive letter campaigns to influence local affairs. The allied organizations sometimes combined to bring in outside speakers, distribute propaganda pamphlets, engage in picketing, heckle and censor "controversial" speakers, and conduct educational workshops and discussion groups.[10]

The members of these groups were particularly active in their efforts to limit and restrict the freedom of speech of individuals of whom they disapproved. From the fall of 1951 through the summer of 1952, the Red Scare activists succeeded in canceling at least three major speaking engagements and forced another speaker to move to a different location. Several other speakers overcame spirited campaigns of protest to speak in Houston, only to find their audiences filled with and disrupted by hostile people. The Minute Women never publicly acknowledged any connections with the protests and always vigorously denied involvement in such activity. Adria Allen, one of the charter members, admitted, however, that the Minute Women initiated chain letters and telephone campaigns against individuals or issues when alerted by their leaders. Houston's newspapers encouraged these activities. Allen, who was known for concluding her protest letters with "Sincerely and with the utmost disgust," recalled later, "We were effective in canceling speakers . . . the [Houston] *Chronicle* gave us wonderful publicity to get the public aroused against outside speakers."[11]

As Adria Allen indicated, the Minute Women were effective. In September 1951, the Houston Chamber of Commerce invited Dr. Willard Goslin, former superintendent of schools in Pasadena, California, to be guest speaker on Business Education Day in the public schools. Five days after the announcement, the Chamber of Commerce canceled Dr. Goslin's speech because of "problems involved in consummating the program." The chamber gave no other official reasons for the action at that time, but a spokesperson later admitted that it had received thirty-four telephone calls protesting the appearance of the educator. In 1950, Dr. Goslin had been forced to resign as superintendent of the Pasadena schools after a campaign against him in which pamphlets of Minute Women favorite Allen Zoll played a decisive part. His Pasadena enemies charged Dr. Goslin with being "too progressive." The Houston Minute Women, informed about Goslin's past through their various right-wing newsletters, protested the educator's invitation. The women's harassment proved effective. John E. Price, Sr., member of the Chamber of Commerce committee, told reporters, "Pretty nearly everybody in town seems against him."[12]

The Houston *Press* eventually discovered that "pretty nearly everybody" meant the Minute Women and two of their most influential cohorts, school board member and CFPM activist Ewing Werlein and Houston Lighting and Power president W. Alvis Parish. Werlein declared that it would be a "very serious mistake" for Goslin to come to Houston. When a reporter asked Werlein to explain, Werlein replied, "He's a very controversial figure. I don't know anything about the man. I have read about the Pasadena case . . . it makes him controversial." Parish told the *Press*, "I just don't believe in the welfare state and progressive education that he stands for. I'm against him."[13]

A few weeks later, Dr. Goslin, who was on the faculty of George Peabody College at the time, received another invitation to speak in Houston. The Texas State Teachers Association (TSTA) invited Dr. Goslin, Dr. Edward C. Lindeman of Columbia University, and Dr. Ethel Alpenfels of New York University to speak at its state convention in Houston. The Minute Women discovered through Helen Thomas that Dr. Lindeman had connections with Columbia's School of Social Work and Dr. Alpenfels had written *Sense and Nonsense about Race.* To the Minute Women the mere mention of "social work" implied the dreaded dangers of creeping socialism. *Sense and Nonsense about Race* attacked racial discrimination; to the Minute Women, such an attack had to be Communist inspired. The Minute Women charged that Alpenfels' book advocated "a hybrid race," a "thesis that should be repugnant to all races." The American Legion led the public protest against the three speakers, distributing a circular charging that Alpenfels belonged to the World Peace Conference, "a vicious Communist front," and had recommended to her college classes twelve books written by "commie fronters." According to the circular, Lindeman served on the editorial board of a "communist youth magazine" and belonged to the Citizens Committee to Free (former CPUSA leader) Earl Browder as well as the American Civil Liberties Union. All three of the invited speakers "belong to the Progressive school of academic thought . . . which stresses human relations, World Government, and the Welfare State." The American Legion told TSTA leaders, "Let's have speakers of unquestionable patriotism and loyalty. . . ."[14]

The Red Scare protest succeeded. The TSTA leadership withdrew their invitations to Alpenfels and Lindeman, but not the invitation to Goslin. The teachers announced that Goslin would appear, despite the protest, because he would be on a panel and would not speak on "controversial matters."[15]

Finding success in their initial forays against threats to Houston's educational philosophy, the Minute Women broadened their activities to other areas. The women supported Idaho Republican congressman John T. Wood's proposed bill to withdraw the United States from the United Nations. Their intense interest in the UN created an incident in December 1951 that revealed the autocratic nature of the Minute Women leadership as well as the extent of the gap between reality and the Minute Women perception of the world.

The Minute Women printed a circular at Biggers' printing shop titled "This Actually Did Happen!! United Nations Seizes, Rules, American Cities." The document consisted of excerpts from an article in extremist Walter S. Steele's *National Republic* magazine that, except to the most careful and thorough readers, appeared to say that troops flying the UN flag had taken over several California cities in a surprise move, throwing the mayors in jail and locking up the police chiefs. An army officer's wife, who belonged to the Minute Women, wondered why the Houston *Chronicle* had failed to mention the UN action and wrote to the Pentagon for information. An upset general quickly replied that the incidents were merely part of a maneuver by the United States Army, carried out with the consent of city officials. The Minute Women member informed her colleagues about their mistake at the next meeting in January 1952. She proposed that the chapter issue a new circular correcting the scare story. The leadership ruled her proposal out of order since no motions could be made from the floor at Minute Women meetings. The Minute Women took no action and the matter died without a public correction. The UN continued to be "controversial" and the Minute Women and their allies eventually made it an issue in the public school curriculum.[16]

The Houston Public Library seemed to be the next Red Scare target when Ida Darden's *Southern Conservative* published a list of "subversive" books on the library's shelves. In the January 1952 issue, Darden claimed the Houston Public Library "promotes the works of subversive writers" such as Arthur Schlesinger, Sr., Henry Steele Commager, Carl Sandburg, Stuart Chase, and Erskine Caldwell. "What chance has a young American to avoid embracing the ideals of Joe Stalin," Darden asked, "when the way is pointed out to him" by the public library? Darden demanded that Houstonians expose the people responsible for placing such books in the library.

Ida Darden's attack on the Houston Public Library failed to elicit any noticeable response in Houston. The Houston library board reviewed Darden's article and concluded that it was of no importance. Houston's public library was of little interest to local Red Scare activists. Unlike public schools, the library had no relationship with the federal government and controversies over federal aid. The library board was composed of solidly conservative members of Houston's social and civic elite who were immune to typical Red Scare charges. Also, during the 1950s the Houston Public Library suffered from official neglect. The nation's twelfth largest city was in fifty-seventh place in support of public libraries. Severely hampered by insufficient staff and budget, the public library maintained such a low profile in the community that it presented an unattractive target for headline-seeking critics. Later, when Red Scare controversies swirled around the public libraries in San Antonio and Dallas, the Houston library board made it clear that it would oppose any local movements to censor its book collection. The board declared that it would "stand firm against branding or burning books on communism or by known or suspected communists." Red Scare participants failed to accept the challenge.[17]

Another event in the winter of 1952 did succeed in gaining the active interest of Houston's Red Scare groups. The national Methodist church had conceived and initiated an annual "Race Relations Sunday" as an attempt to encourage racial understanding and to develop closer ties between whites and blacks within local communities. The special event featured a racially integrated religious service. In several cities, Race Relations Sunday eventually became an event involving groups outside of the Methodist church. In Houston, the Council on Education in Race Relations, which included the Ministers' Association of Greater Houston, Houston Rabinical Association, and the Young Women's Christian Association, sponsored the city's annual Race Relations Sunday. For its 1952 event, the council invited a black man, Dr. Rufus E. Clement, president of Atlanta University, Atlanta, Georgia, to speak to Houston's First Methodist Church on February 10.[18]

The council's announcement brought a quick response from the Committee for the Preservation of Methodism, the Minute Women, and the Americanism Committee of the American Legion, who joined together in an effort to discredit Clement and halt the meeting. This protest marked the first time the three most active Red Scare groups had worked in an alliance.

Several days prior to Clement's appearance, Houston school administrator J. O. Webb distributed a "digest of material" titled "Must a Church Select a Speaker with Communist-Front Record?" This report, which Webb mailed to prominent Methodist, civic, and educational leaders, accused Clement of belonging to seven organizations named by the House Committee on Un-American Activities as Communist front groups. The list included the World Peace Conference, the Joint Anti-Fascist Refugee Committee, Progressive Citizens of America, and the Southern Negro Youth Congress. Webb's circular stated that even though some Methodists might not object to "the program of social mingling of Negroes and Whites," there were many who certainly opposed "an individual with a Communist-front record presiding over their Brotherhood services." Webb told his readers that the warning was "in the interest of the preservation of Americanism and Christianity."[19]

The Minute Women conducted the research for the anti-Clement circular and reproduced it on their office mimeograph machine. Webb's cover letter, which was on Houston school district letterhead stationery and typed by school personnel, asked for concerned citizens to telephone his school office for more information. The American Legion contributed by conducting the public protest. John P. Rogge, the Americanism Committee chairman, acted as the spokesperson for the anti-Clement coalition. Rogge informed Houston's newspapers that the American Legion "resents the Negro educator's appearance" and warned that large numbers of Legionnaires would attend Clement's speech. The *Chronicle* gave the protest supportive publicity with a sensational headline, "Legion Claims Speaker Has Red Connections."[20]

The *Chronicle's* behavior in this affair was another example of the disjunction between the newspaper's public and private positions. The *Chronicle's* publisher, Jesse Jones, knew of Rufus Clement's conservative background and had encouraged his work at Atlanta University. Exactly one year prior to the Clement controversy, Jones had written the black educator an enthusiastic letter conveying his personal endorsement of Clement's school and a $250 donation. Clement, however, refrained from using the Jones letter in his defense, possibly to protect his financial source.[21]

After J. O. Webb's anti-Clement circular was distributed among his Committee for the Preservation of Methodism colleagues, those who were also members of First Methodist Church decided to request a meeting with their pastor, W. Kenneth Pope. The week prior to Clement's appearance CFPM member R. A. Shepherd, who also served as First Methodist's chairman of the board, telephoned Pope, who was on a trip to Dallas, and informed the minister about the charges against Clement and asked him to return to Houston. Pope promptly departed from Dallas and, after arriving back in Houston, agreed to call a special meeting of the church's official board on Friday, February 8. One of the board members brought a copy of Webb's circular to the meeting. Reviewing the charges against Clement, Pope explained that they were unsubstantiated and that he believed the black educator should be allowed to speak. An argument ensued with some board members supporting Pope and the others opposing him. David Bintliff, a CFPM member, offered a compromise. He would personally pay all expenses if everyone would agree to move the Race Relations Sunday event to the Houston City Auditorium. Reverend Pope objected and stated, "I can not, in good conscience, turn my back on having the service in our sanctuary and I can not, therefore, and will not, preside over the service at the auditorium." Pope's firmness carried the discussion as the First Methodist board voted to proceed as planned.[22]

The decision to go ahead with the event was announced in the local newspapers. The American Legion's Americanism Committee spokesman, John Rogge, informed the press that his group would picket the service and attempt to prevent Clement from speaking. Pope felt that Rogge's threat implied that the protest would be violent.

Dr. Clement and Dr. Pope went to First Methodist Church in downtown Houston early on February 10 to avoid a possible incident before the service. They stayed in Pope's office on the fifth floor of the huge church building until it was time for the meeting to begin. Pope warned Clement to walk as rapidly as possible to the pulpit and to look straight ahead and avoid eye contact with the protesters. Pope and Clement took the elevator down to the sanctuary and, as they entered, were confronted by a standing room only crowd. Both men hurried down the outside aisle to the pulpit as planned. After stepping up to the pulpit and turning to face the audience, Pope noticed a large number of men sitting together whom he had never seen before. He went to the microphone and nervously announced that the meeting was a religious service. Pope was placing everyone on notice because it was illegal to disrupt a religious service.

After the minister's announcement, John Rogge stood up from the group Pope had noticed and demanded permission to read aloud the charges against Clement. Dr. Pope rejected Rogge's request and, instead, read some statements he had received about the guest speaker. One was a strong declaration of support for Clement written by Rabbi Robert Kahn of Temple Emmanuel in Houston. He followed this with a telegram that stunned Rogge and his group. Pope announced that he had received a message from Brigadier General Elbert P. Tuttle, past commander of the Atlanta, Georgia, American Legion Post. Tuttle, a conservative, nationally known American Legion leader and a senior partner in one of Atlanta's most powerful law firms, stated that Clement "has been a leader among his race . . . towards the conservative view . . . opposed to the radical leadership of those who . . . stir up Negroes . . . for radical purposes." Tuttle congratulated Houstonians for inviting Clement to speak and declared, "He is an outstanding American."

The Tuttle telegram effectively silenced Rogge and his delegation. Dr. Clement was then allowed to deliver his speech to the fifteen hundred people in attendance. Clement ignored the tension and proceeded to deliver a well-prepared speech that argued for black voting rights and equality before the law but emphasized the importance of good citizenship and patriotism. He vigorously attacked Communism and eulogized "the American Way of Life," declaring forcefully that the "American Negro will never go Communistic." The audience remained quiet throughout the speech and gave the eloquent Clement loud applause when he finished. The American Legion delegation left the sanctuary without further protest. Outside, the tall and lanky Rogge scratched his bald head, frowned, and reluctantly admitted to a reporter that "the speech didn't sound like a Communist." The much-relieved Kenneth Pope later recalled the service as "perhaps the most crucial experience I had . . . during those years" in Houston.[23]

After Clement left Houston, R. A. ("Bob") Childers, a Methodist layman and prominent businessman, wrote a detailed account of J. O. Webb's participation in the episode and sent it to the Houston school board. Childers, a manufacturer of aluminum structures, was an unusual man who refused to be quiet while the Red Scare raged in his community. Enjoying the freedom of financial independence, Childers was an aggressive and vocal opponent of McCarthyism and the anti-Communist hysteria. He and a group of twenty to twenty-five other Houstonians often met informally at their homes or at churches such as Riverside Methodist to discuss the madness that seemed to grip their fellow citizens. Childers, pointing out that Webb had used school stationery and a school secretary, charged the educator with misusing his position as an assistant superintendent and accused him of "bearing false witness" and spreading rumors. The school board asked Webb to answer Childers' charges. He replied that he had acted only as a Methodist lay leader and as secretary of the CFPM and not as an official of the Houston schools. The school board, whose membership included Webb's colleague in the CFPM, Ewing Werlein, as well as Dr. Henry A. Peterson, with whom Webb owned land, asked Superintendent Moreland to caution employees about such behavior in the future. The board ruled the matter closed after receiving a large amount of mail defending Webb's activities.[24]

The Clement affair was an unusually clear example of the willingness of hard-core Red Scare enthusiasts to launch crusades based on inaccurate and misleading data. The anti-Clement protesters failed to understand that Dr. Clement, a follower of Booker T. Washington's philosophy, had a conservative, "Uncle Tom" image among many blacks in groups such as the NAACP. The affair indicated the prominent role racism played in Houston's version of the Red Scare. Although nothing was said in print, except for Webb's comment about "race-mingling," Kenneth Pope and other Methodist clergy and laymen heard several of Clement's opponents refer to him as "that nigger," "that Georgia coon," and other similar racial vulgarisms. Also, J. O. Webb's activities and the Houston school board's subsequent refusal to reprimand him further revealed the connection between Red Scare groups and key school personnel.[25]

The Clement affair also united the three largest Red Scare organizations in a working coalition and provided experience that would prove useful in future endeavors. It created a modus operandi that became standard. Minute Women members would be responsible for obtaining information about the backgrounds of persons selected as potential targets for an attack. The most important part of this process was determining if the person in question had ever been cited by HCUA in any of its numerous lists. This could usually be found by simply checking HCUA publications. These lists, however, were infrequently updated. For fresher information, the Minute Women occasionally relied on a few friendly congressmen who were glad to check current HCUA card files for them.

After his return to Washington in January 1953 as congressman-at-large from Texas, Martin Dies served as an important contact for Houston's

Red Scare activists. Dies was well aware that Houston's Minute Women were among his most enthusiastic campaign workers and he was pleased to send them information. Helen Thomas, after one typical request for material, told Dies that "I never stop being grateful that you are in Washington where your experience and patriotism can be of value."[26]

The problem with Dies, however, was that his alienation from the congressional leadership and Democratic party establishment hampered his ability to get information. Accordingly, Minute Women members would sometimes turn to Price Daniel, who was elected to the United States Senate in 1952. Unlike Lyndon Johnson, who would ignore Minute Women requests, Daniel was happy to have his staff checking HCUA files to determine if an individual had been unfortunate enough to have been named by the committee or by someone testifying before the committee. For example, in response to one request by Anne Harrison for HCUA citations, Daniel promptly located the material and sent it to Houston, writing the Minute Woman that he was "glad to pass this report on to you." In another request, Bertie Maughmer wrote Daniel that the Minute Women "are particularly interested in any 'ultra liberal' activities in which [Frieda Hancock, a member of the Federal Communications Commission] might have been engaged. . . ." Daniel replied within a week, informing Maughmer that Hancock had indeed been cited by HCUA—for being a member of the National Lawyers' Guild. Daniel's cooperation in these matters was much appreciated by Houston's Red Scare activists. After E. M. Biggers praised the senator for his help in the fight against the Red menace, Daniel thanked him and assured Biggers of his "continuing efforts against Communism and all subversive elements that may be found in our government departments."[27]

After the Minute Women obtained the necessary HCUA information, through whatever means, it would go into a circular that would be printed, usually by the Biggers Printing Company but sometimes by another printer by the name of Ned Gill. The printed material would then be distributed to initiate the attack against a selected target. Next, the Minute Women would begin their telephone campaign and join with American Legionnaires and the CFPM in a letter-writing operation. As in the Clement affair, John Rogge often acted as the coalition's spokesperson or "front man," representing anonymous supporters. Local Red Scare attacks would thus be loosely coordinated and would involve a network of usually anonymous persons sometimes stretching back to the halls of Congress.

Coinciding with the Red Scare coalition's campaign against Dr. Clement, the Minute Women conducted a "public education" program about Communism in the schools and churches. This program consisted of discussion groups in the homes of individual Minute Women and the distribution of pamphlets and reprints of right-wing literature. The week-long activities culminated with a speech by George Washington Robnett, Chicago advertising agent and executive secretary of the National Lay-man's Council of the Church League of America. Robnett's organization, founded in 1937, was one of a multitude of right-wing extremist groups in the 1950s whose membership only consisted of a few friends of the founder. The Church League, which specialized in compiling lists of alleged subversives and then selling them to other groups, had no con-nection with any organized church. When not railing against "Reds" Robnett denounced the budding black civil rights movement, calling it "Minorityism" and "a new national disease . . . menacing the American way of life."[28]

The Minute Women asked Hugh Roy Cullen to sponsor Robnett's visit to Houston, which he enthusiastically agreed to do. Cullen arranged for Robnett to speak to the faculty and students at the University of Houston while J. O. Webb arranged for Robnett to speak to the Houston Rotary Club. Webb also provided a junior high school auditorium for Robnett to speak to his Red Scare admirers. Webb, without approval from his boss, Superintendent William Moreland, designated Robnett's speech as an official school activity and issued a formal request to all high school principals and teachers to attend. Webb's staff memo explained that Robnett would inform school staff about radicalism in education and religion.[29]

Robnett's visit to Houston was well publicized by local newspapers, which reprinted his message for their readers. In a speech to the Minute Women and school personnel at the junior high school, Robnett warned that "so called progressive education is unquestionably the greatest danger . . . in the country." Robnett also warned against "Communism, welfareism [sic], minorityism, and Trumanism" and urged Houstonians to begin the "long hard battle" against those elements among them that were encouraging these evils.[30]

Superintendent Moreland received at least one letter that protested Webb's coercive pressures on behalf of his personal political beliefs. The anonymous writer apologized for not signing the letter but explained, "In certain quarters it could bring me . . . misery and brand me . . . as radical and progressive." Moreland held Webb in utter contempt but he knew that some board members endorsed Webb's activity. Moreland chose to ignore his assistant superintendent's insubordination.[31]

Robnett's official appearance at the University of Houston, where he spoke on the "Three Stages of World Revolution Now in Motion," sig-nified the Minute Women's and other Red Scare activists' growing influ-ence over the affairs of Houston's largest university. Hugh Roy Cullen, chairman of the board of regents, played a key role in fostering this influence. Cullen's money had made him the most powerful individual voice among the school's decision makers. The oil man's approval was a necessity for all important university matters. Unfortunately, Cullen's involvement in school affairs often included less important matters that, in most large universities, are traditionally part of the president's responsibilities. His proclivity to intervene in the daily operations of the University of Houston provided Red Scare groups such as the Minute Women an opportunity to have some influence over university affairs.[32]

This influence was vividly demonstrated one month after Robnett's appearance in Houston. A student organization invited John Roy Carlson to speak at the university in March 1952. Carlson, who was to lecture on "The Flame of Nationalism in the Middle East," was a specialist on right- and left-wing subversive activity. Author of *Undercover* and *The Plotters*, Carlson focused on Nazi spy efforts in the United States during World War II and had FBI clearance to lecture at restricted federal government installations.

As soon as the university announced Carlson's forthcoming visit, the Minute Women went to work and researched his background. They eventually discovered an old John T. Flynn newspaper column, written in April 1944, that accused Carlson of being a Communist who had edited a newspaper in Soviet Armenia in the 1930s. Flynn apparently made the false allegation because Carlson had correctly listed Flynn in *Undercover* as a leader of the isolationist America First organization prior to American entry into World War II. The Minute Women sent Flynn's column to Hugh Roy Cullen and demanded that Carlson be banned from the campus. Cullen agreed and ordered President Kemmerer to stop the speech. Kemmerer called a news conference on March 19, 1952, and revealed that the university had received information about Carlson's "following the Communist Party line." The university president declared that because of Carlson's "highly controversial past" he could not allow him to speak on campus.

John Roy Carlson arrived in Houston the next day and bitterly protested the decision. He met with Kemmerer and learned that Cullen was responsible for canceling his appearance. Carlson held a press conference and declared Kemmerer was "taking a rap" for Cullen. Carlson stated that he had lectured at dozens of colleges since 1943 and that the University of Houston was the first to deny him his right to speak. Carlson charged that Cullen was a "divine right philanthropist" who arbitrarily determined university policy and was actually contributing to the growth of the welfare state by attempting to create "rubber stamp Americans." Declaring that he hated Communism, Carlson stated, "I have never been to Soviet Armenia, let alone edited a newspaper there!" He urged Houstonians to check his record with federal agencies, "not with crackpots and slanderers."

The Hillel Foundation defended Carlson and transferred his speech to Houston's Congregation Beth Yeshuran. Rabbi Malev of Beth Yeshuran denounced the accusations against Carlson as "flimsy" and warned Carlson's accusers not to attempt to prevent his speech at the synagogue. Carlson's enemies heeded Malev's warning. Even though Carlson spoke at the synagogue, Red Scare activists had succeeded in their goal of not allowing him to speak at the university.[33]

While the Minute Women, American Legion, CFPM, and their allies waged campaigns against Clement and Carlson, several Houston physicians decided that the city's medical doctors needed their own Red Scare auxiliary. In February 1952, a group of physicians, many of whom had Minute Women wives, formed Doctors for Freedom. Physicians who had long been active in local politics spearheaded the organization, which used suite 511 in the Medical Arts building as its mailing address. These included Dr. Henry Peterson, school board member; Dr. Denton Kerr, a leader in the conservative faction of the city's Democratic party; Dr. William Palm, a Republican party activist; Dr. Alvis Greer, editor of the Harris County Medical Society's weekly bulletin; and Dr. John K. Glen, a CFPM leader and active in school board politics. Dr. J. D. Mabry, the husband of a Minute Women activist, served on the group's executive committee.

The founders of Doctors for Freedom restricted membership to Harris County Medical Society members and declared two goals: "to promote the understanding of individual freedom" and "to oppose Socialism in any form." Like so many other short-lived conservative groups in 1952, Doctors for Freedom seems to have been primarily interested in electing a Republican president in the upcoming fall elections. Truman's occasional pronouncements in favor of some type of federally subsidized health insurance especially irked the physicians. The doctors placed ads in the medical society bulletin inviting doctors to join and fight "Truman [and] his ilk, socialism, and skyrocketing taxes." Doctors for Freedom maintained a low profile and usually acted only in concert with the other members of the informal Red Scare coalition. Its chairman, Dr. W. M. Wallis, admitted that "we cooperate with other groups in this area of like mind. . . ." The organization's members concentrated on "educating" their patients and fellow physicians about socialistic governmental encroachments in health care and raised money to support Red Scare activists and candidates. It apparently never had more than approximately sixty active members, many of whom were husbands of Minute Women.[34]

Red Scare activism accelerated in the summer of 1952. The Minute Women began to screen local newspapers for danger signs of nonconformity. A letter to the editor of a newspaper, expressing any hint of liberalism or progressive thought, assured the writer of finding his or her mailbox clogged for days thereafter with locally mailed pamphlets written by Allen Zoll, Joseph Kamp, John T. Flynn, or other Minute Women favorites. Mrs. T. H. Tennent, leader of the United Church Women, had to install a cut-off on her telephone because she received Minute Women calls every half-hour throughout the night after she defended the United Nations in a public speech. After KPRC radio canceled John T. Flynn's news commentary program, the Minute Women began a chain telephone campaign to the station's management protesting the action. KPRC placed the program back on the air in twenty-four hours.[35]

Members of the Committee for the Preservation of Methodism were also busy throughout the spring of 1952. The Red Scare Methodists monitored the sermons of local ministers, tried to censor material used in Sunday school classes, proselytized their secular political views among church members, and generally kept the local churches stirred up. Dr. Kenneth Pope has written that during this time "the reactionary element wouldn't have minded tearing down the church" since it believed "there was a Communist under every pew and behind most of the pulpits anyhow." The effect of this activity was to make the clergy more cautious about their public statements and circumspect in all phases of their work.[36]

Kenneth Pope, minister at First Methodist, has recalled that "hardly a Sunday went by when some listener in the congregation did not come up after the service and object to something that I had said in the sermon that did not square with his or her conservative views." More often than not, Ewing Werlein, CFPM leader and school board member, was the layman Pope could expect a visit from after the sermon to quibble or argue about some minor point that seemed radical and dangerous to Werlein. Other Methodist ministers experienced the same harassment. Sometimes it came from outside their own congregation. For example, Clarence Lohman, a layman at St. Luke's Methodist and a CFPM leader, was a frequent visitor to the other churches. Lohman, who also served as an officer in the national Circuit Riders, Inc., would call meetings of the lay leaders and announce which items of current church literature should be censored. He would also distribute lists of subversive agents and fellow travelers believed to be lurking in the Methodist membership. Lohman would also request information about the content of the sermons preached by the city's Methodist ministers.[37]

Methodist Minute Women also harassed their clergy. This was not surprising, since many of the CFPM leaders' wives belonged to the women's pressure group. Because of his involvement in having Dr. Rufus

Clement at First Methodist, Kenneth Pope became a special target of these people. Pope remembers the period as being extremely hard on his family. Obscene telephone calls came frequently and his wife, Kate, took the brunt of them.[38]

The overall effect, of course, was to stifle healthy discussion. Just as was the case in other areas of community life, especially in the schools, the "market place of ideas" was being shut down in the churches. To preach on anything resembling contemporary issues or social welfare topics invited an unpleasant protest. Kenneth Pope admitted that the presence of the Red Scare activists, no matter how small a minority of the congregation, made him "careful in the pulpit." Pope states, "I did not want to be misunderstood. You chose some things [to say] rather than other things." Grady Hardin, minister at Chapelwood Methodist, recalled that the Red Scare in the church "scared most of us [clergy] to within an inch of our lives."[39]

While Houston's Methodist ministers seem to have had the worst experience among their religious cohorts, some of the Red Scare also spilled over onto the Episcopalians.

In June, the American Friends Service Committee scheduled its second annual Institute of International Relations. The Friends, who had managed to conduct their first institute in Houston in 1951 with a minimum of harassment, found a new atmosphere in the city in 1952. They now faced an informal but strong Red Scare coalition that had perfected its harassment technique as a result of the Goslin, Clement, and Carlson affairs and other incidents of the previous months.

The American Friends Service Committee selected Autry House, an Episcopalian student center, as the location for their institute. Anna Lord Strauss, United States delegate to the United Nations General Assembly, and John M. Swomley, Jr., a Methodist minister and director of the National Council against Conscription, were chosen as the institute's featured speakers.

The Red Scare coalition responded to the announced Quaker institute by initiating another of its now routine harassment campaigns. Minute Women members, led by Helen Thomas, researched HCUA files and corresponded with Red Scare groups in other states to obtain information on the institute's speakers. This information was then compiled and printed on a circular distributed by all Red Scare organizations. The circular, "Are the 'American Friends' Our Enemies?," contained the standard charges that the Friends' speakers were subversives who would contaminate Houston's pure atmosphere of free enterprise. Swomley and Strauss were both accused of being on HCUA lists. The circular charged that the American Friends Service Committee no longer represented "old-line Quakers" and warned that it would make available dangerous and radical literature, such as *The Races of Mankind* by Ruth Benedict and Gene Weltfish, to Houstonians attending the meetings. Racism dominated the anti-Quaker circular. A Los Angeles *Mirror* news story was reprinted that detailed the arrest and conviction of black civil rights leader Bayard Rustin for "lewd vagrancy." The circular stated that Rustin had spoken at Friends' institutes and implied that the Quakers advocated sexual intercourse between blacks and whites.

The Minute Women and their allies supplemented the circular with an intensive letter-writing and telephone campaign aimed at local Episcopalian leaders, including Bishop Clinton S. Quinn. American Legion members, led by John Rogge, once again provided the public front and appeared as a delegation at the institute. Unofficially accompanied by a group of Minute Women, Rogge and his Legionnaires loudly heckled and booed the institute's speakers. At one point in the evening, one of the protesters wrestled with John Swomley in a brief scuffle on stage. This incident, coupled with disruptions and harassment from the audience, succeeded in closing the Friends' institute. Other than a public expression of regret by Bishop Quinn, who stated that the American Friends were ". . . no more subversive than I am," few Houstonians protested the role played by Red Scare groups in denying freedom of speech to the Friends' speakers. As one clergyman later admitted, "To be a responsible member of the community in Houston during the 1950's was . . . [a] task . . . filled with tension."[40]

By the end of the summer of 1952, Houston's Red Scare activists had established cohesive organizations, tied together in an informal coalition that had gained experience and perfected campaign tactics in a series of protests against allegedly "controversial" speakers. This coalition made important connections at the University of Houston and created a new allied group within the medical community. Its most effective and visible institutional link, however, was with the Houston Independent School District. The school district became the central focus for Red Scare activists who were desperately seeking to preserve their vision of community. The schools were of particular interest to the Minute Women, the dominant group in the Red Scare coalition. As the 1952–53 school year approached, the Minute Women and their allies became more and more preoccupied with the affairs of the school district.

SIX

THE RED SCARE AND THE SCHOOLS

> *It was the time of the Red Menace. The fear of Communists taking over the PTA and Community Chest affected the lives of ordinary people in ordinary towns.*
>
> —*E. L. Doctorow*

> *They like to hunt for Commies*
>   *And pinks of every hue,*
> *But if they can't find Commies,*
>   *Plain liberals will do.*
>
> —*From a skit about Texas performed*
> *at the Women's National Press Club,*
> *Washington, D.C., 1954*[1]

It was inevitable that the Red Scare in Texas' largest city would center on the Houston Independent School District (HISD). A complex set of circumstances made this so. Historically, American teachers have been targets of suspicion and aggression during periods of superpatriotic sensitivity. American educators have always suffered from a lack of job security, low salaries, and low status. As one historian has observed, "Here was a profession it was all too easy to bully and browbeat." This historical pattern reached its national peak in the decade after World War II when political purges cost at least six hundred teachers their jobs. The Red Scare hit New York City's public schools the hardest, with over three hundred teachers purged.[2]

Throughout the United States, extreme anti-Communists such as Allen Zoll called for a thorough educational house cleaning. Speaking on the floor of the House of Representatives in 1946, Republican congressman George A. Dondero of Michigan attracted national attention by charging that the country was being "systematically communized" through its public schools. Dondero claimed that "left-wing theories" were being taught to the young "in an insidious manner" by radical teachers. He demanded that "steps . . . be taken—drastic steps—to trace communistic teachings to their source in America, and then eliminate them."[3]

Dondero's provocative speech, filled with unsubstantiated charges, was subsequently published as a reprint from the *Congressional Record* and widely circulated, along with other "Reds in the schools" literature, among the Red Scare activists. In Houston, Helen Thomas distributed the Dondero speech and Zoll's pamphlets to her colleagues in the Minute Women and to HISD personnel. It is impossible to know how many Houstonians were influenced by this literature, but Dondero, Zoll, and others of similar persuasion were frequently quoted in letters to the newspapers and to the school board and in speeches by school board members. Some Red Scare activists focused on the schools simply because they had become convinced by this literature that the classrooms were at the center of an ideological war between the forces of the "American Way" and "Godless" Communism. For example, to E. M. Biggers "everyone with as much sense as a road lizard knows that the very center piece of communism is the capture of our educational . . . institutions."[4]

This concern about subversive influences in the public schools merely enlarged a theme that had loomed over Texas' teachers since the 1930s. As early as 1935, the Texas legislature, along with those in several other states, required all prospective teachers to satisfy "in some way" the county superintendent as to their loyalty to the United States. In 1941 the Texas legislature passed a new law that required all teachers to take a loyalty oath and provided for the dismissal of any teacher "found guilty of openly advocating doctrines which seek to undermine . . . the republican and democratic forms of government of the United States." The legislators failed to define the word "undermine." The loyalty law applied to all school personnel from yardmen to the superintendent, an inclusiveness adopted by only one other state. The legislature expanded the statute in 1949 to require all school personnel and students to make a formal disavowal of membership in "subversive groups."[5]

In February 1950, the Texas House of Representatives passed without debate a resolution submitted by Marshall Bell directing the Texas Education Agency (the state unit supervising all public education) and the boards of regents of all state universities to remove and destroy any and all literature published by the Soviet Union found in school libraries or classrooms. This included such items as *Soviet Life* and other publications reflecting daily life in Russia. Representative Bell argued that it would be "unwise" to permit such material to remain in the schools "for it can only serve to confuse and mislead the young and immature minds." The material was practically nonexistent in the public grade schools and, since it was merely a resolution without force of law, Texas' university libraries generally ignored it.[6]

In 1951, the legislature required the Texas Department of Public Safety to produce a list of subversive organizations that was subsequently attached to a lengthy affirmation of loyalty to be signed by anyone associated with Texas' public schools. In 1953, at the height of the Red Scare, Representative Marshall Bell expressed concern that subversive teachers might sign the loyalty oath and later, when exposed, be able – with the aid of shrewd and clever radical lawyers – to argue the unconstitutionality of the loyalty law. Bell also suspected some noncompliance with the law. The legislature proceeded to enact a statute requiring that everyone on the state payroll had to sign the loyalty oath, have it notarized, and then file it with the payroll clerk before they could receive their pay. This was too much for the commissioner of education, J. W. Edgar. In a communication to all city and county school superintendents, Edgar emphasized local responsibility in complying with the 1953 law, stating that "you are not required to make any report whatever to the Texas Education Agency" and that no audit would be made to check on compliance. Edgar knew better than to challenge these laws but he clearly had no intention of enforcing them.[7]

Factors other than the simple fear of Communism also made Houston's public schools a Red Scare target. In Texas, beginning in the late 1930s, the conservative business establishment, wary of the New Deal and fearful of taxes and labor unions, became increasingly involved in an effort to control public education. Aware that educated citizens tend to vote more than uneducated and that these votes elect the politicians who make public policies that affect the business environment, the corporate establishment knew the importance of controlling what those citizens learned in school. This is why professors Robert Montgomery, Clarence Ayres, and other members of the Department of Economics at the University of Texas were frequent objects of legislative investigation and harassment. They educated university students about labor unions and the need for the regulation and the equitable taxation of corporations. The dismissal of Homer P. Rainey as president of the University of Texas in 1944 was rooted in Rainey's efforts to defend his faculty and protect the university from corporate control. This effort to control education reached down to the local level.[8]

As Rainey himself observed, the techniques of business control of education are varied.

> There is control of local school boards; there is pressure upon superintendents, principals, and teachers to conform to certain norms. Textbooks are examined, and control of the Textbook Commission, which selects the texts for all the schools of the state, is sought. Teachers' salaries can be kept as low as pos-

sible, and teachers intimidated in many ways—by . . . investigations, by denying them promotions . . . , by subjecting them to loyalty oaths.[9]

In the effort to preserve a rigidly probusiness educational environment, control of the state's largest school district was crucial. Those who wanted control found Red Scare issues and the tactics described by Rainey especially useful in achieving and maintaining it.

Houston's school system also received the close scrutiny of local participants in the Red Scare because it was the one institution in the city that affected nearly every citizen. Since the city government provided a minimum of social services, had little contact with federal programs, and had no control over the public schools, its operations were spared from Red Scare attacks. The school system, however, had to deal extensively and directly with such controversies as federal aid to education and racial integration, both of which stirred strong emotional reactions. To make matters worse, some school administrators and board members openly sympathized with and, in some cases, actively participated in Red Scare campaigns. Red Scare activists became so powerful in the administration that direction of the public schools fell largely under their control for several years in the 1950s. An important ingredient in their influence over the schools was their interaction and cooperation with a powerful administrative machine that existed within the school system itself under the direct control of the business manager, Hubert L. Mills. Officially the Houston schools were administered jointly by the superintendent, William E. Moreland, and the business manager, H. L. Mills, both under the nominal control of the school board. In reality, however, the existence of a powerful machine of school personnel, controlled by the business manager, destroyed the equilibrium within the dual control system. The superintendent, who was responsible for all academic affairs, faced continual insubordination and interference from the business manager's office. That Mills participated in the anti-Communist crusade and Moreland did not exacerbated the problem.[10]

The power struggle within the school administration eventually created a public controversy. Those who supported the dual system assumed the mantle of "conservative" and managed to label their opponents as "liberal." While the two terms are difficult to define in this local context, the conservative faction strongly opposed federal aid to education, racial integration, and nontraditional or progressive education and actively supported the anti-Communist Red Scare crusade of Houston. The liberals, much less homogeneous, embraced a variety of economic and political philosophies. Some opposed federal aid and progressive education as much as the conservatives. All, however, opposed dual administration and supported the strong superintendent system. The liberals also conspicuously refrained from encouraging Houston's Red Scare and, in a few cases, vigorously attacked it.

"Progressive education" alarmed the conservatives most of all. When the conservatives decried progressive education, they were referring to the multitude of new teaching techniques and theories emanating from the work of philosopher John Dewey, among many others. The term very generally described the educational philosophy that focused on relativism and the cultivation of problem solving and conceptualism rather than the rote memorization of facts. It also referred to the creation of new courses of study in human relations and the behavioral and social sciences, the most controversial being sex education. Overall, "progressive education" was a grab-bag term to describe everything from social promotions to the Socratic method of teaching to special education.

The new teaching methods and innovative curricula characterized as progressive education received pertinent and rational criticism from some educators. Many of them, such as Arthur Bestor in *Educational Wastelands,* predicted that the new postwar educational trends would ultimately produce an epidemic of functional illiteracy and a serious breakdown in the effectiveness of public education. Houston school board member Henry Peterson's criticisms—when stripped of their anti-Communist rhetoric—were rational and close to the mark. "Under the so-called doctrine of the 'happy child,' " Peterson complained, "education has become a matter of pure entertainment." Peterson believed, with some justification, that the integration of subject matter such as grammar, reading, and writing into "language arts" and history, geography, and civics into "social studies" would result in the near total neglect of substantive, basic learning. Peterson also denounced the progressive-inspired trend toward "social promotions" through which children would graduate to a higher class level not because of accomplishment but because of "age, size, and physical development; this gives the child something for nothing." Conservatives did not monopolize criticism of progressive education. One of the most vocal and influential liberals in Texas, J. Frank Dobie, persistently criticized teaching methods associated with progressive education. Dobie even questioned the legitimacy of "education" as an academic discipline, frequently referring to professors of education as "elaborators of the obvious."[11]

Any clearly reasoned or thoughtful critiques, however, were overwhelmed by those of the extreme right, which emphasized that the "new" education would create brainwashed drones unable to function in any but a collectivist state. In Houston, the educational conservatives defined progressive education as being "neither progressive nor education." Calling it a system of social reform based on a philosophy that maintained there are no lasting standards of right or wrong, the conservatives charged that progressive education taught nothing "save that which is alien to that taught in the church and the home." According to one Houston pamphlet,

> the child in a Progressive school is made to feel comfortable at all costs. There are no grades—so he cannot fail. The subjects are all lumped together so he can discard one if he doesn't like it and take up another which strikes his fancy. The slowest child in the class is made to feel comfortable, too—the rest of the class is held down to his level. Readin', 'riting and 'rithmetic are neglected as the schemers and the dreamers fill the children's minds with their social reforms. . . .[12]

The conservatives favored an educational program that strongly emphasized the teaching of the "three R's." The integration of geography, history, and civics into a single unit of social studies would, according to the conservatives, create a situation where parents would be unable to recognize one subject from another. This could mean that "any sort of philosophy could be safely hidden in the curriculum." If a social studies course stressed anything but flag-waving Americanism and the sanctity of private property then the conservatives denounced it as propaganda for socialism, world government, and the welfare state.[13]

Some opposition to progressive education stemmed from fear bred by an ignorance of the new social science jargon. Intimidated by the buzzwords of the "new" educators, the husband of one Houston Minute Woman complained that the educators "are so shifty . . . that it is highly difficult to pin them down. Besides, the Progressive Education system itself is so complicated in its inner workings that few people . . . can understand it."[14]

Conservatives often identified progressive education as un-Texan and looked with suspicion on educators from out of state, especially those coming from either the West or East coast. They also strongly opposed the National Education Association (NEA), because "out-of-staters" controlled it and the NEA was perceived as an influential advocate of progressive education. The conservatives believed the association represented a dangerous trend toward centralized control of education.[15]

The public schools thus became the focal point of the Red Scare in Houston. And yet while those in control of local education worried about subversion and socialism, the Houston schools badly needed attention in other respects. Houston, the eighth district in total enrollment in the

United States, ranked near the bottom compared with other districts in proportion of community resources spent for public schools. While school administrators, urged on by the Minute Women, worried about subversive influences, inadequate facilities forced them to hold many classes in school cafeterias, others in school auditoriums, and in one case in the teachers' lounge.

Despite a need for improvement, the conservative faction that had controlled the district for years spent more time protecting the schools from socialism than working on practical solutions for inadequate facilities and funds. George Fuermann, observing the district in the early 1950s, said, "All that saves the system from the fascist mentality is the opposition's tenacity and the fact that the public is informed." While "fascist" may have been too harsh a label, the school district was in the grips of educators participating in the Red Scare.[16]

G. C. Scarborough, the principal of Lanier Junior High School and an influential member of the group in control of the Houston schools, in a public speech attacking the founders of UNESCO said that neither Dr. Julian Huxley nor Dr. Bertrand Russell could be respected by educators because of Huxley's atheism and because Russell had long advocated "free love." Scarborough also opposed kindergarten and nursery school programs as attempts to control young minds "from the beginning." Later, when the National Education Association investigated the Houston schools, Scarborough hysterically exclaimed to the press, "They're trying to destroy me but I'm not afraid. I stand for right. I'm not an atheist. I believe in Jesus Christ."

Louisa Eldredge, principal of Jefferson Elementary School, attracted considerable attention when she rewrote the American's Creed, a pledge that Jefferson students recited every morning to begin the school day. The creed had been approved by the United States House of Representatives in 1916 for use as an official national pledge. Eldredge deleted the word "democracy" from the text because, in her view, Communist affinity for the term had made it a "dirty word." Eldredge explained to angry parents that the United States was not a democracy anyway; it was a republic. The principal also authored a pamphlet called *Americanism versus All Other Isms* that charged that the New Deal had "aided and abetted the destruction of our American Republic."[17]

Another Red Scare activist was J. O. Webb, assistant superintendent in charge of high schools. Webb, who would be active in the John Birch Society in later years, was a leader in the attack on Dr. Rufus Clement. He endeared himself to Houston's more prudish conservatives by inspecting the high school libraries in the district and removing all the art books that contained pictures of nudes. Typical of Webb's methods, this arbitrary censorship occurred without prior approval by either the school board or Superintendent Moreland. Webb succeeded for one year in keeping high school students from attending life classes (which taught methods of artistically portraying the human body) at Houston's Museum of Fine Arts. This action went beyond Webb's statutory authority as assistant superintendent since the students drew pictures on their own time and spent their own money for the sessions. Webb pressured the museum to ban high school students from the classes despite museum officials' admission that no parents had previously objected to the life classes and that Webb was the only citizen to do so.[18]

This clique of right-wing educators received the enthusiastic support of Red Scare activists. When United States senator William Jenner began a series of hearings in Washington, D.C., on Communist influence in education in 1953, Bertie Maughmer wrote Jenner and urged him to seek the testimony of Scarborough and Eldredge concerning "subversion and immorality in our Nation's schools." Maughmer told Jenner that Scarborough and Eldredge "have led the fight here for years and, together with our few remaining conservative administrators, have awakened leading citizens to the extreme dangers from . . . socialistic educators."[19]

The most important member of the conservative group in control of the schools in the early 1950s, however, was the business manager of the school district, Hubert L. Mills, a staunch political conservative and friend and admirer of Congressman Martin Dies. Since its creation in 1923, no one else had held the job of business manager except H. L. Mills. He influenced school policies having little direct connection with the business office. Because of his length of service as head of the district's financial affairs, Mills developed a large following among teachers and administrators and was especially close to J. O. Webb. One teacher in the district called Mills' followers "Junior McCarthys" because of their devotion to ferreting out alleged unpatriotic tendencies in the schools. Mills' extended family made up a significant portion of his clique. Under Mills, nepotism reigned supreme; the district had at least thirteen of his kin on the payroll in 1952. This group included Mills' brother, Coy Mills, principal of Jefferson Davis High School and an administrative power on his own; G. C. Scarborough, Mill's first cousin and principal of Lanier Junior High; and Raymond Scarborough, another cousin who was principal of Berry Elementary School and president of the Houston Association of School Administrators. Mills also had five other relatives who were either principals or assistant principals in the district as well as another five who served as classroom teachers. Mills defended this often-criticized situation by claiming that he had attempted to keep his brother from becoming a teacher and he would be the first to demand the firing of a relative if that person failed to do his job.[20]

While conservative school employees followed H. L. Mills' leadership, the most visible members of the conservative group in control of Houston's public schools held board of education positions. Both liberals and conservatives in Houston fought to control the board. Since the end of World War II, the board had been the city's main forum for debating issues that loomed larger than purely local problems. The welfare state versus free enterprise, the United Nations, federal aid to education, racial segregation, and alleged Communist subversion sometimes monopolized board meetings as subjects of discussion more than mundane educational matters.[21]

Ewing Werlein, a leader of the Committee for the Preservation of Methodism and a school board member, was among the most vocal of those Houstonians subscribing to the view that Communism posed an immediate danger to the local citizenry. When asked his opinion of Joe McCarthy, Werlein said, "Joe McCarthy is a great man. He has never pointed to a single person and named him a Communist that he has not been proved right." Not everyone guilty of perpetrating the Red Scare in the United States fit the dark and sinister stereotype of a Senator Joe McCarthy. Perhaps if they had, American society would have been spared the trauma. Unfortunately, the Red Scare in Houston had the encouragement of too many Ewing Werleins, men and women – pillars of society – who could have just as easily played a far different role.[22]

Werlein, whose father served as a pastor of Houston's First Methodist Church, was a native of St. Louis, Missouri. An attorney, Werlein was deeply interested in education, serving from 1927 until 1945 as dean of Houston Law School, a private night school that produced many of the community's judges. Werlein himself would later end his long career as a judge in the state court of civil appeals. If physical appearance is considered a qualification for a judgeship, then Werlein qualified. A former football player, well over six feet in height and weighing two hundred pounds, Ewing Werlein had the religious convictions and silver-haired grandfatherly visage suitable for an Andy Hardy movie. His personal life seemed right out of the same type of cinema stereotype – a beautiful but not ostentatious two-story home on prestigious North Boulevard, a charming wife, and three children. Werlein was the kind of man to whom a community instinctively turns in times of moral crisis. For example, Werlein agreed to serve as the interim district attorney of Harris County in 1954 after the Texas Senate ousted the previous DA for operating a "bawdy house." But Ewing Werlein's moral and patriotic fervor too often obscured his larger vision. Kenneth Pope, Werlein's pastor and a man often at the receiving end of Werlein's criticisms, characterized him as a man who "would never do something against your back"; his attacks were "eye to eye," said Pope. "He criticized me in love." Another Methodist minister described Werlein as "polite" and in many ways attractive, but he also believed him to be a "true-believer," a bigot, and "not real intelligent." Ewing Werlein enjoyed telling others how to conduct their lives and he always had an audience. On Sunday mornings after church services, Werlein often could be found in the auditorium of First Methodist surrounded by a small group of fellow Methodists, preaching his own narrow view of the state of affairs—in the world, in the nation, in his city, in the church, or in the schools. And people seemed to listen.[23]

Werlein, who once described himself as a "conservative conservative," lived up to his self-portrayal. No other elected public official in Houston in the 1940s and early 1950s exceeded Werlein's consistently vitriolic and vivid railings against anything not in agreement with his political outlook. The ultraconservative attorney was rarely capable of acknowledging the possible legitimacy of an opposite point of view. Examples of Werlein's intemperance abound. When a University of Texas student wrote an article in the *Daily Texan* in 1943 suggesting that Christianity had exerted a less than beneficial role in the political development of Russia under the czars, Werlein was outraged. He wrote university president Homer P. Rainey and demanded that the university take action against the "whippersnapper" who dared to express such an opinion, which was "so much stench in the nostrils of decent citizens." Werlein, who supposedly knew enough about the law to pass a bar exam, informed Rainey that the student had attacked "the religion of our country" and, therefore, the unfortunate young woman was legally "guilty of sabotage and sedition." The zealous Houstonian explained to Rainey that "freedom of speech does not extend" to criticism of Christianity.[24]

When President Truman suggested that the federal government might provide money to help indigent students go to college, Werlein called the idea a "wild-eyed scheme" and charged that it was Truman's personal attempt "to captivate and control the minds of our youth . . . to guide them into the devious and destructive ideology of the so-called fair deal and socialism." In 1952, when the Houston schools were grappling with problems caused by inadequate funds and facilities, Werlein was more concerned about other matters. He issued a memorandum to his problem-beset superintendent, Bill Moreland, asking him to purchase small United States flags, framed copies of the Bill of Rights, and placards imprinted with "In God We Trust." The latter two items were to be situated in a "conspicuous" location in all schools; the flags were to be placed in every classroom. Werlein added that Moreland should also see to it that "In God We Trust" was engraved in the cornerstone of new school buildings.[25]

In 1948, as president of the Houston school board, Ewing Werlein attacked federal aid to education, claiming it would end initiative and individuality. He classified such aid as a "pork barrel," a creator of "decayed societies," and charged that its advocates were "biased, mistaken, and ignorant of history." In that same year the Houston Community Chest ended its program of providing free lunches to indigent school children because it believed the school district should use federal money made available to it through the National School Lunch Act. Led by Ewing Werlein, the Houston school board's conservative majority rejected this proposal out of hand. Rather than accept federal tax money available for free lunches, the school board surprised the Community Chest by conducting its own fund drive. School board member William G. Farrington stated that the trustees refused the $575,000 government grant because the program threatened home rule of schools and "somebody has to start refusing [federal] subsidies sometime." Another conservative board member, Dr. Henry A. Peterson, explained that "it is not the school board's responsibility to provide for indigent pupils." Werlein denounced the free lunch program as "useless," uneconomical, and "unworkable." It would mean federal agents would run the school cafeteria. He added, "If we're ever going to stop this iniquitous practice, we must have courage or we're going right on into a welfare state." Referring to the needy children, Werlein explained that "you can't teach them this fundamental lesson of self reliance and . . . at the same time make them dependent upon a federal dole. . . ." Werlein neglected to add that you cannot teach them much else on a hungry stomach. The school board, which needed approximately $30,000, refused to use part of the $271,000 in lunch room profits to subsidize its own free lunch program and, instead, purchased an ad in the Houston *Post* in an unprecedented effort to solicit private contributions. The ad said, in part, "The board feels that federal grants mean federal control and feels that this is only one step in the direction of federal control of education. Self reliance is the strongest lesson we can teach our youth." Houstonians failed to respond and the city's needy children went without a noon meal. This remained so until 1967, when the Houston schools capitulated and finally accepted federal aid for lunches.[26]

The board received strong support from Houston's conservatives for its stand. Mrs. J. Edward Jones, later a member of the Minute Women, wrote the board that she was outraged at the suggestion of free lunches for anyone, regardless of where the money was to come from. Emphasizing the humiliation sure to result from such handouts, Mrs. Jones declared that other children pointed to pupils getting free lunches and shouted, "I paid for your lunch today!" She charged that when the schools of Houston make "beggars" of children, then "this rich community becomes the laughing stock of the East." Ross Biggers, husband of the future head of Houston's Minute Women, appeared before the board to warn that a federal Civil Rights Commission's report had suggested removal of federal money from any community supporting racial segregation. Biggers, frantically waving a pamphlet, warned that if the district took the lunch funds "it'll mean black children will be going to school in our white schools. It says so right here!" The board received other letters that generally stated that the school district was an educational not a charitable institution. This specter of federal control so terrified the district's conservatives that they refused to purchase meat that required federal inspection. This practice resulted in at least one incident where the district unknowingly purchased horse meat from a company.[27]

In 1949, Ewing Werlein joined with his close friend, Dr. Henry Peterson, in a successful effort to ban further use of Dr. Frank A. Magruder's *American Government* as a civics textbook. The book, adopted by the state in 1928 and used by the district since 1933, was the most widely read textbook in its field. One particular paragraph offended Werlein. A fine print footnote referred to the postal system, federal electric power projects, and progressive taxation as "bits of socialism" and said, "Public free education and old age assistance are examples of communism . . . to each according to his need." Since the book held that the public school system and postal system were worthwhile, Werlein feared this might mislead children into thinking socialism and Communism were beneficial. "I haven't read the rest of the book," Werlein admitted, "but to me the one paragraph cited plants an insidious seed in the minds of students." Hubert Mewhinney, a *Post* columnist who sometimes exhibited views at variance with his newspaper's editorials, commented that "if so shrewd and experienced a man as Ewing Werlein took ten years to catch on to the meaning of that paragraph, the guileless little high school students never caught on at all."[28]

After the board dropped *American Government*, a large group of the district's civics teachers urged the board members to reconsider their action, but they refused. Ewing Werlein explained to the teachers that this was a matter beyond their competence. "School teachers often are idealistic theorists," Werlein said. "They are often duped and misled. They are sheltered in a classroom and are not often exposed to the chicanery of the outside world." Despite the Houston board's action, the Texas State Board of Education readopted the book for a new six-year period as the sole state-approved civics text. The Houston Independent School District thus had to pay for a substitute textbook out of its own funds if it refused to use Magruder. Unfortunately, because of an already inadequate budget, the school board could afford to buy only one set per classroom of an allegedly more patriotic civics book, which resulted in only one book for every five students. Even J. O. Webb admitted that the ban on Magruder's book "would wreck our civics program."[29]

The senior partner of the publishing firm that printed *American Government* (Charles E. Bacon of Boston) responded to the attack by saying, "You might call the Houston board totalitarian itself in banning the book." One year after the schools dropped Magruder's book, a textbook committee consisting of seven teachers examined four other civics books adopted by the state. The committee endorsed Magruder's book as its unanimous choice and declared the other three textbooks unsuitable. The teachers added that Magruder's book appealed to the students' patriotism with references to the achievements made by "democrats" in the American capitalistic system. The request fell on deaf ears. Board member William Farrington told the teachers the entire book failed to meet his personal standards. The board refused to accept the book despite the wishes of the district's educators and the lack of adequate funds to purchase alternative texts.[30] Accordingly, HISD teachers went without a standard civics textbook for five years, until Magruder's was edited to the satisfaction of its Texas critics in 1954. During that period, some of Houston's government teachers opted for John T. Flynn's right-wing books, especially *While You Slept*, which Hugh Roy Cullen had made available free of charge.[31]

The federal lunch aid program controversy returned in the spring of 1951 during the campaign to elect three new members to the school board. The election vividly illustrated the emotional atmosphere in Houston. Most of the candidates competed with each other in vowing to oppose federal aid. Letters to the editor in Houston's major dailies supported the candidates who attacked the free lunch program.

Carl Victor Little, a fearless columnist for the Houston *Press* and an opponent of the Red Scare, spoke for Houstonians tired of the school board squabbles and the controversy about federal aid. Little wrote that he favored acceptance of the federal program and that if anyone "due to colossal stupidity" wanted to brand him a "socialist, a communist, or an SOB first class" because of this then "that's their privilege and to hell with it." Little reminded his readers that when the board first discussed federal aid in 1948 it turned the money down "with dispatch, amid spread-eagle oratory the upshot of which was that Texas would feed her own." Little wrote that children were going hungry in Houston's schools and said, "Uttering the sacred and revered name of Texas, and shouting for states rights and damning the encroachment of the federal government simply has fed no hungry mouths . . . [it] has been found on several occasions that ham sandwiches do not fall from heaven, like the manna did in the days of old, when the magic name of Texas was uttered." To his fellow Houstonians he declared that states' rights had never fed school children; "in fact it has caused quite a few to become undernourished."[32]

With the growth of the Minute Women, the anti-Communist conservatives became even more active in the schools. The Minute Women launched an attack in the schools on the United Nations and its agencies with the aid and encouragement of the Mills machine and their friends on the school board. The primary target of this assault was UNESCO, which the Minute Women accused of spreading un-American ideas in the public schools and of fostering antinationalism and a belief in world government among school children.

In March 1952, the Minute Women mailed reprints of Idaho Republican congressman John Wood's speech published in the *Congressional Record* titled "The Greatest Subversive Plot in History—Report to the American People on UNESCO" to all teachers and administrators in the Houston Independent School District. To make certain that school personnel understood the main points in Wood's speech, the Minute Women printed circulars that listed the major charges against UNESCO and used high school students to distribute them to their teachers and classmates. The circular charged that UNESCO taught children to be disloyal to the United States, "poisoned" the minds of teachers by getting them to suppress American history and discard logical teaching methods, and sought the corruption of morals through sex education courses.[33]

Working in concert with the Minute Women, assistant superintendent J. O. Webb "responded" to their attack by requesting the return of all material from the high schools dealing with a contest held annually in Houston since 1926. The contest, sponsored by the American Association for the United Nations, awarded free trips to New York City and college scholarships to students making the highest scores on a competitive exam about the United Nations. Webb withdrew the material without asking his superior, Superintendent Moreland, who had approved the contest material only weeks before in a board meeting. Although Moreland was theoretically responsible for all decisions relative to the curriculum, the Mills machine demonstrated, through J. O. Webb, where the ultimate authority existed in the district. Not only did Webb arbitrarily withdraw the contest material, he also expunged UN material from the regular curriculum. For example, all reference books on the UN previously listed for students' outside study were deleted from school workbooks, and a debate exercise using the UN as a topic was eliminated from the ninth grade curriculum guide.

The school board eventually asked Webb to explain his actions after the board received several letters of protest. A letter from the Ministers of Christian Churches of Harris County expressed shock at the attitude of the school board and its administrators toward the UN contest. The letter singled out Webb and charged him with "national and racial bigotry." Webb defended his actions before the board. He claimed that the UN was a controversial subject because it had been attacked in the press, on the radio, and in Congress. The UN had divided public opinion; too many citizens believed it threatened freedom of religion and "the American way of life." Because of the controversy, Webb felt that study of the UN should be deleted from Houston's educational program.

Superintendent Moreland told the school board that he had read the contest literature and believed it suitable for school children. He noted that the contest had been held in Houston schools for years, since the days of the League of Nations, and that he personally approved of its use. Unimpressed by Moreland's argument, board member Dr. Henry Peterson warmly congratulated his friend Webb for his courageous actions. The board effectively killed the UN contest in Houston's public schools by asking Webb to head a committee to study the matter further. Webb's unauthorized actions and insubordinate behavior went unpunished.[34]

The school board's action pleased the Houston *Chronicle*. In a supportive editorial titled "Why Should Schools Have U.N. Contest?," the *Chronicle* charged that the UN was "only a step away from the weird one-worldism cult that has seized so many Americans." One-worldism, according to the *Chronicle*, "is contrary to the basic and traditional American concepts" and, thus, Houston's children should not be exposed to such "philosophies."[35]

The UN episode demonstrated to the supporters and members of the Mills machine the practicality and potential usefulness of the Red Scare as a weapon to preserve their power within the school system and to use against their liberal opponents. Not only did the pro-Mills faction of school personnel share the same world view with Red Scare groups such as the Minute Women, it also perceived that Red Scare tactics would be useful in its struggle with the anti-Mills or "liberal" faction. A natural coalition evolved between the Mills machine, Minute Women, Committee for the Preservation of Methodism, Doctors for Freedom, and Red Scare activists from the American Legion.

In the fall of 1952, when four of the seven school board positions stood for reelection, this loose coalition solidified into a quasi-political party with a political manager, office, and a slate of nominees for the school board. Calling themselves the Committee for Sound American Education (CSAE), Virginia Biggers, Minute Women chair, and three other Minute Women leaders, Virginia Hedrick, Faye Weitinger, and Mrs. J.

Edward Jones, met in the office of attorney John E. Price, Sr., with other prominent conservatives to choose four candidates.[36]

In its attempt to maintain the status quo for the business manager's group and ensure the continuation of ideological orthodoxy, the CSAE selected four candidates with solid anti-Communist credentials who would appeal to the patriotism of Houston's voters. The CSAE chose school board incumbent Dr. Henry Peterson to head its slate. Dr. Peterson was company physician to the Houston Lighting and Power Company and a close friend of W. Alvis Parish, the power company's president and a member of the Houston power elite's outer circle. Peterson was also closely allied to the business manager's machine. Aubrey Calvin, an insurance salesman, joined him on the slate. Both Calvin's and Dr. Peterson's wives belonged to the Minute Women. The other CSAE candidates, Dallas Dyer and Bertie Maughmer, were active in the Minute Women and aggressive and vocal supporters of Senator Joseph R. McCarthy.[37]

The conservative business establishment gave the CSAE crucial financial support and community legitimation. Overt supporters included Judge James A. Elkins, Douglas B. Marshall (partner and son-in-law of Hugh Roy Cullen), Hines Baker, W. Alvis Parish, J. S. Abercrombie, and Glenn McCarthy. The Houston *Chronicle* gave the conservative CSAE slate strong editorial support and extensive publicity.[38]

The liberal or anti-Mills group organized the Parents' Council for Improved Schools and nominated a slate of four candidates headed by incumbent school board member Dr. Ray K. Daily, an outspoken critic of the Red Scare and McCarthyism who had served on the board since 1928. Dr. Daily had worked for the woman suffrage movement and a variety of socially progressive programs for over forty years and was a well-known member of Houston's liberal community. Daily, a naturalized citizen and native Russian of Jewish descent, had been the target of bigots in earlier campaigns for the school board. A distinguished eye surgeon and one of the first female graduates of the University of Texas Medical School, in a 1943 broadside she was denounced by anonymous enemies as a "Russian born Red Jewess" under FBI surveillance for Communistic activities. Daily responded to the Red-baiting by denying that she had ever belonged to the CPUSA or had ever engaged in its activities. "I do not even know who the local communists are," Daily said, adding, "I would consider it bad taste to make an open denunciation on communist philosophy . . . when Russia is our ally, and doing an admirable job." She proceeded to win reelection in 1943 as such charges proved ineffectual until the 1950s.[39]

The Parents' Council selected Verna Rogers, an activist in the liberal faction of the Texas Democratic party, to run on the slate with Daily. Rogers was also an incumbent member of the board. Two lesser-known candidates, A. J. ("Jack") Tucker and James Hippard, completed the liberal slate. While Tucker considered himself a Republican and Hippard supported conservative Democrats, they joined with Daily and Rogers in opposing dual control and the power of the business manager's machine.[40]

By October 1952, two opposing slates of candidates for the school board prepared for an inevitably acrimonious and controversial campaign. Because of the importance Houstonians attached to the school board, however, nine other candidates soon filed as independents. Their entrance into the campaign brought a total of seventeen candidates to the ballot.[41]

The Committee for Sound American Education knew that the Parents' Council would campaign against the dual control administrative system and the power of the business manager's machine in the schools. It feared a campaign that would focus on such problems as teacher salaries, over-crowded classrooms, and an inadequate operations budget. Such a strategy would place the conservatives on the defensive since they represented the group that had controlled the schools for years. Clearly, the conservatives needed an issue with which their candidates could wage an aggressive attack. In 1952, at the height of the Red Scare, with Senator Joseph McCarthy filling the newspapers with charges of treason and political writers declaring the omnipotence of McCarthyism as an electoral tactic, the CSAE found a ready-made strategy. The leaders of the conservative faction quickly identified the real enemy for Houstonians: "Creeping Socialism."

The CSAE opened its campaign with a deluge of circulars, pamphlets, and newspaper advertisements that warned Houstonians of the threat to their children. The committee announced that "an educated citizenry will never succumb to Socialism or Communism. Keep America strong by keeping your schools safe from creeping Socialism and abortive Communism. Vote for Men and Women who believe education should be free from all 'isms' except Americanism." Other campaign circulars were equally sensational:

STOP CREEPING SOCIALISM!!!
Are You Aware
That there is a conspiracy spreading throughout the length and breadth of America which bodes evil to YOUR CHILD? That this conspiratorial plot is for the purpose of eradicating the fundamental principles of learning and the spiritual concepts upon which America was founded? Do not permit this conspiracy to take root in the Public Schools of Houston!

KNOW WHAT YOUR CHILD IS BEING TAUGHT!!
VOTE FOR MEN AND WOMEN WHO BELIEVE IN AMERICA
AND ITS PRECEPTS!! VOTE FOR THE COMMITTEE FOR
SOUND AMERICAN EDUCATION![42]

The CSAE told the voters that anti-American thoughts, either deliberately or through carelessness, had infiltrated the curricula and literature of the schools. The CSAE also warned that UNESCO, a favorite Minute Women target, would aid the spread of socialism in Houston's schools. While no one seemed to be able to explain exactly how UNESCO would accomplish this, the implications were that weak-minded teachers would read UNESCO literature and unwittingly pass the insidious propaganda on to students in their lessons. Creeping socialism could only be defeated by refusing federal aid to education, attacking UNESCO, and cleansing the school libraries of subversive literature. The Parents' Council responded that the school board should always be alert for subversives in the schools, but it claimed that no tendency toward socialism existed. Instead, the council charged CSAE with creating a false issue in order to undermine public faith in the Houston schools.[43]

Throughout October, Houstonians witnessed one of the most controversial school board campaigns in the city's history. Although the national presidential contest between Dwight Eisenhower and Adlai Stevenson barely eclipsed the school board struggle in voter interest in Houston, it too added to local tensions. For example, the Hobbys, who had called for a Republican presidential victory since 1940, were working hard to elect General Eisenhower. This included continuing their extreme anti-Communist rhetoric aimed at the Democratic party.

In a televised speech on October 21, 1952, Governor Hobby resorted to Minute Women–style tactics, implying that a Democratic victory could lead to a totalitarian state. Hobby declared that Eisenhower would "save our country from communism and the dictatorship that goes with communism, a dictatorship that can easily result from an administration too long in power." With this and many other like comments from such an influential opinion maker, the CSAE and the Minute Women cannot be accused of activity out of the mainstream of politics in 1952.

Jesse Jones noted with pleasure the aggressive work of Houston women in the 1952 campaign. He wrote a relative that ". . . people finally got aroused . . . and in a big way. Women have never been so aroused nor so active in an election." If the Minute Women were guilty of extremism it would not be unfair to suggest that the Hobbys, Jesse Jones, and Hugh Roy Cullen shared responsibility with them.[44]

Almost daily, conservative school board candidates grabbed newspaper headlines with sensational charges and countercharges, most of them dealing with educational literature. Dr. Henry Peterson attacked a sixth grade teachers' science curriculum booklet produced by the Houston schools' own science department. After close perusal of the conservation section, Dr. Peterson found the statement "Minerals do not rightfully belong to any one group of people or to any one nation." Peterson charged "socialism" and the school district agreed to order its science teachers to ignore the allegedly subversive statement.[45]

Aubrey Calvin, Peterson's running mate, found another suspicious text in the sixth grade curriculum. Calvin charged that *Lands Overseas,* a geography book, "eulogized" and tended to show Russia in a favorable light. He also alleged that his son had checked out of a junior high school library a book published in 1934 titled *Land of the Soviets.* That book, according to the outraged Calvin, "paints a wonderful picture of Russia." The school district answered the charge by announcing that *Lands Overseas* would be replaced by a more current text adopted by the state. *Land of the Soviets,* according to the district, had been removed months before from the library shelves.[46]

Having demonstrated to their own satisfaction that school literature provided a haven for leftist thought, the CSAE candidates hurled new charges against the schools. Aubrey Calvin declared that socialism "is coming in[to the schools] at a dead gallop. Americanism and American history are not being stressed enough." Dr. Peterson called for a better system of selecting textbooks, possibly using a rigid process of censorship, and promised such action if reelected with his CSAE colleagues. Peterson emphasized that censorship was necessary to eliminate subject matter "calculated to infect the fertile minds of youth with foreign isms." Peterson, an intelligent man with degrees from Johns Hopkins and Oxford University, may not have been entirely sincere in his rhetoric. Ray K. Daily later recalled that she and fellow physician Peterson often ate lunch together at Houston's Medical Arts Building. According to Daily, whenever she would scold Peterson for his and the CSAE's Red Scare tactics, he would laugh good humoredly and tell her not to take it seriously, explaining that it was just practical conservative politics concocted as a campaign tactic.[47]

The Minute Women candidates on the CSAE ticket also managed to earn their share of the headlines. Bertie Maughmer specialized in attacking federal aid to the schools and teamed with Peterson and Calvin in seeing "socialistic trends in textbooks." Dallas Dyer, chair of the Minute Women publicity committee, concentrated on warning the voters of the dangers of UNESCO. Dyer quoted Facts Forum's Dan Smoot as saying, "UNESCO is the most evil scheme ever fastened upon the American people." Dyer charged that UNESCO principles were subversive because they criticized nationalism. She feared that they might reach Houston children through their teachers. "The danger of UNESCO," argued Dyer, "is that it teaches children to think, not as citizens of America first, but as citizens of the world."[48]

Despite the efforts of the Parents' Council, Red Scare issues dominated the campaign. The Minute Women held public forums prior to the election to conduct discussion groups about "Reds" in the schools and the threat of UNESCO to religion and the family. Daily and Rogers were denounced as Communists by speakers at American Legion halls. "Letters-to-the-Editor" sections of Houston's newspapers became daily debate forums for both sides. One CSAE supporter wrote to the Houston *Post* that many of the parents supporting Dwight Eisenhower for president because he would cleanse Washington of "Reds" also supported the CSAE because it would do the same thing for Houston.[49]

As election day drew closer, the campaign for the school board intensified. Jim Hippard, a candidate on the liberal slate, opposed Dr. Peterson, the incumbent. His decision to challenge Peterson brought weeks of harassment to Hippard and his family. Anonymous opponents tried to force him out of the race by constantly harassing him at home with telephone calls at all hours of the night. Every telephone ring threatened his family with another message of hate or personal threat. Automobiles parked in front of his house late at night and shone spotlights through bedroom windows. Whenever friends visited the Hippards' home, cars would stop and persons inside of the automobiles could be seen writing down the Hippards' friends' car license plate numbers. The Hippards began escorting their child to and from school for fear she might be harmed by one of the candidate's unknown enemies. Hippard later recalled the campaign of 1952 as one of the most frightening things he had ever witnessed in Houston. Despite the threats, the liberal candidate stayed in the race to the finish.[50]

Houstonians watched the school board campaign with intense interest. Charges and countercharges filled the daily newspapers. The closer election day came, the more heated became the accusations. The campaign placed a tremendous strain on the staff of the Houston school district's curriculum department. It constantly had to spend time tracking down allegedly subversive materials in the schools and defending its curriculum programs. Two weeks before the election, the curriculum department received dozens of telephone calls from people denouncing something titled *Toward World Understanding*. No one, including the protesters, knew if it was a book, essay, short story, or poem. The department held conferences and feverishly searched for the item. Staff members called Rice

Institute and the Houston Public Library for help in the search, but to no avail. The next day, the staff learned that *Toward World Understanding* was the title of a series of UNESCO pamphlets. Dallas Dyer had charged at a public meeting that the pamphlets discouraged the teaching of patriotism and indoctrinated children with "socialistic and one-world ideas." She also implied that teachers in the school district had already been exposed to the UNESCO literature. The superintendent's office responded that not only did they not use the pamphlets but no one had even heard of them before Dyer made her charges.[51]

The accusations directed against the school district curriculum department produced one immediate result. Before the election in October, Superintendent Moreland, thoroughly cowed by the intimidating campaign swirling about him, announced a new program to emphasize the teaching of Americanism. Teachers of all classes, including mathematics, science, and physical education, were required to "create opportunities for the students to study the lives of great Americans and the great American documents." The program also expanded the civics courses to include a more extensive study of the benefits of the free enterprise system. Moreland ordered teachers to initiate classroom projects, conduct assembly programs, and use motion picture films, supplementary readings, and any other technique that could "point up the essential American values." Bill Moreland told reporters that he had called upon the teachers and principals to "mobilize our present strengths and build our future defenses . . . in the battle for the freedom of men's minds." The Hobbys' Houston *Post* praised the new program, calling it a "bulwark against Communism and Communistic lies."[52]

A week before the election, a public debate between all the candidates revealed the emotional tensions of the campaign. The audience clearly divided into two groups, evenly split between supporters of the two major slates. Speeches by the candidates brought forth violent verbal reactions from the audience. Speakers were interrupted by booing; shouts of "Name names or shut up" and "Let's get this out in the open" followed the candidates' speeches. One candidate's husband had to be physically restrained from attacking a speaker. At one point, the meeting's moderator excitedly waved what he alleged to be a subversive book and shouted that he had discovered it in the West University Elementary School library. Unfortunately, the book's title remained unrevealed as the meeting quickly broke up in turmoil with shouting and finger waving on all sides.[53]

Carl Victor Little of the Houston *Press* aptly described the situation with his own penetrating sarcasm. Little wrote that the citizens of Houston had become so upset by the activities of "candidates who are breaking their necks to serve the community for free, that we wouldn't be surprised if many voters go out on election day and get cockeyed drunk instead of voting." Little, tongue in cheek, claimed to have overheard one citizen declare in favor of General Douglas MacArthur for a position on the school board. "He got fired because he was against federal control — even of his own army. Old School Board members never die. They just fade away."[54]

On November 5, 1952, Houston's voters made their decision. The results of the election suggest that more complex factors motivated voting behavior than just the simple issues of creeping socialism or the dual control system. Dr. Peterson and Dallas Dyer, two active manipulators of Red Scare issues, won seats. Yet Verna Rogers and A. J. Tucker, two vocal opponents of the Red Scare, also won. The entire electorate could vote on all four positions so there was no factor of voting by district. The presence of nine other candidates not on either of the two slates complicates an analysis of the results. The other nine candidates, however, were almost equally split between conservative and liberal positions. The personal popularity of individual candidates was probably more important than other factors. For example, the CSAE's Peterson, who won easily, benefited from his incumbent status and was much more widely known than his opponent, a newcomer to school politics. On the other hand, the other successful CSAE candidate, Dallas Dyer, narrowly defeated the well-known incumbent, Ray K. Daily. Dyer's victory may be explained by the fact that, unlike the other CSAE candidates, she emphasized issues other than the threat of creeping socialism. Dyer aggressively attacked Dr. Daily's poor attendance record at school board meetings. Daily later admitted that the absenteeism charge probably contributed to her defeat. A skillful and clever campaigner, Dyer also may have benefited from her status as the only former school teacher in the race.[55]

The two winners on the liberal slate won despite being opposed by the two most outspoken Red Scare participants. Verna Rogers, an easy victor, enjoyed the obvious benefits of being an incumbent. Unlike Dr. Daily, her liberal colleague, Rogers' record provided her opponent, Bertie Maughmer, with no issues that she could easily exploit. Maughmer, who had a "wild-eyed" aura about her and who suffered, as one observer put it, from "foot-in-mouth disease," was no match for the more professional image portrayed by Rogers. A. J. Tucker, the other successful liberal candidate, handily defeated Aubrey Calvin. The insurance salesman leaned more heavily on the use of Red Scare tactics than any other candidate. Incumbency played no role in this race since the incumbent declined to run for reelection. Calvin's exploitation of the creeping socialism issue was clumsy and less subtle than his fellow candidates' tactics. Calvin also suffered from his ineptness as a campaigner, particularly when compared to his more politically talented opponent.[56]

The results of the Houston school board election fail to support assertions that the mass of Houston's citizens encouraged and supported the Red Scare. Nor do the results give credence to the belief that the use of tactics and issues commonly associated with the Red Scare assured electoral victory. The Committee for Sound American Education and independent conservative candidates, with their creeping socialism issue, polled only 41 percent of the total vote while liberal candidates attracted 59 percent. An examination of the 1952 school board election does suggest, however, that the Red Scare in Houston was a phenomenon of the press and community elite, with doubtful appeal at the grassroots level.[57]

Whatever the results imply about the effectiveness of Red Scare election tactics in Houston, the campaign itself indicated that conservative elites readily exploited and manipulated the Red Scare because of its perceived power to enforce conformity and, it was hoped, win elections.

The election failed to change the ideological alignment of the school board. The composition of the new board ensured continued bickering and controversy at future board meetings. The voting alignment would be unpredictable because of the independent behavior of two members who became "swing men" on different issues.

The two "nonaligned" members of the board were James M. Delmar and Garrett R. Tucker, who had been elected in May 1951. Delmar, director of industrial relations at Hughes Tool Company, was an ultraconservative lawyer whose principal mission at Hughes Tool was to keep the company's employees from forming an AFL-CIO–affiliated labor union. This was a job he performed exceedingly well as he succeeded in establishing a company union that lasted for over twenty years. In 1951, however, Delmar was an unknown quantity and actually managed to attract both conservative and liberal support. Houston's liberals later regretted their endorsement.[58]

Garrett R. Tucker represented another unpredictable vote on the school board. Tucker was a member of the prestigious law firm of Baker, Botts, Andrews, and Parish. For a brief period after his election in 1951, Tucker gave the impression of being a faithful conservative who would always vote in a manner satisfactory to Houston's right wing. Tucker denounced the federal lunch program as paternalistic and charged that it would weaken the moral fiber of the American people. He also conceded, however, that if funds could not be obtained by other means, then acceptance of federal aid was still better than allowing one child to go hungry. Later, Tucker began to exhibit a more moderate conservatism.[59]

While James Delmar and Garrett Tucker acted in an independent way, Red Scare activists in the Houston schools could count on two consistent votes, those of Dr. Henry Peterson and Dallas Dyer. Peterson was the senior member of the new board, having served since 1938. An ardent conservative, the grandfatherly appearing Peterson had the full support of Houston's Minute Women. Dallas Dyer's vote was also consistent. Dyer earned name recognition and gained a following before the election because of her many speaking engagements as a Minute Woman on the subject of constitutional government. Although she resigned her membership upon winning election to the school board, the Minute Women considered her vote theirs. She never disappointed them.

The anti-Mills and liberal groups in Houston rallied behind the two members of the board who could usually be counted on to fight against the Red Scare in the schools and to vote against giving more authority to H. L. Mills: Verna Rogers and Jack Tucker. A native of Philadelphia, Pennsylvania, Jack Tucker had lived in Houston since 1946. An engineer by training, Tucker worked as a statistician for Humble Oil and Refining Company. A Republican in national politics, Tucker actively and vocally opposed the Red Scare.[60]

Verna Rogers was one of the most vocal opponents of the Red Scare in Houston. A liberal Democrat and close friend of labor lawyer Chris Dixie, Rogers was a constant thorn in the side of Houston's conservatives throughout her years on the board. She worked with numerous civic and educational organizations, served as a member of the board of directors of the Harris County chapter of the Texas Welfare Association, and was active in the affairs of the Democratic party in Harris County. Rogers opposed racial segregation and led a movement to put blacks into personnel and programs of the YWCA. Facing a conservative community dominated by the Red Scare, Rogers stood by her principles while on the school board and never stopped speaking out against the activities of groups such as the Minute Women. The Houston *Post* belatedly praised her in an editorial after her death in 1971. "Mrs. Rogers never let fear of pressure groups weaken her leadership in any cause she believed to be right. . . . No one ever questioned her courage or her sincerity."[61]

The seventh member of the board, Holger Jeppeson, resigned after the new board members took office in January 1953. Henry Peterson attempted to replace Jeppeson with CSAE leader Aubrey Calvin, but instead the board chose Stone ("Red") Wells. The appointment of Wells, a lawyer and lobbyist for the Tennessee Gas Transmission Company, added a third solid conservative to the school board. Wells, a former football hero at Baylor University, concerned himself with the schools' athletic programs and usually followed the lead of Henry Peterson when voting on controversial matters not related to athletic policy.[62]

Thus, the new school board began 1953 with three conservatives supported by the Red Scare coalition who held a tenuously dominant position of power. Two members, Garrett Tucker and James Delmar, though more independent than the others, could usually be counted on to support the conservative positions of Peterson, Dyer, and Wells. With this alignment, the Mills machine remained safe and intact. The Red Scare coalition could now turn its attention to other problems in the schools that had been postponed because of concern over the election.

Interest in school affairs intensified in 1953. With Dallas Dyer on the board working with Dr. Henry Peterson, the Minute Women and their allies made board meetings one of the city's top entertainment attractions. Carter Wesley, the publisher of the *Informer*, a small Houston newspaper with a largely black readership, attended most meetings at that time and watched in amazement. After observing a typical board meeting, he wrote that the Minute Women poured into the room early to get front-row seats and by the time the meeting began they had two-thirds of the chairs occupied. He noticed that at the mere mention of Delmar's, Peterson's, and Dyer's names the Minute Women would applaud. They also wildly applauded nearly anything those officials said or did throughout the meeting. He also wrote that the conservative board members "played up to their audience from time to time, and one felt that most of what they said was directed to the approval of the Minute Women. . . ."[63]

It was evident at these meetings that the Minute Women and other conservatives wanted to remove Bill Moreland as superintendent. The weak Moreland, however, did not frighten the Houston women nearly as much as the new deputy superintendent, George W. Ebey. His removal became the Red Scare groups' chief project for 1953. Their efforts to drive him out of Houston would symbolize the power of the Red Scare at its peak in Texas' largest city.

SEVEN

THE VICTIM IS A SYMBOL
THE GEORGE W. EBEY AFFAIR

*What am I suspected of? As far as I know, I have committed no
crimes, but perhaps you have a secret list of actions which have
not yet been revealed as crimes but which will be in good time.
How do you avoid committing crimes of whose existence you are
ignorant? How do you purge yourself of sins which could only
exist in the future?*

—Clement Archer[1]

Henry Peterson and Ewing Werlein first became irritated with Bill Moreland in 1951. Although half-hearted and ineffectual, Moreland's attempts
to lessen the Mills political machine's power within the schools displeased
the business manager's friends. The growing intensity of the Red Scare
further exacerbated the relationship between Moreland and the board's
conservatives. After the United Nations contest incident in the spring of
1952, Peterson and Werlein declared that Moreland was "too weak" for
his job and should be replaced. Moreland's "weakness," from the conservatives' point of view, was evident by his moderate political stances
rather than his ineffectiveness in relation to Mills. Moreland's support
of the UN contest also convinced the conservatives that the superintendent was "ideologically undependable."[2]

Bill Moreland, a decent, sensitive, and soft-spoken man, was a sheep
among wolves in his position as head of Houston's public schools. One
friend characterized Moreland as "one of the loneliest men in Houston"
because of his isolation from the conservative power base. He was in an
impossible position with Mills in control and Ewing Werlein and Henry
Peterson backing Mills. He disagreed with the ultraconservative school
activists, but he could not stomach confrontations, so he often appeared
passively neutral, which to the conservatives was almost as bad a sin as
opposition. One observer recalls that no one could be an effective administrator in those circumstances. "You had to have a jelly fish in there to
be acceptable to the Mills crowd."[3]

In May 1952, with Moreland's contract due to expire on June 20, the
school board offered him his former position of deputy superintendent.
Moreland refused the demotion and vigorously defended his record.

Because board member James Delmar liked Moreland, he was able to persuade the other members to give Moreland a one-year extension on his contract "in order to prove himself." The board also approved Moreland's request to hire a deputy superintendent so that he could devote more time to board administrative and policy-making duties.[4]

One observer expressed great concern over the news that Moreland could hire a new deputy. Mrs. W. J. Edwards issued a pamphlet that was an ominous portent of future trouble for the school district. The pamphlet, *Can Houston Afford Another 'Liberal' School Administrator?*, charged that Moreland would choose a liberal to occupy the post and warned that Houston's conservatives should closely watch the situation. She urged citizens to contact the conservatives on the school board and inform them about the dangers of allowing liberals in the schools. Mrs. Edwards warned that the board should not accept anyone suggested by Moreland without thoroughly checking the candidate's background. The pamphlet, which circulated among the Minute Women, also expressed the fear that Moreland would select a deputy from outside the Houston school system, perhaps even from outside Texas. Such an appointee would have no allegiance to the Mills machine and might even be an adherent of federal aid to education, racial integration, and progressive education. Whomever Moreland selected, Houston's Red Scare activists had served notice that the new deputy superintendent would have to be a conservative to their liking. Moreland chose to ignore this advice.[5]

Despite the ominous tone of Mrs. Edwards' pamphlet, Superintendent Moreland decided to conduct his search for a distinguished educator without regard to political beliefs. At the same time, Moreland made a decision that assured the hostility of the Mills faction. He concluded, after reviewing local candidates, that he would prefer to hire someone from another state who was "wholly unattached and unacquainted" with the Houston school system.[6]

Moreland's plan to bring in an outsider to Houston's schools was an idea not in keeping with the traditional localism of the district. The conservatives would automatically perceive an outsider as a threat to their control of the schools. Nonetheless, in the spring of 1952, Moreland notified leading universities and placement officers across the nation of the search for a deputy. The district received dozens of files, with Oregon's George W. Ebey among them. Moreland soon eliminated all others and selected Ebey as the prime candidate because of glowing recommendations from Stanford University and, more important, from Teachers' College, Columbia University. Moreland also received favorable comments and evaluations from a list of school administrators who had previously supervised Ebey's work. On that basis Moreland decided in July 1952 to contact Ebey, who was with the Portland, Oregon, schools, and offer him the job with at least a one-year contract. Moreland told Ebey that he believed the school board would support a three-year contract but emphasized that any such action would be subject to its approval. Ebey decided to go to Houston to acquaint himself with the community and the school system before making a decision.[7]

Ebey traveled to Houston in July 1952 for an interview with Moreland and the school board. When Moreland introduced Ebey to the board, he stated that "he was unusually well-qualified from the standpoint of experience and background." Holger Jeppeson and Henry Peterson were absent from the meeting, but Ebey favorably impressed the five other members. At the urging of James Delmar, the board unanimously agreed to offer the position to Ebey.[8]

Ebey learned from some teachers, however, that Houston's educational climate was highly politicized, so he decided to return to Portland to contemplate the offer. Before leaving Houston, he told Moreland that he would accept the job if he could sign a three-year instead of a one-year contract. After informal discussions with several board members, Moreland later telephoned Ebey on July 23, 1952, and promised him a three-year contract. He explained, however, that this could not be made official until the next board meeting on August 18. Because of Moreland's assurance that he would receive a three-year contract, Ebey agreed to come to Houston.[9]

Armed with a three-year contract, Ebey felt secure enough to make the long move from Portland, Oregon, to Houston, Texas. The deputy superintendent's job in a large and expanding city school system placed him one step closer to his goal of being superintendent in some other district. In George Ebey's view, the positive aspects of career advancement clearly outweighed the risks involved in going to Texas. This optimistic view changed in a matter of months as Ebey's arrival in Houston initiated a year-long Red Scare controversy in which he became a symbol for the diverse "evils" Red Scare activists fervently opposed.[10]

An ambitious and talented man, George Ebey was forty-five years old, married, and father of two children when he came to Houston. Born in San Jose, California, in 1907, Ebey's youth typified the "all-American, boy-next-door" image of the high school hero in the 1920s. At San Jose High School, young Ebey became head cheerleader, star athlete, sports editor of the school newspaper, and campus leader and, despite these extracurricular activities, graduated as valedictorian of his senior class. In 1924, after high school graduation, Ebey entered San Jose College where he continued his successes as a student. He played on the varsity football and basketball teams, served as a cheerleader, acted in college plays, was a debater, and performed as an all-around campus leader. In short, George Ebey personified the American Dream of pre-Depression America. In 1927, he entered Stanford University, the alma mater of another symbol of the 1920s, Herbert Hoover.

At Stanford, Ebey majored in economics with a minor in English and speech while working his way through college in such diverse jobs as messenger for a railway freight office and gas station attendant. After graduating with a fine academic record in 1929, he began work with a fruit cannery in California. After two years, despite a promotion offer from his company, George Ebey decided that teaching was his real love. In 1931 he returned to Stanford and earned his master's degree in education one year later. Upon completion of his training at Stanford, he accepted a job at the Kamehameha School in Honolulu, Hawaii, where he remained until 1937.[11]

While in Hawaii during the Depression, Ebey exhibited a decidedly pro–New Deal frame of mind. His fellow teachers considered him a liberal and "left of center" but never questioned his loyalty. Spain was in the throes of a terrible civil war at this time and Ebey became interested in the "Republican" or Spanish Loyalist cause against the army of General Francisco Franco. He joined the local chapter of the Medical Aid Fund of the American Friends of Spanish Democracy, became its secretary, and sent out appeal letters that raised $212 for the support of the fund's six hospitals in Spain.

In 1936 Ebey again demonstrated his liberal views by reacting to a rash of teacher loyalty oaths passed by the legislatures of several states. He wrote a letter to the Honolulu *Advertiser* questioning the motive behind such oaths, asking why teachers should be singled out. Ebey declared that these oaths were symbolic of the type of nationalism that caused the First World War. Such nationalism, Ebey argued, was running rampant in Germany, Italy, and Japan. He added that a legislated loyalty oath could never adequately express his strong feeling for his country, a feeling "which transcends ostentatious flag waving Americanism."[12]

In 1937 Ebey left Hawaii to earn his doctor of philosophy degree in education, first working at Stanford and finally receiving his degree from the Teachers' College of Columbia University in New York City in 1940. Ebey's association with Columbia's Teachers' College would haunt him in Houston. The city's Red Scare activists considered Columbia University to be the center of progressive education. J. B. Matthews, a prolific writer of extreme anti-Communist tracts, would later refer to Teachers' College as the "Mecca" for this "insidious" philosophy. "From [Teachers' College]," Matthews wrote, "there spreads across the entire land the intellectually envenoming and morally disintegrating view that how-to-teach is more important than what-to-teach and how-to-learn more important than what-to-learn."[13]

Before his graduation from Columbia, Ebey became an instructor of education at Arizona Teachers' College in Tempe, Arizona. In Arizona Ebey was known to his colleagues as a believer in progressive education and a vocal supporter of Franklin D. Roosevelt. His ideas frightened no one, however, nor did anyone question his loyalty.[14]

Thus, before 1952, Ebey had lived the life of a typical young educator climbing the academic and professional ladder, rung by rung, toward the top. Nothing in his background gave the slightest indication of his being anything but a moderate New Deal liberal, a position shared, apparently, by the majority of American voters if FDR's massive electoral victories are any indication.

In 1942, George Ebey's career was interrupted by the onset of World War II. He volunteered for the army air corps and received a commission as first lieutenant. After graduation from officers' school, Ebey's talent and accomplishments in handling a variety of administrative jobs soon attracted the attention of his superiors in Washington, D.C. In July 1944, the army promoted Ebey to major and assigned him to be a staff planning officer for the army air corps in the nation's capital.

As a staff planning officer in "A-5" (long-range strategic planning) Major Ebey served under the direct supervision of General Lauris Norstad on General Henry H. ("Hap") Arnold's personal staff. He prepared numerous important plans relating to the size, composition, organization, and training of the peacetime air force. This work necessitated strict secrecy and Ebey was subjected to a strenuous security check. One of Ebey's staff papers won special praise from General Norstad and the excellence of Ebey's overall staff work earned him the Legion of Merit, awarded to him by command of General Arnold.[15]

After the war, George Ebey returned to Stanford, where he worked as a lecturer until September 1946, when he became a professor of secondary education on the faculty of Chico State College, a small school in northern California. Ironically, in light of his experience later in Houston, Ebey left Stanford at the request of the chairman of the Department of Education because he thought Ebey was too conservative for Stanford's experimental education programs. Nonetheless, the education department thought highly of Ebey's professional skills and found him the position at Chico.

The first tinge of controversy in George Ebey's career occurred while he taught at Chico State. In 1947 a grand jury investigated a marriage and family relations course being conducted in the Chico High School. The Tenney Committee, controversial California state Senate model of the federal House Un-American Activities Committee, subsequently investigated the textbooks used in the course and denounced them as "communistic." The committee's chairman, Jack B. Tenney, labeled the course "filthy sex education." At the time, George Ebey served as a curriculum adviser for the Chico public schools and his name became associated with the investigation. Even though the grand jury found absolutely no evidence indicating that Ebey had anything to do with the textbooks or the course, the mere fact that he was mentioned in the controversy provided ammunition for his enemies later in Houston.[16]

A much more significant affiliation was Ebey's membership in the American Veterans' Committee. Formed in January 1944, the AVC was for GI's returning from the Second World War a progressive alternative to the older, more conservative American Legion and the Veterans of Foreign Wars. Its motto, "Citizens First, Veterans Second," reflected its founders' view that the veterans did not want special privileges, they wanted a better society. At its peak, the AVC could count 100,000 members. Although this figure paled in comparison with the American Legion's more than two million, the AVC could boast of a high-profile membership that included Ronald Reagan, Senator Henry Cabot Lodge, General Henry ("Hap") Arnold, Franklin D. Roosevelt, Jr., Merle Miller, Congressman Jacob Javits, Douglas Fairbanks, Jr., Dean Rusk, and future Supreme Court justice Arthur J. Goldberg. Influential columnist Walter Lippmann served as a founding adviser. At its 1946 national convention, the AVC issued a list of positions and goals that revealed its politically liberal outlook. The organization called for international control of atomic energy, cooperation between the United States and the Soviet Union, a guaranteed annual wage, and an end to discrimination against labor unions, blacks, and Asian-Americans.[17]

George Ebey's deep involvement in the AVC eventually led in 1947 to his election as chairman of the important California state organization, which had a membership of twelve thousand veterans. As chairman, Ebey actively sought to promote the AVC cause. Under his guidance the California chapter lobbied for state public housing programs and initiated an antidiscrimination campaign that featured a "racial and religious cooperation week." In April of 1947 Ebey, as AVC California chairman, addressed the National Conference of Social Work in San Francisco. His speech, later published in the *Social Service Review*, denounced bigotry and racism of all kinds, attacked the growing "red mist of hysteria" as a threat to liberty, and called for a strengthening of the United Nations' police powers in order to ensure world peace.[18]

Ebey's affiliation with the AVC and his own social and political ideas as stated in his address to the social workers provided the basic elements in the charges made against him by Houston's Red Scare activists. That he belonged to liberal organizations and publicly advocated progressive social programs might have been sufficient grounds in themselves for an attack by Houston's conservative establishment. The essential problem of his involvement in the AVC was compounded, however, by an internal struggle within the organization between Communist and anti-Communist members.

With the onset of the Cold War and coming of the Red Scare, the AVC's conservative faction initiated a purge of leftists and Communists in 1947 that threatened the existence of the veterans' group. Ebey, as California chairman, tried vainly to hold his state chapter together by working with a neutral faction within the organization called "Build AVC" that attempted to mediate between the Communists and anti-Communists. Nevertheless, the CPUSA members were eventually purged. Ebey later explained that at the time he believed the Communists could be controlled and that they should be allowed to remain in the organization. He feared that allowing the domination of either faction would destroy the AVC and its program. Nevertheless, he only succeeded in winning the enmity of both sides in the struggle. The Build AVC position was analogous to the position a large number of other non-Communist Americans had taken in the early postwar period concerning relations with the Soviet Union. As late as 1947 George Ebey and many other loyal Americans still believed in the possibility of peaceful coexistence between the Communist and non-Communist worlds and his activities with the AVC reflected this hope. Nonetheless, by 1948 Ebey had decided to withdraw from the fratricidal battle in the AVC. A job offer from Portland, Oregon, gave him his opportunity.[19]

George Ebey's relocation to Portland in 1948 removed him from the AVC struggle but not from so-called controversial activities. While at Portland, he joined the Urban League, an action that stemmed from his belief in racial equality. As assistant superintendent, he worked with a special education program, cosponsored by the Oregon State Department of Labor and the Urban League, that established racially mixed classes in select schools. The program drew praise from religious, business, and educational organizations in Oregon. Ebey's direct association with the intercultural program and its emphasis on harmonious race relations in the classroom later led some Houstonians to fear that he might seek to promote racial integration in Houston.[20]

By the time Bill Moreland persuaded Ebey to come to Houston in the summer of 1952, the educator had compiled a record of activities and beliefs that made him an easy target for the Red Scare. Moreland selected Ebey because of his impressive recommendations from Columbia University and his extensive administrative experience. Moreland had no idea that the deputy superintendent's past harbored elements of possible controversy. Actually, Ebey's political beliefs were moderate and reflected the then current ideas of Cold War liberalism. His association with various liberal organizations indicated a gregarious personality and ambition and reflected his professional view that educators need to be community-oriented. George Ebey was a typical "joiner," an ambitious educator who happened to subscribe to a New Deal–style political philosophy. His background alone would not have been particularly important, except that Ebey, as he came to Houston in 1952, entered a city in the grip of a Red Scare. The combination of Houston's Red Scare climate and George Ebey's liberal background made confrontation inevitable.[21]

When Ebey accepted Dr. Moreland's offer, it seemed to be a major step forward in his career. Ebey never thought, even after his first trip to Houston, that he would become a symbol to be attacked by those in Houston caught up in the Red Scare. In April of 1952, however, three months before his departure for Houston, George Ebey gave a prophetic speech to the general session of the North Central Association in Chicago. As he discussed curriculum improvement in public schools, Ebey digressed for a moment and stated, "In almost every community in our country there are members of the crackpot fringe ready to take a vicious swing at public education. Frequently they are aided and abetted by elements which fundamentally are not interested in public education." Within three months, Dr. Ebey's personal experiences in Houston would attest to the truth of that statement.[22]

Red Scare activists in Houston immediately noted Dr. Ebey's appointment. In August 1952, a few days prior to Ebey's arrival in the city, Mrs. W. J. Edwards circulated a mimeographed booklet titled *We've Got Your Number, Dr. Ebey.* Bitterly attacking Ebey, the booklet charged that Bill Moreland had hired a liberal and highly controversial educator from out of state. Edwards claimed that Ebey had been a "storm center" in Portland because of his racial attitudes. The right-wing pamphleteer charged that Ebey had forced literature on the Portland schools that called for "the training of children in non-discriminatory behavior." She indignantly pleaded, "Will those communities which cherish their prejudices allow the introduction of intergroup education?" In Edwards' opinion, only Communists and fellow travelers espoused theories that supported such radical social experimentation. She reminded her readers that ". . . responsible citizens of both races in [Houston] prefer the traditional American manner of social living to that advocated by Socialists and Communists." Ebey was also condemned for being a member of the Urban League of Portland. According to Edwards, George Ebey would come to Houston with "two strikes against him": he was a controversial figure with a possible subversive background who already held dangerous racial ideas. The crudely produced pamphlet concluded with a promise that more information about Ebey's past would be forthcoming.[23]

Edwards and her allies received most of their information about Ebey's background from right-wing allies in Portland. A Red Scare activist in Portland named Virgil Holland was the chief source. Holland, a member of the Constitutional party, engaged in activities similar to those of the Minute Women, accumulating material about the past organizational memberships and associations of Portland school administrators. Holland specialized in harassing the public schools and Ebey's former boss, Portland superintendent Paul A. Rehmus. Rehmus reported to Ebey in February 1953 that Holland had written to Rehmus' past employers in Michigan asking for a list of the superintendent's previous group affiliations. Rehmus complained to his friend in Houston that "it is annoying to have a small man like Holland do this. . . ." As the attack on Ebey mounted, it became even more obvious that Holland and his associates were furnishing information to Houston's Red Scare activists.[24]

George Ebey arrived in Houston on the night of August 17, 1952, and was met at the airport by Bill Moreland and a reporter from the Houston *Post*. Ebey told the newsman that he was very pleased to be in Houston and that he felt his new position afforded him a "splendid professional opportunity." When the reporter asked Ebey to comment on Mrs. Edwards' pamphlet, Ebey replied that he would not run from people who wrote scare letters. He laughed at the charge that he would be a "storm center" and controversial in Houston. Dismissing Mrs. Edwards' attack, Ebey declared that he had left Portland with the highest of recommendations.[25]

Nevertheless, the Edwards pamphlet did puzzle Ebey when he arrived in Houston. His suspicions increased the next day when Moreland confessed that the local situation had become "uncertain" and that he had decided not to ask the board to extend Ebey's contract for three years. Moreland pointed out that he had a one-year contract himself and that they should both wait until a more propitious time to ask for extensions. Ebey agreed, but with great reluctance, particularly since his decision to come to Houston had been based on the security of a three-year contract. Moreland had perceived the situation correctly, however, because the conservative majority on the school board had agreed among themselves to give Ebey a three-year contract but reconsidered when Edwards began her attack.[26]

The Minute Women leadership noted Ebey's appointment with deep concern. To the Minute Women, his coming symbolized the threat of progressive education, racial integration, and a host of unwelcome ideas. They believed that with his Ph.D. from Columbia University, George Ebey was surely tainted with progressive education concepts. His association with integrated schools in Portland scared many of the members who were obdurate racists. Several of the Minute Women specifically disliked Ebey because he was an "outsider" and a Californian. Many of the Minute Women had been frightened by the right-wing propaganda magazines that charged that Communists had captured the Hollywood film industry. These booklets enjoyed wide circulation among the Minute Women members. Ebey's California origins allowed some Minute Women to associate him with this alleged Communist subversion of Hollywood. Another important reason for the opposition to Ebey centered around the fear that, as Moreland's chosen deputy, Ebey would be a threat to business manager Mills' control of the Houston schools.[27]

The Minute Women held a meeting a few days before George Ebey's arrival to discuss the Edwards pamphlet and to organize an attack. Armed with information from the pamphlet, several of the Minute Women decided to go to Ebey's first scheduled appearance before the school board and confront him and the board members with this "incriminating" evidence. Following their policy, however, they agreed to appear before the school board as individual citizens rather than as an organized group. Norma Louise Barnett and Anne Harrison volunteered to serve as the spokespersons. Mary Drouin, who was not a member of the Minute Women at that time but knew many of them, also appeared at the board meeting and presented her own charges against Ebey.[28]

Although the Minute Women denounced Ebey before the school board on that August night, the board seemingly remained unalarmed. No one, not even the conservatives, acknowledged agreement with the protesters. James Delmar, board president, admonished the women to gather more information before they tried to attack Ebey again. The next day, in a letter to Houston attorney and future federal judge Woodrow Seals, Delmar wrote that the Edwards pamphlet on which the Minute Women had based their attack was completely unethical. Bill Moreland defended Ebey in a letter to Norma Barnett, one of the Minute Women speakers at the meeting. Moreland called Ebey "a patriotic American of highest integrity" and stated that Ebey denied he had ever heard of Albert Maltz, had ever seen the controversial film that Barnett had cited, and denied responsibility for its being on a proposed list for use in the Portland project. A month later, the Reverend Kenneth Pope, himself no stranger to such affairs as a result of the Rufus Clement episode and the continuing machinations of the Committee for the Preservation of Methodism, informed Ebey that "such incidents are not entirely new in a rapidly developing community and in such times as these." He assured the new deputy superintendent that "you may therefore feel that you have already made a special contribution to the growing maturity of this community."[29]

News of the attack quickly reached Oregon. Portland school superintendent Paul Rehmus wrote Ebey, "Nothing has quite galvanized public opinion in Portland more than the attack on you." The Portland *Oregonian,* an independent Republican newspaper, attacked Edwards' pamphlet and stated that the incident typified the "sinister attacks that make the honest school administrator's life far from pleasant these days." The *Oregon Daily Journal,* in an editorial titled "Our Apologies to the People of Houston," pointed out that Ebey had a fine record as a citizen and educator and that his performance in Portland had been outstanding. The *Daily Journal* believed Ebey's Houston problems stemmed from his opposition to racial discrimination. The Portland paper declared, "We honor him for it." The presidents of the Portland unit of the Oregon Educational Association and the Portland Council of the Oregon PTA wrote letters to the Houston school board defending Ebey and lamenting that Portland had been shamed by its association with the smear.[30]

Bill Moreland was pleased by the reaction from Oregon. He wrote the superintendent of Portland schools that Ebey had lived up to recommendations and assured the Portland official that "I have not for one moment doubted the wisdom of our selection for a deputy superintendent." It appeared to Moreland that he and Ebey were safe and could now look forward to the work of getting the schools back in operation after the summer vacation.[31]

Unbeknown to both men, however, the relative quiet of the coming weeks was only the calm before the storm. Ebey's enemies were not going to give up that easily. Preoccupied with the forthcoming local and national election campaigns during the fall of 1952, they decided that little could be done immediately to persuade the school board to remove Ebey before the expiration of his one-year contract. While the Minute Women concerned themselves with other matters, however, they did not forget Ebey and the schools altogether. Adria Allen wrote the board in September 1952 to remind it about the threat of Communism in public education and "progressive-modern" teaching trends. She stated that she intended her letter to be a "preventive measure," hoping only to alert the board to possible dangers, and declared, "Let's keep our schools AMERICAN!"[32]

George Ebey heeded the warnings. Faced with an unfair choice between strict adherence to previously articulated views or long-term employment in Houston, the Californian, like most American liberals during the Red Scare, opted for job security. During the first two months of the school year, Ebey spoke at several meetings in Houston, always careful to pay his respects to patriotism and the "American Way." Speaking at the Houston Teachers' Institute early in September, Ebey interjected patriotic statements at every opportunity. He began to present views somewhat inconsistent with those of his AVC days, backing away from his belief in a strong and active federal government. Speaking to an assembly of regional school boards, Ebey pointed out that the federal government could deliver the mail and carry out other vital services, but ". . . we don't want Federal or even state government exercising final control in the education of our school children." He emphasized that "education . . . operates best under independent local boards of education." On October 22, for an appearance before the Pilot Club of Houston, Ebey used the manuscript of an old speech he had given back in Portland. For his Houston speech, however, he carefully scratched out a paragraph attacking Red Scare groups and Minute Women favorite Allen Zoll, choosing instead to avoid the subject entirely.[33]

These and Ebey's many other attempts to avoid controversy are examples of the Red Scare's insidious effect on freedom of speech. Countless other unknown Americans refrained from revealing their actual opinions or expressing anything at all. The effects of the Red Scare would have to include those millions of small instances when individual Americans chose to be quiet rather than risk saying something, anything, that another American might misinterpret or not like. Isolated and considered individually, those instances may have been relatively insignificant, but when multiplied many times over, the national effect was the substitution of banality and conformity for creativity and constructive dialogue.

George Ebey's cautious behavior was not only a response to the initial attacks against him, but also a result of that fall's school board campaign. As discussed in the previous chapter, the 1952 school board campaign heightened Houston's Red Scare atmosphere. The Committee for Sound American Education believed Red Scare techniques could effectively draw attention to its candidates. Imitating Senator Joseph R. McCarthy's tactics in the national presidential campaign, Houston's Red Scare activists gave the Communist subversion issue a local meaning that other Houstonians could not easily ignore. This anti-Communist rhetoric helped set the stage for another attack on Ebey by calling the attention of many Houstonians to the plausibility of a local Communist menace.

During the contentious turmoil of the board election, George Ebey performed his duties as deputy superintendent without further controversy. A telephone call on January 21, 1953, however, hinted an end to Ebey's tranquility. A reporter for the Houston *Chronicle* informed Ebey that the *Chronicle* had received an inquiry from the Associated Press asking if Ebey was in danger of losing his job. An Oregon newspaper had received anonymous phone calls asserting that Ebey would soon be dismissed. Bewildered, Ebey assured the *Chronicle* reporter that he knew nothing about any moves to have him fired.[34]

A few days after the telephone call, a new brochure appeared in Houston attacking Ebey. A six-page photostatted document, the pamphlet at first appeared unsigned, but the persistent Mrs. Edwards soon admitted authorship. She had delivered her latest work to all three major daily newspapers and demanded that they publish the allegations. Concerned about libel, the newspapers refrained from printing the material and, instead, notified the Houston Independent School District. Mrs. Edwards also sent copies to each school board member as well as to school officials in Portland, Oregon.[35]

The new report admitted Ebey had never been cited by any official agency as a Communist or as a member of a Communist front organization. It did reveal, however, that Ebey had served as chairman of the California American Veterans' Committee and that the California Un-American Activities Committee, headed by state senator Jack B. Tenney, called the California AVC "communist dominated" in 1948. Not only had the Tenney Committee referred to the AVC as Communist-dominated but Edwards also proclaimed that the West Coast Communist party newspaper, *Daily People's World,* had carried a news item reporting Ebey's selection as head of the AVC in California. Edwards reasoned that if a Communist newspaper carried an announcement of Ebey's election then the Communists must have elected him.

Edwards' brochure failed to mention that the Tenney Committee's report did not include the AVC among the alleged 172 Communist front organizations it listed in 1948. Nor did the federal House Committee on Un-American Activities list the veterans' organization as a Communist front. Critics have charged that the Tenney Committee had merely attempted to embarrass the liberal organization by briefly referring to it within the body of its report. Edwards' brochure also neglected to say that Ebey had left California and resigned his office in the AVC prior to the Tenney Committee investigation.[36]

Ebey reacted angrily to this second attack. He decided to write a formal denial, which he titled "Reply to Mrs. W. J. Edwards." Tracing his genealogy back to 1715, Ebey asserted that his family's patriotism was beyond reproach. He repudiated Edwards' sources (the Tenney Committee and *Daily People's World*). Ebey cited editorials by the Los Angeles *Daily News*, the San Francisco *Chronicle*, the Sacramento *Bee*, and other California newspapers criticizing the Tenney Committee. He also included other denunciations of Tenney issued by various California religious groups.

Jack B. Tenney had used McCarthy-type tactics and methods years before Senator McCarthy himself adopted them. Working only within California, Tenney copied the tactics of Martin Dies and the HCUA. His committee became the most notorious of the various state-level "un-American" legislative investigatory bodies. The San Francisco *Chronicle* once quipped, "A communist is any, who disagrees with Tenney." In 1952, Tenney ran for vice-president of the United States on Gerald L. K. Smith's Christian Nationalist ticket with General Douglas MacArthur as the candidate for president. MacArthur never accepted or acknowledged the nomination.[37]

After criticizing Edwards' use of the Tenney Committee records in her pamphlet, Ebey defended his work in the AVC. Proud of his membership in the veterans' group, Ebey listed Henry Cabot Lodge, Harold Stassen, and other prominent Americans who were members of the organization. Ebey dismissed the use of the *Daily People's World*, arguing that it was obviously unreliable because it was a Communist party newspaper. He said that no one in California considered the paper to be factual or authoritative. This was somewhat beside the point, however, because the paper merely reported Ebey's election, which was, indeed, a fact.

After writing his defense and allowing his anger to subside, Ebey concluded that he and his attackers were only pawns in a larger game. He believed that someone had encouraged Edwards, as well as the Minute Women, to act as surrogates for Ebey's unknown enemies. Ebey realized that he only symbolized an obstacle to what Ebey believed his anonymous enemies really wanted—complete control of Houston's public schools. Ebey also believed that someone in Portland, Oregon, aided his accusers in Houston. The telephone call from the *Chronicle* in January asking about the rumors in Portland seemed to verify that. Also, the Edwards pamphlet contained material that could have come only from Oregon.[38]

After the board received the Edwards brochure in February, James Delmar asked Ebey to read his written defense in an open board meeting. Unfortunately for the deputy superintendent, he was asked to speak on the night the board had scheduled to vote on Superintendent Moreland's contract renewal. Ebey feared that bringing up his personal controversy might hurt Bill Moreland's chances for renewal. Out of deference to his boss, Ebey changed his plans minutes before the meeting and withheld his reply.

The school board subsequently held a closed personnel meeting to consider Moreland's future status. In an informal vote, held in closed session, only Henry Peterson voted against renewing Moreland's contract. In the public meeting following the closed hearing, Peterson voted with the rest of the board, including Dallas Dyer, to approve Moreland's contract for a new three-year period. The conservatives in the school district still preferred someone else in the superintendent's job, but James Delmar and Garrett Tucker favored Moreland. As long as Delmar served on the board he would never support a move to oust Moreland. The conservatives declined to make an issue of it as long as Moreland refrained from interfering with business manager H. L. Mills.

At the closed personnel meeting held to consider Moreland's contract, James Delmar made a surprise announcement that Ebey did not have to defend himself after all. Without further explanation, Delmar claimed that a friend of his "with the FBI" had checked Ebey's background and declared the deputy superintendent to be "clean as a whistle." Ebey listened with relief. Now that Bill Moreland had his three-year contract, Ebey also wanted to extend his contract in accordance with Moreland's original promise. Moreland preferred to wait until May, however, when the board would consider renewing Ebey's original one-year contract.[39]

Delmar's "clearance" of Ebey temporarily protected the deputy superintendent from further attacks. Nevertheless, the Ebey family grew restless under the constant harassment. The Houston job was becoming less attractive with the passage of each day. Ebey's wife, Leonor, a beautiful and intelligent woman of Hispanic descent, disliked the city and felt that the move had been a mistake. She longed for a return to the West Coast. A person with liberal political and social views, Leonor could not adjust to Texas or Texans, and the fringe group accusations against her husband made Houston all the more unbearable. Her unhappiness affected George, who was also tiring of having to defend himself. He began to think about seeking another job somewhere else. In the meantime, Ebey's troubles continued, only this time they did not involve the school board.[40]

In February 1953, the University of Houston's College of Education asked George Ebey to help conduct a conference for area school counselors. Ebey persuaded an old friend, Dr. William O'Dell, the dean of the College of Education at Stanford University, to appear as the main speaker at the conference. The counselors' conference provided the Minute Women with yet another opportunity to harass Ebey and the American Legion's John P. Rogge now joined the attack.

On February 10, 1953, Rogge sent a letter to University of Houston president W. W. Kemmerer to protest the appearance of Dr. O'Dell. Rogge charged that the Tenney Committee cited O'Dell as a cosponsor of a reception for Paul Robeson, the internationally known black singer and actor who openly supported the American Communist party. Rogge also protested the appearance of Dr. Henry N. Wieman, a professor of religion and philosophy at the University of Houston, and charged that the HCUA had cited Wieman for affiliation with Communist groups. He demanded that Kemmerer cancel O'Dell's and Wieman's appearances. A few days before the conference, Rogge also argued that local Methodist minister Durwood Fleming's lecture on premarital counseling would be "a dangerous business"—such sensitive discussions were best left to the privacy of the home.

Despite Rogge's charges, the university's conference went as scheduled and Dr. O'Dell gave his speech without further hindrance. When the Stanford educator arrived in Houston he told George Ebey that he had never sponsored, attended, or even heard of the reception for Robeson. He also did not know about the Tenney Committee citation, although he admitted that it was not surprising, as Tenney had compiled a tedious list of several thousand Californians whom Tenney had implied were fellow travelers. Rogge failed to continue the protest against Dr. O'Dell because he apparently just wanted to help build a case against Ebey. The Minute Women and their allies were not that interested in the counselors' conference; it just added more controversy to Ebey's reputation. The Minute Women left Ebey alone during the rest of the spring of 1953. They decided to wait to continue their attack until May, when the board considered contract renewals.[41]

While Rogge protested the counselors' conference at the University of Houston, Methodist participants in the anti-Communist movement were confronting their fence-straddling bishop, A. Frank Smith. The bishop, although as conservative politically as many of the CFPM members, rejected their more extreme viewpoints. His personal opinions, however, remained largely a private matter that he refused to express publicly. Criticized by liberals among the leaders of the national Methodist church for not denouncing the CFPM or other Red Scare groups, Bishop Smith now began to draw the ire of those on the ultraconservative right. Smith was finding it increasingly difficult to maintain his public position of neutrality. To Red Scare activists, neutrality was tantamount to treason. Early in 1953, as the pressure on Smith to take sides mounted, the bishop finally agreed to meet with a group of Houston's Methodist ministers and CFPM members. The CFPM people also intended to confront some of the ministers, such as Kenneth Pope, who they felt were on the wrong side of the Methodist anti-Communist movement. As one participant declared, ". . . we came down here to get some preachers' scalps."

At the meeting, however, the CFPM members directed their criticism at Bishop Smith. One person asked Smith why he had not taken a forthright stand in favor of the anti-Communists and declared, "It is time you got off the fence and came over on our side." The CFPM also wanted Smith to denounce his fellow church officials who had been affiliated with the Methodist Federation for Social Action. Smith retorted that most of the people in question had resigned from the MFSA and should not be persecuted for their former associations. A CFPM leader told Smith that they should have followed their resignations with public announcements against the federation. This statement left many of the CFPM leaders vulnerable to a similar criticism, however, and the bishop was quick to take advantage of it. He looked around the room and said, "There are men sitting right here in this room who were Ku Klux [Klan] members when I came to Houston [in 1922]. I never heard it publicly announced that they withdrew, but I'm not going to get up and call them Ku Kluxers now just because they were twenty-five years ago."

This declaration had the intended effect, as the tension "just dried up." Smith went on to say that the Methodist church was "a great church that is nation-wide in membership and interests" and that the CFPM members could not expect all of Methodism to reflect only the ideas of Houstonians. The bishop revealed that he had "scars" on his body that he would "bear to the grave" because he had refused to denounce the extreme anti-Communists. "And now you turn on me . . . and denounce me because I haven't come out against the other side," Smith said.

Having defended his church, the conservative Smith then cast blame in another direction. "The seat of what you men call the radical leftist movement is in Washington," the church leader charged. "I have voted the Republican national ticket ever since Woodrow Wilson," Smith declared. "The men here who voted to keep Roosevelt . . . and Truman . . . are far more responsible for . . . this thing you are deploring than any preacher. . . ."

Bishop Smith's tactic of reminding some of the CFPM leaders about their former Ku Klux Klan association and deflecting their accusations from the church to the national Democrats placated the laymen. Someone finally announced, "I guess we better go home," and the meeting ended. Some of the ministers present at this confrontation admitted that Smith had succeeded in relieving much of the pressure on the clergy. His statement about Roosevelt and Truman and the "radical leftist movement" was pragmatic. He succeeded in partially alleviating a local and immediate problem by displacing it with a more abstract and distant one about which the Houston Red Scare Methodists could do very little. A. Frank Smith once said, "I am a pragmatist if I can be one without sacrificing principle for expediency." In the matter of the Red Scare, Smith, an opponent of the New Deal, could be expedient without sacrificing his own idea of principle. The Red Scare in Houston's Methodist churches did not go away after this incident, but it did redirect its focus more toward national issues and less toward local concerns.[42]

While the Methodists continued to grapple with their problems, the Minute Women decided to deal with one of their few public critics in Houston: W. W. Kemmerer, the president of the University of Houston. Kemmerer had rejected John Rogge's demand that Dr. O'Dell be banned from the counselors' conference in February. Not only did Kemmerer spurn Rogge's demand, he bitterly denounced Rogge and identified him and the Minute Women as enemies of academic freedom and a danger to public education.[43]

Even Kemmerer, however, underestimated the Minute Women's influence. Unknown to him, in January 1953, several Minute Women enrolled in classes in the College of Education and the College of Arts and Sciences. Although the University of Houston was a private school controlled and financially supported by the city's power elite, including Hugh Roy Cullen, Gus Wortham, and Judge James A. Elkins, the Minute Women believed that the faculty and administration harbored "socialistic intellectuals." They were especially suspicious of the College of Education and feared that advocates of progressive education were indoctrinating future teachers. As one conservative declared, "The University of Houston is the Columbia University of the South. It trains the teachers for the Houston system in Progressive Education methods and in no other educational philosophy." As a result, the Minute Women began in the spring semester of 1953 to place "monitors" in certain classes to spy on university faculty members.

The university had the equivalent of an open admissions policy and welcomed the enrollment of older adults in search of a college education. This facilitated the Minute Women monitoring campaign since members could readily enroll in targeted classes. They especially favored summer school courses because of their brevity. The object, of course, was to listen to lectures and carefully note any political heresies. The tactic had the potential of creating an extremely troublesome problem for the university since any lecturer could easily be misinterpreted in a classroom setting. The common teaching technique of playing the devil's advocate, of taking positions not actually subscribed to by the professor so as to make a point or clarify an issue, was one example of an area fraught with potential misunderstanding. This was particularly true if the "observer" was hostile or already suspicious of the teacher in question. The university benefited, however, from an unanticipated ally. Some of the Minute Women, like their fellow classmates, were quickly bored by the dull drone of some professors reading old lectures from paper yellowed with age. Other Minute Women became disinterested when forced to contemplate lectures obfuscated by buzzwords. Some were discouraged by their inability to follow an abstract and technical discourse. In short, few had the intellectual capacity or patience to last a semester, so "drop-outs" were frequent.[44]

In March 1953, shortly after Kemmerer publicly denounced the Minute Women, Esther Nelson, an education professor, told one of her classes that she believed the Minute Women themselves were subversive. Unfortunately for Nelson, a Minute Women monitor heard her remark and duly reported it to Virginia Biggers. The Minute Women leader and her fellow officers decided to confront Kemmerer and demand that he force Nelson to apologize for the remark.

On April 11, Biggers and two other Minute Women met with Kemmerer in his campus office and demanded an immediate apology. Kemmerer promised that he would investigate and, if Nelson made the remark, he would ask her to apologize. After an hour of heated discussion, Biggers and her friends stormed out of Kemmerer's office, unsatisfied with his offer and insulted by his demeanor.

This meeting provided the excuse for a concerted attack on Kemmerer by Houston's Red Scare activists. The Minute Women initiated another of their highly effective letter-writing campaigns and flooded the office of Hugh Roy Cullen, chairman of the board of regents, with letters attacking the university's president. Unfortunately for Kemmerer, while the Minute Women pressured Cullen and his associates on the university board of regents, anonymous persons distributed to all campus organizations a twenty-four-page pamphlet titled *The Southern People's Common Program for Democracy, Prosperity, and Peace.* The pamphlet, published by the Southern Regional Committee of the Communist Party of the U.S.A., attracted the attention of the press, which played up the incident with front-page Red Scare headlines such as "Communist Pamphlets Flood Texas Colleges." The FBI got into the act by sending an agent to the University of Houston campus "to investigate," which in reality meant little more than walking around the grounds on a nice spring day. The incident, which was repeated on other Texas campuses (including the University of Texas), was much ado about nothing, but it only added to

Kemmerer's problems. Joe Worthy, a radio talk show host who served as the self-appointed broadcasting voice for Houston's Red Scare, urged his audience to "help us get rid of those Commies out at the University of Houston."

Hugh Roy Cullen and the men who were on the board of regents were power elitists who were not susceptible to public pressure and were unaccustomed to responding to demands from citizen groups. Unfortunately for Dr. Kemmerer, however, Cullen and his fellow board members, particularly his son-in-law, Corbin J. Robertson, and the powerful Judge Elkins, had already become dissatisfied with the president's administrative policies. The university's regents were displeased with Kemmerer's propensity for innovative but expensive programs, such as the new educational television station. Kemmerer's less than enthusiastic support of the university's growing intercollegiate athletic program also directly clashed with Corbin Robertson's views. Thus, for reasons totally unrelated to the Red Scare, the board of regents decided to fire Kemmerer. The Minute Women campaign, however, gave them a more emotional and simplistic excuse to explain their action.

Cullen summoned Kemmerer to a meeting in his office on April 17 and showed the president large boxes filled with letters demanding his removal. Cullen then explained that he and the other regents had decided to "look for another president." He asked Kemmerer to resign, "for reasons of health," effective September 1, 1953. Kemmerer knew that to fight Cullen would be futile. He agreed to resign for "personal reasons." The delighted Cullen promptly promised Kemmerer that a campus building would be named for him and agreed to pay him two years' salary.

The university's student body and faculty protested the popular Kemmerer's resignation. Student strikes and demonstrations were threatened but Kemmerer himself diffused campus tensions with a conciliatory speech delivered to a student assembly. Aware that his forced resignation was actually the result of very definite and specific policy differences between himself and the board of regents and that the Minute Women campaign only provided the superficial excuse, Kemmerer accepted his fate. If he had fought the board of regents' decision, then he would have risked having Cullen use the Red Scare charges against him in public. By quietly agreeing to the decision, he avoided the taint of the Red Scare and possible blacklisting.[45]

The Kemmerer affair and the internal contentions within Methodism in Houston during the winter and spring of 1953 were provided an appropriate background by the Texas legislature in Austin. While Houston's Minute Women and their associates scurried about doing their work and

prepared for the inevitable confrontation with George Ebey, the legislators continued the work they had begun in previous legislative sessions.

Representative Marshall O. Bell, responsible for the Communist Control Act passed in the previous session, decided that the act's registration requirement was inadequate. The law, he thought, needed to be
strengthened by a provision allowing the issuance of general search warrants to seize "books, records, pamphlets, cards, receipts," and other
material of suspected Communists. As usual, Bell trotted Colonel Homer
Garrison out before the legislature to testify to the dire necessity of such
a provision, despite Garrison's admission a month later that "we don't
know of any . . . Communists in Texas."[46]

Representative Bell also submitted HB 21 to combine all current state
employee loyalty oaths into a single oath. The legislator from San Antonio included provisions in the loyalty bill that would also require authors
of public school textbooks to sign the oath. If the author was no longer
living, then the textbook publisher would have to file the oath for the
deceased. Not even the grave could hide a traitor. Bell's loyalty oath bill
passed both houses of the legislature in February 1953 with little discussion. For the next fourteen years, Texas state employees and college
students duly signed the loyalty oath. In 1966, Everett Gilmore, Jr., a part-
time music teacher at Dallas' El Centro Junior College, refused to sign
and was promptly fired. The American Civil Liberties Union subsequently
represented Gilmore in a class action suit to enjoin enforcement of the
loyalty oath. In 1967, a three-judge federal panel in Dallas declared the
oath unconstitutional, a decision that was later upheld by the United
States Supreme Court.[47]

The search warrant addition to the Communist Control Act ran into
legislative difficulty, however. Representatives William H. Kugle, Jr. (Galveston), Doug Crouch (Fort Worth), Edgar L. Berlin (Port Neches), and
Maury Maverick, Jr. (San Antonio) all fought against it. Kugle told his
colleagues that "we don't want to run roughshod over civil liberties in
chasing straw men." Edgar Berlin argued that the bill would "allow flag-
waving witch-hunters . . . to infringe on the basic rights of individuals."
Representative Crouch criticized Marshall Bell, declaring that he "imposes
upon the members of this House with his incessant array of bills which
are of doubtful constitutional validity." Crouch charged that Bell's introduction of Red Scare legislation was "a highly irresponsible endeavor and
immature in every respect."[48]

While legislators debated his search warrant proposal, the ever-
imaginative Bell introduced yet another Red Scare bill. Bell now proposed
to ban from the public schools all books that "discredit the family as an

institution, ridicule the Constitution on freedom of religion, scorn American or Texas history, and advocate the violent overthrow of the government." In addition, school officials would be forced to stamp in red ink
all books written by members of the CPUSA, Communist fronts, or other
subversive organizations. This new bill won praise from several legislators, including Joe Pool of Dallas and William Miller of Houston. Representative Miller was so inspired that he wrote his own Red Scare resolution. Miller, no doubt with one eye looking back home to Houston,
submitted a resolution calling for the Texas House to create a state un-
American activities committee patterned after the federal version. Miller
declared that Reds had penetrated "into the very heart of this state for
the purpose of subverting our people." Marshall Bell quickly enlisted as
a cosponsor of Miller's resolution.[49]

The proposed legislative anti-Communist actions won the immediate
endorsement of Houston's American Legion. Adolph Blieden, district
chairman of the Legion's own un-American activities committee, praised
the idea of a state committee. His praise was joined by Albert Brown, Jr.,
of Austin, state American Legion commander. While debate continued
in the Texas legislature over the need for new loyalty laws, FBI director
J. Edgar Hoover inadvertently helped the Texas Red Scare cause. In a
statement featured on the front page of Texas newspapers, Hoover told
the national wire services that "subversive activities across the nation have
materially increased" and that the CPUSA had become a "dangerous
shadow organization."[50]

Nevertheless, the various Red Scare proposals floating around the legislature continued to be attacked by representatives Crouch, Berlin,
Maverick, and Kugle as well as representatives "Barefoot" Sanders of
Dallas, Anita Blair of El Paso, A. D. Downer of Center, and others. This
group succeeded, with the help of Hulon Brown, a conservative legislator from Midland, in severely weakening Bell's textbook ban and labeling acts. Representative Brown persuaded the House of Representatives
to remove the red stamp provision and replace it with a requirement that
school officials merely post a list of such books in the schools. Representative Sanders, a future federal judge, succeeded in altering Bell's bill to
allow local school officials to decide if any books should be banned—an
authority they actually already possessed. Brown, arguing for these
amendments, stated that everything should be done to eliminate Communism "as long as we still permit free thought and free speech. I believe
[Bell's] plan would hurt more than it would help." Representative Downer
called it a "rabble rousing . . . McCarthyism type of legislation . . . that
will bring back the old book-burning regime of the Nazis." Bell's "red
stamp" bill, crippled by amendments and hamstrung by its opponents'

procedural maneuvers, failed to come to a final vote before the end of the regular session. Miller's un-American activities committee suffered the same fate. Bell's search warrant bill never left the Senate, although it would find new life in a future special session.[51]

By the first of May 1953, while legislators grappling with Marshall Bell's continuing Red Scare machinations were attracting headlines and the Kemmerer affair was quickly coming to a close, Houston's Minute Women made plans to renew their attack against another easy victim. Early in May 1953, the Minute Women allegedly held a closed meeting in which Virginia Biggers, Virginia Hedrick, and Faye Weitinger announced that John Rogge would file formal charges against Dr. Ebey at the school board's May 11 personnel meeting. They appointed two members to accompany Rogge to the board meeting and warned that no one was to know the Minute Women had any connection with Rogge's charges.[52]

George Ebey's enemies thus prepared for another attack. His opponents included members of the H. L. Mills machine within the schools as well as board members Henry Peterson and Dallas Dyer. One important incident revealed the supporting role played by these people. In April 1953, J. O. Webb mysteriously ordered a delay in the printing of the program for commencement exercises for Lamar High School. The scheduled speaker for the event, to be held on May 29, 1953, was Dr. Ebey. Obviously, if Rogge appeared before the board on May 11 and the board agreed to fire Ebey, then the high school would need a new speaker. Incredibly, when Bill Moreland demanded an explanation, Webb answered that he meant to have Ebey's fitness as a speaker examined before printing the programs. This was a blatantly insubordinate action, since Ebey was Webb's boss. It should have resulted in a severe reprimand, but the timid Moreland was fearful of Webb's influential connections and thus did nothing. Webb's actions prior to May 11 imply that he knew of the Minute Women's and Rogge's plans. Webb and the other members of the Mills machine played an active part in the behind-the-scenes maneuvering against the deputy superintendent.[53]

On May 11, John Rogge stood before the Houston school board and announced dramatically that he had information, provided by anonymous clients, proving that George Ebey had belonged to Communist front organizations, had associated with Communists and fellow travelers, and had expressed subversive ideas and opinions before coming to Houston. He then submitted a collection of evidence to support his charges.

James Delmar replied that the board would have to read and study the material before it could make a decision to investigate Ebey. He added that Rogge would be given an opportunity to elaborate in detail his charges against the deputy superintendent in a closed personnel conference immediately following the public meeting. Ebey's contract would not be voted on until the closed meeting.

Verna Rogers immediately protested and pleaded that holding Ebey's contract would make it appear as if the board considered him guilty before he had been investigated. She made a motion to go into a personnel conference to consider the entire reelection list. Garrett Tucker responded that he wanted to make it clear that holding Ebey's contract did not indicate the board believed him to be guilty. He only wanted to approve the other teacher contracts in order to expedite business. Garrett Tucker then moved to elect the entire school list except for Ebey, who would be considered in a closed personnel conference.

The board passed Garrett Tucker's motion by a 4 to 2 vote with Stone Wells abstaining. Wells objected to the conference being held immediately after the public meeting because Ebey had not had time to prepare a defense. Ebey replied that he was all too familiar with the charges and could refute them easily at the meeting.

After clearing the room of spectators and reconvening in closed session, the board asked Rogge to explain his charges. Rogge emphasized that he represented concerned taxpayers who understood the personal sacrifices each board member suffered in discharging his or her civic responsibilities. His clients, therefore, did not blame the board for any mistakes in hiring personnel since it was the superintendent's duty to inform them about candidates. He and his clients believed that candidates for jobs in the Houston schools had an obligation to disclose all facts about their background, which, he claimed, Ebey had failed to do. Rogge and his backers had, therefore, taken it upon themselves to enlighten the board. He admitted that he based his charges on second-hand sources and did not know for certain if the deputy superintendent was the same Ebey mentioned in the AVC material.[54]

Rogge's material contained information initially printed in the Edwards brochures. It had some important additions, however. Regarding the AVC, Rogge included reproductions of records, newspaper stories, and pictures. He particularly emphasized the speech Ebey gave in April 1947 at the National Conference on Social Work in San Francisco. Rogge argued that the speech was a revealing and extensive expression of Ebey's beliefs as it dwelt on "democratic ideals, civil rights, veterans' housing, and the veteran's role in society." Rogge denounced Ebey's remark that "the Communist Party is to be abhorred" but that free thought and free speech should not be suppressed to fight Communism.

Much of Rogge's material dwelt on racial issues. Ebey's involvement with the intercultural program served as primary evidence. One picture showed a Portland teacher in a racially mixed classroom. Someone had typed on the photograph the teacher's name with the word "Negro" in parentheses and no other comment. Another photograph portrayed a racially mixed class with a caption "True Americanism knows neither race, creed, nor color." Across the top of the page was written, "Dr. George Ebey was assistant superintendent in charge of instruction at this time." Rogge emphasized that the curriculum, the supervisory staff, and all teaching materials came under Ebey's jurisdiction and implied that he had been personally responsible for Portland's integrated classrooms. Rogge concluded his charges by declaring Ebey had belonged to the Urban League of Portland, an organization dedicated to the improvement of black employment opportunities.[55]

Rogge's attack focused on two issues of primary importance to Red Scare activists in Houston: Communism and racial integration. The material had three points touching one or both of those issues. Ebey had headed the American Veterans' Committee in California—an organization charged with being Red dominated. He participated in a controversial and "progressive" educational program involving racially integrated classrooms. A third point merged both issues: he belonged to the allegedly Communist front Urban League, which had a biracial membership striving for black economic rights.

After Rogge's presentation, the board allowed Ebey, consumed with rage, to respond. He defended himself by repeating the information he had prepared in February in his "Reply to Mrs. W. J. Edwards." The board then asked Rogge and Ebey to leave the room. After a lengthy and contentious deliberation, in which Verna Rogers and Jack Tucker objected to the entire proceeding, Ebey was called back into the room. James Delmar informed Ebey that the board had decided to investigate him. Ebey was crestfallen and bewildered. He thought Delmar had cleared him through the FBI back in February and could not understand why a new investigation was now necessary.[56]

After Delmar announced the board's decision, news reporters swarmed around both Ebey and Rogge as they tried to leave the building. Ebey claimed that he welcomed an investigation, even though he privately resented the board's action. He questioned Rogge's motives, demanded that he reveal his backers' identity, and called for an investigation of Rogge's background.

Rogge labeled Ebey's demand for an investigation of himself a "red herring." He claimed that he represented a "heterogeneous group of citizens" and could not name them for fear that he might overlook one or accidentally leave out a name. Rogge stated that he would gladly answer any questions under oath but only if they pertained to his connections with Communist groups and only if Ebey did the same.[57]

Two weeks after Rogge's appearance, the school board hired the General Research Company, a newly formed business operated by former FBI agents, to conduct the investigation. After consulting with attorneys, Ebey signed a release agreement with the General Research Company to free it from threat of a libel suit. The release authorized a complete reputational investigation that could use data from unidentified sources, provided the sources were "evaluated" by the investigators. They could also make the results public, subject to authorization by the board. The board hired the General Research Company to investigate Ebey's loyalty. One of the investigators, Roland S. Torn, told the board that his company would conduct an impartial study and produce an objective report that would allow the board to judge Ebey's qualifications for employment. This implied that the investigation would include things not pertinent to the question of Ebey's loyalty, which was an unsolicited broadening of the report's scope. Ebey's attorney assured him of the company's competence and advised him to sign the agreement.[58]

While the Red Scare coalition planned the attack on George Ebey, its constituent groups continued to work in other areas. Throughout the months of March, April, and May individual Minute Women and CFPM members sought the removal of five of Houston's Methodist ministers. The "hit list" included such obvious candidates (from the Red Scare point of view) as W. Kenneth Pope and Grady Hardin. Pope's involvement in the Rufus Clement affair and Hardin's vocal opposition to the Red Scare groups made targets of both men. Red Scare activists also pressured three conservative Methodist ministers: Neal Cannon of St. Paul's; Stewart Clendenin, a district superintendent; and Durwood Fleming of St. Luke's. These three were criticized together with Hardin and Pope for being in favor of "pre-marital counseling." Fleming, for example, attracted the attention of John Rogge for his participation in the University of Houston counselors' conference in February. Premarital counseling was in reality a rather modest attempt to educate young couples about the basics of marital sexual relations as well as the general responsibilities of marriage. In the view of some Red Scare activists, such counseling might lead to the dangerous possibility of couples deciding to get a head start in their sexual relationship before the actual marriage ceremony. To these people, premarital counseling meant "sex education," which they identified with debauchery and promiscuity, which, in turn, would lead to the moral collapse of the United States. The "Reds" could just walk into power, presumably because Americans caught up in the inevitable sexual frenzy would either be too weak or too occupied to do anything about it. The criticisms of Cannon, Clendenin, and Fleming never amounted to much, and Pope and Hardin also survived. But the pressure continued to take its toll on freedom of thought, speech, and action among them all.[59]

An outsider drew more heat from Houston's Red Scare Methodists than did local clergy during 1953. The CFPM intensified its vocal attacks on Bishop G. Bromley Oxnam of Washington, D.C., in the first three months of the year. They were joined in this effort by the renegade Methodist minister Rembert G. Smith, now retired from his Oklahoma church and living in Houston, who printed an almost incoherent tract titled *Garfield Bromley Oxnam, Revolutionist?*

The CFPM and Rembert Smith, using material first published by John Flynn in *The Road Ahead,* accused Oxnam among other things of writing essays during World War II in praise of Soviet premier Joseph Stalin. They also charged that Oxnam was the real power behind the CFPM's bugaboo: the Methodist Federation for Social Action. Oxnam had resigned from the MFSA in 1947, but that did not matter to Houston's Red Scare Methodists. The Houstonians made so much noise that in March 1953 Representative Donald J. Jackson, a member of the House Committee on Un-American Activities, quoted their "impressive" criticisms against Oxnam in a national radio debate. The bishop, whom one clergyman described as a fierce "Viking" and whom another observer noted "usually gave as good as he got," retorted on the national broadcast that "when anyone quotes this little organization of a few reactionary laymen down in Houston as impressive, it's the least bit sad."[60]

Oxnam's on-the-air comments about the CFPM during a nationally broadcast radio program sent Houston's Red Scare Methodists into a frenzy. Bishop A. Frank Smith, a friend of Oxnam's and deeply concerned about the matter, advised his clergy that it might help if Oxnam came to Houston and allowed himself to be confronted by the CFPM and his other local Methodist critics. Accordingly, Neal Cannon, pastor of the church with the most prominent CFPM membership, arranged to have Bishop Oxnam come to the city on May 26, 1953. Dunbar Chambers, a wealthy businessman and lay leader in Cannon's church, agreed to make his large River Oaks home available for the confrontation.

Approximately seventy CFPM members, including Ewing Werlein and Clarence Lohman, and a few ministers, including Cannon and Pope, assembled at Chambers' home the evening of May 26. Bishop Smith, having encouraged the meeting, nevertheless found it necessary to be out of town that night. The meeting was private and a policeman was hired to keep the press and uninvited guests away. Oxnam, accompanied by his wife and full of wrath, made an abrasive and condescending speech, managing to insult nearly everyone present, including those sympathetic to his plight. The bishop was especially rude in a question-and-answer session following his speech and managed to humiliate Clarence Lohman, the true-believing extremist leader of the Circuit Riders. One witness who was favorable toward Oxnam recalled that "here was this ungracious little man [Oxnam] cutting this little ignoramus [Lohman] down to size and more people felt sorry for Lohman than proud of Oxnam." Nevertheless, despite Oxnam's unwillingness to "talk sense" to the CFPM, some members of the group made an attempt to declare a truce. As one witness remembered, the majority of CFPM members were "really meek little men when face to face in private with a big bad force like Oxnam, who was willing to take them on one at a time or as a group." One layman stood up and admitted that he believed the charges against Oxnam were "greatly exaggerated . . . we ought to drop it . . . this man's not guilty." Oxnam's uncompromisingly hostile behavior, however, precluded a peaceful resolution and the meeting ended as it began.[61]

Although the Oxnam meeting proved unsatisfactory in terms of making peace with the combative bishop, the episode seemed to indicate that the CFPM was losing its zest for the fight. In addition, Grady Hardin and his more liberal colleagues believed the time was right for the Texas Conference to the Methodist Church to pass an anti-CFPM resolution. When the conference met in its annual session in Houston in June, while the Ebey investigation continued, Hardin drafted a strong statement critical of the CFPM and gave Bishop Smith a copy. The bishop spent hours persuading the Spring Branch minister to moderate the draft. Hardin finally agreed to allow Smith to rewrite one of the paragraphs and, on Smith's recommendation, took a copy to the Vinson, Elkins law firm, where R. A. Shepherd rewrote another section. Hardin submitted the new watered-down version to the annual conference.

The resolution recognized the right of the CFPM to organize and to have differences of opinion with the church. It also reaffirmed "the unequivocal stand" of the church against Communism. The "critical" portion, however, merely requested that the CFPM "state clearly in all its material . . . that as far as The Texas Conference is concerned it is an unofficial body." Even such a moderate and factual statement as this troubled some of the delegates who feared CFPM retaliation. Hardin and a layman from his church, L. H. Moon, were forced to read the resolution to the conference themselves because the secretary considered it too controversial. The resolution passed, however, because word had spread that Bishop Smith and R. A. Shepherd had helped draft it. Individual members of the CFPM denounced the conference and Hardin for the action. Hines H. Baker complained to Bishop Smith that "pastors in high places of leadership" were responsible for the unfair resolution. Baker felt that he and his associates on the CFPM had been "officially and publicly rebuked." Bishop Smith, a close friend of Baker, paid the corporate lawyer a personal visit and eventually succeeded in soothing his feelings about the matter, although Baker continued to be active in the CFPM. The CFPM continued its pressure tactics after the incident, but Grady Hardin had succeeded in winning a minor victory. Weak though it was, the passage of the resolution indicated that the CFPM did not control the Texas conference. This in itself helped alleviate some of the fear within the church. Even a minor victory counted for something at a time when the Ebey affair raged in Houston. Victories were hard to come by for anyone opposed to the Red Scare in the summer of 1953.[62]

While the Methodists were passing Hardin's weak but nonetheless courageous resolution in June, secular Houston continued to debate John Rogge's charges against the deputy superintendent of schools. The charges against Ebey and the subsequent investigation initiated a two-month period of tension, controversy, and heated debate in Houston. Houstonians gossiped and argued over backyard fences and businessman's luncheons about the possibly subversive, mysterious background of the Californian serving as deputy superintendent. John Rogge puzzled many Houstonians as well. Who had backed the right-wing lawyer? The city quickly divided into pro-Ebey and anti-Ebey camps as the controversy raged for the rest of May and throughout the month of June 1953.

The Houston Teachers Association, an independent organization representing the classroom teachers in the public schools of Houston, promptly announced support of the accused administrator. In a letter to the school board, the board of directors of the HTA expressed approval of the investigation. They expected the investigation would clear Ebey completely and expressed the hope that as much publicity would be given to his clearance as the newspapers gave to Rogge's charges. The HTA also urged Rogge to disclose the identity of his clients and stated, "It is un-American for those who have cast aspersions on the patriotism of Dr. Ebey to hide behind a legal front." The Parents' Council for Improved Schools, composed of citizens who had opposed the Committee for Sound American Education in the school elections in 1952, joined in the demand for Rogge to reveal the identity of his backers or withdraw his charges.[63]

The Minute Women quickly responded to these criticisms. Mrs. J. Edward Jones wrote the Houston *Chronicle* that the teachers' association's support of Ebey did not impress the people of Houston because the association had also supported the appearances of controversial speakers such as Dr. Willard Goslin. Jones said that Houston's teachers should not allow the association to represent them and urged the teachers to ". . . see to your own house-cleaning."[64]

The debate over George Ebey's loyalty grew louder. People crowded into the school board's meeting room circulating literature both pro and con. Besieged by letters and telephone calls, John Rogge became a minor celebrity. He invited the public to come to his office in downtown Houston and see the "documentary evidence" he had collected on Ebey. Rogge also announced that he would be available to appear before civic and educational organizations to explain his position. Numerous groups accepted his offer and Rogge soon had more invitations than he could handle. Besides making personal appearances in behalf of his cause, Rogge bought an $800 advertisement in the Houston *Chronicle* that appeared on May 25. The newspaper ad occupied one-half page with the heading, "DO *YOU* WANT George W. Ebey reappointed as Deputy Superintendent of Houston Public Schools?" It asked readers to review the list of charges and decide for themselves. Rogge ended his plea with "THERE IS TOO MUCH AT STAKE TO TAKE A CHANCE!" He urged readers to telephone the board and voice objections to Ebey's reappointment. Only John Rogge's name appeared at the bottom of the page as he continued to refuse to reveal the identity of his associates.[65]

The Minute Women, among those responsible for Rogge's attack, initiated a letter campaign to the city's major newspapers. For example, in separate letters, Minute Women members Mrs. Henry Clay Lee and Anne Harrison defended Rogge. Mrs. Lee wrote that Rogge was ". . . highly esteemed and respected by all who know him and what he stands for — the USA, first, last, and always." Anne Harrison defended Rogge as a loyal patriot and gentleman who would never interfere with anyone's freedom of thought.[66]

Other Minute Women took different approaches. Mrs. J. Mart Wren wrote to the *Chronicle* that James Delmar should not be surprised at the attack on Ebey since some of the charges had been made in September 1952. She recalled that Delmar promised an investigation then but nothing came of it. Mrs. H. W. Cullen (unrelated to Hugh Roy Cullen) praised the board for its decision to investigate and wrote that the education of children should not be left in the hands of ". . . controversial or even doubtful persons."[67]

Other groups joined the attack on Ebey. For example, the president of the Property Owners Association of Houston, Inc., J. B. Adoue, wrote an urgent letter to his fellow members attacking Ebey for advocating while in the AVC the establishment of a public housing program. Adoue warned that Ebey had supported a move for the California legislature to establish rent control. Ebey had also supported legislation to prevent racial segregation and discrimination in housing projects. The Property Owners Association president charged that Ebey's ". . . bold stand on many controversial issues does not in any way qualify him as an educator and indicates more that he is a social reformer." He urged all members to write and demand Ebey's dismissal.[68]

The Ebey controversy even involved Houston's barbers. One barber, J. H. Stewart, wrote and distributed a circular addressed to "All Houston Barbers." Stewart's circular indicated the role racism played in the attack on Ebey. It began by stating, "Do you want a social reformer meddling in your barber business?" The circular cited Dr. Ebey's speech before the National Conference on Social Work in 1947 and stressed that Ebey had opposed racial segregation in housing and education and had criticized a California barber who refused to cut a black war veteran's hair. These statements, Stewart argued, revealed Ebey to be a ". . . social revolutionary instead of an educator." He urged all barbers to protest the reappointment of the deputy superintendent because he would be a ". . . rabble-rouser and a troublemaker."[69]

Despite the vociferousness of his opponents, the besieged educator also had supporters. Almost immediately following Rogge's attack, Tom Friedman, head of the local Jewish Anti-Defamation League (ADL), began to work closely with Ebey to gather information for the educator to use in his self-defense. Because of the Minute Women's association with anti-Semitic writers, Friedman and the ADL had monitored the group for months prior to the attack on Ebey in May 1953. In concert with the ADL office in Los Angeles, Friedman accumulated material on the California Un-American Activities Committee as well as information on local Red Scare activists. Other Houstonians offered moral support. Eddie Dyer, a former professional baseball player and owner of an insurance agency in Houston, wrote Ebey, "All of us . . . resent most highly the unfair and unjustified accusations made against you." Kenneth Fellows, personnel director of Houston Natural Gas Corporation, wrote Moreland of his "grave concern over the malicious, subversive attacks to which Dr. Ebey has been exposed."[70]

While Houstonians argued and took sides and the General Research Company conducted its investigation, news of the Ebey controversy spread to Portland, Oregon. Many Oregonians reacted to Rogge's charges in the same manner they had reacted to the previous attacks on Ebey's record — with shocked indignation and outrage. A member of the Portland school board declared that Ebey's performance in Portland ". . . does not warrant investigation by any other community excepting to justify the fine position he held in our system and community." Residents of

Portland, its teachers and principals, who knew Ebey best, defended their former administrative head. The Portland High School Teachers Association wrote James Delmar of its deep concern about the affair, calling it an attack upon public education. A school principal in Portland wrote the Houston *Press* that Ebey had been a community leader, an outstanding educator, and a loyal American while in Oregon. He stated that "to imply Communistic leanings to Dr. Ebey is absurd."[71]

The Associated Press and United Press International noted the attack on George Ebey and spread the news across the United States. In Chicago, Harold Fey, managing editor of the *Christian Century*, a monthly Protestant magazine, wrote to a friend in Houston, ". . . the battle you are waging for Ebey in Houston is as important for the future of our nation as any that is being fought in Washington or Korea. The Rogge [attack] is character assassination at its worst."[72]

The Houston *Chronicle*, which had helped create the atmosphere that allowed the Ebey affair to occur, charged that men "shrieking" about violations of academic freedom wanted to violate the first principle of academic freedom — the search for facts regardless of the consequences. Jesse Jones' newspaper declared that anyone who opposed investigating the political beliefs of school teachers was "undemocratic." The *Chronicle* supported Rogge's efforts while the *Post* and *Press* remained quietly neutral.[73]

During the public debate of May and June, the school board members were subjected to intense pressure by people supporting both sides of the emotional issue. None of the board members gave any public indication of how they might vote once the report was finally submitted. Nonetheless, people on both sides knew Henry Peterson and Dallas Dyer would vote against Ebey. Likewise, Verna Rogers and Jack Tucker would probably vote for the deputy superintendent unless sensational new information surfaced. The unknown votes belonged to James Delmar, Garrett Tucker, and, to some extent, Stone Wells.

The General Research Company investigators submitted the long-awaited report a week early, on Friday, July 10. George Ebey did not receive a copy until Monday, July 13, the night the board was scheduled to make its decision.[74]

The investigators, Roland S. Torn and William H. Storey, had traveled to California and Oregon to research Ebey's background. This research consisted of 117 different interviews with various individuals purporting to be able to provide the researchers with pertinent material. Ebey himself submitted a list of persons for the company to contact. The report attempted to cover five areas of Ebey's background. The researchers investigated his loyalty record and his role in establishing racially integrated schools in Portland, Oregon. Also, the General Research Company studied his role in placing black teachers in white classes in Portland as well as his participation in a Portland debate over a curriculum change that switched the emphasis from home economics and manual training to arts and crafts in several grade schools. Finally, the investigators sought opinions about Ebey's personality. Thus, a large portion of the report went far beyond the board's original authorization and delved into areas unrelated to Rogge's accusations.[75]

The report covered George Ebey's general activities from his birth in San Jose, California, to his employment in Houston. Forty-five years of the deputy superintendent's life were spread over the 348 pages. As they read Ebey's story the board members became aware of the obvious. Ebey was not subversive, disloyal, or a fellow traveler. The report, however, did imply that Ebey had not taken a strong stand against the Communists in the American Veterans' Committee. The testimony of several members of the anti-Communist faction of the AVC provided the most serious charge in the report. These witnesses, who had fought Ebey while he served as chairman of AVC's California division, charged that he had been fully aware of Communist infiltration. He did not actively fight for Communist expulsion, they asserted, because he believed that he could control them and preserve the unity of the AVC. The investigators managed to avoid any of Ebey's AVC supporters. The most sensational summation of George Ebey's AVC career came from a man identified mysteriously as "GR-7." Supposedly some type of governmental secret agent, GR-7 had allegedly infiltrated the Communist party and thus could not be identified because of his secret work. GR-7 claimed to have known Ebey and to have been active in the AVC. He told the General Research Company that the "Reds" felt they could control Ebey and have their policies implemented while he served as California chairman. GR-7 inaccurately claimed that the Communists controlled the AVC in California, yet Ebey refused to oppose them because he enjoyed the power and publicity of being chairman.[76]

Overall, except for GR-7, even Ebey's harshest critics failed to question his loyalty. Most felt that Ebey was a "New Dealer" but not disloyal by any standards. Not one person accused Ebey of being a Communist or sympathetic to Communism. Some testified that the very questioning of his loyalty seemed incredible. One aspect of the interview, however, shocked Ebey and his wife. Both friend and foe alike responded. Some of these people portrayed Ebey as an overly ambitious, "tactless," overbearing man with a superiority complex who should not be employed in a job where he would have frequent contact with the public.

Later, after the report was made public, several Oregon educators and civic leaders expressed indignation at what the researchers had attributed to them. Some accused the investigators of "putting words in their mouths" and committing errors of fact. The interviewees especially resented remarks attributed to them about Ebey's personality. They claimed many of the words were statements that the investigator had made as leading questions or were statements expressing the investigator's own views. For example, Norman K. Hamilton, assistant superintendent of Portland schools, wrote the Houston school board and charged that "some of the key words attributed to me . . . and used with a derogatory slant were not even my own." Portland school district official Joy Gubser charged that paragraphs credited to her about Ebey's personality included statements never made and "carry a tone never implied."[77]

The other portions of the report that frightened Houston's Red Scare activists included discussions of Ebey's 1936 letter to a Honolulu newspaper protesting loyalty oaths and his support of the Loyalist forces in the Spanish Civil War. Other areas of concern included his belief in racial equality and his participation in the integrated school program in Portland.

On Monday night, July 13, the school board met to consider the appropriate action to take on the deputy superintendent's contract. Weeks before the meeting, George Ebey hired Jack Binion as his attorney. Binion, a highly respected senior partner of Butler, Binion, Rice, and Cook, a major Houston law firm, also served on the State Board of Education. Because of his own liberal educational beliefs, Binion could identify with his client's predicament. Binion was also a political conservative who had an intimate knowledge of the power structure in Houston opposing Ebey. Binion's past clients included Jesse Jones, Brown and Root, Inc., and the Houston *Post*. His law partner, George Butler, was Jones' nephew-in-law. Binion was also close to Governor Allan Shivers. When asked why he had helped Dr. Ebey, Binion replied, "Because he was entitled to counsel." When Ebey asked Binion about the lawyer's fees, Binion replied, "You don't owe me one red cent, podner."[78]

On the day of the meeting to decide Ebey's future, Jack Binion asked James Delmar for a copy of the report for his client to prepare a defense. Delmar refused and said the board did not want Ebey to see it. Eventually, a few hours before the meeting that night, Delmar gave Binion a copy of the report. He told Binion that the deputy superintendent could "thumb through it pretty fast" before the meeting if he wished. Ebey's preparation for his defense against the report had to be based on a hasty glance over the 348-page document.[79]

The Board of Education meeting room filled to capacity long before the vote on Ebey's contract. From 250 to 300 people crammed into the small room, filling every seat, while many others stood along the walls. An overflow crowd waited outside in the corridor. Conspicuous by his absence was John P. Rogge.

After taking an unbearable two hours to conduct routine business, James Delmar finally asked Superintendent Moreland for his recommendation on Ebey's contract. Before Moreland could respond, Jack Tucker proposed a delay to allow Ebey adequate time to prepare a defense. Tucker explained that anyone under an investigation had the fundamental right to complete knowledge of the accusations against him and should be able to testify on his own behalf. Verna Rogers quickly seconded Tucker's motion. An extended debate followed between Jack Tucker on one side and Henry Peterson, Dallas Dyer, and James Delmar on the other. Peterson and Dyer opposed Ebey and neither of them hid that fact at the meeting. James Delmar also emerged as an Ebey opponent, however. All three argued for an immediate vote on the deputy superintendent's contract. Delmar, openly hostile, argued, "We gave Ebey . . . a full and complete hearing on May 11. I've noticed Dr. Ebey sitting out here for more than two hours watching us transact routine business when he could have gone down the hall to his air-conditioned office and read the report." During the debate, Delmar insisted that Bill Moreland deny or affirm that he had told him privately that he would recommend keeping Ebey. Moreland replied that he could find nothing in the report to change his mind about renewing Ebey's contract. Delmar declared that Moreland's recommendation surprised and disappointed him. Jack Binion urged the board to give Ebey a chance to read the report and defend himself. Turning to Delmar, Binion said, "I see you're prejudiced, so I appeal to the rest of you . . . give this man a chance."

After the debate, the board voted 4 to 3 in favor of Jack Tucker's motion to postpone the vote for two nights. Jack Tucker and Verna Rogers won the vote with the unexpected help of Stone Wells and Garrett Tucker. Delmar followed this with a motion to make the "Ebey Report" immediately available to the public. After a brief discussion, the board agreed and the report was released to the public that night.[80]

The Houston school board reconvened on Wednesday night, July 15, to decide Ebey's future with the Houston school system. So many people appeared at the meeting that many had to stand along the walls of the board room while others stood in the outside hall. At the front of the room, filling the first few rows of chairs, sat an organized cheering squad of Minute Women, accompanied by John Rogge. On the first few rows were some of the group who had been most active in attacking Ebey. This group included Ida Ward, Mrs. H. W. Cullen, Norma Louise Barnett, Anne Harrison, Elsie Daniel, Mrs. N. H. Agopian, and one of the Minute Women leaders, Virginia Hedrick.[81]

An incident two hours before the meeting increased Ebey's anxiety and frustration. Moreland urged Ebey to resign before the board could vote on his contract. The superintendent explained that a resignation would relieve him of the responsibility of making a speech in Ebey's defense. Such a speech would place him in an "unfavorable light" with the board majority. Ebey angrily rejected Moreland's suggestion and told him he would stay and fight it out.[82]

The school board held a closed personnel conference with Ebey, his attorney Jack Binion, and Superintendent Moreland prior to the public meeting. At this closed personnel session, Ebey presented his defense. Before the deputy superintendent spoke, his legal counsel, Jack Binion, asked to be heard.

Binion reminded the board that Rogge had accused Ebey of disloyalty to the United States. With that in mind, Ebey had consented to the public investigation. Once the report had been released, Ebey discovered that certain board members, as well as others in the city, now accused him of committing a new offense. Ebey was now guilty of being controversial. Binion argued that "this is a new type of delinquency in American life." He urged the board members to ask how anyone can protect themselves from being found guilty of being a controversial figure. The issue, according to Binion, "is whether a man falsely accused . . . is to be punished for having been an innocent victim of a situation he did not create." He pointed out that the research report did not include a discussion of Ebey's total philosophy, it just gave examples of a few cases where Ebey had held views that might differ in some respects from some of the board members. "If you consider the whole man," said Binion, "the important thing would be the areas of agreement, not the differences." Binion briefly defended some of the controversial views Ebey had held. Referring to the 1936 loyalty oath letter, Binion argued that educators all over the United States had expressed the same opposition at nearly every professional educational society meeting held in 1936. Binion also discussed Ebey's participation in the drive for medical aid for the Spanish Republic in the 1930s. He pointed out that the Gallup Poll reported that 65 percent of the American people favored the Republican forces against General Francisco Franco. Arguing that Ebey's views were moderate, Binion cited his stand in favor of public housing programs. He read an article published in the Houston *Post* that reported that a majority of people questioned on the issue favored government-sponsored public housing.

Binion stressed that Ebey's activities were in the public record. Ebey had made no effort to conceal his expressions or actions in the past. His loyalty had been proven. His only guilt stemmed from the fact that John Rogge had made him "controversial" simply because Rogge had accused him of being controversial. The attorney concluded by warning the board that they would never find people of intelligence and courage if they could not hire anyone holding controversial views at some time in the past.[83]

After Binion's presentation, George Ebey read his own defense statement. He declared that the research report overwhelmingly established his patriotism and devotion to his country. The major reason for the report had thus been satisfied. Friend and foe alike, Ebey continued, had testified to his loyalty. Ebey stated that his position needed no "Monday morning quarterbacking." In 1947 the United States was fresh from its military alliance with the Soviet Union; neither Korea nor the Cold War had yet begun. He declared that when one ". . . considers the period of history, it is evident that I was vigorously anti-communist."

Ebey then stated that this left the question of other aspects of his fitness for his job. He reminded the board that no question of his fitness had been raised in his four years in Portland, Oregon. His recommendations indicated this. The same held true for his performance while in Houston. He asked that since the disloyalty charge was false, then why should the board apply different standards of fitness to him than would have been applied before Rogge made his charges?

The deputy superintendent assured the board that he loyally supported official policies and that he realized his position did not involve policy-making responsibilities. Despite his belief in racial equality, he told the board that "it is not the role of an educator to tell the people what to do." Though "all men of good will" approved the promotion of racial and religious harmony, Ebey insisted, "Its implementation will differ with the circumstances." He believed southerners could solve their racial problems themselves and that he personally had no plans to intervene.

On the opinions about his personality, Ebey said that this had no relation to Rogge's charges. He could not have advanced professionally if the "uncomplimentary" remarks were true. If so, the people of Portland, Ebey charged, would not have been so spontaneous in coming to his defense, nor would have citizens in Houston.

Ebey declared that the board could absolve him of the disloyalty charge by renewing his contract for one year. If evidence surfaced that his effectiveness as an administrator had been impaired, he would resign. Ebey stated, "I have tried to act with courage and honor and respect for this board during these trying times for my family and me. All that I ask is a decision based upon fairness and justice."[84]

Almost immediately the board went into open session. The school board president, James Delmar, asked Moreland to begin the public meeting with his official recommendation. Moreland announced that while reading the "Ebey Report" he found no evidence of Ebey's having been a Communist or any proof of disloyalty. Based on the evidence, plus the fact that Ebey had performed his job in an "excellent manner" while in Houston, Moreland told the board that he could not withdraw his recommendation that Ebey be rehired. Delmar asked Moreland why he had told him privately on May 11 that he should not have recommended Ebey in 1952 nor would he ever recommend him for the superintendent's job. Moreland replied that he would not have originally hired Ebey if he had known of his vulnerability to charges of being controversial. Now that Ebey had worked with Moreland for a year, he had to recommend him because he had proven himself by his excellent work. He still could never recommend him for the superintendent's position because of the current controversy. After hearing Superintendent Moreland, Delmar called for a vote on whether to accept Moreland's recommendation in favor of renewing Ebey's contract.[85]

Verna Rogers voted first. The board's most vocal liberal surprised no one when she voted in favor of Ebey. Rogers stated that she could find no evidence in the General Research Company report indicating that Ebey was disloyal. To her, the evidence proved that Ebey was a patriotic American and an able administrator.

Predictably, Henry Peterson voted against renewing Ebey's contract. The physician told the audience that while he did not believe Ebey to be a Communist, the report revealed that Ebey worked willingly with known Communists in the AVC. If he did not mind working with Communists then, why would he mind working with Communists someplace else? Peterson declared that he would never work with subversives. Responsible people such as himself actively fought against the evils of Communism.

Dallas Dyer admitted that she could find no legal evidence in the report that Ebey belonged to the Communist party. Dyer insisted, however, that she could not find in the report that Ebey was a good and loyal American. Placing an emphasis on the testimony of GR-7, Dyer charged that Ebey had "walked on a tightrope to keep from offending the Communists" in the AVC. She believed Ebey had compromised with the Communists. To Dallas Dyer, Communism was evil and she did not compromise with evil. She said that of over one hundred persons interviewed not one could point out one single "act, deed, or statement" that Ebey made against the Communist party. She could not vote for Dr. Ebey's continued employment because "I do not think he is the best man for the job." Dyer made a point to disavow any influence by the Minute Women on her decision. She declared, "I am responsible to no . . . pressure group that may pack this board room."

A. J. Tucker, Verna Rogers' liberal colleague, evened the vote at two for and two against when he voted for renewing Ebey's contract. Jack Tucker stated that Bill Moreland's recommendation on professional grounds was an adequate reason to support Ebey. Tucker could find no evidence indicating Ebey had ever been disloyal or had ever "deviated from the principles of Christian American Democracy." As for his AVC activities, Tucker concluded that Ebey had not been dominated by any factions within the organization. Instead, Ebey had prevented the Communist faction from taking over by using his skill to work with all sides.

The four "obvious" votes had been cast. Now the audience, as well as Dr. Ebey, would find out which way the "swing" votes would go. Garrett Tucker went first. His earlier actions seemed to indicate a favorable view toward Ebey, but no one could be sure. Garrett Tucker stated that Dr. Ebey had tolerated Communists in the AVC at a time when those people could be members under the organization's membership rules. He reminded his colleagues that this also occurred at a time when the United States was trying to cooperate with its wartime ally, Russia, and when a president of the United States had referred to Joseph Stalin as "good old Joe." Tucker stated that this was before most Americans had awakened to the dangers of Communism. He could not condemn Ebey for making the same mistake. To vote against Ebey would condemn him as being disloyal in the view of many Americans. Tucker also feared it would end Ebey's career as a public school administrator. A vote against Ebey, Tucker argued, ". . . is a vote for John Rogge and for the anonymous forces behind him. . . ." Such people would then feel free to attack other school employees with whom they disagreed. Garrett Tucker voted for rehiring Dr. Ebey.

With the vote 3 to 2 in Ebey's favor, James Delmar asked Stone Wells for his vote. Wells had given no prior indication of how he would vote, but he had told reporters that Ebey had never been a Communist. Wells announced that his decision was based solely on whether Ebey possessed the proper qualifications for the job. He then declared, "I can't, to save my life, come here tonight and vote for reemployment of a man who has on so many occasions failed to take a stand. . . ." The General Research Company report, according to Wells, revealed that Ebey had failed to fight Communism when he had the opportunity. Wells believed that Ebey's weakness disqualified him from being deputy superintendent.

The vote stood at a deadlock, 3 to 3. James Delmar's vote would settle the question. Only a few held out hope over Delmar's vote because the board president had been hostile toward Ebey since Rogge's charges in May. Delmar quickly removed any lingering doubts about his feelings. He agreed that Ebey had not been a Communist. Delmar charged, however, that not only had he failed to oppose the Communists in the AVC, he had helped them by opposing the anti-Communists. According to Delmar, Ebey did this for personal gain and a desire for power. Another problem concerned Ebey's personality. Delmar felt the report revealed Ebey's inability to handle personnel matters, which could not be tolerated in a man of his position. Delmar reminded the board that Bill Moreland had admitted he could not recommend Ebey to be his successor. The board would be wasting its time employing a man as deputy superintendent who was not qualified to step up and become superintendent. Delmar declared that Ebey's personal ambitions, as indicated by his AVC activities, did not fit into the "scheme of a harmonious working program." The controversy "caused" by Ebey had split "our entire community," Delmar charged, and if Ebey remained in the school district he could only see a continuation of the conflict.[86]

After voting 4 to 3 not to rehire Dr. Ebey, the board adjourned. Confusion reigned in the room as scores of people rushed the rostrum praising or condemning the board members and Ebey. Heated shouting debates broke out around the room. Shoving and pushing incidents occurred in the outside hall. John Rogge quickly became the center of attention as the crowd swirled around him. Many people stopped to shake his hand, while others passed by and shouted "fascist" at him. Newspaper reporters eventually surrounded Rogge. Their interrogation was interrupted by a man shouting that Rogge had remarked in a barber shop that he opposed all public education. Rogge pushed his way past the journalists and, waving his arms, shouted at his fleeing accuser, "You're a damn liar!"[87]

The reporters asked Rogge who had backed him. He shot back, "It's none of your business who they are." One reporter asked if he planned any new attacks and Rogge replied that if he saw a fire he would attempt to put it out. Rogge told the reporters that his clients were so numerous, "literally hundreds," that he could not identify them all. A reporter for *Time* magazine asked about the Minute Women and Rogge mentioned that he had heard of them but they had not put up the money to pay his fee. Anyway, Rogge said, no one had made anonymous accusations: "I signed them." He also paid for the newspaper ad in the *Chronicle*. Rogge announced that he had come in contact with very few people who disagreed with him on the Ebey case. He had noticed that his opponents were "misled idealists and shallow thinkers," including Verna Rogers, A. J. Tucker, and Garrett Tucker. Rogge had decided that "every person who believes in the school system which made this country great agrees with me." He praised the four board members who voted against Dr. Ebey and declared that the rest of the United States could "well emulate" the "good example" provided by the "courageous" educators and school officials in Houston.[88]

Reporters also swarmed around the deposed deputy superintendent. An ashen-faced Ebey admitted that the board's decision had made him "heartsick" and that it was not easy to sit by and listen to people slur his character. He told the press that he only hoped his "firing" might make Houstonians aware of the character of some of the people on the school board. "I tried," Ebey said, "to act with courage, honor, and integrity under these circumstances originated by gossip and rumor."[89]

News of Ebey's dismissal spread across the nation. *Time* magazine, which featured a prominent article about the event, called Rogge's charges "absurd." *Nation*, in an editorial on the Ebey affair, called it the "zaniest of the poison-pen attacks on public education since they began in 1949." According to *Nation*, "Dr. Ebey was not the issue . . . the issue . . . was the control of public education." The *Christian Century* charged that Houston's educational system had been caught in the "grip of a conscienceless machine" and urged an investigation by the National Education Association. Other reactions to Ebey's treatment ranged from a spokesperson from Columbia University denouncing it as an "outrage" to the bishop of the Methodist church in San Francisco comparing the firing to justice in Nazi Germany.[90]

In Oregon, the Portland Urban League charged that Ebey's career had been sacrificed at the "altar of bigotry and racism." The *Oregonian,* in its editorial "Setback for Freedom," declared that the Houston school board fired Ebey on the basis of the "flimsiest" of accusations and that the episode would encourage "bigots and cranks" to wage a "hit and run war" on American public education. The *Oregon Daily Journal* denounced Ebey's firing as "indefensible" and stated that the episode was a "clear warning" to those citizens believing in basic freedoms.[91]

Oregon's educators also reacted to Ebey's dismissal with shock and outrage. The Oregon Education Association declared that the Ebey affair directly concerned its organization and that the case had "important implications for our American way of life." The association urged Texas members of the National Education Association to request an investigation of the episode. The Oregon teachers warned that they would request an investigation if their colleagues in Texas failed to fulfill their obligations in the matter.[92]

Back in Houston, the Ebey affair activated a small portion of the community. When Ebey lost his job, he received flowers, gifts, telegrams, and several offers of financial assistance. One Houstonian offered to share $50 a month of his salary with Ebey as long as he stayed in Houston.[93]

The protest against Ebey's firing as well as offers of help came from a cross section of the city's economic, social, and religious groups. John Crossland, the secretary of the local Oil Workers International Union (CIO), urged the national office to investigate the "fanatic fringe" groups in Texas responsible for the Ebey affair. Crossland noted that these same groups were openly hostile to labor unions. The city's Jewish newspaper, the *Herald-Voice*, charged that the school board fired Ebey ". . . the moment it was discovered he was . . . a 'liberal.' " The paper urged that Houstonians not forget the people responsible for the dismissal, "now, or next week, or at the ballot box."[94]

The Houston *Post*, which referred to the affair as the number one news story in Houston during 1953, favored retention of Ebey as deputy superintendent. The *Post* noted that the episode was part of a larger, national movement and was symptomatic of the "morbid feeling of insecurity which has gripped the country." The *Post*'s "Sound-Off" column of letters to the editor printed eleven letters in favor of Ebey for every one letter against him. The *Chronicle*, however, denounced Ebey and strongly supported the school board's action. The Houston *Press* was more impartial. In an editorial column, the editor of the *Press*, George Carmack, stated that he would not have fired George Ebey. He added that he meant no criticism for any board member and that he believed both sides had acted with honor and a "clear conscience." The editor criticized John Rogge's methods, which, he declared, revolved around the use of innuendo and gave the Ebey case a "distasteful air." Carmack, however, also criticized George Ebey. He declared that he could not agree with Ebey's philosophy of government and charged the dismissed educator with "over-dramatization."[95]

The *Press*'s caustic columnist Carl Victor Little, however, openly ridiculed the views of the school board's majority. Little wrote that he had received a letter from a man named "Uriah Heep" asking for Dr. Ebey's job. "Mr. Heep" admitted that he had no experience in the academic world, no degrees, and had never watched educational television. Little, tongue firmly in cheek, declared that "Heep" possessed all the qualifications necessary to please the board: he had never held an opinion on anything; he had never been interested in his community, nor served on any committee, nor belonged to any organizations; he had never held an idea that would not coincide with views of the board majority; and he would work to delete from textbooks any mention of controversial figures such as George Washington, Andrew Jackson, Alexander Hamilton, Aaron Burr, and Abraham Lincoln. "Heep" added that the Civil War was "dynamite" so it would also be deleted. Little stated that "Mr. Heep" wants children to breathe the "pure air of free enterprise," so he would be against telling them about Social Security, federal aid, and old-age pensions. Letters to the *Press* indicated that conservatives failed to appreciate Little's humor.[96]

The successful use of Red Scare tactics in the Ebey affair indicated that anti-Communism was a symbolic issue representing locally perceived preservationist impulses. George Ebey provided a single target for those in the community who wanted to attack many different enemies. Racism was obviously a major element in the attack, since Ebey attracted the opposition of those who feared racial integration of the schools and other public services. Eighteen months after his departure from Houston, Ebey, reflecting on what had happened to him, emphasized "the strong undercurrent of prejudice directed toward me because of my views on racial harmony. . . ." Ebey recalled that the epithets hurled at him by hostile spectators in the school board room the night of his dismissal included "nigger lover." From the very beginning racial prejudice hovered over nearly every charge made against Ebey. Minute Woman Anne Harrison accused him of "race mixing" in the Portland schools during that first confrontation in August 1952. Racial fears were stirred in Mrs. Edwards' and John Rogge's accusations as well.[97]

Ebey's New Deal liberalism attracted the opposition of those who feared the advances of big government and the growth of the welfare state. Ebey's entire ideological record presented a challenge to the postwar conservatives in Houston who defended such doctrinal positions as limited government, states' rights, the inviolable nature of private property, and a strongly nationalistic foreign policy. Most of his opponents were conservative Republicans and the attack also reflected partisan political animosities.

Ebey also symbolized the progressive education that many of his attackers feared. Progressive education resembled Communism in its intangibility and vagueness as an issue. Some equated it with Communism, since they perceived it to be a necessary stage to prepare children for the socialist state. Ebey had graduated from Columbia University, the school where John Dewey first articulated his educational philosophy. Dewey's philosophy led to the methods of progressive education; thus, Houston's Red Scare activists viewed Columbia Teachers' College with deep suspicion. Anti-intellectualism and provincialism formed other elements of the attack and they too stemmed from Ebey's Columbia background. One of Ebey's opponents wrote to the *Post* that Columbia University had provided "a fertile field for . . . infamous radicals. . . ." An essential source of the discontent against the native Californian was traditional

Texan and southern distrust of the outsider. Ebey's enemies often made references to his nonsouthern origins, with several statements directly charging him with the crime of being an "outsider."[98]

The bitter struggle between conservatives and liberals for control of the Houston schools was yet another reason for the Ebey affair. George Ebey represented a threat to the powerful Mills machine within the school district because of his independent personality. A simple, pragmatic power struggle certainly influenced some of the support for his removal as deputy superintendent. One can only speculate, but the Ebey affair might have had a different resolution had Bill Moreland been a stronger man. Ebey believed the episode would not even have occurred if Moreland had kept his original promise of a three-year contract because Ebey would not have been vulnerable at a crucial time in the Red Scare. Certainly Moreland's weakness played a significant role in the event, but a stronger man would not have been allowed to be superintendent.

For some individuals Ebey symbolized mainly a frightening if illusory enemy. Some of his opponents can be classified as sincere but uninformed anti-Communists who genuinely believed that George Ebey represented a direct Communist threat to the safety of their homes and children. Uninformed anti-Communism obviously interacted with the other elements of the attack in varying degrees. Still, the Ebey affair symbolized much more than pure anti-Communism; the charge of Communism merely provided an easy, simple, and popular means of attacking more complex and pluralistic evils.

Finally, the Ebey affair must be seen as a part of a larger attack on public education that was national in scope. There are striking similarities between the Ebey case and the Willard Goslin episode that occurred two years earlier in Pasadena, California. Dr. Goslin, the superintendent of schools in Pasadena, was dismissed in 1951 after an intense and sensational campaign by a Red Scare citizens group called the School Development Council (SDC). The SDC was analogous to Houston's Committee for Sound American Education. While the SDC's main purpose was to keep school taxes low, it emphasized the dangers of progressive education, UNESCO, and other "subversive" influences creeping into Pasadena schools. The SDC's membership was dominated by small businessmen, women from the Daughters of the American Revolution, and American Legionnaires. In addition, women belonging to a national right-wing patriotic pressure group called Pro-America played leadership roles in the SDC. Pro-America was especially strong on the West Coast, having been founded in Seattle, and some of Houston's Minute Women, including Virginia Biggers and Virginia Hedrick, belonged to the national organization. The SDC anti-Goslin campaign featured the propaganda pamphlets written by Allen Zoll, who was also a favorite of Houston's Minute Women. Similar comparisons could be made with incidents in Denver, Minneapolis, San Diego, Los Angeles, New York City, and Philadelphia during the period 1945 to 1960. Historian David Caute has counted at least six hundred educators (380 in New York City alone) who fell victim to the post–World War II Red Scare. In many places the pattern was nearly the same as that of the Ebey and Goslin affairs.[99]

That an informal but effective national network existed to exchange information and disseminate literature can be easily deduced. Cross-fertilization among such groups as the American Legion, the Minute Women, Pro-America, the Circuit Riders, the DAR, and other organizations was rampant, especially since some persons held memberships in several of these groups at the same time. The Ebey affair, while rooted in distinctly local causes, had ties to the overall national uproar over public education. Two years before the Ebey case, David Hulburd warned with prescience in a book about the Goslin affair that "an analysis of what happened in Pasadena provides a lesson of grave importance: any school system in the country is alarmingly vulnerable today [1951] to attack from outside the local community as well as from within." Unfortunately for George Ebey and the public schools, Hulburd's warning went unheeded in Houston.[100]

George Ebey and his family returned to California in August of 1953. Although he was able to join the staff of the prestigious Stanford Research Institute in Menlo Park and subsequently received a federal security clearance to work on government defense contracts, Ebey's public school career was over. He never achieved his goal of being superintendent of a school district. Recalling those bitter and anxious days in Houston, Ebey later observed: "I find it a bit ironic . . . that probably my most significant contribution to education came from being lynched professionally by savages in a community where I was relatively a stranger."[101]

EIGHT

"OVETA DOESN'T BROOK BACK-TALK"

*And what is one reason that people are speaking up? Because
. . . old conservatives, rich people, even the elite . . . are being
painted pink. I laugh! It may be sadistic, but when all of us were
getting our brains beat out, no sympathy came from them.*
                                        —*Maury Maverick, Sr., 1954*[1]

By the fall of 1953, Houston's Red Scare seemed to be unopposed and
uncontested. With a growing roster of victims that included a high-
ranking public school official and the president of the University of
Houston and a list of successful censorship campaigns against public
speakers and school textbooks, potential Red Scare targets waited in fear,
wondering who would be next. This was especially true of many of the
city's educators. Teacher morale had plunged to a new low as a result
of the Ebey affair.

A radio commentator in search of higher ratings made matters worse.
Joe Worthy began a series of programs on radio station KATL called
"Worthy Speaks Out" that contributed to the fear among public school
teachers. The program had a talk-show format in which listeners could
telephone opinions and questions about local affairs while Worthy provided commentary. To attract a large audience, Worthy would spread
outrageous Red Scare rumors and conduct local crusades against alleged
subversives as a regular feature of his program. The show soon became
one of the most controversial in Houston broadcasting history. One
hostile listener observed that Worthy "is most effective, and as vicious
as [he] is effective. He browbeats his listeners into believing that he
stands between them and destruction by the Reds. He tells them that
they can identify themselves as 100% red-blooded Americans by pa-
tronizing his sponsors." The Minute Women in particular enjoyed his
commentary. One member wrote the Houston *Press* that Joe Worthy
was a "vivid and interesting radio personality, a young man dedicating
his time and talents to a crusade against Communism and all other
'isms' except Americanism."[2]

Carl Victor Little of the *Press* reacted to Worthy in a different way. Little wrote, "If you don't agree with that great 119 percent patriot Worthy
. . . you not only are a dangerous Red, a two percent American and one

of the subversive scum but an 18-carat what-Truman-called-[Drew] Pearson as well. (And we have the California records to prove it, too.)"[3]

Before coming to Houston, Joe Worthy worked briefly at several radio stations from Hawaii to Florida and became distinguished only by an inability to maintain listener ratings and an ability to insult various groups within each community where he worked. At one time or another, Worthy managed to attack Jews, blacks, Asians, Methodists, Quakers, the YMCA, the YWCA, labor unions, and the American Civil Liberties Union, among others, in his radio shows. Radio Station KOOL in Phoenix, Arizona, fired Worthy because he could not refrain from unauthorized editorializing while on the air. Station WGBS in Miami released him because of "unreliability" in reporting for work and because of alleged connections with gamblers. Unfortunately for the controversial news "analyst," his talent for on-the-air rumor spreading was not the only reason for his moving from place to place. Worthy also had an alleged bad habit of marrying more than one woman at a time and wound up with a bigamy charge for his carelessness. Worthy also had the misfortune of being accused of operating con jobs on the side. In one community, a group of citizens sued him for selling worthless "water-softening" devices. Such habits required frequent travel, so Worthy found himself in Houston in 1953.[4]

Worthy perceived that in his new city educational issues were particularly vulnerable to exploitation. He made frequent attacks on progressive education and "liberal" teachers and charged that socialistic ideas had infiltrated Houston's public school curriculum through subversive textbooks. The University of Houston and its president, Dr. W. W. Kemmerer, also attracted Worthy's verbal darts. In May 1953, after his forced resignation, Kemmerer publicly denounced the controversial radio personality as an "ignorant critic" and asserted that if he had followed Worthy's advice the University of Houston would have had to burn most of its books. Kemmerer contended that even the dictionary and the Bible seemingly failed to meet Worthy's patriotic standards.[5]

Joe Worthy also participated in the Ebey affair. On May 20, 1953, he dedicated a two-hour program to the Ebey dispute and allowed John Rogge to answer questions "over the air" from his concerned listeners. Since Rogge appeared alone and Worthy opposed Ebey, the program became a lengthy public harangue against the school administrator. Worthy provided Rogge an unchallenged forum to embellish his formal charges with innuendos that he could not have used before the school board. As if by script, Worthy played the straight man, setting Rogge up with helpful leading questions. For example, Worthy told Rogge that he was very concerned about Ebey's religious beliefs and wondered if he knew anything about them. Rogge answered on the air that he had "over-heard someone" say that Ebey was an atheist. Ebey's religious opinions were thoroughly discussed at the closed personnel conference on May 11, Rogge admitted, but, regrettably, the American Legion crusader could not reveal what had been said due to the confidentiality of the proceedings. Worthy then went on to another topic, leaving the distinct impression that Ebey was an atheist. In reality, Ebey had informed Rogge and the school board in the executive session that he belonged to one of Houston's largest Methodist churches.[6]

After listening to the Worthy-Rogge performance, Carl Victor Little compared Worthy to the nationally syndicated right-wing radio commentator Fulton Lewis, Jr., and wrote, "We hope Fulton Lewis Jr., Junior and Comrade Rogge never look into our past and find out the Oklahoma Legislature once passed a resolution branding us a commie after we insulted the representatives for attempting to mooch theater passes for themselves and all their kinfolks. We hope the 'Watchdog Twins' never dig up the dirt that we once belonged to the Red Hibiscus Literary Society, a commie front in Oregon."[7]

In September 1953, Worthy announced the formation of a "club" composed of parents with children in the schools. The club, appropriately called the Watchdogs, would place a "spy" in every grade school and college classroom in the city. These spies would be students who would report to their parents what their teachers said in class and what materials their teachers gave them to read. Anything that smacked of progressive education would be reported to the Watchdog organization, which would, in turn, provide the information to Worthy for use on his program. Worthy warned his listeners, "There is poison being taught in our schools. . . . We are interested in finding teachers who tell the children that we cannot get along without . . . the UN." The next night, Worthy promised to make his Watchdog organization anonymous and that he would not reveal the names of his informers. He again warned that "UNESCO is the greatest danger to free men. We do not have to tolerate these rats!"[8]

Worthy's attacks had the full endorsement of the Minute Women, with one prominent member, Mrs. J. D. Mabry, allegedly contributing funds to help keep Worthy's program on the air. Worthy's Watchdogs eventually proved to be nothing more than a publicity hype. Worthy himself was uninterested in creating an actual organization. The Red Scare was just another con game that Worthy hoped would attract enough listeners to keep his program ratings high. Nonetheless, Worthy gave Houston's Red Scare a radio voice that increased pressures on Houston's school teachers to adhere to conservative educational orthodoxy.[9]

These pressures were already great. For example, University of Houston professors knew about Minute Women "monitors" because of the complaints about Esther Nelson's lectures and the fact that some of the women could be easily identified in class. Also, a visiting Minute Women speaker had publicly congratulated the group on its spying program in March 1953. Worthy's invitation to regular students to also become spies created a chilling atmosphere inimical to academic freedom. The mere idea that a disaffected student, upset by a low grade, could yell "Red!" with a fair chance of being believed was a sword of Damocles hung above the head of every teacher. In addition, after Ebey's dismissal a rumor swept the University of Houston campus that the Red Scare coalition had already selected several professors for a purge. The university administrators understandably took all of this with great seriousness. For example, United States history courses were deleted from the pioneering educational television channel for the fall semester of 1953 due to a fear that Houston's ideological censors might find some comment "un-American." With a popular president having mysteriously resigned, spies in classrooms, rumors of purges, and a right-wing Red Scare oil man with little understanding of the complexities of higher education in firm command of the institution, long-time faculty would remember the fall semester of 1953 as a dark and unhappy time.[10]

While many of Houston's educators grappled in their individual ways with the specter of the Ebey affair and the pressures of the highly charged political climate, the city's Red Scare supporters were busy paying homage to their national hero, Joseph R. McCarthy. The forty-five-year-old Republican senator thrilled his fans in September 1953 by marrying his attractive assistant, Jean Kerr. E. M. Biggers, the father-in-law of Minute Women chair Virginia Biggers, presented a new six-thousand-dollar Cadillac Coupe DeVille to Senator McCarthy as a wedding gift. Biggers paid for the automobile by soliciting donations from Texans who wanted to show their appreciation for McCarthy's work. Although Biggers claimed to have received nearly two thousand individual donations of from $100 to $200 within days after he publicly announced his plan, McCarthy biographer Thomas C. Reeves labeled the story a "yarn." According to Reeves, the majority of the money came from Biggers and twenty others. Biggers also claimed that so much money poured in that he faced a problem of what to do with the surplus. He decided to add air-conditioning and set aside a gasoline fund. Biggers' son told one reporter, "We put more gadgets on that car than any Cadillac ever had in Houston. . . . We gave the car everything except a left turn indicator . . . and we figured Joe didn't need that." This story is also challenged by Reeves, who interviewed Jean McCarthy. Reeves says that Mrs.

McCarthy caused a delay in delivery because she had asked the Texans for a plusher model than they had envisioned.[11] Whatever the case, the presentation finally occurred in Washington, D.C., and included the reading of a proclamation signed by Texas governor Allan Shivers that declared, "Joe McCarthy—a real American—is now officially a Texan." As he handed McCarthy the keys to the new car, a proud E. M. Biggers announced, "We Texans approve the work you are doing, the methods you are employing, and the results you are getting." The event was highly publicized in Texas. The *Dallas Morning News* commented in an editorial about the "Texas" Cadillac that McCarthy "has had some pretty hard knocks lately from some nogoodniks, and we'd kind of like to show how we feel about it." McCarthy later wrecked the car in Wisconsin when he hit a deer. Biggers and his friends "promptly and quietly" replaced it with a new one.[12]

Despite these outward indications of a seemingly omnipotent Red Scare movement in the fall of 1953, there were also signs that some heretofore quiescent individuals and organizations were unwilling to allow the situation to continue. The Ebey affair served as a catalyst to motivate moderate and liberal Houstonians to speak out against the witch-hunt in the city. Two weeks after Ebey's dismissal, Curtis Quarles, a local businessman, wrote to the Houston *Post* demanding that the newspaper assign a top reporter to conduct a thorough investigation of the Minute Women and expose its membership and motives. Unknown to Quarles, his letter asked for an action that the *Post* had already begun.[13]

As discussed in a previous chapter, the *Post*, owned by Will and Oveta Culp Hobby, had helped legitimize Red Scare activists with its own anti-Communist editorial rhetoric. Although Oveta Hobby had failed to persuade "The Governor" to restrain Ed Kilman and moderate his more extreme editorials, she did keep the *Post* from ever endorsing the activities of Senator McCarthy. Unlike the *Chronicle*, and contrary to the *Post*'s own Red Scare editorial record, the *Post* openly criticized McCarthy. The Republican senator was often referred to as "the loud Wisconsin solon" in *Post* editorials. Nevertheless, despite the Hobbys' distaste for McCarthy and Oveta's personal dislike of Kilman's reactionary conservatism, the *Post*'s Red Scare rhetoric actually increased during the two years prior to the 1952 presidential election. Practical political strategy dictated this editorial policy.[14]

In Texas the Hobbys had allied themselves with the conservative faction of the Democratic party because of the realities of a one-party state. In national politics, however, they worked vigorously for moderate Republicans. They supported the Republican party's Thomas E. Dewey for president in 1944 and 1948.

During the bitter struggle between Senator Robert Taft and Dwight Eisenhower for the Republican presidential nomination in 1952, the Hobbys and Houston oil man Jack Porter played a key role in building a pro-Eisenhower movement to control the Texas Republican delegation. Texas' ultraconservative Republican regulars who supported Taft deeply resented the Hobbys' aggressive support of Eisenhower in the party primary. They viewed the Hobbys and their Democratic allies as opportunists and "one-day" Republicans who not only wanted to deny the presidential nomination to Taft but who also threatened the authority and power of the small clique that had ruled the GOP in Texas for years. As one Taft supporter later complained, "Needless to say how we feel about 'Oveta' [Hobby], how did she get on Ike's bandwagon?"[15]

In the spring of 1952, during an extremely contentious battle between the two forces to select delegates to the national Republican convention, the Taft faction resorted to the use of Red Scare tactics against its "newcomer" challengers. Throughout Texas, Taft workers distributed literature written by Joseph Kamp that featured such headlines as "IKE CODDLED COMMUNISTS WHILE PRESIDENT OF COLUMBIA UNIVERSITY" and "REDS, NEW DEALERS USE IKE IN PLOT TO HOLD POWER."

Despite sensational right-wing tactics, the Texas Eisenhower forces eventually triumphed and were accepted as the official Texas delegation at the national convention in Chicago in July. Much of Eisenhower's success in Texas can be credited to the Hobbys and the Houston *Post*. Eisenhower biographer Herbert Parmet has observed that Oveta Culp Hobby "used her newspaper resources for great partisan effect" during the delegate fight.[16]

Many Minute Women and other Red Scare activists worked for the Taft faction. Once Eisenhower won the Republican nomination, most of the members of the rival factions united in the campaign to oust the Democrats from the White House. A few Minute Women, such as Virginia Biggers, bitterly refused to support Eisenhower, however, and announced in favor of the Constitutional party, which had nominated General Douglas MacArthur for president.[17]

Oveta Hobby worked in New York City and served as a leader of the national Citizens for Eisenhower organization during the presidential campaign. Will Hobby remained in Houston to run the *Post* and help the campaign in Texas. He was joined in support of the Eisenhower campaign by Democrats Allan Shivers and Price Daniel, who ran for governor and senator, respectively. The Texas Democrats for Eisenhower alliance was held together not only by a mutual hatred of the New Deal and Fair Deal, but also by Adlai Stevenson's position that Texas did not own the submerged oil lands, or tidelands, extending from its shores in the Gulf of

Mexico. Texans argued that the 1848 Treaty of Guadalupe Hidalgo between Mexico and the United States gave the land to Texas. The United States Supreme Court in 1947 ruled that California did not own its tidelands, thus implying that Texas did not own its tidelands either. The issue of ownership was no small matter since millions of dollars of state revenues were at stake. Eisenhower supported state ownership. The tidelands issue dominated all others for many of Texas' oil men. The average Texan had less interest, however, so the issue was submerged beneath the "Communists in Washington" theme.[18]

The anti-Truman and the splinter MacArthur group thus relied heavily on McCarthyism and other Red Scare tactics to defeat Adlai Stevenson in November 1952. In Texas, the deep animosities between moderate Eisenhower Republicans and the smaller, right-wing faction of the pro-Taft movement surfaced almost as soon as Eisenhower assumed office in January 1953.

The main source of friction between moderates like the Hobbys and the extreme right wing was their different perceptions about the nature of the Communist threat. For moderates and some of the Taft supporters, the Red Scare was a symbolic partisan issue that could be manipulated to win political office. Once Eisenhower restored the Republican party to national power the issue of Communists in government could be muffled if not abandoned. Right-wing Republicans who made up the hard core of the Red Scare perceived the Communist issue differently. They were ideological "true believers" who steadfastly believed much of their own Red Scare rhetoric. Already wounded by their intraparty defeat, right-wing Red Scare activists were shocked when the Eisenhower administration failed to conduct a wholesale purge of the "Communist-infested" federal bureaucracy and return to a pre–New Deal style of government. As a result, Senator McCarthy's claim that "twenty years of treason" had become "twenty-one years of treason" found instant support among such groups as the Minute Women.

Following his inauguration as president in January 1953, Dwight Eisenhower appointed Oveta Culp Hobby head of the Federal Security Administration, the government agency responsible for administering the Social Security Act. Mrs. Hobby accepted the position with the understanding that the agency would be elevated to a cabinet-level government department. This occurred with the creation of the Department of Health, Education, and Welfare (HEW) in April 1953. As Eisenhower assistant Sherman Adams later recalled, Secretary Hobby "ran into rough going" almost as soon as HEW was created. The department began work on a conservative proposal to create a national health insurance plan that would provide federal backing to private companies offering low-cost hospitalization insurance. The American Medical Association (AMA), calling it "socialized medicine," initiated a lobbying campaign that quickly defeated the proposal.[19]

Back in Houston, the Minute Women and the Doctors for Freedom, composed of persons who resented Oveta Culp Hobby's role in defeating Senator Taft's bid for the GOP nomination and who were concerned about Eisenhower's failure to "clean out" the federal government, joined in the attacks on Hobby and her new department. Houston's Red Scare activists openly accused Hobby of Communist sympathies and charged that HEW was "socialistic." Physicians in Doctors for Freedom gave circulars to their patients that declared that HEW would be an "ideal vehicle for the complete socialization of medicine." One member complained that "the whole social security system is alien to America and is more parallel to the USSR than ours." The Minute Women, including Virginia Biggers, Mrs. J. D. Mabry, and Elsie Daniel, launched another barrage of individual protest letters denouncing Hobby and HEW. Mrs. Mabry complained to Martin Dies that "[Oveta] Hobby went high under Truman and now Eisenhower. Anything for advancement—nice business!" Elsie Daniel urged Price Daniel to see that Hobby's agency be "investigated and cleaned up." The majority of letters received at the White House criticizing Hobby's new federal department came from Houston.[20]

The charge that Hobby was "soft on Communism" was ironical in light of the *Post*'s earlier editorial campaign and Hobby's own future behavior as a member of Eisenhower's cabinet. As secretary of HEW, Oveta Hobby suspended the federal research grants of several scholars working on medical projects because they were deemed to be "security risks." The scientists were deprived of their financial support without benefit of charges or hearings on the basis of unsubstantiated and largely scurrilous secret reports from the Federal Loyalty Review Board. Hobby also dismissed Dr. John P. Peters as a special consultant to the Public Health Service and Kenneth M. Cole as a federal food and drug inspector after they were accused, in separated incidents, of being security risks. They were later restored to their jobs by the United States Supreme Court in separate decisions, *Peters* vs. *Hobby* (1955) and *Cole* vs. *Young* (1956). The court ruled that Mrs. Hobby had improperly dismissed both men. Nevertheless, the old resentments over the Taft-Eisenhower struggle, Joe McCarthy's criticisms of Eisenhower policies, and a paranoid fear of the new HEW department obscured everything else for the Minute Women. Virginia Biggers believed that Hobby "represented the reverse of everything the Minute Women stood for."[21]

Concurrent with the Red Scare attacks back in Houston, Senator McCarthy and his supporters were beginning to irritate Eisenhower and the national Republican party hierarchy. His outrageous and irresponsible behavior was rapidly transforming the senator from an asset to a liability in the eyes of Eisenhower Republicans. In the early summer of 1953, veteran journalist William S. White observed in *Look* that "in McCarthy, embarrassed Republican leaders know they have got hold of a red-hot bazooka, useful in destroying the enemy but also quite likely to blister the hands of the forces that employ it. Their private fear is that a lethal rocket may at any moment blast out through the wrong end of the pipe."[22]

In June, McCarthy's hiring of J. B. Matthews as executive director of his subcommittee staff enraged influential Protestant religious leaders throughout the United States. Matthews had charged in a national magazine that seven thousand Protestant clergy were Communists or fellow travelers. In July, McCarthy made the mistake of sharply criticizing Allen W. Dulles, the director of the Central Intelligence Agency (CIA), hinting that he planned to conduct a full-scale investigation of the CIA to search for Soviet KGB agents. Both actions were anathema to the Eisenhower White House team. McCarthy's use of extremist J. B. Matthews was perceived as a political liability for the party, while an investigation of the CIA would challenge the president's own power and might expose a myriad of clandestine activities that could damage national security and embarrass the government. With Eisenhower's approval, Vice-President Richard M. Nixon, presidential aide Emmett John Hughes, and Deputy Attorney General William Rogers stopped McCarthy in his tracks. At a private luncheon, Nixon himself explained to McCarthy that he was dangerously close to having an unpleasant problem on his hands. McCarthy, in an unusual moment of perception, saw the handwriting on the wall and made a rare retreat. Matthews resigned and the CIA hearings never materialized.[23]

While these significant inner White House maneuvers were not public knowledge, the Eisenhower hierarchy knew about them and this surely included cabinet member Oveta Culp Hobby, who was close to both the president and Nixon. Even if Hobby did not know the details about the Matthews and CIA incidents, she was certainly aware of and shared the White House's view of McCarthy and his followers. For example, Eisenhower was becoming increasingly impatient with Hugh Roy Cullen's constant drone of unsolicited advice about how the president should manage foreign affairs. In response to one of Cullen's letters, Eisenhower peevishly wrote, "I must say I was surprised by some of your comments . . . I am astonished by your implied fear that . . . my associates and I might fail to keep up our guard" against the Communists in Korea. No one in the administration, including Eisenhower and Nixon, was prepared to publicly attack McCarthy and wealthy supporters such as Cullen, however. After all, they might still be useful in the upcoming 1954 congressional elections. Republicans were not quite ready to abandon Red-baiting tactics for electoral purposes. The rabid local fringe groups on the extreme right were another matter, however. Personal attacks on Hobby, her new government department, and on "Ike" by a small but vocal pack of troublesome women and their spouses had to be dealt with. As one politically active Houston woman observed, "Oveta doesn't brook back-talk." And while McCarthy could not be attacked, at least his supporters could be, and this would be an indirect assault on the senator himself.[24]

Oveta Hobby had pressed "The Governor" for years about the *Post*'s editorial editor, Ed Kilman, and his Red Scare editorials. Now that the extreme right was attacking Oveta and Eisenhower and the situation was getting out of hand, Oveta got her way. Kilman remained as a figurehead editorial editor but his Red-baiting was stopped and the *Post*'s editorial page became more moderate, although still Republican. Accompanying the editorial change was the decision to publish an exposé of Houston's Red Scare groups. The exposé would appear on the front page and would symbolize the change in the *Post*'s political direction.[25]

George Carmack, the editor of the rival Houston *Press*, believed that the Red Scare exposé was "purely Oveta's decision. I don't think the Governor [Will Hobby] would've cared much about it. It was a real smart decision. . . ." Carmack felt that "Oveta decided that this was a road that the Houston *Post* ought to take; it'll help the *Post*. Oveta did it for what . . . it would do for the *Post*'s . . . image." A series of highly publicized investigatory reports about such fringe groups as the Minute Women would be a sound business move for the newspaper. Not only would it sell the paper, but it would give the *Post* a crusading and progressive image without risk. While the Minute Women and their associates had damaged the schools and caused problems at the University of Houston, the Hobbys and their close friends such as the Browns, Jesse Jones, and Judge Elkins in the local power elite had nothing to fear whatever from the Red Scare groups. The power elite, which had done so much to create the local Red Scare, could just as easily do much to emasculate it.[26]

The *Limelight* affair illustrated the change in the *Post*'s policies. Since 1949 the national leadership of the American Legion had conducted an anti-Communist campaign against the movie industry. The *American Legion Magazine* featured articles that accused Hollywood of being dominated by subversives and un-American influences. One such article, written by J. B. Matthews, claimed that three hundred movie personalities had belonged to the CPUSA at one time or another. Among those actors so accused was Charles Chaplin. Red Scare groups together with the United States Immigration Service (Chaplin was a British citizen) harassed the internationally famous comedian and filmmaker to such an extent that he finally moved in 1952 to Europe, where he remained until his death over twenty years later. Following his self-exile, Chaplin continued to make a few films, *Limelight* being one of them.[27]

In March 1953, just prior to the attack on Oveta Culp Hobby, Houston's Red Scare Coalition, led once again by the Americanism Committee of the American Legion, denounced the owners of a local motion picture theater for showing *Limelight*. The Americanism Committee lodged a formal protest with the theater's manager, who was also barraged by the usual Minute Women letter campaign. The Legion's spokesperson declared that "Americans aid and abet Stalin's Communism when they patronize and pay money to see Limelight." The theater agreed to stop showing the film three days after the controversy began. The Houston *Post* remained silent throughout the affair. In July 1953, shortly after the Minute Women began criticizing Hobby and HEW, another theater tried to show Chaplin's film. Again Red Scare groups demanded that the movie be banned. The American Legion's spokesperson declared that the public must learn that they cannot have anything to do with "Communist" products because "the stake is nothing more or less than the American way of life." The *Post*, which had ignored the incident three months earlier, suddenly became the defender of free speech. It declared that the protesters supported a "false concept of Americanism." The *Post* stated that "it is not the office of the Legion to decide for all the people whether or not the film affects the public welfare." The American Legion responded by saying, "It [is] inconceivable that the Houston *Post* can deny the soundness . . . of the Legion's viewpoint. . . ." Adolph Blieden, chairman of the Americanism Committee, declared that the *Post* must be "tolerant of Communist sympathizers like Chaplin" and "intolerant" of "pro-American views." The *Post* itself was soon inundated with Red Scare mail attacking the editors as "left-wingers" because of their defense of the film.[28]

The *Post*'s stand in the *Limelight* affair was one of the first indications that something new was in the air. It signaled the beginning of the power elite's withdrawal of the sanction of legitimacy for the extreme right's accusations. With the Republicans in power, the establishment was less enchanted by the activities of these fringe groups, especially since Eisenhower Republicans were now becoming the accused rather than the accusers. It was time to pull the plug on the Red Scare. The *Post*'s new attitude would become more evident, however, when the newspaper printed a scathing exposé of Oveta Culp Hobby's enemies in October 1953.

The exposé had its origins in May 1953 when a prominent member of the League of Women Voters went to Harry Johnston, the *Post's* city editor, and gave him a list of 516 names, addresses, and telephone numbers of people she believed to be members of the Minute Women. The George Ebey affair had just ended and the woman told the *Post* that the Minute Women were responsible for the controversy. For several months a *Post* reporter, Ralph S. O'Leary, had pleaded to be allowed to do an exposé on local Red Scare organizations, but Johnston always rejected his requests. Apparently, now that the Red Scare was no longer useful or desirable for the Hobbys' partisan efforts, Johnston could allow the forty-two-year-old O'Leary to do the exposé. As city editor, Johnston was not in the top echelon of the *Post*. George Carmack observed that Johnston did not make decisions as important as the Red Scare exposé. "Harry was just a conduit . . . that was Oveta's decision. . . ." The city editor gave the Minute Women membership list to O'Leary and asked him to write the *Post's* formal attack on Houston's Red Scare.[29]

A native of New Orleans, Ralph Semmes O'Leary was a veteran journalist who had previously worked for the New Orleans *Item* and the St. Louis *Star-Times*. O'Leary remained with the *Star-Times* until it ceased publication in 1951. He was offered a job by Jesse Jones' Houston *Chronicle*, where he began work as a reporter and rewrite man in July 1951. After a year and a half he moved to the Houston *Post*.[30]

O'Leary had been at the *Post* for five months when Johnston assigned him to the Minute Women investigation. O'Leary began his research by tracing the origin of the membership list given to the *Post*. After much effort he found the woman responsible for compiling the roll sheet. The woman, a former Minute Women member, had worked as a volunteer part-time office secretary for the organization, but had quit the group after becoming alarmed at their activities. Before leaving, she typed a membership list based on information she found in the Minute Women office. She willingly answered O'Leary's questions about the Minute Women's activities but adamantly refused to sign an affidavit that would have protected the *Post* from libel charges. She admitted that she would rather flee the city than testify in court and reveal her identity in public. The informant told O'Leary that she believed the Minute Women and their backers were more powerful than the Houston *Post* and could have her fired from her job. She also expressed a fear of the organization's telephone chain. It could be used to harass her day and night and to spread rumors about her to her friends.[31]

The list proved to be invaluable to O'Leary, who subsequently verified more than one hundred members. The list, however, could not appear in the newspaper because of the woman's refusal to sign a statement. Eventually, O'Leary found twenty other former members willing to talk about the group, each of whom provided important information verifying his other sources. Unfortunately, because of fears of reprisal, none of the women would sign a statement to protect the *Post*. In several years of reporting, O'Leary had never seen a situation where not one witness agreed to sign an affidavit. All of the women feared that the Minute Women would initiate a whispering campaign that could ruin their husbands' or their own reputation. Even their children might be intimidated by classmates at school.

One woman gave O'Leary a complete file of national Minute Women newsletters, local bulletins, and other pamphlets used or printed by the Minute Women. But before he could view the papers, the woman had O'Leary cross-examined by her attorney. O'Leary agreed before witnesses that he would not reveal her name and that she would not have to testify in case of a libel suit. The reporter also agreed to keep the material under lock and key at his home and that he would never take it to his desk at the *Post*. Furthermore, O'Leary agreed never to write the woman's name on any of the material and never to mention to anyone that he had even talked to her.

Ralph O'Leary, with the help of some Houston school employees and George Ebey, soon acquired enough information to write his exposé. Most of his sources had to be classified as anonymous because of the refusal of informers to sign affidavits. After two months of work, O'Leary possessed a substantial amount of circumstantial evidence. He decided to verify his material by interviewing Minute Women leaders Virginia Biggers, Virginia Hedrick, and Faye Weitinger. He asked a *Post* photographer to accompany him to the interviews with each of the three leaders in individual and separate sessions. When he and the photographer arrived for the first interview with Virginia Hedrick, they also found Faye Weitinger, the second person O'Leary had planned to question. O'Leary was upset since he felt that the two together could help change the subject or rescue each other from a situation that might reveal more about the Minute Women than they might desire. They refused to allow the *Post* photographer to enter the house, so O'Leary was forced to conduct the interview alone, without a corroborating witness. Before O'Leary could ask questions, Virginia Hedrick turned on a tape recorder and she and Faye Weitinger proceeded to conduct their own interview. They believed that Governor Hobby ran the Houston *Post* as a "front" for someone else, perhaps the CPUSA. To their irritation, O'Leary had no information to offer on that subject. They then asked O'Leary questions about Oveta Culp Hobby and tried to get him to admit that she had personally assigned him to investigate their organization because of her "left-wing" beliefs. O'Leary had nothing to offer in this matter either. The two Minute Women gave up and allowed O'Leary to ask his own questions.

During the two-hour interview Hedrick and Weitinger inadvertently confirmed most of the vital information O'Leary had received. The reporter kept the women off guard by taking no notes and acting uninterested when they mentioned something important. When O'Leary revealed most of the details about their secret meeting to organize the attack on Ebey, Faye Weitinger angrily interrupted him and said that "women rats" had infiltrated their group. She asked how he knew so much about the Minute Women and demanded the names of his informers. The interview soon ended on a strained note.

When O'Leary returned to the *Post* and typed what he remembered of the interview, he realized that he had received confirmation of enough material to write his Minute Women series. O'Leary tried to get a copy of the tape recording of the Minute Women interview the next morning. When he telephoned Virginia Hedrick, she refused to send him a copy. The two women had played it to their husbands and decided that it was an unfavorable interview. They had put the tape recording into a safe and intended to keep it there.

O'Leary took the notes from what he felt was his best interview in twenty-five years of newspaper work and combined them with his other sources to produce an eleven-part series of articles in the Houston *Post*. The series, placed prominently on the front page, began on October 11 and continued until October 21, 1953.

In his series, O'Leary charged that "there . . . is a large-scale Red scare under way in the community." His research revealed that the overwhelming majority of Houston's residents had taken no part in the Red Scare. The names of a comparatively small number of persons had turned up again and again as active in the anti-Communist campaign. According to O'Leary, most of these persons belonged to the Houston Minute Women. A less active role had been played by a small number of American Legion members, members of the Committee for the Preservation of Methodism, and more informal groups composed of remnants of the defunct 1948 Dixiecrat movement. Because its members had taken part in nearly every Red Scare attack in recent years in Houston, O'Leary's inquiry centered on the Minute Women.[32]

The Minute Women series caught the rapt attention of much of the city. Copies of the Houston *Post* became hot items in great demand for ten days after the initial article. Houstonians learned in detail who had spearheaded the Red Scare in their city. Throughout the series, O'Leary emphasized that Houston was "remarkably free of Communistic influences." But, thanks to the "well-meaning" organizations and citizens described in his series, a "reign of terror" existed among many concerned Houstonians. Understandably, O'Leary neglected to discuss the significant role played by his own newspaper and the *Chronicle*, not to mention his

bosses, the Hobbys, and their friends among the 8-F Crowd in helping
to create the "reign of terror." Reacting to O'Leary's statement that there
were very few Communists actually in Texas, one Red Scare supporter
reminded the *Post* editors that "the only place I ever read . . . there were
a lot of communists in Texas was in the columns of the Houston *Post*."
O'Leary was personally very aware of this hypocritical omission. Nevertheless, the journalist was a realist, grateful to be able to at least go after
the activists of the Red Scare if not its creators.[33]

The series had a dramatic impact on the public. It was as though people had been holding their breath to the point of pain and could now
breathe with relief. A flood of mail poured into the offices of the *Post*.
So many requests came in for copies of the series that the *Post* rushed
to publish ten thousand special reprint editions. A fascinated public
absorbed these so rapidly that the *Post* had to publish another ten thousand. The American Federation of Labor and the National Education
Association's Defense Committee in Washington, D.C., distributed thousands of copies throughout the United States. In all, individuals and
organizations from across the nation requested over 120,000 copies of
O'Leary's work, an amazing figure for a local newspaper reprint. One
group in Connecticut requested copies to distribute to the members of
the Connecticut state legislature because of O'Leary's discussion of
Suzanne Stevenson. In Georgia, the editor of the Atlanta *Constitution*,
Ralph McGill, wrote in an editorial column that the *Post* had provided
a public service in the best traditions of journalism and "Americanism."
The St. Louis *Post-Dispatch* commended the Houston *Post* and Ralph
O'Leary for having the courage to investigate the cause of the spreading
fear in Houston. *Time* magazine featured O'Leary's exposé and declared,
"The *Post's* . . . careful, unhysterical tone was a model of how a newspaper can effectively expose irresponsible vigilantism." O'Leary's work
received even greater national exposure when *Nation* magazine printed
a three-page condensation. *Nation* made the article its cover story in
January 1954 and titled it "Daughters of Vigilantism."[34]

In Houston, O'Leary's exposé received endorsements from the small
but growing circle of anti–Red Scare civic leaders. For example, Nina
Cullinan, daughter of Joseph S. Cullinan (the founder of the Texas Company [Texaco]) and an active and progressive civic leader, congratulated
the *Post* for showing "initiative and courage." Miss Cullinan felt the Red
Scare had reached a turning point in Houston because of the series and
that the atmosphere of "repression and fear" had been relieved. The
Hobbys' son, William P. Hobby, Jr., wrote O'Leary from his naval officer
training school to congratulate him on the series. The young Hobby, a
future lieutenant governor of Texas, said, "What a masterful job of reporting, researching, and writing the series was! I think you have done

Houston—and the *Post*—a service that will be much noted and long remembered. It was a job that needed to be done in the worst way. . . ."[35]

Other Houstonians joined with these individuals in praising the exposé.
Among them was independent oil man Jubal R. Parten, who had long
been an opponent of the Red Scare and McCarthyism. As chairman of
the University of Texas board of regents, Parten had faced down a challenge from Martin Dies and foiled attempts to fire Dr. Robert Montgomery. Parten had become a director of the newly formed Fund for the
Republic, an organization based in Santa Barbara, California. The fund
was created to provide financial support through grants to organizations
and individuals working to defend constitutionally protected freedoms.
Initially supported by the Ford Foundation, the fund served, among other
purposes, as one of a handful of national organizations opposed to the
Red Scare. Parten read O'Leary's exposé in amazement, not because he
was unaware of the Red Scare but because the Hobbys had printed it.
The oil man was well aware of the influential role played by Houston's
newspapers in creating local fear. As a New Deal Democrat, Parten himself had suffered from the *Post*'s editorial tactics. The *Post* had prominently
featured a false political accusation made by Governor Allan Shivers
against Parten during the presidential campaign of 1952, but later buried
the news that disproved Shivers' charge.[36]

Despite his views about the *Post*, Parten was nevertheless delighted
about O'Leary's exposé. He clipped the articles as they appeared and
mailed them to David Freeman, secretary of the Fund for the Republic.
Parten wrote Freeman that "so far as I know this is the first time that any
Metropolitan newspaper in Texas had made any effort toward giving piti-
less publicity to some of the political activities which have for so long
tended to smother the educational system in this state." He suggested
that Freeman acquire reprints of the series and distribute them to the
other directors of the fund. To push this idea further, Parten also sent
clippings to his friend Dr. Robert M. Hutchins, former chancellor of the
University of Chicago, who was the associate director of the Fund for the
Republic, and to Clifford Case, the fund's president. Subsequently, at
their November 1953 board meeting in New York, the fund's directors
asked Case to investigate the Minute Women articles to determine
whether or not the fund should help disseminate the material or support
a more thoroughly researched book on the subject. Following the meeting, Case told Parten that "Houston's experience, past and present, . . .
holds a great many valuable lessons as to effective ways of approaching
problem situations" relating to the Red Scare phenomenon.[37]

This initial enthusiasm, however, was somewhat cooled by an evalu-
ation of the exposé by the fund's educational consultant, Harold C. Hunt
of the Harvard University Graduate School of Education. Hunt advised

against the fund's distribution of O'Leary's series. The consultant felt that O'Leary's research was shallow and that the Houston situation's "roots are far deeper . . . than the Houston *Post* series . . . reveals." Hunt accurately argued that Houston's Red Scare was more complicated than just being a case study of the actions of local extremists. He reported that the situation in Houston revolved "around personalities, ambitions, jealousies, and the ebb and flow of power over many years." Hunt advised the board to do its own research and publish a pamphlet about the national educational crisis that would emphasize "a constructive approach" to solving the problem.[38]

Clifford Case agreed with Hunt, and added that he feared that "wide publicity might actually help the Minute Women." Nevertheless, although the fund failed to distribute the *Post*'s articles, knowledge about the Houston problem did result in the fund's decision to sponsor a scholarly study of fear in education. The fund subsequently commissioned Dr. Paul Lazarsfeld of Columbia University to conduct the project. Lazarsfeld, with the aid of Wagner Thielens, Jr., eventually produced *The Academic Mind: Social Scientists in a Time of Crisis*. Based on 2,451 interviews of teachers in 165 colleges in 1955, the Lazarsfeld study provided quantitative evidence for the charge that higher education was being severely challenged by the effects of the national Red Scare.[39]

Meanwhile, O'Leary's work was noted elsewhere. In March 1954, O'Leary received the American Newspaper Guild's Heywood Broun Award for "disclosing a growing climate of fear" in Houston. The judges, who included Eric Sevareid of CBS News, stated that it took courage for the *Post* to print the exposé in an area of the nation in which the "suppressionist spirit is especially strong." O'Leary also won the Sidney Hillman Foundation Award and the National Headliners Club Award.[40] Not all of the reaction was so favorable, however. A small bomb exploded in the doorway of O'Leary's home shortly after the end of the series, causing minor damage but no injuries. Fortunately for the O'Learys, most of the negative reactions were expressed in a less violent form.[41]

The Minute Women series appeared during the Eighth American Legion District (Harris County) annual convention. Irate Legionnaires, including John Rogge, submitted a resolution to the convention denouncing the series. The resolution denied O'Leary's allegation that the Legion had interfered with freedom of speech and stated that the organization did not oppose the appearance of any speaker so long as churches and schools were not used as forums for "propaganda we consider inimical to the best interests of America." Referring to the Clement affair, the Legion resolution claimed that "Negro American Legionnaires here were in full accord with our project" against the black educator. Finally, the resolution denied an O'Leary charge that a Legionnaire had physically attacked John Swomley at the American Friends Service Committee's Institute of International Relations meeting in 1952. The convention, led by Americanism Committee chairman Adolph Blieden, narrowly rejected the resolution in a voice vote. Blieden, although sympathetic, opposed the resolution for several reasons. A Legionnaire may have been involved in the altercation with Swomley, Blieden argued, and "we would look rather foolish if it could be proved" to be so. Blieden also said that the statement about black American Legionnaires supporting their attack on Clement was "another assumption in my opinion," since no one had ever bothered to ask them. Finally, the Americanism Committee chairman declared that it was "stupid" to say the Legion only opposed un-American speakers appearing at churches and schools in Houston. "I am against them speaking, period," Blieden proclaimed. "I don't give a damn if we hang them."[42]

The Republican Women's Club of Harris County (Houston), an organization dominated by Minute Women and former supporters of Senator Taft, issued a resolution in October soon after the series ended that praised the Minute Women and attacked the *Post*. The Republican women also declared that the *Post*'s recent coverage of Senator McCarthy was intended to discredit him. The resolution warned that President Eisenhower had swung to the left and had used the *Post* and other papers "under his control" to prepare the public for an even more "radical swing to the left." The *Post* had attacked the Minute Women, according to the right-wing Republican women, because its members had fought against creation of the Department of Health, Education, and Welfare. The Republican party of Harris County, which represented the dominant pro-Eisenhower faction, formally repudiated the women's resolution and charged that they represented a small minority of Republicans in Houston.[43]

The *Chronicle* held steadfast in its Red Scare policy while the *Post* moved toward a more moderate position. Jesse Jones had undergone an emergency gall bladder operation earlier in the year and had endured several days on the critical list as a result. The seventy-nine-year-old newspaper publisher was left in a weakened physical condition and never fully regained his health, although his death would not occur until 1956. Jones' condition meant that the *Chronicle*'s editorial policies would be even more reflective of men such as Emmet Walter than of himself.[44]

The *Chronicle* denounced the *Post*'s attack on the Minute Women and declared that Houstonians were not victims of any "thought control." According to the *Chronicle*, "One gets the idea that a reign of terror has all but paralyzed the clergy and the educators of Houston." The newspaper announced that it had failed to find any person in the city fearful of speaking up on any issue. The *Chronicle* concluded, "Anti-anti-communists . . . scream 'thought control' at anyone who is sensible enough to reject their weird philosophy." Referring to criticism of Joe Worthy, the *Chronicle* charged that the only attempted thought control had been by "radical liberals" who wanted to censor radio shows. The *Chronicle*, however, would eventually edge closer to the *Post* after Joe McCarthy's attack on the army.[45]

Naturally, the strongest protest against the *Post* and O'Leary came from the Minute Women. On October 22, 1953, the group invited the public to an open meeting at a local American Legion hall. With approximately two hundred people present, Bertie Maughmer began the meeting with a review of a new book by Paul W. Shafer and John H. Snow entitled *The Turning of the Tides*, which declared that socialists were using the public schools to remake the United States along "collectivist" lines. Virginia Hedrick followed Maughmer and charged that the nation's schools had failed to teach American history properly. To support her argument, Hedrick quoted a survey indicating that only 6 percent of college freshmen could name the original thirteen colonies.

After Maughmer and Hedrick finished their portion of the program, the husbands of three Minute Women leaders stood and read statements that accused the Houston *Post* and Ralph O'Leary of attempting to intimidate and silence a group of patriotic housewives through the use of insinuations and innuendos. They stated that the articles contained "unfounded allegations, half-truths and falsehoods" and had made patriotic citizens appear to be un-American. According to the men, the *Post* had attempted to "suppress freedom of speech and freedom of action of individuals to perform their duty toward schools, churches, and government." The O'Leary series violated "honest newspaper reporting and the ethics of newspapermen" because the series did not appear on the editorial page and statements were printed without reference to sources. Finally, they demanded that the *Post* identify the person or persons responsible for promoting the series. They challenged the *Post*, "in the spirit of fair play," to give the Minute Women an equal amount of front-page space to refute O'Leary. They demanded that a *Post* spokesperson debate Minute Women leaders on radio and/or television over the questions raised by O'Leary.[46]

The Houston *Post* replied in an editorial that it stood "on its full, careful report" and that it had performed the function of a newspaper in reporting the activities of the Minute Women. The *Post* explained that O'Leary wrote his eleven articles thoughtfully and carefully after working for "months" gathering a mass of material. The *Post* rejected the debate challenge and stated that the columns of the newspaper were open to any noteworthy news of Houston or Houstonians. The *Post* refused to give the Minute Women the space they demanded.[47]

The Minute Women were forced to pay for advertisement space in Houston's newspapers to publicize their defense. This limited their effort to a small announcement that declared the Minute Women of the U.S.A. to be

> a non-profit, non-partisan, non-sectarian, educational organization which stands:
> FOR God and Country
> FOR the Constitution of the USA
> FOR States Rights
> FOR Free Enterprise
> FOR a Free Press and the Truth
> FOR Patriotic Teaching in Our Schools
> AGAINST Socialism and Communism

The ad charged that those who opposed the Minute Women evidently did not believe in the above-stated principles.[48]

As criticism of the Minute Women mounted in Houston because of the O'Leary series, Virginia Biggers continued her attempts to get the Houston *Post* to print the group's refutations. Finally, in December 1953, the *Post* printed Biggers' "corrections" of O'Leary's series. The Minute Women chair's letter specifically challenged O'Leary on only a few points and did more to verify O'Leary's articles than to refute them.

The Minute Women denied O'Leary's claim that Houston was relatively free of Communists. They recalled that the Communist party had operated openly in the city until 1950. The Minute Women cited the incident in April of 1953 when University of Houston students found Communist party literature in their cars. Also in April, the letter charged, a speaker at Rice Institute told an audience that he opposed only "Russian Communism." Their last proof of Communist activity in Houston centered around Louis Budenz's book *Men without Faces*. Budenz, a former editor of the *Daily Worker* and perhaps the best known ex-Communist informer of the postwar period, charged that it was impossible to discover Communists because they disguised themselves as loyal, good Americans. This being "true," then the *Post* could not possibly say there were no Communists in Houston.

Virginia Biggers also denied any involvement in the Ebey affair. She claimed that the school board made its decision on the basis of an investigation by an independent private firm. "The Minute Women," wrote Biggers, "had no policy whatsoever concerning Dr. Ebey." Other than a few words defending the administrative structure of their organization, the Minute Women failed to refute any other portions of the eleven-part series, including the indirect quotes O'Leary used from his interview with Virginia Hedrick and Faye Weitinger. The latter woman was so enraged by the *Post*'s attack that she wrote Texas governor Allan Shivers. "I am a Minute Woman," Faye Weitinger stated. "Mrs. Hobby has forced O'Leary on unsuspecting Houstonians." She wanted Shivers to do something about it; a futile request given Shivers' strong ties to the Hobby family and his dependence on *Post* support in his upcoming campaign for reelection to an unprecedented third term.[49]

The Minute Women were likewise stymied in an attempt to smear O'Leary as a subversive. Faye Weitinger asked Martin Dies to locate material on the *Post* journalist in HCUA files. Dies agreed but failed to find "any reference to Mr. O'Leary" in the records. Undeterred, Weitinger asked Dies to check HCUA files for information on Julius Klein, a former newspaper collaborator of O'Leary's in St. Louis. "It is very important that we have this information," Weitinger declared. "Something must be done to help us . . . we have no money except what we take from our household accounts which is a drain on a few of us. Very few, as you so well know, care enough for their countries [*sic*] Welfare to donate toward its preservation. Is it not possible to get the *Post* and *Nation* Minute Women smear listed [in HCUA files]? Maybe we should sue the *Post*." This tactic also proved futile, as Dies replied that nothing could be found about Klein. No longer a member of HCUA, Dies ignored the request to have the *Post* cited in the committee's files.[50]

After the Houston *Post* attacked the Minute Women and their allies, the National Education Association prepared its own attack on the Red Scare coalition. The National Education Association (NEA), the nation's largest teachers' professional organization, had created the National Commission for the Defense of Democracy through Education in 1941 to defend public education against "unjust attacks" and to investigate charges against teachers, schools, and educational methods. This NEA commission now gave its attention to Houston.[51]

Two days after the Houston school board failed to rehire George Ebey, the Oregon Education Association asked the NEA's defense commission to investigate the situation in Houston. The commission, however, could not investigate a school district unless invited by the local NEA affiliate. The NEA sent the defense commission's executive secretary, Dr. Richard B. Kennan, to Houston on July 30 to confer with George Ebey, Houston Teachers Association (HTA) leaders, and others to gather facts on the case. His visit encouraged the HTA and its forceful president, Margaret Bleil, to urge the Texas State Teachers Association (TSTA) to file a request for the NEA to go into Houston.[52]

In October, the TSTA's executive committee held hearings in Austin to determine the need for an investigation. Margaret Bleil, convinced that the school board had treated Ebey unjustly, told the TSTA's committee that the Minute Women were responsible for the Ebey affair. She described the Houston situation as being "fraught with politics and pressures and generally a mess" and warned that Houston's problem was contagious but could be stopped if publicly exposed. Bleil admitted that the NEA could not force the school board to rehire Ebey but she believed it could at least clear his name. Opposition testimony came from Charles Poe, president of the Houston Association of School Administrators and a member of the Mills machine, who declared that everything had "quieted down" in Houston. Poe warned the TSTA that it would be a mistake to ask the NEA to investigate because it would only promote confusion in the schools. Besides, Poe charged, the executive secretary of the NEA was against state possession of tidelands and favored UNESCO, "that new world social and economic order."[53]

The TSTA appointed a subcommittee to conduct a preliminary investigation to determine if the TSTA should ask for help from the NEA. After a brief probe, in November 1953 the subcommittee reported that a "climate of uneasiness and uncertainty" existed in Houston's schools and that "75 to 85 percent" of the teachers wanted an investigation. The subcommittee noted that Superintendent Moreland had publicly announced that he supported the school board, but the committee members felt that he privately wanted an investigation. As a result of the report, on December 10, 1953, the executive committee of the TSTA voted 19 to 10 in favor of asking for an NEA investigation.[54]

Houston's Red Scare activists greeted the TSTA's announcement with open hostility. The NEA had been attacked by the conservatives in Houston's schools for years. The Minute Women issued a statement calling the NEA an "American Gestapo." One Minute Women member wrote to Houston's newspapers and asked, "Texans, are we going to tolerate this infringement upon our rights as a free people to govern ourselves?" The letter announced, "This is the Houston INDEPENDENT School District! . . . NEA . . . keep your nose out of our business!" Minute Woman Anne Harrison hinted possible reprisals against those responsible for the TSTA request and called for the publication of a list of teachers who had signed petitions supporting the NEA probe. John Rogge told the Houston *Press* that the investigation would be a "hot potato" for the NEA when it learned the real facts of the case. He suggested the NEA could save time by just reading the General Research Company report on Dr. Ebey.[55]

School board members reacted to the NEA probe with differing feelings. Verna Rogers and Jack Tucker both supported the investigation, with Tucker declaring, "We need someone from the outside to look us over." The conservatives on the board felt differently, however. James Delmar argued that "outsiders don't have any right poking around here." Dallas Dyer agreed and stated, ". . . local control of schools is one of the few rights we have left." She charged that only local people could correct local problems. Henry Peterson expressed surprise that Houston's teachers would desire an investigation. Bill Moreland, very much a man on a hot seat, wrote a letter to the NEA opposing any investigation. Calling the Ebey case a "closed issue," Moreland warned that a probe would do no good.[56]

Predictably, the Houston *Chronicle* denounced the TSTA's request and tried to discredit the investigation. It announced Moreland's position with a glaring front-page headline: "Moreland Says Forget Ebey Case." In an editorial, the *Chronicle* charged that the NEA "is entirely out of sympathy with the school philosophy of the Houston School Board and Houstonians generally." The newspaper stated that liberal organizations such as the TSTA and NEA caused the confusion in Houston's schools instead of nonteacher influences. According to the *Chronicle*, teacher organizations possessed no legal or moral authority to dominate schools because teachers are public employees under the control of the school board and thus have no right to investigate legitimate actions of their employer.[57]

The *Chronicle* also published a six-part series of articles "exposing" the NEA. The series featured questionable or "pro-communist" statements issued by NEA leaders in past years and made a vigorous attempt to link the NEA with socialism and Communism. *Chronicle* columnist Ina G. Grotte wrote, ". . . as an unreconstructed states' righter, I don't want any group of 'furriners' investigating . . . Houston schools." Miss Grotte suggested that teachers who "find our conservative requirements too binding" should, like asthma sufferers, "seek a climate which is healthier for their ideas."[58]

The *Chronicle* went to great lengths to convince Houstonians that the city needed an investigation of local subversives rather than an NEA investigation of anti-Communists in the schools. Just prior to the arrival of the NEA committee, the *Chronicle* printed a front-page interview with the head of the Houston Police Department's "subversive squad." Police officer Larry Fultz told the *Chronicle* that there were at least fifteen "known subversives" in Houston. Fultz claimed that these subversives included businessmen, office workers, professional people, and laborers and that the police had attended meetings "all over the city" to gather information about their activities. The *Chronicle* commented that this meant "the Communists . . . are pretty active" in Houston. The newspaper also cited the Wittenburg deportation case (which had occurred five years earlier) as substantive proof of Communist activity in the city. The *Chronicle* followed the "subversive squad" interview with a sensational front-page editorial demanding that Governor Allan Shivers and the Texas legislature outlaw the Communist party in Texas.[59]

Despite the hostile atmosphere, some of Houston's teachers openly indicated their full support of an NEA investigation by signing petitions endorsing a probe. A citywide drive for signatures was slowed considerably, however, after James Delmar issued a warning "to stop politicking in the classrooms." This frightened some teachers from signing. At Milby High School the principal and assistant principal held a "strife-torn session" with a group of pro-NEA teachers that ended when the administrators seized the NEA petitions and threw them into a wastebasket.[60]

Ignoring opposition from the *Chronicle*, Minute Women, and others in Houston, the NEA readily agreed to the TSTA request and appointed a seven-member committee to conduct an investigation of Houston schools. All seven members came from the South and represented a variety of backgrounds. The chairman, John W. Letson, was superintendent of schools in Bessemer, Alabama. Other members included a professor of education from Louisiana State University, a classroom teacher from Columbia, South Carolina, a businessman from Savannah, Georgia, an attorney from Tennessee, and the dean of the College of Education at the University of Mississippi.[61]

The NEA investigating committee began its hearings in Houston on January 27, 1954, by inviting teachers and any other citizens with information about the alleged problems in the public schools to come forward and testify. The committee gave witnesses the choice of testifying at open or closed hearings. Margaret Bleil and other HTA officers testified first. The HTA officers claimed that the Mills machine controlled Houston schools and the Houston Association of School Administrators (HASA). According to Bleil and other HTA leaders, the Mills machine wanted to destroy the teachers' organization. They also charged that school principals pressured teachers to vote for CSAE candidates in school board elections. The next day, Ralph O'Leary testified at a closed hearing that had to change rooms several times because of reporters attempting to eavesdrop on their fellow journalist's testimony. O'Leary repeated the accusations he had made in his exposé. On January 29 a group of over five hundred teachers swept into the committee meeting room and interrupted the hearings to protest the investigation. The teachers charged that a clique controlled the HTA and therefore did not truly represent Houston's teachers. Several of these teachers, however, later admitted that they did not know what the meeting was about. They had been told by their principals to attend the hearings at a scheduled time.[62]

On January 30, the final day of the hearings, sixty school principals appeared before the committee. The administrators repeated the charge that HTA represented a minority of Houston's teachers and that the group had tried for years to wrest control of the school district from the school board. The principals denied they had pressured teachers and warned the committee to "stop meddling" in Houston's affairs.

After the hearing with the school principals, the NEA committee faced the Houston school board in a meeting broadcast over local radio and television. The NEA refrained from questioning the board members. Instead, the committee answered the board's questions and listened politely while the conservatives attacked its investigation. Surprisingly, this passive tactic worked. The meeting began with Jimmy Delmar telling the committee to "go home . . . your communities need you more than we do." It ended with him saying that "on the surface the committee seems to be most sincere." The board agreed to supply the committee with any information it needed. Verna Rogers wryly commented, "We all had on our company manners. It was a nice little tea."[63]

The NEA investigation ended on February 2, 1954. As the committee left Houston it issued a statement declaring that it found "numerous expressions of unrest . . . and even bitterness" in the city's schools. The *Chronicle* responded with a scathing editorial that excoriated the committee for failing to invite any Minute Women or American Legion members to testify. The newspaper compared the NEA's closed meetings to the tactics of the Ku Klux Klan, "where people were charged without an opportunity to . . . know who their accusers were. Certainly that is not the American way."[64]

Once the NEA left Houston, the Red Scare activists in the public schools decided to deal with school personnel that had actively lobbied in favor of the investigation. The Mills machine, led by J. O. Webb, selected two teachers at John Reagan High School to use as examples to demonstrate to other independent-minded teachers the penalties for nonconformity. Although Webb and his associates wanted to make examples of the two young teachers, the school administrator's behavior in the matter also provides a vivid example of the mind-set and tactics of the people in control of the Houston public schools during the 1950s. It also explains why many of the district's teachers would later tell NEA investigators that they taught in an atmosphere of fearful pressure.

Peter Jaeger and Robert Gilmore were two English teachers at John Reagan High School in Houston Heights, an old streetcar suburb near downtown. They were idealistic, popular with their students, naive, and as bored as their pupils by the unimaginative and unchallenging textbooks adopted by the school board for use in sophomore English. To create interest in literature and writing among their brighter students, the two teachers would read aloud in class selected portions of the writings of nonapproved authors such as D. H. Lawrence and Philip Wylie and ask students to write theme papers in reaction to what these authors had written. The teachers were careful to avoid sexually provocative material, choosing to read, for example, Lawrence's satirical writings in *Studies in Classic American Literature.* The results were heartening to the two teachers as dozens of parents called them and said that their children were showing a new interest in books and libraries. The parents were pleased. One of their teaching colleagues, however, was not.

One of the hazards of teaching in the Houston schools during the Red Scare was the informal spy system used by the Mills machine in which teachers either eager for favor or out of a sense of political duty would "report" on the politics and views of fellow teachers. Such a system seems to have existed at Reagan High School. During the fall semester following the Ebey affair, one of Jaeger's and Gilmore's teaching colleagues went to Reagan principal R. H. Williams and told him about their heretic teaching methods and, more important, their teachers' lounge diatribes against the Minute Women, Joe McCarthy, and the school board's treatment of George Ebey. Williams, an ultraconservative friend of J. O. Webb, a supporter of H. L. Mills, and ill-informed about English literature, was outraged. He immediately acquired a copy of Lawrence's *Studies in Classic American Literature* and asked his assistant principal, Harlan G. Andrews, to read it and give him his opinion. Andrews replied that Lawrence was "un-American and anti-American," especially since Lawrence had made fun of Benjamin Franklin by writing a humorous version of Franklin's thirteen points on morals. Jaeger and Gilmore had read Lawrence's satire of Franklin to their classes. Williams reported Jaeger and Gilmore to J. O. Webb and school district personnel director Richard Jones. Webb did "some checking on this D. H. Lawrence" and failed to find any evidence that he was a Communist, although Webb did agree with Williams and Andrews that the eccentric Lawrence wrote the "vilest kind of literature" and was obviously perverted and un-American. Since Gilmore and Jaeger were troublemakers opposed to the anti-Ebey faction and used Lawrence's writings, then they too were un-American. Besides, as Webb later admitted, "It wasn't merely . . . the literature, which of course was the main issue, but the fact that the individual had refused to conform." Personnel director Jones decided to write the police department in New York City (where Jaeger had once lived) and the House Committee on Un-American Activities to see if they had information on the two rebel teachers. Jones later explained that he wrote to HCUA "quite often" about Houston teachers "because we want to be sure that we have founded information and not hearsay [and] . . . gossip. . . ." The hearsay and gossip accumulated by HCUA thus became "factual information" when in the hands of persons like Jones, John Rogge, and the Minute Women's Helen Thomas. Nevertheless, neither the police nor the HCUA had any record of the teachers.

While their inquisitors waited for more information, Jaeger and Gilmore, unaware of the case being prepared against them, committed another rebellious act. In January 1954, as the National Education Association prepared to begin its investigation of Houston schools, Reagan principal R. H. Williams, in concert with other pro-Mills administrators, asked his teachers to sign a petition critical of the investigation, stating that morale was high in the schools and that the NEA probe was unnecessary and unwanted. Although eighty-one of their colleagues signed, Jaeger and Gilmore refused. They both paid an immediate price: Gilmore was assigned a fifth English class (the normal load was four) and Jaeger, identified as Gilmore's "mentor," was given an inferior room adjacent to the faculty restroom. Gilmore complained to Williams about his teaching overload and argued that the students would suffer from his inability to give them individual time. The principal, however, refused to change Gilmore's new assignment.

In late February 1954, after the NEA had left Houston, Williams and assistant principal Harlan Andrews confronted their two teachers. Williams pulled a copy of Lawrence's *Studies in Classic American Literature* out of his desk and, tossing it on the desk top, stated that he had determined that Lawrence was a Communist. Williams informed Jaeger that, since he knew the teacher owned a copy of the book, Jaeger obviously endorsed its contents and its author. Even worse, since Jaeger had read portions aloud to his class, then Jaeger's actions were "tantamount to practicing communism." Williams charged that Jaeger had loaned this "vile" book to a student and warned him not to let his parents see it, a charge Jaeger vehemently denied. Andrews jumped in and said that clearly Jaeger was "tearing down all of our great American principles" and was "teaching un-Americanism." At this point, the reason for Jaeger's placement in the classroom adjacent to the restroom became evident when Williams charged him with taking two female students into a toilet stall in the restroom for "immoral purposes." The administrator quickly dropped this ploy when Jaeger refused to resign under threat of making the charge public. The charge had been totally trumped-up. In exasperation, the principal ended the meeting.

Following this confrontation, the student to whom Jaeger had loaned the book went to tell Williams that Jaeger had not told him to hide or conceal the book from his parents or anyone else. Williams told the student "to get out of the office, it was none of his business."

Williams called J. O. Webb and asked him to get resignations out of Jaeger and Gilmore. Another meeting with the teachers was subsequently held, but this time J. O. Webb was present. Webb stared at Jaeger and Gilmore and demanded that they confess they were Communists. Both indignantly refused. Webb pressed on but neither Jaeger nor Gilmore would break down. Webb gave up, and, turning to Williams, said, "Well, he's non-cooperative, call the personnel office and have him fired." The meeting was over.

Jaeger and Gilmore hired attorneys and appealed their case to the school board. Before the hearing, Verna Rogers telephoned Richard Jones and questioned why Jaeger was being harassed. Jones, alluding to the false restroom charge, said, "You don't want to defend a person with a morals charge, do you?" When the case came before the board, however, nothing was said about any "morals charge."

Prior to the school board's meeting to consider the request to fire Jaeger and Gilmore, their students signed a letter addressed to Superintendent Bill Moreland stating that their teachers had explained that Lawrence should be read critically and that his views were subject to debate. The students declared that "neither . . . Benjamin Franklin, our American-ism, nor our religious convictions" had suffered as a result. In addition, the student to whom Jaeger had loaned the book signed a notarized state-ment denying Williams' charges that Jaeger had asked him to hide the book. Unfortunately for Jaeger, school board president Jimmy Delmar announced, "We will not bring the students into this" and refused to accept the affidavit or see the student.

At the board meeting, Webb, Williams, and Andrews repeated their views about the teachers' "un-Americanism" and, because of the student protest letter, they added the charge that Jaeger was guilty of "agitating" the students against authority. Williams also charged that Jaeger had read aloud to his classes some passages from Philip Wylie's *The Disappearance.* Stone Wells asked Williams about Wylie's book and the principal replied, "No, I'll tell you, . . . I haven't read the book. I don't know anything about it." Williams said he merely read a review in the Chicago *Tribune* and that newspaper did not think the book was very good. The *Tribune,* Williams stated, had said that *The Disappearance* was "a one-man mono-logue which forecasts a holocaust or possibly a hallucination, when for four years there is a world without women for the men [at this point Stone Wells interrupted and blurted out, "That ain't good, is it?"] and Mr. Wylie indulges in . . . conversational forays . . . [about] sex and deviation such situations provoke."

Showing signs of impatience and possibly embarrassment at this dia-logue, Garrett Tucker, addressing Harlan Andrews, who was sitting with Williams and Webb before the board, asked, "Did [the students] learn

English from [the teachers] or didn't they?" Andrews admitted that he did not know, this question had not come up before. Webb added that in his view one of the points about Wylie and Lawrence was that the "average home" would not have "this kind of literature around" and that would be one reason for not having it in the classroom. Webb seemed to be unaware of the fact that, using his standard, most of the world's greatest literature would be prohibited from the classroom.

The school board allowed Peter Jaeger to defend himself. He called Williams and Andrews "self-appointed inquisitors" and declared that the charges stemmed from his criticisms of the Mills machine and refusal to sign the anti-NEA petition. Nevertheless, the thirty-year-old, six-foot-tall native of New Jersey lost the argument. The board, with Verna Rogers abstaining, voted for dismissal. Gilmore was more fortunate, however. With Rogers voting no, the board ordered Bill Moreland to transfer him to San Jacinto High School to teach driver education and have a "second chance."

Gilmore's troubles were not at an end, however. The Houston *Chronicle,* congratulating the board for rooting these subversive educators out of the schools, accused Jaeger and Gilmore of "attempting to destroy children's faith in the American heritage." Gilmore, only two days at his new position teaching kids how to drive, wrote an angry rebuttal to the *Chronicle* that also criticized the school board. J. O. Webb and Richard Jones quickly retaliated, leveling nine charges against the twenty-eight-year-old Gilmore and requesting that he too be fired. The charges repeated the old ones about reading D. H. Lawrence aloud in class. They also included some new ones, such as writing the critical letter to the *Chronicle* and leaving school early without permission. In addition, Jones charged that Gilmore had kept an "obscene" poem by E. E. Cummings in his desk drawer while teaching at Reagan. Jones had a photostat copy of the poem, written in Gilmore's own hand, that Jones and Williams had discovered while searching the teacher's desk without his knowledge. Gilmore admitted that it was his personal copy—he enjoyed Cummings' poetry—but denied ever using the bawdy poem in class or ever showing it to a student.

Gilmore now saw the handwriting on the wall; he was finished in Houston. He refused to resign, however, and decided to force the school district to dismiss him. Gilmore told Richard Jones that until the board considered his case he would no longer teach driver education. He demanded his old job of teaching English at Reagan. Bill Moreland seized this opportunity to avoid further controversy and ruled that Gilmore's refusal to report back to duty at San Jacinto constituted his resignation. Gilmore was removed from the payroll.

Nonetheless, in April Gilmore was able to make one final appearance before the board to make a statement. The six-foot, three-inch-tall native Houstonian stood up at the board meeting and denounced Communism, "Joe McCarthy," and the "lady Minute Women." Gilmore stated that he was "the victim of an organized, insidious conspiracy" to have him fired. "It is my honest conviction," Gilmore argued, "that there is a . . . powerful machine that so dominates this school system that no teacher would dare to bring a grievance through proper channels . . . at the expense of that machine." Gilmore charged that H. L. Mills ran the machine and J. O. Webb "reports to him."

Peter Jaeger sued Webb, Williams, and Andrews and received an out-of-court settlement. He returned home to New Jersey and secured another teaching position. Robert Gilmore joined an oil company and moved to Salem, Oregon.[65]

Unlike the Ebey case, the Jaeger-Gilmore affair was not highly publicized. Classroom teachers did not enjoy the same status or visibility as an administrator such as Ebey. The "crusading" Houston *Post* kept silent about the matter. The absence of any large-scale concerted effort to save their jobs also illustrated the extent of fear among Houston's teachers. Certainly the Ebey affair and the Jaeger-Gilmore dismissals provided vivid and disturbing evidence that Houston teachers should keep their mouths shut and maintain as low a profile as possible.

After the Red Scare activists in control of the public schools made examples of Jaeger and Gilmore, they attempted to eliminate the effectiveness of the one school organization willing to challenge them: the HTA. Conservative teachers, cooperating with the Mills machine, created an "alternative group," the Congress of Houston Teachers, and announced as their main goal the building of harmonious working relations with the school board. At its first meeting Dallas Dyer addressed the new group, which was the equivalent of a company union, and read a laudatory and approving letter from Henry Peterson. Dyer told the teachers that she hoped they would "turn the spotlight on the good things about the school system."[66]

Not content with organizing an opposition faction among the teachers, Dyer and Henry Peterson attacked the leadership of the HTA. Dyer made a motion, seconded by Peterson, to suspend the contracts of Margaret Bleil, HTA president, and Dr. Kate Bell, newly elected president of the TSTA. Bleil and Bell were among the most active HTA leaders trying to get the NEA to investigate Houston. Dyer particularly disliked Margaret Bleil, describing her as a "very militant type of woman." Dyer charged both educators with insubordination to Superintendent Moreland and accused them of creating fear and confusion in the schools by "alleging there is a bad educational climate in Houston." The purge failed because of Jimmy Delmar's reluctance to support it. Margaret Bleil continued to suffer from her activities, however, when Superintendent Moreland, despite enthusiastic endorsements from parents and teaching colleagues, declined to nominate her for a Ford Foundation fellowship several months after the NEA investigation.[67]

1953 had been an eventful year for Houstonians embroiled in the Red Scare. The extreme anti-Communist coalition enjoyed significant victories in its successful attacks against W. W. Kemmerer and George Ebey. Yet 1953 also included the first major assault against the Red Scare coalition at the local level. The Houston *Post*'s exposé and the NEA's investigation heralded the coming of another contentious year in 1954. The Red Scare continued unabated but more and more voices were being raised against it – nationally as well as locally.

NINE

DEMAGOGUES IN AUSTIN
McCARTHY AT SAN JACINTO

Allan [Shivers] really doesn't like to demagogue, but he was about to lose the race.

         —A Shivers lieutenant

Joe [McCarthy] has put quite a few out of circulation, but has he ever harmed an innocent person?

         —E. M. Biggers[1]

In the final weeks of 1953 and early months of 1954 Houston's Red Scare coalition, still intact despite the Houston *Post*, shifted its focus away from the local scene as events in Austin and Washington temporarily dominated affairs. In Washington, the isolationist attempt to restrict the president's power in the realm of foreign policy attracted the keen interest and personal involvement of many of Houston's Red Scare activists, especially those in the Minute Women. In the state capital, the Red-baiting rhetoric of the governor and his allies in the legislature dominated local headlines and, to the delight of the Minute Women and others, seemed to refute the *Post*'s declaration that Houston and the Gulf Coast were free of Communist activity.

Despite this further escalation of extreme anti-Communism, 1954 would be a decisive year in the history of the Red Scare at the national and local levels. The political environment stabilized and became less conducive to fear tactics. Senator McCarthy, after making a final, controversial appearance in Houston, would soon self-destruct on national television and deprive the Red Scare of an important national symbol. In Houston, the anti–Red Scare coalition would strengthen and succeed in temporarily capturing control of the Houston school board. For the Minute Women and their allied pressure groups, 1954 would mark the end of their effectiveness as formal organizations, although the Red Scare impulse would remain healthy and very much alive.

In the months immediately following the O'Leary exposé, the Minute Women concentrated on providing support for Ohio senator John Bricker's proposed constitutional amendment to make the president's executive agreements subject to the same process of congressional approval as that required for treaties. This so-called Bricker Amendment was an unsuccessful right-wing cause célèbre throughout the early 1950s.[2]

In their effort to have Congress pass the Bricker Amendment, the Minute Women joined in a national campaign that produced a separate organization for this single issue. The organization, led by women in Illinois and Wisconsin, was called Vigilant Women for the Bricker Amendment. With Virginia Hedrick acting as Texas coordinator, the Vigilant Women conducted petition drives to influence congressmen to vote for the Bricker Amendment. Houston Minute Women and the American Legion assumed local responsibility for soliciting signatures for the petitions and set up tables throughout the city to garner the autographs of passersby. The *Chronicle* helped with supportive publicity and published a photograph of Jesse Jones posing with Virginia Hedrick while signing a petition in support of the amendment in the lobby of his Gulf Building.[3]

The Minute Women's lobbying on behalf of the Bricker Amendment culminated in January 1954. In that month, the Red Scare coalition, once again with the help of publicity from the Houston *Chronicle*, mounted an impressive letter-writing campaign aimed at Texas' congressional delegation. On January 20, George E. Reedy, Jr., an aide to Senator Lyndon B. Johnson, reported to his boss that the office had received an unusual amount of mail that week because of the Bricker Amendment issue. Johnson's staff counted 1,325 postcards, letters, and telegrams from Texas in favor of the amendment and only 90 against. The vast majority of the Bricker mail came from Houston. A sample of the letters revealed that a large proportion was signed by physicians and women. Reedy noted that the mail from the women was "obviously 'inspired' . . . one block of 35 postcards came from Houston and most of those from the same typewriter." He also noted that the Houston postcards had the appearance of having been "handed out at a meeting."[4]

Senator Johnson, not wanting to get caught napping on this issue although he privately opposed it, asked Sam Low, his political liaison in Houston, for an on-the-scene report. Low replied that "local Republicans, former Dixiecrats and many uninformed people . . . are 'hopped-up' over the Bricker Amendment." He reported that the Houston *Chronicle*, the American Legion, and the Minute Women were using tactics that "are nauseating in the extreme but they have stirred up public sentiment which can be compared with that on the Tidelands during the 1952 campaign." Low warned Johnson to "tread softly" on the issue.[5]

Lyndon Johnson's briefing about the Bricker Amendment's potency in the largest city in his constituency proved timely. The national leaders of the Vigilant Women for the Bricker Amendment staged a two-day march on Congress to lobby for the constitutional change. A delegation of Houston Minute Women led by Virginia Hedrick and including Virginia Biggers, Mrs. J. D. Mabry, and Elsie Daniel dutifully traveled to Washington to participate. While there, the women called on Texas senators Price Daniel and Lyndon Johnson. Daniel assured the women of his strong support for the amendment; Johnson found it more convenient to be elsewhere.[6]

Although Johnson eluded them, the women had better luck with representatives Martin Dies and Kit Clardy, a leading member of the House Committee on Un-American Activities, and senators Joe McCarthy and William Jenner, the chairman of the Senate Internal Security Committee—four men who constituted a veritable Mount Rushmore of the congressional extreme right. Virginia Hedrick told the press that she and her colleagues were "very fond" of Dies, who amiably posed with the women for a wire service photograph. The Houston delegation returned home happy after seeing their heroes, but empty-handed nevertheless. President Eisenhower, Secretary of State John Foster Dulles, and a majority of the Congress opposed the Bricker Amendment and it never passed the Senate.[7]

The Houston women returned home in time for a Minute Women rally on February 1 that featured Rabbi Benjamin Schultz, head of the American Jewish League against Communism, Inc., and a celebrity of the extreme right wing. Virginia Biggers, Virginia Hedrick, Faye Weitinger, and another Minute Woman, Mrs. Henry Clay Lee, met Schultz's train at Houston's Union Station where he conducted an impromptu news conference. The next night Schultz told his audience at the Hermann Park Garden Center that opponents of the Minute Women and Senator Joseph McCarthy were members of an "intellectual fifth column" serving the Kremlin. He charged that radical "fringe groups" controlled the NEA and that Ralph O'Leary was himself a "very controversial figure." Schultz delighted the Minute Women by holding above his head a copy of *Nation*, which had condensed the O'Leary series, and declaring that the journal was "known even to socialists as a notoriously left-wing weekly."[8]

As the Minute Women busily worked for the Bricker Amendment and held publicized meetings, they had every reason to feel confident about their credibility and the ultimate righteousness of their cause. Events in the state government in the months immediately following the O'Leary series seemed to vindicate the women as public officials attracted widespread publicity in an effort to drive "Reds" from Texas.

Governor Allan Shivers, a Democrat in name only who had supported Dwight Eisenhower for president in 1952, was preparing to run for an unprecedented third term in office. The conservative Shivers enjoyed substantial support from Houston's 8-F Crowd and other Texas establishment powers, but he faced some severe problems. His administration was tainted by an insurance scandal and charges that the governor had participated in unethical real estate deals. Shivers was also violating a venerable Texas political tradition by breaking the two-term rule. His administration had accomplished little and his behavior in 1952 had alienated a large bloc of Texans still loyal to the national Democratic party. To make matters worse, Shivers was being challenged by Judge Ralph Yarborough, a feisty and energetic liberal Democrat from east Texas who would attract labor and minority votes as well as the ballots of national Democrats alienated by Shivers' pro-Eisenhower stance.

Shivers did not want to lose and the Texas establishment did not want someone like Yarborough breathing down their necks. Shivers was a man who needed an issue other than his own record. Despite the anti–Red Scare ramblings in Houston, anti-Communism still hung heavily in the air, a convenient and useful campaign tool for a candidate in need of an issue. Shivers knew his Red Scare tactics would not draw adverse reaction from the "crusading" Houston *Post* since Governor Hobby had personally telephoned him and pledged his strong support in the campaign. The *Post*'s dislike of Red-baiters extended only to those who Red-baited Eisenhower and Mrs. Hobby. Thus, Governor Shivers, no stranger to Red Scare tactics anyway, fell back into his old habits. Shivers' Red Scare mentality became so pervasive that it surfaced in some almost comical ways. For example, in a statement issued to the people of Texas about the need to curb the rapidly increasing death rate due to accidents on the state's expansive highway system, Shivers declared that reckless driving and Communism were both equal "threats to life and happiness" in Texas.[9]

The governor's obsession with the "Red threat" also had less amusing results. Shivers' anti-Communist ploy was aided in November 1953 by a recognition strike conducted by CIO workers in Port Arthur. Although the CIO had purged its radical faction in the late 1940s, Shivers and Texas' antilabor attorney general John Ben Shepperd knew an opportunity when they saw one. Both men wasted no time in denouncing the strike leaders as "Communists." The governor appeared on H. L. Hunt's "Facts Forum State of the Nation" television program on December 1, 1953, and repeated his accusations that subversives were involved in the Port Arthur strike and that these "Reds" were trying to organize the entire Gulf Coast. Such accusations delighted the Minute Women. Now, only one month after Ralph O'Leary had declared Houston "remarkably free of communist influences," the governor and attorney general of Texas, men who would certainly know, had revealed that "Reds" were all over the Texas coast! The Minute Women wrote "we told you so" letters to

Houston's newspapers. They asked, who should we believe, a hack "leftist" muckraker or our distinguished and courageous governor? [10]

With much fanfare, Shivers appointed a five-man State Industrial Commission (SIC) to investigate Communist infiltration in coastal unions. The commission included L. E. Page of Carthage, American Legion state commander; Walter Buckner of San Marcos, conservative newspaper editor and publisher; and a rancher, C. E. Fulgham of Lubbock. The newly reorganized SIC went to work almost immediately, conducting hearings in Austin in December on "communist infiltration of Texas." After hearing Homer Garrison, several DPS officers, and other witnesses, the SIC issued a preliminary report on December 7, 1953, declaring that subversives posed "a clear and present danger" to the state. The SIC concluded that "the present laws of Texas are inadequate to deal with this menace" and announced that the commission would recommend "adequate legislation" to ensure elimination of "such groups and their agents." [11]

In January 1954, while his State Industrial Commission looked into CIO activities, Shivers announced that he was calling a special session of the Texas legislature to convene in March to consider a teacher pay raise. Attorney General John Ben Shepperd hinted a few days later that the legislature might also be asked to pass more stringent anti-Communist laws. Shivers verified this while again appearing on Hunt's "Facts Forum State of the Nation" with a startling observation that Communists were traitors and if treason was an offense punishable by death, why not give the same punishment to Communists? "I'm in favor of doing anything we can to a Communist . . . ," Shivers told his delighted program hosts "We're going to crush them under our heels every way we can." Shivers stated that he hoped the special session would consider such action. The Austin *American*'s editorial writer, R. O. Zollinger, was stunned by Shivers' statement. In a published commentary, Zollinger observed that many persons "steamed up to a high pitch of emotionalism" would agree with Shivers' solution to the Communist problem. "Kill them, they will say,. . ." the journalist wrote, "and we can live happily ever after." Zollinger declared that Shivers' idea "is a greater threat to the national destiny than anything the domestic breed of Communists ever could think up." [12]

Despite some shocked reactions, Shivers proceeded with his idea. On February 15, the governor announced that he would ask the legislature to make Communist party membership illegal and punishable by death in the electric chair. "Membership in the Communist Party is worse than murder," Shivers asserted. "It is mass murder." Shivers' recommendation threatened to transform the Red Scare in Texas into the ultimate stage of maximum terror. He was undoubtedly influenced by the precedent already established by the federal government's execution of Julius and Ethel Rosenberg on June 19, 1953, for allegedly passing atomic bomb secrets to the Soviet Union. Also, Massachusetts, Indiana, Pennsylvania, and Georgia had already led the way in outlawing the CPUSA, although none of those states was so bold as to provide the death penalty as punishment.[13]

On March 9, the State Industrial Commission issued its final report on subversive elements in the Gulf Coast CIO unions. The SIC admitted that it had been frustrated in its search for Reds and had failed to find a single CPUSA member. Commissioner Page argued that they did not find any Communists because "their raid on Texas backfired. They came to recruit members and raise money. They left with bloody heads." The commissioners nonetheless saw fit to recommend two laws to the governor that would "make it tough" on those phantom radicals. With Attorney General John Ben Shepperd's office providing legal advice, the SIC urged that the state outlaw the Communist party and create a five-member loyalty review board to investigate charges of subversive activity against persons or organizations. This loyalty board would be empowered to subpoena witnesses and punish contempt with a jail sentence. It would also have the authority to punish "disloyalty" with a prison sentence of up to twenty years. The proposed loyalty board would, in effect, enforce the proposed law to prohibit Communist party membership.[14]

John Ben Shepperd frankly admitted that he personally favored this process because it would be easier to obtain convictions in an administrative hearing than in a normal jury trial because the standard of proof of guilt was less rigorous in such a procedure. In other words, Shepperd, Shivers, and their friends would do away with such troublesome obstacles as juries and other safeguards of legal due process. The attorney general argued that loyal Texans had nothing to fear. The proposed loyalty board legislation would allow a jury trial appeal. Shepperd failed to mention that automatic appeal was not required by the law, but was left to the sole discretion of a judge as to whether the appeal was justified. The SIC commissioners simply emphasized that only "Communists and subversives" had reason to fear the board. The SIC report did disappoint Governor Shivers, however, by recommending a maximum prison term of twenty years rather than electrocution as punishment for being a Communist. The SIC chairman admitted that the death penalty was a good idea, but the SIC feared that timid juries would fail to convict some subversives if conviction resulted in the defendant's electrocution. L. E. Page, the American Legion member of the SIC, argued that he personally favored "stringing up every Communist" but admitted such a procedure would be "impractical." Besides, Page lamented, such punishment "would attract the . . . bleeding hearts who come around and bleed for the rights of man every time we try to do anything about Communism."[15]

The SIC and John Ben Shepperd had gone a little too far. The situation was getting out of hand. Wasting no time, the *Dallas Morning News,* a bellwether of Texas establishment orthodoxy, immediately called a halt. The *News* stated that the SIC's solution to Communism "is not a happy one. In final analysis, it is quite probably an unconstitutional one." The Dallas paper argued that a loyalty board "is a poor substitute for grand jury action." The *News* patiently explained to the attorney general that ". . . a charged offender is due his day in court . . . a loyalty review board is not a court." The editorial suggested that the legislature provide adequate funds to strengthen the attorney general's office so that existing state laws could be enforced. The SIC's loyalty board, said the *News,* is "not . . . the right answer." The *Dallas Morning News* was seconded by the San Antonio *Express,* which called the SIC proposals "fraught with grave questions." The loyalty board recommendation, the San Antonio paper argued, "raises sharp issues of due process of law. . . ."[16]

Governor Allan Shivers reluctantly agreed to go along with the SIC recommendations, although he stated that he still believed the death penalty to be more appropriate punishment. The governor claimed that 75 percent of his mail supported him on this issue. Nevertheless, Shivers sent the more "moderate" SIC recommendations to the legislature, where state senators Rogers Kelley of Edinburg and John Bell of Cuero accepted sponsorship. Representative Robert Patten of Jasper refused to back off, however, and submitted to the House his own death penalty bill for CPUSA membership. Not to be outdone, Representative Dudley T. Dougherty of Beeville, who was preparing to run for the United States Senate against Lyndon Johnson in the Democratic primary, submitted a bill that would prohibit subversives from voting, holding public office, making speeches in public, speaking on radio or television, or publishing in any periodical. Fearful that not to submit an anti-Communist bill could reflect on their political reputations, several other legislators hastily prepared their own proposals. This included Marshall O. Bell, who proposed a bill to prohibit state employees from invoking the Fifth Amendment's protection against self-incrimination when testifying about their Communist affiliations. Bell's patently unconstitutional bill was largely ignored by his colleagues, however.[17]

The legislative hearings conducted by the Criminal Jurisprudence

Committee to consider the various anti-Communist bills became a "theater of the absurd." Representative Bill Daniel, the brother of United States senator and future governor Price Daniel, became agitated because of an unexpectedly large audience at one of the hearings. Daniel interrupted the proceedings and anxiously demanded, "I would like to know if any Communists . . . are here today." Glaring at a group in the rear of the room, Daniel repeated his question, "Are there any of you here today?" After a prolonged silence, someone nervously blurted out, "I'd like to say that I'm not a Communist!" As the audience laughed, the irritated Daniel complained, "You've all got your coats on; how do I know you're not carrying guns?" The committee chairman, Jim Bob Paxton of Elkhart, eventually got Daniel to sit down. Paxton left the hearings early but told the clerk to get the name and address of every spectator. C. F. Sentell of Snyder, who replaced Paxton as presiding officer, told reporters not to mention the name taking in their news stories. With great forbearance, the journalists explained to Sentell and the paranoid Daniel that the committee had no authority to censor news accounts of a public meeting. Whereupon the surprised Sentell blamed the censorship request on the absent chairman, Jim Bob Paxton. Two other committee members, Bill Kugle of Galveston and A. D. ("Buffalo") Downer of Center, ordered the clerk to record their official opposition to Paxton's attempted censorship.[18]

In the hearings, the committee members listened to Colonel Homer Garrison testify: "I think everybody knows [the Communists] are in Texas, there's no doubt about that." Representative Downer asked Garrison for some specific proof, maybe a name or two. The colonel refused. The committee would just have to take his word for it. The legislators heard their fellow representatives, Robert Patten and Dudley Dougherty, testify in favor of their different bills. Patten admitted that, sure, he hated to see anyone electrocuted for his political beliefs, but, after all, he loved his country more than his fellow man. Dougherty, discussing his bill to deny freedom of speech to subversives, suggested that such a law should probably also be applied to Puerto Rican nationalists, if any should ever come to Texas. When someone suggested that it might violate the federal constitution to outlaw a political party, Dougherty charged that the CPUSA "is not a bona fide political party; it is a criminal organization." One of the few to testify against the proposed laws was liberal attorney Robert Eckhardt, who appeared for the Texas CIO. Eckhardt, a future Texas congressman, declared that the legislation denied due process of law. "A man could be tried and his reputation ruined on hearsay testimony" in a board hearing, Eckhardt argued. Representative Waggoner Carr, a future Texas attorney general, rebuffed Eckhardt, and retorted that under present law a man's reputation could be ruined in court by accusing him of running a whorehouse and asking for an injunction. Carr asked, "Why should it be different for Communists?" As the Houston *Post*'s Hubert Mewhinney observed about Texas at this time, "All mimsy were the people."[19]

An altered bill, close to Shivers' original proposal, eventually went to the floor of the Texas House for consideration. Three representatives, A. D. ("Buffalo") Downer, Edgar Berlin, and Maury Maverick, Jr., the son of the former New Deal congressman, dared to speak against the pending legislation. Maverick delivered a defiant speech that others had wanted to give, but, cowering beneath the shadow of the Great Fear, could not. The San Antonio legislator looked at his colleagues and noted that it had been said that to oppose the bill would be political suicide. "If it is," said Maverick, "let me write my own political obituary." He admitted that "once or twice I've run on this terror legislation, but I'm never going to run [on it] again—not once." Maverick warned the representatives that "we cannot put the ideology of communism in an electric chair or in a prison. You cannot lynch communism. You cannot burn communism. If we, in fighting communism, adopt totalitarian tactics . . . then we, by our own hands, will destroy ourselves. Under the broad limitations of this bill a cop can go into your home, knock down the door and see what you're reading. . . . This is a goose-stepping, storm trooper bill."[20]

Representative Fred Meridith of Terrell countered Maverick's speech with one of his own. Meridith declared that the Department of Public Safety had frightening information "that indicates the vital necessity for this law." Meridith lamented, however, that to release this information would endanger the public welfare. Nevertheless, he could assure his fellow citizens that the Communists in Texas "have managed to sneak . . . their dastardly henchmen into our schools, into our churches, into our labor unions, yes, even into the American Legion." Meridith argued that these people must "be dealt with immediately, decisively, and firmly as [we] would a common murderer." Becoming emotional, Meridith invoked the obligatory Texas analogy of William Barret Travis drawing a line with his saber in the dirt of the Alamo. "Today, 118 years later, another line is about to be drawn," Meridith announced. "I sincerely hope that you . . . [will] step across that line with me. Just as Colonel Travis said: 'Who will be first?' " The House chamber erupted in applause as Meridith sat down. Edgar Berlin, an irritated expression on his face, stood up and said he regretted Meridith's use of the "time worn and much-abused story of the drawing of the line at the Alamo." Such false analogies masked the reality of the situation, Berlin argued. "Mass hysteria" and bills such as the one being considered created "a greater . . . danger to our democracy than all the Communists in the Western Hemisphere."[21]

Maverick's and Berlin's arguments fell on deaf ears. The Loyalty and Subversive acts of 1954 passed the House by a 107 to 7 vote. Maury Maverick, Jr., Edgar Berlin, A. D. Downer, and Doug Crouch of Denton were among the seven casting negative votes. After the vote, Buffalo Downer charged that "at least one-half if not more of the membership of this House" had privately expressed their personal opposition to the bill, but when the final vote was cast they voted in favor of the bill "in order to be reelected." After the bill passed, several of Maury Maverick's colleagues came by his desk on the floor of the House to tell him that although they voted for the Red Scare legislation they really agreed with him about it. They could not afford to vote against the bill because they would be Red-baited back home. More than one of these legislators told Maverick not to worry about the law, the courts would overturn it anyway. "Let the judges kill it," said a representative. "They won't suffer for it." Maverick, who did not run for reelection because of personal financial reasons, later remembered that the worst aspect of the Red Scare "was not really what the evil people were doing but what the good people *weren't* doing."[22]

There being no "Mavericks" in the Senate the bill passed by a 29 to 0 margin. The new law had been shorn of its loyalty board provision. It also prohibited "advocacy, conspiracy, participation, or assistance in any other way in the overthrow of the government by force" rather than simply outlawing the Communist party per se. It retained a penalty of twenty years in prison and a fine of $20,000. The law also allowed any local judge, upon the affidavit of one credible witness and the application of a district attorney, to order the search of any establishment and the seizure of "subversive" literature. A private home could be raided upon the affidavit of two "credible" witnesses. Governor Shivers signed the law on April 15, 1954. The governor told reporters that he still favored the death penalty for Communists but he was willing to try the new law. The Houston *Post* stated that Governor Shivers and the legislature had felt strongly that a stringent anti-Communist law was needed. The *Post* asserted, however, that "they were much more deeply concerned about it than the general public is. Well, the law is now on the books, for better or for worse. Let us hope it is for better."[23]

Unfortunately, it was not for better. The passage and signing of the Suppression of the Communist Party Act on April 15, 1954, resulted in the creation of a special Department of Public Safety police school in Austin in July 1954. Funded by the state legislature, the school was staffed by FBI agents, DPS officers, and a few members of the University of Texas faculty. Its students consisted of local Texas law enforcement officers who attended classes for three weeks, studying such topics as "subversive ideologies," economics, propaganda, espionage, sabotage, and counter-intelligence. The DPS explained that the school's purpose was to train local police to combat "all subversive activities" in Texas. The ultimate result of the DPS' efforts would be the investigatory excesses and civil rights abuses by its own officers as well as local police in such cities as Houston in the 1960s and 1970s. The Houston Police Department's Criminal Intelligence Division used many of the skills learned at the DPS school to wire tap illegally, spy, and compile over one thousand "non-criminal" dossiers on liberal politicians such as black mayoral candidate Curtis Graves, Congresswoman Barbara Jordan, former school board member Gertrude Barnstone, Congressman Mickey Leland, and Houston mayor Fred Hofheinz.[24]

Maury Maverick's warning that under the broad scope of the Communist Suppression Act "a cop can go into your home . . . and see what you're reading" eventually proved to have been prophetic. On December 27, 1963, state and county law enforcement officers, accompanied by two Texas assistant attorneys general, entered the San Antonio home of John W. Stanford, Jr. Under the authority of a warrant sanctioned by the Communist Suppression Act and issued by Judge Solomon Casseb, Jr., the police proceeded to search Stanford's house for books and records related to the Communist party. Stanford, a self-admitted Communist, operated a bookstore from his home under the trade name All Points of View. The police ransacked Stanford's home for over four hours, seizing magazines, pamphlets, letters, and anything else they deemed to be subversive. Among the items packed into fourteen boxes and hauled off to the Bexar County courthouse were materials written by Karl Marx, Earl Browder, and Fidel Castro. Also seized as subversive, however, were the writings of C. Wright Mills, Hans Bethe, Erich Fromm, Linus Pauling, Theodore Draper, Jean Paul Sartre, Pope John XXIII, and Supreme Court justice Hugo L. Black. The officers failed to find any records of the Communist party or any membership lists or dues payments. They did find the Stanfords' marriage certificate, insurance policies, household bills, and personal correspondence, which they also impounded.

In a twist of irony, Maverick himself agreed to represent Stanford in his legal attempt to recover his property. The United States Supreme Court eventually reviewed the case. In the conclusion to his brief before the Court, Maverick argued that "this business of playing havoc with a mail order bookstore in a citizen's private residence under a vaguely worded search warrant, based on an application and affidavit which did little more than spread a rumor, and where no specific violation or any crime was alleged, was as contrary to the ways of a civilized state as it was to the Constitution. It was tyranny. It was a monkey-see, monkey-do reminder of a dictatorship. It was unworthy of the great State of Texas. It cannot stand before the Constitution of the United States of America." The Supreme Court agreed, and, in a unanimous decision on January 18, 1965, ruled that the general search warrant allowed by the Communist Suppression Act violated constitutional requirements for such warrants. Justice Potter Stewart, writing for the Court, declared that the "indiscriminate sweep" of the search warrant used by Texas authorities in the case was "constitutionally intolerable." Stewart wrote that "the Fourth and Fourteenth Amendments guarantee to John Stanford that no official of the State shall ransack his home and seize his books and papers under the unbridled authority of a general warrant. . . ." The Supreme Court's decision in *Stanford* vs. *Texas* rendered the Communist Suppression Act ineffective. And Maury Maverick, Jr., one of only seven legislators to oppose the act in 1954, could enjoy the satisfaction of playing a key role in making it ineffective a decade later.[25]

Viewed out of context, Governor Shivers' antics and the Texas state legislature's hysterical paroxysm in the spring of 1954 seem to indicate that there was no relief in sight for Houstonians opposed to the Red Scare. At the national level, Senator McCarthy had lost whatever restraint he may have once had and was busily at work attacking the United States Army and—by implication—President Eisenhower. As historian David Caute has written, McCarthy was now "capable of subpoenaing God Almighty." In reality, however, the Red Scare and its national symbol were tottering at their peak, on the verge of decline. The decline would be rapid and end in disaster for McCarthy; it would be gradual and less final for the anti-Communist impulse that fed the Red Scare and the fringe group activists who led it.[26]

Even as the Texas legislature engaged in its attack on the Bill of Rights and Governor Shivers prepared for a Red Scare–style gubernatorial campaign for reelection, forces were at work changing the political environment at the national, state, and local levels. Since one of the most important underlying causes of the Red Scare in Houston as well as the nation was the political frustration of the Republican party and anti–New Deal Democrats, the election of Dwight Eisenhower to the presidency and a Republican majority in Congress in November 1952 removed a primary driving force behind the phenomenon, although its effects were delayed. Frustrations and resentments over the stalemate in the Korean War, during which twenty-five thousand Americans died, were relieved by an armistice in July 1953. Soviet premier Joseph Stalin's death in March 1952 initiated a Kremlin power struggle that eventually produced a leadership with a less rigid foreign policy, resulting in a thaw in the Cold War in 1954. Joe McCarthy—already privately detested by the Republican leadership—had charged that in the highest levels of the military, Red sympathizers were protecting Russian spies. Secretary of the Army Robert T. Stevens, according to McCarthy, had tried to blackmail him and his staff by claiming (correctly) that the senator and his counsel, Roy Cohn, had pressured the army to extend privileged treatment to Cohn's close friend, draftee G. David Schine. McCarthy's tactics had finally provoked Eisenhower, who told his press secretary, James Hagerty, "This guy McCarthy is going to get into trouble over this. I'm not going to take this lying down." The president's reaction and McCarthy's refusal to retreat would produce the Army-McCarthy hearings and, ultimately, lead to McCarthy's censure by the United States Senate.[27]

In Houston, the negative community reactions resulting from the Ebey affair and the Ralph O'Leary exposé intertwined with international and national events to begin gradually to lessen local Red Scare pressures. As it was with the beginning of the Red Scare, so it was with the end; there is no event or date that can be singled out as its terminus. In Houston, however, the symbolic climax of the Red Scare was embodied by the reappearance of the man who symbolized its beginning.

On March 27, 1954, after the Texas legislature had begun its special session in Austin, the Sons of the Republic of Texas (SRT), a patriotic fraternity consisting of the descendants of Republic of Texas (1836–1845) citizens, announced that Senator Joseph McCarthy would present the principal address at the annual celebration of the anniversary of the Battle of San Jacinto on April 21. The festivities would be held, as traditional, on the grounds of the battlefield at the base of Jesse Jones' monument to the 1836 victory. McCarthy was chosen after Hugh Roy Cullen agreed to serve as honorary chairman of the event. Cullen personally extended the invitation to his friend, who accepted without hesitation.

McCarthy, needing to escape Washington due to the heat from his confrontation with the army, decided to use the speech as an excuse to take a brief vacation in Texas with his oil friends. Cullen proudly declared, "Senator McCarthy is an outstanding speaker and great patriotic American. It is fitting he should speak on the battleground where Texas won its independence." Cullen added that, of course, McCarthy's speech would be completely "non-partisan and patriotic." The Houston oil man, noting the mounting criticism of the senator, asserted, "I am for Sen. McCarthy because . . . he is doing more than any other man to fight the Communist conspiracy in this country." Cullen urged Houstonians to show their appreciation by coming to the battleground. Roderick J. Watts, an admirer of McCarthy who, as managing editor of the Houston *Chronicle*, joined with Emmet Walter in shaping the right-wing aura of the newspaper, was also president of the local SRT chapter. Watts made the actual public announcement and thanked Cullen for getting "such a fine speaker."[28]

News of McCarthy's planned speech was not met with universal praise. The growing disenchantment with McCarthy and the Red Scare soon produced some unfavorable reactions. In a March editorial prior to the announcement, the *Post* called for support of the Eisenhower administration's "effort to prevent [McCarthy] from wrecking its plans for the country's good." The Hobbys continued their journalistic assault by printing a series of hostile "analytical and biographical" articles about McCarthy that ran for several days just prior to the senator's arrival in Houston. The state executive committee of the Young Democrats voted unanimously to denounce McCarthy's visit to San Jacinto. Approximately eight hundred University of Texas students held a campus protest in the Texas Union building in Austin. Led by student body president Franklin Spears (who later became a justice of the Texas Supreme Court), *Daily Texan* editor Bob Kenny, and Ronnie Dugger, future publisher of the liberal *Texas Observer*, the students issued a statement charging McCarthy with undermining "the basic American principles of fair play and free speech." Kenny and Dugger went to Houston and delivered a forty-foot-long petition to Hugh Roy Cullen's office signed by 1,571 students protesting McCarthy's appearance. The petition stated that McCarthy's selection as guest speaker was "offensive to the good judgment of Texans everywhere" and called the Wisconsin senator "an irresponsible demagogue." Dugger later recalled that after Cullen welcomed the two students into his office, he sat behind his desk and solemnly asked if they were Communists. Both replied no and Cullen grinned and said, "All right, let's talk about this thing!" The students explained their position and Cullen replied politely that he could not withdraw his invitation to McCarthy. Dugger remembered that "we left on pretty good terms. After he got his blood question out of the way, he was a southern gentleman." The Young Democrats' and the university students' actions were highly publicized by the *Post*, which ran a photograph of Cullen receiving the petition.[29]

While extreme anti-Communism still retained an appeal to such politicians as Allan Shivers, John Ben Shepperd, and various state legislators, McCarthy was increasingly being perceived as a political liability. The legislature, although involved in its own Red Scare circus, refused to take advantage of McCarthy's presence in the Lone Star State. Representative Jack Fisk of Wharton proposed a resolution inviting McCarthy to speak to the Texas legislature on the subject of Communism. On April 5, the House tabled the resolution by a 73 to 54 vote. Representative Charles Hughes of Sherman, referring to the senator's attempt to get special treatment for army private G. David Schine, thought McCarthy should speak on "political influence" in the army. "In my opinion that's the one thing he's an expert on," Hughes stated.[30]

Developments in Washington nearly accomplished what the Texas protests failed to do. Eleven days before McCarthy accepted the invitation to speak at San Jacinto, his Senate subcommittee voted to conduct hearings on the army's accusations against him. At that time, the subcommittee failed to set a date since it was asking for the approval of the full Senate. Several days after McCarthy agreed to speak in Texas, the subcommittee scheduled the hearings to begin on the same day. There was an immediate uproar from Houston's Red Scare groups and the Sons and Daughters of the Republic of Texas. To them, the Senate action only confirmed their wildest conspiratorial theories. The Senate was attempting to silence their hero. Rumors spread that Oveta Culp Hobby had somehow personally convinced the subcommittee to schedule a conflicting date.[31]

A delegation of women went to Hugh Roy Cullen's office on April 8 to ask him to intervene through his contacts in the Senate. Cullen agreed to do whatever he could. His office had received telegrams and telephone calls from all over Texas protesting the nefarious "plot" to keep McCarthy from speaking at San Jacinto. Cullen quickly discovered just what a hot potato McCarthy had become among his fellow senators. Ordinarily, no one would even notice the postponement of a hearing by one day. But these hearings were different. They were so unusual that the television networks planned to broadcast them live over the national cables, a historic event in itself. McCarthy's enemies were depending on the army hearings to damage the senator's public reputation. It is highly unlikely, however, that the event was purposely scheduled to conflict with McCarthy's speaking engagement. McCarthy was always speaking somewhere and his Senate colleagues did not keep his calendar. Besides, Karl Mundt, who was serving as temporary chairman of the subcommittee, was a close ally of McCarthy's. Nonetheless, now that a date had been announced, everyone involved, friend and foe alike, did not want to be accused of tampering with the hearings for any reason.[32]

Cullen had telephone access to many of the members of the United States Senate. As soon as the irate women left his office, Cullen called Karl Mundt and asked him to postpone the hearings until April 22. Mundt, sensitive to charges of purposeful delay by the Democrats, told Cullen that Senate Minority Leader Lyndon Johnson would have to approve a delay. Foiled, Cullen called Texas' junior senator, Price Daniel, who promised to talk to Mundt but admitted that he could do little else. Cullen telephoned Everitt Dirkson, Republican senator from Illinois and a member of McCarthy's subcommittee. Dirkson also equivocated. Cullen grew more irritated. Dirkson refused to request a postponement. Instead, he told Cullen he would ask Johnson to ask Mundt to postpone. This buck passing angered Cullen. He would have to talk to Johnson directly.

Cullen finally telephoned the Texas senator. He asked Johnson to request from Mundt a day's postponement. "No reason why they shouldn't do that," Cullen asserted. "We want to get Joe McCarthy [to Houston] because people here want it." Cullen told Johnson that he had also talked to Price Daniel. Johnson refused, explaining that McCarthy himself had to ask Mundt for the delay. Cullen, becoming frustrated by everyone's reluctance to take a stand on what he considered a minor point of procedure, repeated, "Mundt asked me to ask you." Johnson became impatient. "I have got nothing to do with it. Price [Daniel] has nothing to do with it." Finally, Johnson explained the problem to Cullen. "I don't want Mundt to try to put me on the spot and say these Democrats are trying to delay something," Johnson said. Cullen replied, "This whole state is roused up. Figure it's a double cross and figure Oveta Hobby has done it. People don't like it. This thing is going to be [in] the interest of our country." Johnson finally relented and told Cullen that if McCarthy would first ask Mundt for a delay, he would call Mundt and support it. Cullen's access and persistence worked. The Sons and Daughters of the Republic of Texas would have their speaker.[33]

Seemingly oblivious to the uproar, McCarthy and his wife, Jean, arrived in Texas a week early to enjoy a brief respite from the battles in the nation's capital. After a visit to Dallas, the McCarthys flew to Galveston where they went deep-sea fishing with the Douglas Marshalls, the son-in-law and daughter of Hugh Roy Cullen, aboard the Marshalls' 112-foot yacht, a converted submarine chaser. Following the fishing expedition, the McCarthys joined Hugh Roy Cullen for dinner at the enormous Cullen mansion in Houston's River Oaks. McCarthy, dogged every foot of the way by wire service news reporters, refused to comment about Governor Shivers' proposal to execute members of the CPUSA. The next day Dallas oil man Clint Murchison, Sr., sent his private airplane to Houston to fly the McCarthys to Tyler, where Murchison joined them on yet another fishing expedition. After a quick trip back to Washington to talk to his fellow subcommittee members about final details in preparation for the hearings, McCarthy returned to Houston to make his much-publicized appearance.[34]

Because San Jacinto Day is a traditional holiday in Texas, all municipal and county governmental offices as well as the public schools in Houston were closed. Cullen predicted that a crowd of at least 100,000 people would come to see McCarthy. Cullen's guess proved to be wildly optimistic. Estimates of crowd size varied from five thousand to nine thousand persons. Actually, this was a considerable improvement over attendance figures for the San Jacinto ceremonies in the preceding decade. The ceremony the year before had attracted only three hundred spectators.[35]

Except for Cullen, Houston's entrepreneurial power elite avoided the San Jacinto ceremony. Mayor Roy Hofheinz, a liberal Democrat, had earlier refused a request to stage an official city welcome for McCarthy. Hofheinz took the opportunity to leave town on April 21. City council members also excused themselves due to "prior commitments."[36]

Senator McCarthy and his wife arrived at the monument in a limousine with Mr. and Mrs. Hugh Roy Cullen. The two couples, with Jean McCarthy on crutches due to an ankle injury, walked up the monument steps past an ROTC honor guard from the University of Houston. Because of anonymous threats to disrupt the ceremony, McCarthy was accompanied by an unusually large security force from the Houston Police Department. Norma Louise Barnett, one of the Minute Women who had attacked George Ebey at his first school board meeting, began the program by singing "The Star Spangled Banner." After several other ceremonial rituals, Hugh Roy Cullen walked to the podium. Cullen introduced McCarthy, calling him a "real American and a champion of freedom." After prolonged applause and a drum roll by the American Legion Band, McCarthy delivered a blistering attack on the "Reds in the Army." He charged that the upcoming hearings were designed to hamstring his investigation of traitors. Standing at the base of the San Jacinto Monument, the tallest of its type in the world, the senator gazed at the stone star on top and declared, "Luckily for the free world, there were no 'Fifth Amendment' Texans at . . . San Jacinto. . . ."[37]

Joe McCarthy's appearance on April 21, 1954, symbolized the decline of the Red Scare in Houston. The announcement that he would speak at the San Jacinto monument had been met with criticism that would have been unthinkable only a year earlier. McCarthy had soiled his own nest. Even the Texas legislature avoided him. Politicians, wet fingers in the wind, realized that the gale had become a breeze. National polls substantiated that view. After McCarthy returned to Washington, the Army-McCarthy hearings began and nearly the entire nation watched the Republican senator dig his own political grave on live television as he bullied and verbally abused witnesses.[38]

The growth of the Red Scare in Houston and its subsequent influence had little to do with Joe McCarthy. Its sources were rooted in other soil and it actually began without him. McCarthy came late to the national Red Scare and, likewise, he was not responsible for it. McCarthy's significance in Houston sprang from the fact that he soon became the embodiment of the Red Scare everywhere, especially in Houston, where he attained the status of folk hero among the Minute Women and their associates. In Houston, to support the local anti-Communist purge was eventually to extend unshakable support to Joe McCarthy. This strong identification with McCarthy by Houston's Red Scare activists would play a role in their decline. When McCarthy lost face, so by extension did the Minute Women. As David Caute and others have noted, McCarthy played a role that eventually proved historically healthy. He gave the Red Scare a face and, once he was finally discredited, his local followers also lost much credibility. Likewise, except for a few less sophisticated types such as Hugh Roy Cullen, elites in Houston who had provided crucial legitimation to Red Scare activists through their rhetoric in the Houston *Chronicle*, Houston *Post*, and local Chamber of Commerce publications were also affected by McCarthy's behavior. He embarrassed them, he was attacking *their* institutions such as the army and the Eisenhower presidency, and he had become a political liability. One by one they began to distance themselves from McCarthy and, though less so, the tactics he symbolized.[39]

A month after McCarthy's San Jacinto speech, *Fortune* magazine published an article revealing that the Wisconsin senator was faltering in Texas. *Fortune* asserted that "there are significant signs that the McCarthy spell, if not broken in Texas, is beginning to lose some of its earlier potency." It noted that McCarthy had enjoyed "more appeal to Texas businessmen than to those of any other region, with the possible exception of the Chicago area." Nevertheless, the magazine emphasized, when McCarthy began to criticize the Eisenhower administration and when the president himself publicly questioned McCarthy's ethics and competence, "a number of Texas businessmen began to have second thoughts about their 'third senator.' "

Fortune interviewed several wealthy Texas businessmen about McCarthy. Oil millionaire Sid Richardson of Fort Worth, a previous McCarthy enthusiast, declared that the senator "is doing more harm than good." Clint Murchison, Sr., one of McCarthy's most important financial brokers, stated that his "enthusiasm had cooled" and that he suspected McCarthy's ambitions had gone out of control. Murchison admitted that he used their recent fishing trip near Tyler to urge McCarthy to assume "a proper spirit of humility." The Houstonians *Fortune* interviewed, however, generally stood fast in their support of McCarthy, although their enthusiasm had waned noticeably. Jesse Jones, as usual keeping his own counsel, uttered a meaningless but generally positive platitude about the senator. Hugh Roy Cullen sang McCarthy's praises. The ultraconservative Ewing Werlein declared, "Joe McCarthy is a great man." General Maurice Hirsch, a conservative and socially prominent attorney, would only state that he was "in accord with McCarthy's objectives." Three of those interviewed, however, had never supported McCarthy. Independent oil men R. E. ("Bob") Smith and Jubal R. Parten both criticized McCarthy, and Jesse Andrews, a powerful corporate attorney who moved among Houston's 8-F Crowd, declared, "I judge him a baneful influence and wish he never happened."[40]

Members of Houston's Red Scare coalition tried to ignore the mounting criticism of their hero and themselves. They continued their political pressure group tactics despite the rapidly changing environment. In May 1954, President Eisenhower nominated former Harris County Republican chairman Joe Ingraham to succeed Thomas Kennerly as federal district judge. The Minute Women, including Mrs. Henry Clay Lee, Mrs. H. W. Cullen, and Faye Weitinger, launched a strenuous protest. They unleashed their usual avalanche of postcards and letters on the Senate judiciary subcommittee in an effort to stop Ingraham's candidacy. The Minute Women opposed Ingraham because of his close association with Houston oil man and Republican activist Jack Porter and the fact that Ingraham and Porter had led the Eisenhower movement in Harris County in 1952. The right-wing coalition opposed Ingraham because of old political animosities and it wanted to get even. The Houston *Post* publicized the Minute Women opposition and Porter publicly denounced them. The Senate proceeded to approve Ingraham's nomination. Not only had the Minute Women protest failed but the mere fact that they were the ones protesting was used to advantage by their opponents.[41]

In the summer of 1954, the owners of the Houston *Press*, the Scripps-Howard newspaper syndicate, also decided to join in the anti-McCarthy boom and the *Press* followed suit. Scripps-Howard wanted to criticize McCarthy without leaving its newspapers open to charges of being "soft on communism," so it unleashed its own Red-baiter, Frederick Woltman, on the senator. Woltman wrote a scathing five-part attack on McCarthy that was carried by the *Press*. As one historian of the press, Edwin Bayley, has observed, "It was clear from Woltman's stories that the change [in editorial policy] resulted from McCarthy's attacks on the Eisenhower administration . . . it was time to get rid of him."[42]

For the members of Houston's Red Scare coalition, however, the most brutal blow occurred on June 2, 1954. To their bewilderment and shock, the Houston *Chronicle* also turned against McCarthy. In an editorial titled "Law unto Himself—McCarthy's Controversy-Filled Career," the *Chronicle* belatedly joined the ranks of the senator's critics. The editorial itself was rather peculiar. Instead of using the *Chronicle*'s usual straightforward editorial style, this one tried to make a point without clearly stating it. This was an indication, no doubt, of Emmet Walter's and Jesse Jones' displeasure at having to confront the McCarthy issue honestly. Yet there could be no mistake, the *Chronicle* was criticizing Joe McCarthy.

The editorial discussed three controversial episodes in the senator's pre–Red Scare career. It repeated charges made against him when he was state judge and was reprimanded for destroying evidence in a case. The editorial pointed out that McCarthy later violated Wisconsin state law by not resigning his judicial position while running for the United States Senate in 1946. It also lamented the senator's behavior in an affair in which McCarthy received a $10,000 payment from Lustron, a housing company, to write a brief article on the postwar housing problem. The implication had been that Lustron had "bought" McCarthy's influence, which was actually incorrect. The editorial abruptly concluded with a final comment that referred to the attack on the army: "The Senator apparently makes his own rules—and now challenges the President of the United States."[43]

The *Chronicle*'s editorial was revealing from the standpoint that the three incidents for which it criticized McCarthy had been well publicized since 1952. The *Chronicle* had ignored them for two years. Also, the charges had no relation to McCarthy's anti-Communist tactics and Red Scare behavior. The final sentence mentioned only his challenge to Eisenhower and implied that McCarthy had placed himself above the law. That McCarthy and his allies had unnecessarily ruined the lives of scores of innocent people and had wreaked havoc on the nation escaped the *Chronicle*'s attention. This was an understandable omission since in those areas the *Chronicle* management shared much of McCarthy's guilt. The *Chronicle* had criticized McCarthy, not his supporters (as had the *Post*) or the extreme anti-Communist impulse.

Despite the narrowness of the *Chronicle*'s attack, the Minute Women felt deeply betrayed. Because identification between McCarthy and Houston's Red Scare activists had become so close, to criticize one was to criticize the other. Besides, to the Minute Women the Houston *Chronicle*'s editorials were equal to gospel. Fretful Minute Women letters deluged Emmet Walter's office. Eleanor Watt declared that the editorial was "so out of character for the *Chronicle* that I wonder if it could have been written by a reporter from the Houston *Post*." "You can imagine the astonishment of this lifetime *Chronicle* reader," Watt wrote, "to find her favorite newspaper using documentation from the [CPUSA's] *Daily Worker*." Faye Weitinger responded to the editorial with a letter including a detailed refutation of the Lustron charges. Weitinger stated, "At first I thought you had made a mistake and had reprinted Drew Pearson's column in your editorial space." One Minute Women member asked, "What has happened to my nice, conservative newspaper . . . have you changed editors, editorial policy, or what?" Another cried, "I never thought I would live to see this day! The *Chronicle* . . . lending aid and comfort to the traitors of this country. I would . . . also challenge the President . . . as long as he tries to act like a dictator as Eisenhower does. Eisenhower is power mad like Truman and Roosevelt before him." Mrs. J. D. Mabry wrote that she and her husband were "shocked" by the editorial; "in fact, we could hardly believe our eyes." Mabry pleaded with Emmet Walter not to go "Left Wing" and claimed, "Your paper is our last and only hope for the facts to be given to the people of Houston." Elsie Daniel told Walter that her friends were blaming Jesse Jones for the editorial. She asserted, "I am defending the *Chronicle* with my last breath and I keep saying . . . that we can count on it to be fighting the CAUSE of America. . . ." Daniel admitted, ". . . it just breaks my heart to think that I must waste time having to defend the *Chronicle*. . . ." Many other letters repeated this sample's tone and content. Emmet Walter duly reported the response to Jones but he expressed no interest. The power elite had regained its consensus. Legitimacy and acceptability had been withdrawn from Houston's extreme anti-Communist activities.[44]

In the summer of 1954, Houstonians witnessed one final major attempt to rely on the simplistic weapons of the Red Scare in a political campaign. This time, however, the Red-baiting occurred at the state level in Allan Shivers' effort to win reelection to a third term as governor. Shivers had already attracted extensive publicity for his proposal to electrocute Texas' CPUSA members. Faced with a serious challenge from Judge Ralph Yarborough, Shivers proceeded to remind the voters of his aggressive anti-Communist activities. Yarborough had the endorsement of most labor unions, black organizations, liberals, and party loyalists, groups that were easy targets for a Red-baiter like Shivers. "While I know my opponent is not a Communist," Shivers proclaimed, "I feel that he is a captive of certain people who do not approve of being tough on Communists." Shivers' rhetoric and his ultraconservative politics attracted Houston's Red Scare supporters. Hugh Roy Cullen gave a substantial amount of money to his campaign. The Minute Women joined with other conservative women and formed Women for Shivers.[45]

The Houston *Post*'s exposé, however, had made the Minute Women a marked group. Ralph Yarborough's aides, involved in one of the bitterest political campaigns in modern Texas history, knew the climate was changing. They went on the offensive and used the Minute Women against Shivers. The Yarborough staff purchased full-page advertisements in Houston newspapers that accused Governor Shivers of being a Minute Women candidate. The ads asked, in large type, "Why Are *Minute Women* Fighting So Frantically to Keep Shivers in Office?" The names of several members, including Virginia Biggers, Bertie Maughmer, and Dallas Dyer, who also belonged to Women for Shivers, were prominently displayed. The ads included quotes from the O'Leary exposé. Like McCarthy, the Minute Women themselves were being perceived as a political liability.[46]

Yarborough shocked the state Democratic party establishment on July 24 by trailing Shivers by only 23,000 votes out of 1,350,000 cast and forcing the incumbent into a run-off election. Shivers, now really running scared, escalated the Red Scare rhetoric. In an intemperate radio speech, Shivers excitedly charged that all the "Reds, radicals, Communists, and goon squads" in Texas favored Yarborough's election. The governor declared that "Reds" were creating an extensive network of labor unions along the Gulf Coast and, when completed, "the pushing of a single button in Moscow" would paralyze the entire state. Shivers won the run-off with approximately 53 percent of the vote.[47]

It is impossible to gauge the effectiveness of Shivers' demagoguery in the outcome because of other factors. Shivers was able to spend unprecedented millions of dollars in his campaign while Yarborough spent no more than $500,000. Other issues also render a judgment difficult. The most important issue other than Communism was racial integration. The 1954 gubernatorial campaign was the first to occur after the Supreme Court's decision in *Brown* vs. *Topeka Board of Education* in May 1954. The Shivers forces seized the racial issue and used it against Yarborough as much as the Red Scare. The increasingly visible specter of racial integration was beginning to surpass the less tangible fear of Communist subversion as a dominant concern for Houston's and the state's right-wing radical fringe. Although the two were often mixed together with the charge that the civil rights movement was "Communist inspired," such accusations seldom meant much to white racists confronted with a powerful challenge. In Houston, this new fear soon diverted attention away from the Red Scare, replacing it with something much more real to local racists.[48] The dominance of racial integration as an issue in Houston still lay ahead, however, as school patrons began to prepare for another potentially controversial and hotly contested school board campaign.

By the summer of 1954, an informal anti–Red Scare coalition began to coalesce and become visible. This informal group included Eisenhower Republicans, moderate and liberal Democrats, anti–Mills machine school patrons, university professors, journalists, clergy, black leaders, labor leaders, and a handful of prominent civic and cultural leaders. Of course, Methodist ministers W. Kenneth Pope and Grady Hardin as well as the Jewish Anti-Defamation League's Thomas Friedman had been early critics of anti-Communist extremism. They were now joined by individuals activated by the Ebey affair. These included Nina Cullinan and Ima Hogg, two of the most widely respected cultural leaders in Houston. Others included such civic leaders as Mrs. Walter Fondren, the widow of a founder of the Humble Company; Will Clayton, one of the founders of Anderson, Clayton Company and former under secretary of state in the Truman administration; William A. Kirkland, an influential banker and a prominent member of one of Houston's oldest families; Major Jubal R. Parten; and J. Newton Rayzor, a wealthy philanthropist. Scholars from Houston's institutions of higher learning, such as Dr. R. A. Tsanoff, Dr. Hardin Craig, and Dr. Lee Sharrar from Rice Institute, Dr. Louis J. Kestenberg of the University of Houston, and Dr. W. W. Kemmerer, former president of the university, also publicly criticized Red Scare groups. Some of these individuals joined with liberal political activists such as former mayor Neal Pickett (a brother-in-law of Ralph Yarborough), liberal Democratic leader Mrs. R. D. ("Frankie") Randolph, labor leader Don Horn, civil rights activist Sid Hilliard, independent oil man E. Pliny Shaw, R. A. Childers, Eleanor Ball, Ray K. Daily, and Verna Rogers in a concerted effort to remove Red Scare activists from their institutional stronghold, the Houston Independent School District.[49]

Many of these individuals helped to organize the Parents' Council for Improved Schools with the intention of placing three of its representatives on the Houston school board in the November 1954 election. Up for reelection were Garrett Tucker, Stone Wells, and James Delmar. The Parents' Council, which became known as the "liberal" faction, wanted Garrett Tucker to run for reelection on its slate, but Tucker, tired of the continuing school controversies, decided to retire from the board. Since Delmar and Wells had voted against George Ebey and were considered to be allies of such groups as the Minute Women, the liberal faction ran candidates against them. George Eddy, an attorney, was picked to oppose Delmar; Mrs. A. S. Vandervoort, a wealthy socialite from a prominent "Old Houston" family, opposed Stone Wells; and W. W. Kemmerer was selected to run for Garrett Tucker's vacated position.[50]

The Parents' Council proposed a six-point platform with five of the points aimed at destroying the power of Red Scare pressure groups in the schools. The liberal faction announced that, if elected, it would abolish the dual control administrative system and diminish the power of the business manager. This was a direct attack on H. L. Mills. It also proposed to take the school board out of politics, promote cooperation among board members, and leave administrative matters to administrators. If elected its three candidates would join Verna Rogers and A. J. Tucker to form a new liberal consensus on the board. Only Dr. Peterson and Dallas Dyer would remain from the old conservative majority. Referring to the Minute Women, the fifth platform point declared that the "liberal" candidates would "resist pressure groups." The only part of the platform not directly attacking the Red Scare faction was a pledge to promote a rational long-range school building program to alleviate the problem of over-crowded schools.

The Minute Women and other supporters of H. L. Mills and his school machine resurrected the Committee for Sound American Education (CSAE) to offer its own slate. The committee persuaded the previously independent Jimmy Delmar to lead its ticket, which also included Stone Wells. The CSAE chose Edwin J. Smith to run for Garrett Tucker's position.[51]

As in the 1952 campaign, both sides presented voters with clear-cut, distinctly different options. George Eddy urged election of the Parents' Council slate "to unshackle the schools from the grip of anonymous forces" and to rid the school district of the "unholy atmosphere generated by . . . the Minute Women. . . ." The Houston *Post* continued its anti–Red Scare policy by endorsing the Parents' Council candidates and declaring that "they offer the best hope of ending the current factional strife. . . ."[52]

Despite changing conditions, the CSAE continued its old habits and relied heavily on Red Scare tactics. Houston businessman Neil T. Masterson, a CSAE spokesman, dug up the bones of Henry Wallace's Progressive party and claimed the "liberals" were supported by former members of the party. Masterson charged that Hobart Taylor, a local black lawyer who would later become associate counsel to President Johnson, supported the Parents' Council and that Taylor's home had been the site of a reception for Henry Wallace, Paul Robeson, and Herman Wright in 1948. "The Progressive Party," declared Masterson, "has joined the progressive educators in an attempt to take over our schools." If Houstonians still did not understand their choices, a CSAE supporter made it simple: "This is a contest between conservatives, who believe in the time-honored methods of instruction," and the liberals, "who would toss aside all that we know to be good and true and sound. . . ."[53]

It appeared that all the ingredients were present for a repeat performance of the Red Scare school board election of 1952. There were some crucial differences, however. The most important was the active hostil-

ity of the *Post* toward the CSAE. The *Post* refused to publicize the Red
Scare charges of the CSAE as it had in 1952. Even the *Chronicle,* despite
its official endorsement of the CSAE, refrained from making the school
board campaign the same type of media event that it had been two years
earlier. Another important difference was reflected by the published list
of CSAE supporters. Conspicuous by their absence were such previous
elite backers as James A. Elkins, Glenn McCarthy, Hugh Roy Cullen,
Douglas Marshall, Gus Wortham, and Herman and George Brown. Only
James Abercrombie and W. Alvis Parish allowed their names to be publicly associated with the CSAE.[54]

The most crucial difference between the 1952 and 1954 campaigns was
the atmosphere in which the campaigns were conducted. The 1952 campaign occurred concurrently with the presidential race, with Senator Joe
McCarthy and his partisan allies at the peak of their credibility. Houston's
elite sustained the CSAE with a common front, financial support, and
appropriate newspaper encouragement. In the fall of 1952, support of the
Red Scare in Houston was an "acceptable" position, overlaid with establishment approval. Things had changed by 1954, mostly in subtle ways.
Red Scare activities had become much less acceptable. Houston's power
elite, with a few exceptions, had quietly abandoned the Red Scare as a
practical and realistic method of dealing with its perceived enemies. Ralph
O'Leary's scathing exposé and the NEA's highly publicized investigation
certainly damaged the Minute Women and severely weakened the
CSAE's candidates' positions.

The results of the school board election in November 1954 revealed that
the Red Scare had loosened its strong grip on the city. The Parents' Council placed two of its anti–Red Scare candidates on the school board when
Dr. Kemmerer and Mrs. A. S. Vandervoort defeated Stone Wells and
Edwin Smith. They joined Verna Rogers and Jack Tucker to form a "liberal" majority on the school board. Kemmerer's victory was especially self-
satisfying since his opponents were basically the same as those who had
forced him out of the University of Houston. CSAE supporters spread
rumors about the reasons for the resignation but the strategy failed.
Mrs. Vandervoort's wealth and social connections protected her from
anti-Communist charges. Vandervoort was firmly entrenched among
Houston's aristocracy. Ironically, although his newspaper printed an
editorial in favor of the CSAE candidates, Jesse Jones personally voted
for Vandervoort. Of the CSAE's slate, only James Delmar won. Delmar
was opposed by two anti–Red Scare candidates: George Eddy of the
liberal slate and Wellington Abbey, an independent who vowed to "clear
George Ebey's name." Delmar's opponents split their votes and he
was reelected.[55]

A month after the Houston school board election, on December 2, the United States Senate voted 67 to 22 to condemn Joseph McCarthy for contempt and abuse of Senate committees. Texas senators Lyndon Johnson and Price Daniel both voted for the condemnation. In the debate about the resolution Johnson asserted that McCarthy's description of the committee members investigating his record as the "unwitting handmaidens of Communism" did not deserve to be in the *Congressional Record*. It "would be more appropriate on the wall of a men's room," Johnson declared. Throughout the debate, Houston's Minute Women, along with other Texas McCarthyites, bombarded Johnson's office with pro-McCarthy mail and telephone calls. Johnson, however, had just won reelection to another six-year term in the Senate and was very aware of McCarthy's loss of popularity among Texas' power elite. He led the Democratic forces in getting the resolution through the Senate. The condemnation devastated McCarthy. As his biographer, Thomas Reeves, has written, "The censure destroyed McCarthy's spirit, accelerated his physical deterioration, and hastened his death." McCarthy's influence was at an end, although his humiliation and fall discredited but did not destroy the style and technique that had become known as "McCarthyism." Houston's Red Scare groups, already in retreat, shared in McCarthy's defeat. The Wisconsin Republican, a victim of his own political excesses and alcohol abuse, died on May 2, 1957.[56]

In Houston, the new board majority took over the public schools in January 1955. The event marked the first time that the so-called conservative or Mills machine faction had failed to be in control of the school district. The new majority assumed authority armed with the long-awaited NEA report, which had finally been issued in December 1954.

The NEA report included the results of a poll conducted by an independent research firm that substantiated the Houston Teachers Association's charges about the existence of educational unrest in Houston and the need for an investigation. Two-thirds of the respondents indicated they believed Houston needed the NEA investigation. Forty-one percent of the teachers believed the board of education did not understand their problems. One-third of the teachers complained about the lack of grievance procedures and charged that politics played too large a part in determining promotions. Twenty-six percent of the teachers believed that academic freedom in the schools had been stifled. Many teachers reported being pressured to slant their teaching to agree with the political view of their principal or a school administrator. Some of these teachers also accused their superiors of pressuring them to vote for certain political candidates.[57]

The NEA report concluded that "deep-seated suspicion" and a highly emotionalized factionalism had caused widespread cleavages within Houston's school system. This factionalism resulted in controversial school board elections characterized by dogmatism and extremism. The NEA also discovered a strong underlying sense of anxiety among teachers that reprisals might come at any time from forces in the community bent on making examples of certain teachers. In this regard, the Minute Women were named 308 times as the source of community pressure.

The NEA severely criticized the dual control system that allowed the business manager to share direction of the schools with the superintendent. The report noted the claim that H. L. Mills had developed a "large following" in the district through which he influenced school policies having no direct connection with his responsibilities. "There could be little doubt," the report stated, "that the . . . dual system . . . has been a disrupting factor . . . and a major cause of unrest." Therefore, the NEA urged that the system be abolished.[58]

The NEA report also evaluated the Ebey affair. The committee concluded that the board of education had the right not to renew the deputy superintendent's contract since the position did not carry tenure and no law required the board to give a reason for its decision. The report stated, however, that the board's decision left doubt as to Dr. Ebey's loyalty, "whereas no such decision was warranted from the record prepared by the Board's own investigators." The report charged that the board acted rashly in investigating the Ebey case because John Rogge refused to identify his backers and admitted to having no firsthand knowledge of Ebey's past. The NEA knew of no other case where a major investigation had been launched on such flimsy evidence. The school board should have carefully evaluated the charges before it hired an investigation firm. If the board's action established a precedent for future personnel relations, then any person could cause another major investigation of any teacher on the basis of unscreened charges. The report concluded that the episode had been handled in such a way as to cause anxiety among loyal and dedicated employees. The Ebey case convinced many that any employee deemed controversial might be the target of unwarranted attacks, reprisals, and the object of a public investigation. The NEA declared that it could find no reason to believe the Houston schools harbored disloyal or Communist teachers. It urged, however, that charges like those made in the Ebey case be fully screened before any teacher "be subjected to a public investigation on the basis of rumor, supposition, or innuendo."[59]

When the NEA issued its report the Houston *Chronicle* responded with a vituperative editorial. The NEA, according to the *Chronicle*, "smeared everybody who has dared to oppose the attempts of the NEA to control the public schools in the United States and establish the socialistic philosophy of education known as Progressive Education." The *Chronicle* charged that the NEA investigation was an example of "pseudo-liberalism which goes berserk at any opposition and attempts to brainwash everyone into conformity with so-called liberal ideas." The newspaper stated that the report "is propaganda, pure and simple"; people who oppose "socialization" of schools and the children in them will continue to oppose professional educators who decide "to smear anyone who opposes their schemes."[60]

The remaining members of the conservative faction of the board reacted in a similar manner. James Delmar charged that the NEA had "stuck its nose into our business . . . we don't need any of their suggestions . . . whether they are good or bad. The report is an outrage." Dr. Henry Peterson, a native of Maine, said, "It's not unusual for itinerants from afar to come to Texas and tell us how to think, politically, economically, and educationally. Texans believe in Texas and local control." H. L. Mills agreed with Peterson: "These people who come from far-away places and visit Houston usually end up giving us a kick in the britches." Mills noted that the report urged abolishing dual control of the Houston schools and replied that it would take a "superman" to conduct both the business and academic affairs of the district.[61]

Once in power, the new board followed through with its main campaign promise. It abolished the dual control system and gave "supreme authority" to the superintendent. The business manager's position was considerably weakened and subordinated to that of the superintendent. Assistant Superintendent J. O. Webb, possibly the most vociferous Red Scare activist in the school administration, was charged with insubordination, demoted, and eventually placed on indefinite suspension. The *Chronicle* called the board's decisions "shocking" and "drastic" and declared Webb's demotion "cruel and unfair."[62]

The board majority carried out other, less dramatic changes, but before it could do much more, the new faction fell victim to a CSAE that had been renewed and strengthened by white reactions to the immediate threat of federally imposed racial integration. Although the Red Scare coalition had lost much of its cohesion, white response to black demands would allow the Red Scare ethic to maintain a base of power in the Houston public schools.

TEN

BERTIE AND THE BOARD

God grant . . . the strength to continue the fight until America's children are again taught to love and honor their own God, their own country, and their own homes!

—Bertie Maughmer[1]

The national Red Scare seemed to evaporate during the somnolent second term of President Dwight Eisenhower. With McCarthy gone and the Korean War over, American society settled down, enjoying unprecedented economic prosperity at home and "Pax Americana"—enforced by the nation's military might—abroad. All was not what it seemed, of course. A great civil rights movement was brewing and other forces were stirring beneath the seemingly placid surface of American society, forces and feelings that would break forth in a disruptive torrent in the late 1960s. But this would be in the future. Americans in the last half of the 1950s seemed to be more concerned with hula hoops, rock and roll, and sputniks than with Reds and subversives. And Texans were no different.

In many ways, however, the demise of the Red Scare was a delusion. Although the press and national opinion makers turned their attention to other matters, the virulent strain of extreme anti-Communism in the American culture remained a potent force. Its most obvious manifestation could be seen in an American foreign policy that continued to define the world in stark black and white terms of either "pro" or "anti" Communism with no ground in-between. Vietnam would be the inevitable result. But extreme anti-Communism also continued to influence domestic life. Because no one at the national level filled the void left by McCarthy's utter ruin, the impression remained that the Red Scare had been banished. In reality, however, entertainers continued to be blacklisted from television, radio, and the movies; loyalty oaths continued to be signed; and the House Committee on Un-American Activities proceeded unabated with its own inquisitions. At the local level, veterans of Red Scare pressure groups continued to warn their communities of the imminent dangers of Communism. The atmosphere in the late 1950s was different, of course. Fewer people paid attention and the press was less likely to encourage right-wing political extremism. But in little pockets throughout many communities in the United States the Red Scare mentality still held sway.

In Houston, a community continuing to endure the contradictory stresses of rapid change, a pocket of influence remained in a predictable place: the Houston Independent School District. Although the fallout from the Ebey affair had helped to elect a liberal school board majority promising to ease political tensions within the schools, that majority was doomed to be short-lived.

The United States Supreme Court's decision on May 17, 1954, in the Brown case, which declared that racial segregation in public schools was unconstitutional, set forces in motion in Houston that would end liberal control of the school board. Many Red Scare activists such as the Minute Women leaders drew new energy from opposition to the growing civil rights movement. For example, in September 1955 the Minute Women, by now a smaller organization due to the developments of the preceding year, began to conduct public forums to discuss the specific issue of racial integration. The Minute Women, still led by Virginia Biggers, now added the civil rights movement to their list of dangers threatening the "American Way of Life." Their efforts in this area, however, were largely co-opted by other newly formed groups such as the Citizens League for School Home Rule, which included CSAE supporters Joe Reynolds, Loren Stark, Stone Wells, and Ewing Werlein. The Citizens League vowed "to oppose the integration of white and negro students in our schools by all lawful means." Other opponents of racial integration such as Dr. Denton Kerr and school principal G. C. Scarborough helped form a local chapter of the White Citizens Councils of America, Inc.[2]

In February 1956, aware of the need to accommodate to change and respond to the intensifying racial issue with an equitable but moderate plan, the liberal-dominated school board began public discussions that it hoped would eventually end segregation. Unfortunately, racial segregationists disrupted the hearings by singing "Dixie," heckling, and waving protest signs in the school board meeting room. This incident and others exerted enough pressure on the liberal school board to force it to postpone racial desegregation at least until new school buildings could be built. Despite the pressure, however, the board did order the integration of the school administration.[3]

Throughout the summer of 1956 it became clear that the Red Scare mentality in Houston's school politics was regaining its strength as a result of the increasingly tense racial situation. At the state level, however, there were signs that extreme anti-Communism was actually losing its attractiveness as a campaign tactic.

In the campaign between Senator Price Daniel and Judge Yarborough to succeed Allan Shivers as governor, Red-baiting was conspicuously lessened. Although Daniel occasionally charged that Yarborough's election would allow the NAACP and the CIO to control state government, the overall campaign between the two major candidates was in stark contrast to that of 1954. Two other candidates attracted the extreme right while Daniel appealed to the middle of the road. One candidate on the extreme right was a familiar household name, former governor W. Lee O'Daniel. The other was well-known Texas historian and cattle rancher J. Evetts Haley. Both men ran campaigns that dwelt on the dangers of the civil rights movement. They both mixed anti-Communism with racism, but Haley's style was so extreme that he attracted only 88,800 votes. O'Daniel, however, had strong enough name recognition to draw 347,750 votes. Price Daniel defeated Yarborough by a 629,000 to 463,400 vote. Although Price Daniel had never been the Red Scare advocate that Shivers had been, the 1956 gubernatorial campaign seemed to indicate that Texas politics had returned to its pre–Red Scare status, less skewed by extreme anti-Communism.[4]

In Houston, the potency of the racial integration issue in school politics became obvious in the fall of 1956. In September, after unsuccessful attempts by black children to enroll at white public schools, the Committee for Sound American Education augmented its standard "creeping socialism" warning with an overtly racist and prosegregation platform. Anti-Communism still dominated the world view of some of the CSAE's most ardent supporters, but race was now a more promising campaign issue.

To recapture control of the Houston school board in the upcoming November 1956 election, the CSAE rallied behind two of its incumbents: Dr. Henry Peterson and Dallas Dyer. Two other positions were up for election, however, and the CSAE chose Stone ("Red") Wells, who had voted against Ebey and had been defeated in 1954, to run against Jack Tucker, the liberal incumbent. For the fourth position, held by the formidable Verna Rogers, CSAE leaders such as Aubrey Calvin and Dallas Dyer preferred a conservative civil engineer named J. L. Williams. Minute Women activist Bertie Maughmer coveted the position, however, and announced her candidacy. She demanded CSAE endorsement, but Dyer and her colleagues, who considered Maughmer a pushy social climber and a neurotic, resisted. Maughmer refused to bow out and threatened to split the ticket with Williams with the probable result being the reelection of Verna Rogers, the one person the conservatives most wanted to defeat. Although the CSAE's endorsement would bring votes to Williams, Maughmer's greater name recognition would win many other conservative votes. She had run unsuccessfully for the school board in 1952 and had kept her name in the newspapers through her activities as head of the Houston Police Officers' Wives Association and as parliamentarian of the Houston-area Parent-Teacher Association's Council.[5] Maughmer was also well known for her Minute Women activities and for her active support of Allan Shivers in the 1954 gubernatorial campaign. Her husband, Earl, was a popular member of the Houston Police Department who had served as president of the police association. The CSAE decided not to risk the probable reelection of Rogers through a split conservative vote and accepted Maughmer for its slate. Williams subsequently withdrew and announced in favor of Maughmer. Dallas Dyer was displeased, but decided that "sometimes in life you make a compromise rather than have everything shot to pieces."[6]

The liberal school board group resurrected the Parents' Council for Improved Schools and chose Jack Tucker to stand for reelection against Stone Wells. The council recruited James B. Giles, an economics professor at Rice Institute, to oppose Dallas Dyer. The council also supported Verna Rogers, who surprised everyone, however, by abandoning her board position to run against her arch foe Henry Peterson. The liberal slate chose oil man E. Pliny Shaw to run in Rogers' old position against Maughmer.[7]

As the school board campaign gathered momentum in October 1956, the issue of racial integration dominated all others. CSAE candidates Dyer, Peterson, and Maughmer mixed the Red Scare tactic they had used together in 1952 with a "Black Scare" tactic more appropriate for 1956. In the campaign, Dallas Dyer and Henry Peterson stressed their belief in "separate but equal" schools for blacks, with Peterson declaring that "racial segregation . . . offers the best educational opportunities for both races." Stone Wells, an attorney, offered a legalistic argument in favor of segregation. Bertie Maughmer, however, chose a less paternalistic, more openly racist position. She spoke frequently to Houston's White Citizens Council (accompanied at least once by Dallas Dyer) and declared that "race mixing" was anti-Christian. In the event anyone might have misunderstood her views, Maughmer later declared, "I'd rather go to jail than see my kids go to school with niggers."[8]

The liberal candidates attempted to campaign on the progressive record of the 1954–1956 school board majority, but the race issue overwhelmed them. The liberals argued that desegregation was now "the law of the land" and that Houston must take every step to comply. This argument, however, failed to attract much support in a community where the racist legacy of the Old South still held sway.[9]

On November 7, 1956, after a campaign later described by *Time* magazine as "the most vicious . . . in Houston history," the CSAE reclaimed the city's schools by sweeping all four of the board positions up for election. Using the issue of racial integration, Dyer, Peterson, Wells, and Maughmer achieved an easy victory on the same day Dwight Eisenhower won reelection to a second term as president. The next day, to allay any doubts about her campaign promise, school board member-elect Maughmer announced to the Houston newspapers that "I will certainly do my utmost to live up to my platform which is segregation in the public schools. . . ." She, Dyer, Wells, and Peterson now joined Jimmy Delmar to form a five to two majority over liberals W. W. Kemmerer and Mrs. Vandervoort.[10]

Although the conservative majority had been elected on a prosegregation platform, race was not their only concern. The return of the CSAE group also meant a heightening of the Red Scare environment in Houston schools. Right-wing political pressures had continued in the schools even during the two-year term of the liberal majority in 1955 and 1956. The Mills faction was too deeply rooted throughout the district for the liberal board to do much about it. For example, Sam Gibbs, a math instructor at Sam Houston High School, was warned by his fellow teachers to refrain from discussing his liberal political views in the teachers' lounge. The teachers told Gibbs, who openly supported Adlai Stevenson for president, that they were all being watched by some of their colleagues and that his ideological heresy would be reported to Mills machine school administrators. Gibbs, feeling protected by the liberal school board majority, brashly rejected this advice. In 1957, shortly after the CSAE returned to power, the school board fired Gibbs for "incompetence." The dismissal occurred despite the fact that two-thirds of his students achieved scores higher than the national average on a standardized math test. Gibbs elected not to appeal the dismissal. Because of his contempt for those now in control of the schools, he no longer wanted to remain in the district and promptly got a teaching job elsewhere.[11]

Before the Gibbs dismissal, however, the CSAE majority served notice almost immediately after their election that the Red Scare mentality was back on the school board. A few days after her reelection, Dallas Dyer succeeded in getting the lame duck board to deny expense money to Nelda Davis to go to the National Council for Social Studies convention in Cleveland, Ohio. Davis, a social studies supervisor and an employee of the district for twenty-nine years, had been invited to give a lecture on the problems of rapid learners in secondary schools. Dyer killed Davis' request by charging that speakers with "un-American" backgrounds were scheduled to appear at the social studies convention. Dyer made it clear that teacher requests for funds to attend such meetings affiliated with the National Education Association would continue to be denied in the future. This threat was subsequently made an official board policy. Nelda Davis paid her own expenses and went to the meeting anyway.[12]

In January 1957, when the CSAE took formal control of the school

board, Dyer was elected board president and Bertie Maughmer parliamentarian. Under their guidance the board embarked on a two-year campaign to continue the war against potential "un-American" tendencies
in the schools, to fight off racial integration, and to preserve the Mills
machine's power over the district's teachers. During these years the board
allowed the University of Houston's educational television station to
broadcast its weekly meetings. These televised meetings became a public sensation as a result of the behavior of the CSAE majority and the futile
opposition offered by remaining liberals Kemmerer and Vandervoort.
Stone Wells, Dallas Dyer, and Bertie Maughmer quickly became the
"stars" of these programs. Wells, who cultivated a country-bumpkin
image, enjoyed telling funny anecdotes during the televised meetings that
belittled people with doctoral degrees. Dallas Dyer often monopolized
air time with lectures about the evils of the NEA and the need to teach
American heritage courses in the schools. During one meeting early in
1957, Dyer sadly announced to the board and her television audience that
a mother had discovered in an American history textbook used by Houston school children the statement that George Washington "lost more battles than he won" during the Revolutionary War. Dyer expressed deep
regrets about this heresy and declared, "We would like to find books that
are objective . . . and stress American heritage and those qualities which
in the past we have considered fine in our leaders." These televised performances, which were called "Bertie and the Board" by *Time* magazine
and the "Monday night fights" by many Houstonians, provided stiff competition for the television networks' situation comedies. One conservative board member later recalled that his colleagues "loved to perform"
on television with the result that "we were the best show in town."[13]

Neither Wells, Dyer, nor Peterson, however, could match Bertie
Maughmer's performances. Maughmer, who continued after her election
to make speeches at White Citizens Council meetings denouncing racial
integration, garnered the most publicity. She managed to get into the
newspapers so often with her Red Scare–style antics that she began to
stuff her many press clippings in her purse and would proudly display
them at public forums. During board meetings, Maughmer—under the
spell of klieg lights and television cameras—was prone to ramble incessantly about the dangers of federal aid to education and subversive textbooks. In March 1957, for example, she convinced her board colleagues
to ban from the schools two state-adopted economics textbooks and two
geography textbooks. Maughmer described the two geography texts,
Geography and World Affairs, published by Random House, and *Geography of the World,* published by Macmillan, as being "completely undesirable" because she believed them to be slanted in favor of the United

Nations and "one-worldism." Maughmer attacked *Applied Economics* because it suggested that citizens can sometimes save money by buying items collectively through cooperatives. Hearing this during the board meeting, a startled Stone Wells blurted out, "That's socialism, isn't it?" Maughmer also denounced *Economics and You* for being "too objective" in its discussion of capitalism and announced that the textbook's suggested reading list recommended such "fellow travelers" as historian Allan Nevins and novelist Edna Ferber. The usually quiet superintendent, Bill Moreland, growing increasingly wary of all this, felt compelled to remind Maughmer that these books were published by "free enterprise system publishing companies" owned by wealthy capitalists. Nevertheless, the books were banned.[14]

Maughmer's textbook attack and an attempt by Henry Peterson to make White Citizens Council leader G. C. Scarborough deputy superintendent proved to be the final humiliations for Bill Moreland. After twelve years of similar episodes and the future full of complex problems revolving around the issue of racial integration, Moreland gave up. Citing "personal reasons," he submitted his resignation in April 1957. *Time* magazine stated that it was extraordinary that the moderate Moreland had "managed to last so long" and concluded that "Houston's school board has chalked up as impressive a record of sheer orneriness as any big-city board in the nation." George Carmack, editor of the Houston *Press,* called the departure of sixty-one-year-old Moreland "a black day for Houston" because he was "just about the last brake" keeping the schools from "plunging into a mad whirlpool of uncontrolled extremism. . . ."[15]

The conservative majority replaced Moreland with his political enemy, fifty-one-year-old G. C. Scarborough, a first cousin of H. L. Mills and a right-wing extremist dedicated to preserving racial segregation. Scarborough's appointment was made on an interim basis until the selection of a permanent superintendent by September 1957. There was an implication, however, that Scarborough would eventually receive the permanent job. Stone Wells, delighted by this development, declared that Scarborough would make certain that "the American way of life will be taught, the Texas way of life will be taught, and conservatism will be taught" in the schools.[16]

Almost immediately Scarborough supervised a major overhauling of the social studies curriculum. The hated term "social studies," viewed as progressive education jargon, was eliminated altogether. World history and world geography were postponed until the tenth grade. The trouble with world history was that it was exceedingly difficult to teach without at least a mention of Karl Marx and the Russian Revolution. Likewise, in world geography one could not ignore that huge nation stretching from the Pacific to Poland sitting astride two continents. It would be better not to risk confusing youthful minds about such complex subjects. In their place, the school board approved five years (grades three through seven) of local, state, and American history and geography. This included three years (grades three, four, and seven) of Texas history and geography.

Time noted that the new curriculum would "keep Houston's younger generation safe from learning anything at all about three-fourths of the globe." Mrs. A. S. Vandervoort warned her fellow board members that "we will just create a bunch of little Davy Crocketts and little Daughters of the Republic [of Texas]. I hate to see us get so narrow." W. W. Kemmerer charged that the conservative majority was "encircling the state with a cotton curtain to prevent the children from peeping out." Henry Peterson replied that "these little seventh and eighth graders are not going to discuss world history . . . anyway. They are going to discuss their new party dress or something else." Scarborough was more to the point, however. He told the board that the new curriculum was necessary to keep "propaganda" out of the classroom.[17]

Bertie Maughmer and her colleagues' behavior, as unintentionally amusing as it may have been to some, was anything but funny to many teachers. One teacher has described 1957 as "a hellish nightmare" because of "Bertie's antics" and the fear stalking the school halls. The primary fear was of losing one's job, perhaps because of some politically heretical remark accidentally uttered in an unguarded moment in front of a soft drink machine in a shabby teachers' lounge. Principals warned their teachers at staff meetings never to express a personal opinion anywhere—in the classroom, in the lounge, in their friends' homes, in church—and never to deviate from a rigid adherence to their curriculum guides. Open class discussion was best avoided; better to show an approved film such as the ones recently distributed by conservative Harding College in Arkansas—the ones that featured maps showing how the United States was rapidly being surrounded by Communist governments painted in blood-red with huge hammer and sickle emblems marking them off from the shrinking free world. Nor was a hard-earned summer vacation in an exotic place a good idea; a rumor circulated that at least one teacher had been reported to the FBI by a colleague because of her vacations to Mexico and Europe. Joe McCarthy might be dead and the Minute Women pariahs but the Red Scare raged on in the public schools of Houston in 1957.[18]

Nor had it entirely disappeared in other areas of the community, although the environment was nothing like the days prior to 1954. Nonetheless, vestiges remained. Herman Wright and Arthur Mandell, for instance, were plagued by their past anti-establishment political activities. When Wright became vice-president of the National Lawyers Guild in May 1956, Houston newspapers publicized the event in terms implying that Wright and the guild were both un-American. The Houston *Press* emphasized that the Lawyers Guild was on the attorney general's list of subversive organizations. The *Press* also reported Wright's office and home addresses in case anyone might be interested.[19]

In the summer of 1957, the Grievance Committee, Houston district, of the State Bar of Texas suspended Wright's, Mandell's, and Ben Ramey's law licenses for ninety days. The bar association charged the three attorneys with solicitation of clients for personal injury suits. Although they denied the charges, the firm decided not to appeal. Wright always believed that their political activities as well as their success in winning personal injury suits against local industries were responsible for the bar's action.[20]

That same summer, the United States Department of State ordered Arthur Mandell to sign a non-Communist affidavit before it would allow him to travel outside the country. Mandell refused since it was not required as a part of the standard application. An employee of the State Department admitted to a reporter for the Houston *Press* that a confidential source in Houston had sent the department information about Mandell that "made it seem advisable to ask him to sign a certificate on Communist Party membership." When Mandell refused to sign the affidavit, the State Department informed the immigration authorities and ordered them to keep him from leaving the United States. Mandell subsequently returned his passport with a cover letter stating that he "did not need it anymore." Eventually, in April 1958, Mandell gave in, signed the affidavit, and had his passport returned. Three months later, in an unrelated case, the United States Supreme Court declared such passport procedures unconstitutional.[21]

In the schools, many of Houston's teachers faced the new year of 1958 with a sense of deepening dread. The CSAE's Red Scare outlook now seemed in total control of public education with G. C. Scarborough holding the superintendent's job. Unexpectedly, however, the old McCarthyite group dominating the school board began to self-destruct.

Shortly after Scarborough became acting superintendent, Henry Peterson and H. L. Mills asked him to fire several teachers, including Kate Bell and Nelda Davis. These teachers had supported Peterson's and Bertie Maughmer's opponents in the 1956 election. To Peterson's and Mills' great shock, Scarborough rejected this request. Scarborough was not so reckless as to initiate a teacher purge while serving merely as acting superintendent. In addition, he was acutely aware of W. W. Kemmerer's public charges that he replaced Moreland to carry out exactly what Peterson was now requesting.[22]

Scarborough's refusal and Peterson's and Mills' reaction began a feud
that eventually destroyed the old CSAE coalition. The first loss was Jimmy
Delmar, who resigned in February 1958. Delmar had tired of the constant
school board battles and the growing public criticisms of the CSAE's
extremism. He had decided against running again in the upcoming election in the fall. His early resignation would allow the CSAE majority to
appoint another conservative to the board whose incumbency would
benefit the campaign. That all was not peaceful within the CSAE, however, became apparent during Delmar's last board meeting. Delmar
shocked his colleagues by declaring that H. L. Mills did not know how
to run his department properly, accusing Henry Peterson of being "long-
winded," and criticizing Dallas Dyer when she failed to recognize his
request to make a point during a debate. Ten days after Delmar's resignation, the CSAE majority elected Dr. John K. Glen to replace him. Glen,
a fifty-nine-year-old pediatrician, was a former member of Doctors for
Freedom. His wife had been an active Minute Women member.[23]

The CSAE's old guard continued to crumble in the summer of 1958.
Accusations by the Houston *Post* that H. L. Mills was violating state laws
by circumventing bidding regulations governing the awarding of contracts
led to an investigation of the business manager's office. The school board
paid local attorney William N. Bonner $7,500 to examine the *Post*'s
charges. In July, Bonner produced a sixty-five-page report exonerating
Mills and the board gave the sixty-eight-year-old business manager a vote
of confidence, although Mrs. Vandervoort called the action "a white-
wash." Despite the vote of confidence, Mills had now lost much of his
influence within the CSAE.[24]

In the midst of Bonner's investigation of Mills' business practices, the
silent feud between Peterson, Maughmer, and Mills on one side and Scarborough on the other became an open public dispute that resulted in Scarborough's early retirement. In June 1958, the school board had to decide
if it would make Scarborough the permanent superintendent or hire a
new person. Job applications had been received in the preceding months
and the board needed to make a decision. On June 20, Henry Peterson
and Bertie Maughmer shocked Houstonians by voting with liberal board
members Kemmerer and Vandervoort to defeat Stone Wells' motion
to appoint Scarborough permanent superintendent. Dallas Dyer and
John K. Glen voted in favor of Scarborough. Peterson was angry because
of Scarborough's refusal both to fire the teachers and to take orders from
Mills. Maughmer disliked Scarborough because he had opposed one of
her frequent book-banning forays and because she usually followed Peterson's lead. When Scarborough realized the votes were against him he
requested and was granted early retirement. The strange new board
majority of Peterson, Maughmer, Kemmerer, and Vandervoort then

proceeded to hire Dr. John McFarland as the new superintendent of Houston schools. McFarland was a self-described "middle-of-the-roader" who had previously been head of the Amarillo public schools.[25]

The old guard Red Scare school board faction was now deeply divided. This fundamental rift prevented the CSAE from offering an official slate of candidates in the school board election of November 1958. Nevertheless, an unofficial conservative slate was composed of Aubrey Calvin against W. W. Kemmerer; John K. Glen opposed to two candidates, including a black woman named Mrs. Charles White; and Mrs. H. W. Cullen versus several others. Mrs. Vandervoort decided to retire from the board and did not file for reelection. Due to the confused political alignments, the liberals also failed to organize a campaign organization. Most of the confusion stemmed from the surprise endorsement of the liberal Kemmerer by his former archfoes Bertie Maughmer, Henry Peterson, and H. L. Mills.[26]

The 1958 school board campaign marked the first time since the 1940s that anti-Communism and extreme right-wing rhetoric failed to play any role in political strategy. The Red Scare leaders were too busy attacking each other. Aubrey Calvin publicly accused Peterson and Maughmer—two of his former 1952 running mates—of "stabbing me in the back." Dallas Dyer called her two former ideological colleagues "utter liars." Epithets, insults, charges, and countercharges filled the air as the old Red Scare coalition committed public suicide. This schism cost the former CSAE activists dearly as Kemmerer defeated Calvin and Mrs. Charles White, a former teacher and graduate of Prairie View A&M University, became the first black ever to be elected to the Houston school board. Mrs. H. W. Cullen, a housewife and former Minute Women activist, won her election, but political analysts believed her victory was the result of having the same last name as Hugh Roy Cullen rather than because of her right-wing political views. Mrs. Cullen was not related to the millionaire oil man.[27]

Cullen's victory provided but little comfort to the conservatives. They were horrified by the election of a black to a school board locked in a legal struggle to avoid racial integration. Mrs. White's victory and the threat of impending NAACP law suits forced Peterson and Maughmer to hold their noses and vote with Dyer, Wells, and Cullen on most school board issues in 1959. But this fragile coalition was forged on racism, not extreme anti-Communism.

After the CSAE schism of 1958, the Red Scare style of the 1950s largely disappeared from the Houston school board, although the pressure on teachers to conform rigidly to the conservative viewpoint of education continued unabated. Except for Dallas Dyer, the principal leaders of the Red Scare in Houston schools left the scene during the 1958–1960 period.

H. L. Mills, still suffering from the hints of scandal associated with his handling of school contracts, retired on August 31, 1959, after thirty-seven years as business manager. Upon Mills' retirement, the school board delegated supreme administrative authority over all facets of school management, including the business office, to the superintendent. The emotional controversy over dual administration that had marked school board elections throughout the 1950s was now forgotten. The conservative faction had supported dual management solely as a means to preserve H. L. Mills' power. With Mills gone, dual administration lost its real reason for existence. Although still dominated by the CSAE, the board voted unanimously to end the system. The fact that John McFarland, the current superintendent, was a conservative (although not an extremist) certainly helped clear the way for this structural change.[28]

H. L. Mills' retirement in 1959 was followed the next year by that of his close friend Henry Peterson. After twenty-two years of board membership, CSAE leaders told Peterson that they would oppose his reelection in November 1960. Peterson, now anathema to the majority faction of the CSAE, decided to retire. Peterson's decision, however, was but a postscript in the two-year-long demise of the old Red Scare school board leadership. The sensational and symbolic end of the Minute Women/McCarthyite dominance over school affairs occurred just prior to Peterson's forced retirement.[29]

A few minutes after eight o'clock on the evening of July 3, 1960, police lieutenant Earl Maughmer began to dress in the bedroom of his modest east-side home as he prepared to report for night duty at the city jail. Maughmer was anxious to go to work. His relationship with his wife, Bertie, had degenerated into one of constant bickering and frequent physical altercations. Divorce had been discussed but never followed through with. The day of July 3 had been no different; he and Bertie had argued violently about his going on a boat ride without her.

As Earl stood in front of his closet clad only in his underwear, Bertie called his name. The policeman turned and confronted the cold reality of his .357 magnum pistol being pointed at him. "I've been trying to warn you and trying to tell you that it was going to turn out like this," Bertie said in a calm voice. She squeezed the trigger and a bullet passed through his right elbow, tearing into his stomach. Earl fell to the floor in agony, screaming, "No Bert! Don't do that" as his wife continued toward him, still aiming the gun. Earl managed to tackle Bertie's legs, pull her down, and wrestle the gun away from her. The critically wounded policeman somehow got back to his feet and scrambled down the stairs, where he collapsed, still holding his revolver. A suddenly contrite Bertie telephoned Jeff Davis Hospital and an ambulance soon delivered her husband to the emergency room. Before losing consciousness, Earl, thinking he would die and not wanting to leave a scandal behind him, told his police friends that the shooting was an accident. Bertie quickly agreed. She told the policemen that she and Earl were worried about prowlers and Earl had been trying to teach her how to fire the gun when he slipped and accidently shot himself.

Earl Maughmer survived, however, and on July 12 decided to tell the truth. This news was spread across the front pages of Houston's newspapers in lurid headlines. Bertie Maughmer, Red Scare leader and school board member, was arrested and suffered the indignity of having the entire process of being booked documented and presented to the public in a series of photographs featured in the Houston *Press*. One picture showed a grim-looking Bertie posing for a mug shot, a plaque with her police number hanging from her neck. She was spared the humiliation of a jail cell, however, as her husband's friends allowed her to sit in a waiting room until her attorney secured her release.[30]

On August 10, 1960, the Harris County Grand Jury, influenced by Earl's wishes, Bertie's status as a civic leader, and letters of support from Henry Peterson, H. L. Mills, and others, decided not to indict her. Bertie Maughmer subsequently resigned from the Houston school board, although she had tenaciously clung to her position even after admitting that she had intentionally shot her husband. She and Earl divorced and Bertie disappeared from public view.[31]

The departure of Mills, Peterson, and Maughmer from the public scene by 1961 marked the end of the post–World War II Red Scare era in Houston—the Red Scare identified with Joe McCarthy and McCarthyism. Such local Red Scare pressure groups as the Minute Women, Doctors for Freedom, the Committee for the Preservation of Methodism, and the Americanism Committee of the American Legion had lost their effectiveness in Houston affairs by the time of Joe McCarthy's death in 1957. But some of the old Red Scare activists, using the vehicle of the CSAE and feeding on the fear of racial integration, maintained a conspicuous pocket of influence in the Houston schools.

The extreme anti-Communist impulse that had fueled the city's Red Scare in the 1950s remained, still nurtured by members of the local political fringe. But for the period between 1958 and 1961, with the easing of international tensions, relative calm within the national and state political environments, the loss of elite sanctions and press support, and the conflict among Red Scare school leaders, this extremist fringe lost its tight grip on local affairs. The Red Scare in Houston was over, but in the early 1960s the extreme right would soon regain some of its power, especially in the schools, as a new phase in the continuing history of traditional domestic American anti-Communism would begin.

ELEVEN

CONCLUSION: BEYOND THE RED SCARE

*The Devil is alive in Salem, and we dare not quail to follow
wherever the accusing finger points!*
— *The Reverend John Hale*[1]

Recalling her activities during the second American Red Scare, a former Minute Women member stated, "America was great until Roosevelt and Truman. Then things got bad and you could see it right here in our own city. My friends and I wanted to help return America to the old system of free enterprise and the best place to begin was at home. I'm afraid we failed." Despite her feelings of failure, this former Minute Women member did not give up the fight. She and her surviving colleagues continued their work beyond the Red Scare, throughout the 1960s and 1970s.[2]

During the 1960s many of those Houstonians and other Americans who had been deeply involved in the activities of Red Scare groups in the previous decade transferred their memberships and their attentions to organizations and issues identified with the so-called Radical Right. Although the second Red Scare was over, extreme anti-Communism retained a vitality, especially in the Sunbelt regions such as southern California, Arizona, Texas, and Florida. The election of John F. Kennedy to the presidency in November 1960 helped feed this new brand of radical anti-Communism. Kennedy's Catholicism, his eastern elite background, his inability "to do something" about Fidel Castro in Cuba, and his support of civil rights legislation for blacks spawned a mélange of new hate groups and political action organizations.[3]

Texas, which continued to be a center for those who noisily opposed change and the modern world, contributed its share to the Radical Right. In Houston during the early 1960s this included active chapters of the John Birch Society, the Christian Anti-Communist Crusade, Freedom-in-Action, the Christian Crusade, and others more ephemeral and blurred in identity. Those Red Scare groups of the 1950s such as the Minute Women, the Committee for Sound American Education, and the Americanism Committee of the American Legion that had managed to survive in some form also contributed to the rising din of protest. The Minute Women chapter, however, was but a shadow of its former self.

This new burst of right-wing reaction in the early 1960s, combined with the ongoing fight against racial integration, enabled the CSAE to maintain its control over the Houston Independent School District. New CSAE leaders emerged such as Robert Y. Eckels, an insurance salesman and former industrial arts teacher; John M. Robinson, a lawyer and former FBI agent; J. W. McCullough, an accountant and American Legion leader; and Joe Kelly Butler, an independent oil operator. These men joined with Red Scare holdovers Dallas Dyer and Mrs. H. W. Cullen to maintain the CSAE school board majority throughout most of the 1960s.[4]

Although H. L. Mills and his friends Henry Peterson and Bertie Maughmer were no longer on the scene in the 1960s, the Red Scare mind-set that the Mills machine had encouraged and sustained remained as its long-lived legacy in Houston's schools. For teachers and students, the new decade brought little relief from the political pressures of the 1950s.

For example, Charlene Potter, HISD's supervisor of history, geography, civics, and other related courses, dedicated much of her time in the early 1960s to the education of teachers and students about the threat of an imminent Communist takeover. In 1961 Potter initiated an in-service workshop series to instruct the teachers under her supervision on methods of anti-Communist indoctrination aimed at high school students. Potter later arranged a series of weekly night classes at Jesse Jones High School for an organization she helped sponsor called Teens against Communism. Potter's voluntary night school featured extreme anti-Communist films produced by the Church of Christ's Harding College in Searcy, Arkansas, the U.S. Army, and the House Committee on Un-American Activities. William P. Strube, Jr., a Houston insurance executive and national vice-president of the Christian Anti-Communist Crusade, served as primary lecturer at these high school meetings. A series of early morning classes was also organized. Strube, an evangelical Christian fundamentalist with a flair for oratory, used the school meetings to preach a militant Christian anti-Communism. Strube would stress that "the best way to enlist" in the anti-Communist struggle "is to enlist . . . in the Army of Jesus." Although the school board never required students to go to these meetings, several teachers later recalled that "it was understood" that they were expected to pressure their pupils to attend.[5]

At the board level, the new members acted as though it was 1953 again. Kenneth Parker, a high school history teacher, resigned in April 1961 after the school administration investigated him for subversive activities. Nancy Hale, a twenty-six-year-old member of the Minute Women, had complained to Dallas Dyer about Parker's liberal political views and Dyer ordered the investigation. The investigation cleared Parker of any wrongdoing, but he decided to resign due to intensive administrative harassment, which Parker claimed included administrators spying on his class lectures and making frequent demands that he resign.[6]

In May 1961, while Strube used school facilities to preach his Christian anti-Communism, the board refused to allow the American Civil Liberties Union (ACLU) use of a school auditorium for a free public speech by ACLU national director Patrick Malin. Before rejecting the ACLU request, J. W. McCullough read aloud to his fellow board members from an American Legion pamphlet published in 1952 that accused the ACLU of being a subversive organization. Joe Kelly Butler, who would eventually become head of the Texas State Board of Education, supported McCullough and also denounced the ACLU. The school board later required anyone asking for permission to use a school facility for a public meeting to sign a loyalty oath.[7]

In June 1961, Superintendent John McFarland recommended Margaret Bleil for a promotion to the position of registrar at Bellaire High School. Bleil, a Phi Beta Kappa with over thirty years of teaching experience in Houston, had supported George Ebey and demanded the NEA investigation of Houston schools in 1954. The CSAE had not forgotten. Bob Eckels alertly noticed Bleil's recommendation buried in the personnel list and blew the whistle. Mrs. Cullen vehemently denounced Bleil as "controversial" because of her connection with the NEA probe. The board rejected the proposed promotion. After the decision, the *Texas Observer* declared, "No doubt about it, the Minute Women . . . mentality continues to dominate the Houston board."[8]

There were other indications in 1961 of a resurgence in extreme anti-Communist activism in Houston and not all of them were coming from the school district. For example, William P. Strube, Jr.'s Christian Anti-Communist Crusade was attracting attention outside of the classroom. Strube seemed to be everywhere, presenting his lectures and films to evangelical Protestant churches, civic and fraternal clubs, parent-teacher associations, veteran and patriotic groups, and small gatherings in private homes.

Strube's Houston organization was a chapter of a larger worldwide movement founded in 1955 by an Australian physician named Fred C. Schwarz. The crusade's basic thesis was that Communism would "conquer" the United States by 1973 unless Americans "joined with Christ," prayed, and donated money (preferably no less than $100) to the crusade. In 1961 Strube claimed that his local group had sponsored three hundred programs attended by over sixty thousand Houstonians. Schwarz himself made several appearances in Houston, Austin, and other Texas cities in the early 1960s.[9]

Another national right-wing group, the John Birch Society, also began to assert itself in Houston in 1961. Founded in 1958 by a former Massachusetts candy manufacturer named Robert Welch, the Birch Society became a symbol of the Radical Right throughout the 1960s. Welch's group generally held the same social and economic views as most post-war right-wing conservatives. A significant difference, however, was Welch's elaborate and fantastic conspiratorial theory of history that he articulated in his bible, *The Blue Book.* The Massachusetts candymaker believed that Communism was merely a screen for a secret and diabolical conspiracy to conquer the world planned by a mysterious cadre of men called the Illuminati. Welch claimed this evil (and mythical) group supposedly originated in 1776 in Europe and was responsible for the French Revolution. Welch acquired this conspiratorial view from John Robison's *Proofs of a Conspiracy against All the Religions and Governments of Europe,* first published in 1797. To Welch, this invisible group has been responsible for every war and revolution on earth since 1789. Welch saw its hands in small events as well. To him, the Illuminati have been behind every social and economic reform in American history, especially the federal reserve banking act, the personal income tax, and the direct election of senators.[10]

The Birch Society always perceived itself as a small cadre, eschewing mass appeal in order to be more effective as a "striking force." Accordingly, the Houston chapter admitted to having only fifteen members in April of 1961. Despite its small size, the group's unusual ideology and vocal aggressiveness attracted much attention in Houston as well as in other sections of the United States such as southern California, where the society was especially strong. Although he had larger chapters elsewhere, Robert Welch always contended that Houston was the most promising "Birch City" in the United States.[11]

The chairman of Houston's tiny Birch chapter in 1961 was Garland B. Rowland, owner of a small cleaning and laundry company. Rowland allegedly sold his country club membership, boat, ranch, and other personal property and donated the funds to the Birch Society. Rowland admitted that he had body guards and carried a pistol in his automobile to protect him from "the lunatic fringe." The Houston chapter eventually opened an American Opinion bookstore that featured John Birch Society publications and those of other extreme right-wing groups. The Houston chapter also had a telephone number that could be dialed to hear a prerecorded polemic on current events. Robert Welch saw the society's mission as an educational one and the Houston chapter functioned accordingly.[12]

Although the new groups of the Radical Right dominated the extreme anti-Communist movement in Houston in the early 1960s, the Minute Women resurfaced occasionally in incidents such as the Kenneth Parker affair. Still led by Virginia Biggers, the group cosponsored a "patriotic" rally on July 4, 1961, at Houston's Hermann Park. Biggers appeared on the platform with the main speaker, Dan Smoot of H. L. Hunt's "Life Line" radio program. Addressing an unruly crowd of approximately fifty thousand people anxiously awaiting a heavily publicized fireworks show, Smoot declared that "liberalism" was just another word for "Communism." The rally was cosponsored by Houston's Junior Chamber of Commerce ("Jaycees"), which had become a local vehicle for a variety of conservative Republican activities.[13]

The major citywide manifestation of this renewal of Houston's organized anti-Communist ethic occurred in early 1962 during another attempt to establish land use zoning. The Greater Houston Planning Association, a group of realtors opposed to the zoning proposal, dusted off the old Red Scare charge that zoning was a Communist plot. Morris W. Lee, temporary chairman of the association, labeled compulsory land use restrictions "socialized real estate." The association was joined in its antizoning effort by the Birch Society's Garland Rowland, who led a protest march of one hundred persons to a Houston City Council meeting. The campaign also distributed right-wing literature, including articles by Dan Smoot, that repeated the argument that zoning was un-American and Communistic. On November 6, 1962, Houstonians once again voted down zoning, this time by a 57 percent margin. One historian has concluded that the anti-Communist tactic was effective and contributed to the election's outcome; "there is no doubt that many opponents sincerely believed zoning was communistic. . . ."[14]

During this flurry of Radical Right anti-Communist activity in Houston, writer and editor Willie Morris of the *Texas Observer* visited the city to report on political conditions. Morris concluded that the city was experiencing a new surge of reaction similar to the Red Scare of the 1950s. "The Houston Minute Women," Morris declared somewhat incorrectly, "are now as active as ever. . . ." He found the city beset by a "proliferation of ultra-right organizations." Morris' observations about Houston's Radical Right received nationwide attention in the fall of 1961 when *Harper's Magazine* published a slightly different version of his *Observer* series in an article titled "Houston's Superpatriots." In the *Harper's* article, which President Kennedy is supposed to have read and been disturbed by, Morris claimed that the 1950s "were nothing more than a gestation period" for the city's extreme anti-Communists. "The Houston patrioteers," Morris wrote, "have got going as never before."[15]

Although Morris and others perceived a continuation of the old Red Scare in Houston in the early 1960s, that perception was inaccurate. There *had* been a break in anti-Communist tensions in Houston from about 1958 until 1961. During that break, the old Red Scare of Joe McCarthy took on a different tone and was transformed. The label "Radical Right" is most often used to differentiate the 1960s activists from those groups and individuals who led the anti-Communist reaction of the second Red Scare. Certainly the two right-wing responses shared many of the same views, especially in regard to the welfare state, the civil rights movement, and foreign policy. But some important differences were also evident.

One major difference was in organizational tactics and strategies. The Radical Right groups of the 1960s were better organized and more sophisticated in style. The Christian Anti-Communist Crusade typified this difference. The crusade prided itself on its slick, "Madison Avenue" style, using the advertising techniques and technologies of modern mass culture. Unlike such Red Scare groups as the Minute Women, which urged their members to send letters to targeted politicians and other leaders, the crusade and other Radical Right organizations relied on a direct mail technique aimed at the ordinary public. The crusade used newly perfected automatic typewriters with electronically punched tapes to produce large quantities of attractive and personally addressed form letters at relatively low cost. The crusade also made extensive use of portable slide/tape programs, which were mass produced on special recording equipment in the Houston office. This slick "personalized" form letter direct mail approach was a precursor to the tactic favored later by the conservative political action committees of the "Reagan Right" in the late 1970s.[16]

Another difference with implications for the future was the strong identification of much of the Radical Right with fundamentalist evangelical Protestantism. The postwar Red Scare was certainly involved with religion, but not in the same way. Red Scare groups attempted to purge alleged subversives from their clergy, churches, and religious organizations. Little effort was made at altering religious philosophy or in espousing a particular creed. Much of the Radical Right, on the other hand, was marked by a religious zealotry whose intent was not just to purge but to convert. To groups such as Schwartz's Christian Anti-Communist Crusade or Billy James Hargis' Christian Crusade (based in Tulsa, Oklahoma) the anti-Communist campaign was nothing less than a "holy war" against religious infidels. This marriage between religious fundamentalism and extreme anti-Communism was not a new development in American history, but the bond became much stronger and more visible in the 1960s.

There were other significant differences. Red Scare activists often referred to alleged domestic Communist subversion in conspiratorial terms such as McCarthy's famous allusion to "a conspiracy so immense," but the "conspiracy" was never fully elaborated. The John Birch Society, however, espoused a finely tuned conspiratorial theory. Other Radical Right writers of the early 1960s such as Phylis Schlafly and John Stormer stressed different versions of this theory but nonetheless traded just as fully in conspiratorial ideas. Schlafly's *A Choice Not an Echo*, for example, charged that from 1936 to 1960 the Republican party had been controlled by "a small group of secret kingmakers" who conspired to keep the party out of power.[17]

Also, there was less mention of the Soviet Union as an immediate threat to the physical security of the United States or of Soviet spies in the government. Soviet difficulties with China and its Eastern European allies mitigated the old view of "monolithic" world Communism. Some of this attention—probably due to the evangelical influence—shifted to a serious concern about a rapidly liberalizing society that was breaking many of the traditional social taboos in the realm of racial, familial, and sexual relations. These same social concerns had been articulated by Red Scare groups in attacks against sex education courses in schools, but the Red Scare had occurred at a time when the traditional social patterns largely remained intact.

Although there were other differences marking off and setting apart the Red Scare of the 1950s from the Radical Right of the 1960s, no difference was as significant as that of the degree and depth of opposition each faced in its own time frame. The Red Scare ran roughshod over American society for nearly ten years. No aspect of American life was left untouched by it. Opposition was almost nonexistent at its height and what little did exist was generally ineffective.

The Radical Right in Houston as well as the rest of the nation operated in a different environment. It faced a stronger, more intensely hostile and effective opposition. The Radical Right attracted much publicity and some adherents in Houston, but its influence never compared with that of the Red Scare groups of the 1950s. Political leaders, operating in a new political climate, openly attacked the Birch Society and its associated organizations. Even Republican conservatives distanced themselves from the John Birch Society. For example, when the Houston Birchers nearly captured control of the Republican party in Harris County, they were thwarted by the personal intervention of conservative Republican senator John Tower and his supporters, who understood that Birch control would be a political disaster.[18]

The old Red Scare ploy of guilt by association was turned against the Radical Right as Democratic politicians often accused their conservative opponents of being "Birchers" or at least sympathetic to the tenets of the society. Labor unions, civil liberties groups, and religious organizations that had been silent during the Red Scare rediscovered their courage in the 1960s and vigorously joined in the attack. Such organizations as the liberal Harris County Democrats, the Houston Association for Better Schools, the Young Democrats, and the local councils of the AFL-CIO all vied with one another in issuing vituperative press releases denouncing the Birch Society, the Christian Anti-Communist Crusade, and other elements of the Radical Right.

The most important difference between the 1950s and 1960s, however, was the behavior of the press. In Houston, the *Post* and even the *Chronicle* featured periodic exposés of Radical Right groups, especially the Birch Society, because its ridiculous theories, insignificant membership, and lack of elite support made it an easy target. Houston's newspapers (the *Press* ceased publication in 1964) remained solidly conservative but, unlike during the Red Scare, the local press failed to sanction Radical Right activism. This journalistic moderation can be partially attributed to changes in the composition and political ties of Houston's power elite.

Hugh Roy Cullen died on July 4, 1957. Although he had never been a member of the inner circle of Houston's power brokers, Cullen's immense wealth and generous philanthropy provided him a public platform that he used to raise public awareness about his right-wing political views. Cullen's money also played an important role in support of extreme anti-Communist activism in Houston as well as in other sections of the nation. After his death, no one in Houston came forth to take his place, probably because the simplistic and lovable Cullen was one of a kind. The loss of Cullen's rhetoric and money, however, was not as crucial to Houston's extreme anti-Communist fringe of the 1960s as was the new political environment and the elite's place in it.

In the early 1960s, as the Birchers and their allies raved and ranted about dark conspiracies and insidious foreign influences in the White House, Houston's power elite sat back and enjoyed its own influence in Washington. Where Houston's Radical Right saw devils and traitors, such local power brokers as George and Herman Brown, who had taken the late Jesse Jones' place at the top of the establishment ladder, saw political leverage and financial opportunity. Their close friend, Lyndon B. Johnson, had become vice-president of the United States and head of the nation's new space program. Their congressman, Albert Thomas, was chairman of the House subcommittee that oversaw the budget of the National Aeronautics and Space Administration (NASA). This combination proved crucial to Houston's eventual selection as the site for NASA's new Manned Spacecraft Center in 1961. The Brown brothers' construction company became the major architectural and engineering contractor for the $125 million project. And the bountiful financial largess increased after Johnson became president. Other prominent Houston business leaders such as Gus Wortham, James A. Elkins, Oveta Culp Hobby, and Jesse Jones' nephew John T. Jones (who had become publisher of the *Chronicle*) also enjoyed their Washington connections.

Thus, the voices of the establishment, the Houston *Post* and the Houston *Chronicle*, which for partisan political reasons had encouraged Houston's Red Scare in the early 1950s, had no such political need in the 1960s. The political environment had changed and the editorial pages of the city's newspapers reflected this new reality. This was also due to changes in the editorial offices of both newspapers. After Emmet Walter became the *Chronicle*'s "consulting" editor in 1961, that newspaper's editorial page lost some of its former right-wing tone. Walter finally retired in 1966. The *Post*'s Ed Kilman also retired in 1961, but the *Post*'s editorials had fallen under the control of moderates years earlier. Kilman continued to write a Texas history column for the *Post* until his death in 1969.[19]

The altered relationship between Houston's powerful and the federal government was especially evident after John F. Kennedy's assassination in Dallas on November 22, 1963. Kennedy's murder, which was widely perceived by the general public as having been encouraged by the hate atmosphere created by the right-wing "lunatic fringe" in Texas (especially in Dallas), began a backlash that inflicted a mortal wound on the Radical Right in Houston as well as in the nation as a whole. The coup de grace, however, did not occur until Lyndon Johnson won a landslide victory over Senator Barry Goldwater in the presidential election of November 1964. Johnson received enthusiastic and visible support from Houston's power elite and its two newspapers. Although the Birch Society actually increased its membership nationally during the two-year period following Kennedy's death, whatever effectiveness Houston's Radical Right may have enjoyed in the 1960–1964 years was greatly curtailed by the Kennedy assassination and Barry Goldwater's electoral disaster.[20]

The impulse and mind-set of the extreme right, however, remained in Houston as well as in the rest of the nation. It would be transformed by the political and social upheavals of the late 1960s and resurface as a visible and cohesive entity in support of Alabama's George Wallace in his effort to win the presidency in 1968. The old constituency of the Radical Right in Texas found Wallace especially appealing. Wallace's Texas campaign committee was dominated by Birch members and Bard Logan, Wallace's state chairman, was a long-time Birch Society leader. Wallace's campaign headquarters in Houston distributed Birch Society literature.[21]

Later, in the 1970s, the extreme right matured into the "New Right," a sophisticated and effective movement that would provide much of the energy behind the election and reelection of Ronald Reagan. The change in federal election campaign laws, which encouraged the creation of political action committees (PACs), the further refining of mass marketing techniques, and the appearance and proliferation of single-issue groups concerned with perceived threats to the traditional family such as abortion, homosexuals, and "women's liberation" have all been factors significant to the growth of this new version of the extreme right. The New Right, however, has not relied on McCarthy-like Red-baiting, although one pro-family organization claims homosexuality "causes" Communism and Ronald Reagan has charged that the anti-nuclear movement is "Communist inspired." But despite its different manifestations and leaders and causes and—in 1984—significant electoral success, extreme anti-Communism has never resurfaced in American society in such a fundamental and pervasive way as it did in the postwar decade.[22]

Although the Red Scare had loosened its firm grip on Houston and Texas by the early 1960s, the phenomenon's effects were felt for two more decades. Public employees and students in Texas continued to be compelled by law to sign loyalty oaths until the late 1960s. The state anti-Communist law, passed during the legislative frenzy of the Red Scare years, continued in effect and culminated in the seizure of John Stanford's political library in San Antonio in 1964. State and local police "Red Squads," created during the extreme anti-Communist fervor of the 1950s, expanded and intensified their unconstitutional activities well into the 1970s, wire tapping and spying on Texans whose only crimes were political views that differed (in some cases only slightly) from those of the conservative establishment.

Because the Red Scare in Houston occurred primarily within the city's public schools, its long-term effects were most evident there. Indeed, the Red Scare style lasted longer in the schools than it did in the society at large. The Houston school board continued to be dominated by the ultra-right well into the 1970s. School teachers continued to suffer from political pressure and fear that what they said in the classroom or in the teachers' lounge might be interpreted by their principal or curriculum supervisor as politically dangerous. Many teachers, fearful of guilt by association, dropped out of civic, professional, and educational organizations. Membership in the NEA had been stigmatized by the Red Scare school board and, as a result, over five hundred Houston teachers were frightened into resigning from the association by 1960. For many years the Houston NEA chapter remained one of the weakest in the nation.[23]

The attacks on curriculum and the efforts to censor textbooks that began in the late 1940s in Houston with the banning of Magruder's *American Government* did not diminish with the passing of the Red Scare. Until the 1970s, the Houston school board and its administrators continued to insist on outdated approaches to the social sciences and right-wing political propaganda in history and government classes. John T. Flynn's extreme anti-Communist works were still used as supplemental readings in civics and economics classes without any counterbalance. J. Edgar

Hoover's *Masters of Deceit* was standard reading with no other viewpoint available. The United Nations and UNESCO remained off-limits as topics of discussion. Classes in economics were little more than indoctrination sessions in support of right-wing conservatism. Educational quality inevitably suffered. Louis Galambos, an associate professor of history and political science at Rice University, claimed at a Texas State Teachers Association meeting in 1963 that the Houston Independent School District was about thirty years behind then-current scholarship in economics. Galambos warned that "as long as the extremist mentality prevails . . . Houston will fall further and further behind . . . in social science."[24]

Houston's Red Scare censorship movement had effects well beyond the city limits. The Houston school board's ban against the Magruder text spurred an effort to banish the book throughout Texas. The Texas chapter of the Daughters of the American Revolution (DAR), whose leadership included Minute Women such as Virginia Biggers, created a Subversive Texts Committee that carried the censorship battle to Corpus Christi, Abilene, and Dallas and to small towns such as Brenham, Beeville, and Richmond. The DAR circulated literature statewide that instructed local citizens on how to examine a textbook for subversive material. Other groups quickly formed, including one led by J. Evetts Haley, that focused on the Texas Education Agency and the State Board of Education. These Red Scare–inspired groups and individuals lobbied with much success to control the ideological content of books used in Texas schools.[25]

The legacy of the censorship efforts of the Ewing Werleins, Dallas Dyers, and Bertie Maughmers remains in Texas in the 1980s, sustained and promoted by Mel and Norma Gabler of Longview. The Gablers, who have been called "the most effective textbook censors in the country," have turned censorship into a nationwide industry. They represent a continuation of the Red Scare style combined with evangelical Protestant fundamentalism. The Longview couple has lobbied incessantly for years against textbooks that encourage open-ended classroom discussion of a diverse range of topics, including death, racism, national health insurance, sex, Darwinian theories of evolution, aging, stress, childhood rebellion, welfare, and woman's rights. Their efforts succeeded in a Texas Board of Education rule in 1974 (rescinded in 1984) that restricted the textbook teaching of scientific theories of evolution in public schools. The Gablers are firm believers in a literal interpretation of the biblical explanation for biological creation. Because Texas is the second largest purchaser of textbooks in the nation, publishers have rewritten their textbooks to comply with Texas regulations influenced by the Gablers, thus affecting public schools throughout the United States. One critic has charged that the Gablers have had "by far the greatest negative impact on science education in the entire country during the past nine years."[26]

Another legacy of the Red Scare in Houston was the continuation of highly contentious, controversial, and sensational school board election campaigns. Liberals and conservatives continued their bitter struggle for domination of the public schools. As the years passed, however, racial integration overwhelmed all other issues as the primary point of contention. Although race replaced progressive education and subversion as a framework for school politics, the result was the same: a highly unstable school board and administration marked by severe disputation. In 1970 a "liberal" faction won control of the board and hired Dr. George Garver, an educator from Michigan, as the new superintendent. Eighteen months later the CSAE regained control and, in an action similar to the Ebey affair, fired Garver. The Garver dismissal differed from Ebey's, however, in that no "smoke screen" excuse such as Communism or disloyalty was given. The CSAE-controlled board fired Garver because he had been appointed by the liberals; no other justification was necessary. The liberals returned to power, however, and rehired Garver in 1972. This contentious and disruptive pattern continued until the late 1970s.[27]

Complicated social and demographic forces together with a change in the method of electing school board members seem to have ended the destructive pattern of school board politics. During the 1970s "white flight" to Houston's suburban school districts eventually resulted in the HISD's becoming a black majority system. By 1980 the district school population was 45 percent black, 27.5 percent white, and 27.5 percent Hispanic. White flight and the resulting demographic transformation simply shifted many of CSAE's supporters to other school districts. The most significant development, however, came in 1973 when the legislature changed the method of electing school board members from the single district system to an at-large system. This structural alteration made coalition school "slates" or parties more difficult and ensured appropriate ethnic and racial representation on the board. School board campaigns and school board meetings are now peaceable affairs that attract little attention compared to the school boards of the 1950s. Severe educational problems partially due to the legacy of disruption stemming from the battle over racial integration and ideological control still remain in the system, but there have been encouraging signs recently that some progress is being made in the effort to improve the quality of education in the HISD.[28]

The Red Scare in Houston was the product of a complex mechanism of legitimation that gave a small fringe group of extremists credibility. Central to the local causes of Houston's Red Scare was the fact that the city was in a period of transition as a result of significant economic, demographic, and cultural changes stemming from World War II. Accompanying and inherent in any period of transition are social strain, community confusion, and fear. Sociologist Talcott Parsons argues that neither individuals nor societies can undergo major changes without producing a degree of "irrational behavior." Such transitions tend to bring forth value distortions and an alteration of the normal beliefs about the facts of situations. Such promptings to irrational action also tend to be strongly emotional. In Houston, stimulated by the strains of rapid change swirling about them and encouraged by the local press, normally inactive upper-middle-class professionals, small businessmen, and upper-middle-class housewives joined with the always present extremist fringe to attack a variety of perceived evils. This alliance focused on what it felt to be the sources of strain and difficulty: "outsiders," progressive education, cosmopolitanism, "big government," the United Nations, advocates of racial integration, progressive or liberal religious theologies, labor unions, and "radical-liberals" of any sort. In other words, a psychological formula operated to prescribe a set of beliefs that certain specific, symbolic agencies are responsible for the present distress and they have "arbitrarily" upset a satisfactory state of affairs. If "they" could be eliminated the trouble would disappear and society would return to a condition modeled after an idealized and largely mythical past.[29]

Also crucial to the legitimation of Houston's Red Scare were the actions and inactions of the city's power elite. This entrepreneurial elite controlled the city's organs of communication and information, its banks, law firms, construction, real estate, city government, and educational institutions. This group also responded to changes, both of a national and local nature. These community leaders individually, never as a group, spoke out against their own set of perceived evils, which were largely political in nature. Elite rhetoric against big government and the Democratic party coupled with financial and rhetorical support of Senator McCarthy were significant factors in creating and sustaining the Red Scare at the local as well as at the national level.

A brief flurry of "radical" activism in Houston in the late 1940s also contributed to the legitimation of Red Scare activism. An internal struggle between anti-Communists and Communists within the National Maritime Union, which was active in Galveston and Houston, became a public squabble duly reported by the local press. A handful of local Communists openly operated in the city in this period and garnered sensational headlines by distributing "peace petitions," copies of the *Daily Worker*, and Communist party propaganda leaflets. Constantly harassed by the local police, these party members were represented by a group of local lawyers. The activities of these lawyers, who were also active in Henry Wallace's Progressive party campaign in 1948, were highly publicized and contributed to community fears.

A concentration on local factors should not, of course, ignore the obvious influence of national and international events on Houston's Red Scare. The Cold War and its associated "shocks," combined with the rhetoric of national leaders such as McCarthy, provided the overall framework for the local Red Scare. Theodore White, writing about Texas at the time, noted that the dominant reason for the state's Red Scare climate was the Cold War. White believed that "in Texas, nerves have cracked generally worse than elsewhere in the U.S. because to the emotions of [the Cold War] have been added all the other strains which that state is experiencing. For it is an enormous strain on human minds . . . to change as swiftly as Texas has changed."[30]

The strains produced by the Cold War were imposed on a society undergoing significant internal changes that had themselves been sources of strain. The effect was to superimpose one kind of strain on another. Thus, the Cold War and the national phenomenon of McCarthyism played key roles in shaping the direction of local protest. It was Senator McCarthy who put together a single package to attract disparate elements in the population by personifying their various fears in the name of anti-Communism. Seymour Martin Lipset labels this phenomenon "simplism . . . the unambiguous ascription of single causes and remedies for multifactored phenomenon."[31]

In Houston, the Red Scare was simplism, an easily understandable explanation for the disconcerting changes caused by World War II and the transformation from city to metropolis. The Red Scare served as an effective, simplistic device to symbolize a plurality of complex issues for conservative pressure groups. The Ebey affair, for example, indicated that anti-Communism was a symbolic issue representing a multiplicity of preservationist impulses. George Ebey was not personally as important as what he symbolized. He provided a single target for those in the community who wanted to attack many different enemies such as racial integration, New Deal liberalism, and progressive education.

Memories of the Red Scare in Texas and in Houston have faded, and the fact that the state and its largest city experienced their own version of the phenomenon has become obscure and little known. This is also true of other Texas cities, including San Antonio and Dallas, which are beyond the scope of this book but which suffered their own versions of the Red Scare.[32]

This lack of knowledge and awareness of Texas' recent past is to be regretted. The Red Scare mentality has never gone away, especially in Texas. The fear of change, disorder, and the unknown is a primal instinct, a natural and ineradicable component of the human condition. At its most basic level, the extreme anti-Communist reaction as well as other reactions rooted in fear are products of this element, which simmers to some degree in us all. When natural fear is matched with disordered social, economic, and political environments and encouraged by influential individuals and institutions, outbreaks of intolerance and oppression seem to be the inevitable result. Houston's Red Scare was a product of such a process and American history is pockmarked with examples of similar reactions. The potential for yet another Red Scare type of political and cultural suppression is great, both at the national and state levels.

As this is being written, relations between the United States and the Soviet Union have plunged to their lowest depths since the worst years of the Cold War. The executive branch of the United States government is controlled by men who have resurrected the provocative and fear-inducing rhetoric that typified the behavior of conservative elites in the late 1940s and early 1950s. The press, of course, is less open to manipulation and generally more sophisticated in its editorial approach due to the experience of Vietnam and Watergate. But there are indications that the press' ability to serve as a critic and watchdog may be severely hampered in the coming years. The Reagan administration has expended much energy in an attempt to stifle information about its activities. This includes attempts to censor government employees for life, to destroy the Freedom of Information Act, and the White House's successful attempt to control news coverage of the military invasion of Grenada. Not only is the press having to operate in an increasingly hostile governmental environment, but the nature of the news industry itself is radically changing—and not necessarily in favor of its watchdog role. Rapid technological developments in computers and satellites and in all components of the communications world promise a new day in the realm of information. But these developments also portend greater centralization and the destruction of the competitive influence in the news industry. The new technology not only promises quicker access to more information, it threatens to provide temptingly easy means to control the quality of that information from some central location. More and more independent newspapers are shutting down their presses permanently with the passage of each month. Others are being grabbed by corporate conglomerates and homogenized as a part of larger chains of newspapers. With few exceptions, communities that have undergone such journalistic alterations have gained more color photographs of movie stars and human interest stories but lost much hard news coverage and analysis. The increasing tension between the superpowers, the right-wing scare rhetoric of a Reagan administration bolstered by a massive electoral victory, and the troubling developments in the communications industry do not bring comfort to those who fear the return of a Red Scare type of national psychosis.

A new version of the Red Scare could be triggered by several developments, one of which could be a further deterioration of Soviet-American relations. A glimpse of this possibility was seen in the aftermath of the Korean Airlines tragedy in September 1983. Many Texans and other Americans engaged in a brief but intense anti-Russian reaction. The reaction was generally more ludicrous than dangerous as travel agencies in Austin and Houston announced boycotts of rarely used Russian tour packages and coin-operated computer games were reprogrammed to allow children the thrill of killing Russians from the safe haven of suburban shopping malls. As harmless as this may appear, it is symptomatic of the ever-present strain in American society that can fuel political pogroms.

There are other potential sources for a new Red Scare, but for Houstonians and other urban Texans political and military developments to the south of the Rio Grande could prove to be the most likely source of all. As revolutionary movements—created by abysmal living conditions and governmental oppression—continue to develop in Central America and possibly Mexico, American military intervention is highly probable. Colonel Robert Blizzard, commander of the 147th Tactical Fighter Group at Ellington Air Force Base near Houston, declared in October of 1983 that the most advanced military aircraft were much needed in Texas. He and Colonel Gray Walston of the Texas Air National Guard called on the air force to station F16s throughout the state. "The threat to the South is becoming more and more serious," Blizzard argued. "We're talking about our backyard . . . if push comes to shove, we'd like to have the best aircraft available to carry out our mission." The mission, presumably, would be the bombing of guerrillas in Mexico. In such a scenario those who are the objects of American military actions are likely to retaliate in the only manner at their disposal: urban terrorism. The obvious targets for such terrorism would be those most geographically accessible: the cities and towns of California, Arizona, New Mexico, and Texas.[33]

This would surely result in the militarization of Texas' international border. It would also require antiterrorist civilian law enforcement measures. But based on our historical experience, it could also create a domestic antisubversion reaction that would make the Red Scare of the 1950s seem like a Sunday school picnic by comparison. If some Texans and other Americans behaved as they did when the United States was at the peak of its military and economic power, with no real domestic threat from any credible "subversive" source, how will they behave when conditions are radically different? How will we respond to a real threat? Will we seek the answer at the source and resolve the crisis by altering our role in the affairs of our neighbors to the south? Or, in our effort to protect ourselves, will we carry the Red Scare to its logical conclusion, one only hinted at during the 1950s—the creation of a police state? The threat to civil liberties and basic American freedom would be great. As Terrell Arnold, a deputy director of the State Department, recently warned, "Our response to terrorists should not destroy the fabric of our own society." This need not happen, but if another such extreme reaction is to be avoided (as a result of whatever source), Americans must be aware of the possibility. They must not allow anyone to trample freedom of thought, association, and expression. Most of all, they must not be silent. They must show more courage than they did during the 1950s—during the Red Scare.[34]

ESSAY ON SOURCES

Anyone seriously interested in conducting original research on the historical development of the city of Houston must spend many hours at the Houston Public Library's Houston Metropolitan Research Center (HMRC), located in the beautiful Julia Ideson Building in the heart of downtown. A product of the fertile mind of Dr. Harold M. Hyman of Rice University, HMRC has amassed hundreds of valuable collections documenting nearly every conceivable aspect of Bayou City history. Among those are two collections that have been indispensable to my work on the Red Scare in Houston: the Ralph S. O'Leary Papers and George W. Ebey Papers. The extent of their value may be seen throughout the endnotes of this work. O'Leary's papers consist of the materials he assembled for his series on the Minute Women. The Ebey Papers could also be called the "Ebey affair collection" because they are made up almost entirely of documents related to that event. The Ebey Papers also contain the General Research Company's two-volume report on its investigation of the school administrator.

The newspaper clipping "morgue" of the now defunct Houston *Press* is also located at HMRC. This extensive collection largely consists of valuable photographs and clipping files, but a few manuscripts are scattered throughout. Among these is the typescript of a never published exposé partially written by the Pulitzer Prize–winning journalist Vance Trimble. This exposé and other material in the *Press* collection provided important information relating to alleged radical activities in the Houston-Galveston area in the 1940s and 1950s. The material is full of errors and must be used with extreme caution. The exposé was never published on the advice of *Press* attorney Leon Jaworski, who believed it libeled Arthur J. Mandell and Herman Wright (interview with Leon Jaworski, July 18, 1977, in Houston). I have not used information from the *Press* files (or from the O'Leary and Ebey papers) without corroborating evidence.

Other HMRC collections of use in varying degrees to this work are the papers of W. A. Combs, W. Alvis Parish, Kate Bell, Ray K. Daily, William E. Moreland, and Ed Kilman, the minutes of the Houston Public Library Board, and the minutes of the Houston Independent School District's Board of Education. HMRC has the school board minutes for the late 1950s and early 1960s only. A complete set is available for reading at the HISD administration building.

Just as a visit to HMRC is essential for research in Houston history, a trip to the Eugene C. Barker Texas History Center (BTHC) of the University of Texas at Austin is required for work in Texas history. BTHC's manuscript and archival collections fill over five miles of shelf space. Among those BTHC collections used for this book, the most important are the papers of Jesse Holman Jones. This large collection of correspondence, notes, photographs, and scrapbooks provided invaluable information about Jones and his relationship to the *Chronicle* and its editor, M. E. Walter. The papers also contain incoming correspondence that proved useful for determining the views and perceptions of elites and Red Scare activists. Another extensive portion of Jones' papers is located at the Library of Congress (LC). Although mainly the records of Jones' federal service, the LC collection also includes correspondence related to his postwar political activities.

The BTHC also houses the Labor Movement in Texas Collection, which provided information on the National Maritime Union and labor strikes in the Houston-Galveston area in the late 1930s. Other pertinent collections at BTHC include the Dudley K. Woodward Papers, the Ima Hogg Papers, the Maury Maverick, Sr., and Maury Maverick, Jr., Papers, and a collection of material on the NAACP and the Progressive party in Texas donated by Michael Gillette. BTHC is the repository for the University of Texas at Austin's official archives and I have made much use of the records of the Office of the President (OPR) from that source.

There are collections at other repositories that are useful for research on the postwar anti-Communist reaction in Texas. These include the Senate files of Price Daniel and the papers of Martin Dies at the Sam Houston Research Center (SHRC) in Liberty, Texas; the gubernatorial papers of Allan Shivers at the Texas State Archives in Austin; the Texas AFL-CIO Records in the Labor Archives at the University of Texas at Arlington; the Oveta Culp Hobby Papers and the President's Central and General Files at the Dwight D. Eisenhower Library in Abilene, Kansas; and the Senate Files of Lyndon B. Johnson in the presidential library in Austin. The constituent mail in the Eisenhower and Johnson libraries is a rich source for local and state history. I discovered detailed letters from Houston Minute Women in both collections. The papers of Major Jubal R. Parten are as valuable as they are extensive for a number of important topics, including the one at hand. The Parten papers, although committed for future archival preservation, remain at this date in Major Parten's office in Houston.

Even a cursory glance at the endnotes will indicate my dependence on oral history interviews. Over a period of thirteen years I have personally interviewed nearly one hundred individuals. Many of these persons simply restated information I had already acquired from stronger sources. Others, such as some public school teachers and former Red Scare activists, refused to be quoted or named. Accordingly, I have listed at the end of this essay only those persons whose interviews proved crucial in reconstructing the events of the period. In addition, I benefited from the massive oral history collection housed at HMRC and I have listed those interviews as well. I am aware of the many shortcomings of the oral source as evidence and, with some small exceptions, I have only used information that could be corroborated by other sources.

Printed sources are crucial for writing a history of this period. The most important sources, of course, are newspapers. Not only are they necessary for placing events in time, they reflect the views of elites and political activists. I have viewed nearly every issue of the Houston *Chronicle,* Houston *Post,* and the Houston *Press* for the years 1947 through 1955, paying particular attention to editorial pages. Other newspaper sources include the *Dallas Morning News, The Daily Texan* (University of Texas at Austin student newspaper), and the *New York Times.* Stories in other Texas newspapers were discovered in clipping files, especially those in the Texas AFL-CIO Records at the University of Texas at Arlington. The *Texas Observer* (Austin), although technically not a newspaper, proved to be the single most important journalistic source for reporting Red Scare activities in Texas from 1954 until the mid 1960s. For information about many specific incidents, especially in Houston during the 1958 to 1964 years, the *Observer* is not just a good source, it is the only source.

Other valuable printed sources for this period include the National Education Association's *Report of an Investigation, Houston, Texas: A Study of Factors Related to Educational Unrest in a Large School System* (Washington, D.C., 1954). The NEA report, although superficial in analysis, is required reading for information about the condition of Houston's public schools after the Ebey affair. For the rhetoric and actions of state legislators during the Red Scare, the official journals of the Texas House of Representatives and the Texas Senate (1949 to 1953) provide a wealth of material.

Secondary sources for McCarthyism and the second Red Scare are so numerous as to have created a cohesive body of literature. Space limitations preclude a full bibliography of the phenomenon, but the interested student or reader can find useful lists in Thomas C. Reeves' *The Life and Times of Joe McCarthy* (New York, 1982) and David Caute's *The Great Fear: The Anti-Communist Purge under Truman and Eisenhower* (New York, 1978). Both are superb books and I have relied heavily on them. I have also been influenced by Michael Paul Rogin, *The Intellectuals and McCarthy: The Radical Specter* (Cambridge, Mass., 1967); Robert Griffith, *The Politics of Fear: Joseph R. McCarthy and the Senate* (Lexington, Ky., 1970); Athan Theoharis,

Seeds of Repression: Harry S. Truman and the Origins of McCarthyism (Chicago, 1971); Robert Griffith and Athan Theoharis (eds.), *The Specter: Original Essays on the Cold War and the Origins of McCarthyism* (New York, 1974); Seymour Martin Lipset and Earl Raab, *The Politics of Unreason: Right-Wing Extremism in America, 1790–1970* (New York, 1970); David Brion Davis (ed.), *The Fear of Conspiracy: Images of Un-American Subversion from the Revolution to the Present* (Ithaca, N.Y., 1971); and Richard Hofstadter, *The Paranoid Style in American Politics* (New York, 1965).

Important sources for the political left and labor unions include Bert Cochran, *Labor and Communism* (Princeton, N.J., 1977); David A. Shannon, *The Decline of American Communism* (New York, 1959); Joseph R. Starobin, *American Communism in Crisis, 1943–1957* (Cambridge, Mass., 1972); and Harvey Klehr, *The Heyday of American Communism: The Depression Decade* (New York, 1984). For the existence and influence of power elites in local communities, I drew upon David C. Hammack, "Problems in the Historical Study of Power in the Cities and Towns of the United States, 1800–1960," *American Historical Review* 83 (April 1978): 323–349; Edward Pessen, "Who Rules America? Power and Politics in the Democratic Era, 1825–1975," *Prologue* 9 (Spring 1977): 5–26; and Floyd Hunter, *Community Power Structure: The Study of Decision Makers* (Chapel Hill, N.C., 1953). For the role of the press, I used Kai T. Erickson, *Wayward Puritans: A Study in the Sociology of Deviance* (New York, 1966); James Aronson, *The Press and the Cold War* (Indianapolis, 1970); and Edwin R. Bayley, *Joe McCarthy and the Press* (Madison, Wis., 1981). The work of Ralph Lord Roy sheds much light on the Red Scare and Protestantism, especially *Apostles of Discord* (Boston, 1953) and *Communism and the Churches* (New York, 1960). For the Red Scare and the Methodist church in Texas, Norman W. Spellman, *Growing a Soul: The Story of A. Frank Smith* (Dallas, 1979) and W. Kenneth Pope, *A Pope at Roam: The Confessions of a Bishop* (Nashville, 1976) are important sources.

For Houston and Texas, a number of secondary sources provide useful information. David G. McComb's *Houston: A History* (Austin, 1982) is the starting point for any aspect of the city's historical development. Also valuable is the Work Projects Administration's (WPA) *Houston: A History and Guide* (Houston, 1942) and the various publications of George Fuermann, especially *Reluctant Empire* (New York, 1957). The best reference for Texas politics in the 1930 to 1960 era is George N. Green's *The Establishment in Texas Politics: The Primitive Years, 1938–1957* (Westport, Conn., 1979). Biographies of political and business elites abound, but few are well written, much less good history. Nevertheless, if critically used, Bascom Timmons, *Jesse H. Jones* (New York, 1956); Edgar Ray, *The Grand Huckster: Houston's Judge Roy Hofheinz* (Memphis, 1980); and Ed Kilman and Theon Wright, *Hugh Roy Cullen: A Story of American Opportunity* (New York, 1954) provide information that cannot be found elsewhere. Robert A. Caro's *The Years of Lyndon Johnson: The Path to Power* (New York, 1982), controversial and flawed, is still the best source for the Brown brothers and their political influence. Oveta Culp Hobby, James A. Elkins, and Oscar Holcombe await biographical treatment. The best biography of a Texas Red Scare business leader is Harry Hurt's book on H. L. Hunt, *Texas Rich: The Hunt Dynasty from the Early Oil Days through the Silver Crash* (New York, 1981). Similar work is needed for Jones, Elkins, the Hobbys, and the Browns. Important contemporary articles on the Texas elite and the Red Scare include Charles J. V. Murphy, "Texas Business and McCarthy," *Fortune* 49 (May 1954): 100–101, 208, 211–212, 214, 216, and Theodore S. White, "Texas: Land of Wealth and Fear," *Reporter*, May 25, 1954, 10–17, and June 8, 1954, 30–37.

Four potentially crucial sources proved to be either nonexistent or inaccessible. Oveta Culp Hobby failed to reply to my several letters and telephone calls seeking an interview. The general correspondence files of the Houston Independent School District have extensive gaps, particularly for the period of the Ebey affair. Allegedly, the correspondence for 1953 was destroyed on orders of a school board member. The records of the Houston Police Department are, for all practical purposes, unavailable. An inside source claims that an extensive portion of the police department's records was destroyed in a warehouse fire a few years ago. A fourth potential source, Federal Bureau of Investigation files for Houston during the 1930 to 1950 period, is also alleged to have been destroyed. Repeated attempts to penetrate the Department of Justice and the FBI through use of the Freedom of Information Act proved futile.

Interviews by the Author

Mrs. W. N. (Adria) Allen, January 20, 1972
Mrs. Albert (Eleanor) Ball, July 6, 1971
William Ballew, January 15, 1973
John Barnhart, March 18, 1983
Kate Bell, February 2, 1972
Mrs. Ross (Virginia) Biggers, January 16, February 14, 1972
Jack Binion, March 5, 1972
Margaret Bleil, July 11, 1971
Morris Bogdanow, October 29, 1976
George Carmack, November 12, 1982
Robert A. Childers, July 7, 1971
Ray K. Daily, December 10, 1974
Ida Darden, January 16, 1972
Chris Dixie, March 6, 1983
Mrs. Andre (Mary) Drouin, January 21, 30, 1972
Ronnie Dugger, January 30, 1984
George W. Ebey, July 21–22, 1971
Creekmore Fath, January 5, 1983
John Henry Faulk, July 9–10, 1982
Grady Hardin, January 7, 1983
James Hippard, March 16, 1972
Leon Jaworski, July 18, 1977
Marguerite Johnston, July 8, 1971, January 17, 1984
Louis J. Kestenberg, September 26, 1970, February 15, 1973,
October 10, 1974
Mary Lasswell, December 13, 1980
Maury Maverick, Jr., March 1, 1983
James ("Blackie") Merrill, September 11, 1979
Leopold Meyer, April 19, 1978
William E. Moreland, July 20, 1974
Mrs. Ralph S. O'Leary, October 25, 1970
Jubal R. Parten, July 8, 15, 1983
W. Kenneth Pope, January 7, 1983
Mrs. Loren Stark, January 20, 1972
Emma Tenayuca, September 24, 1983
A. J. Tucker, December 18, 1970
Herman Wright, November 8, 1976

Interviews by Others

(Unless otherwise noted, the following are in the Oral History
Collection, HMRC)
George A. Butler, November 18, 1982
W. A. Combs, August 11, 1977
John Crossland, August 17, 1971, Oral History Collection,
Labor Archives, University of Texas at Arlington
Ben Kaplan, June 18, 1976
Moses Leroy, October 30, 1974
Glenn McCarthy, March 31, 1976
Mrs. Douglas (Dallas Dyer) McGregor, August 1, 1974
Gilbert Mers, September 27, 1977
Leopold Meyer, April 5, 1978
Ben Ramey, July 28, 1973, personal collection of Michael Gillette,
Austin, Texas
Bernard M. Sakowitz, April 21, 1977
Herman Wright, March 29, 1977

NOTES

PROLOGUE

1. Davis, *The Fear of Conspiracy*, xv.

2. George Ebey's perceptions, feelings, and reactions as indicated in this prologue are based on interviews between the author and Ebey. Dates of this and all other oral history interviews are listed in the essay on sources. Additional background information on Ebey is in the Ebey Papers, HMRC.

3. This account of the protest against Ebey on August 18, 1952, is based on the author's interviews with Ebey, William Moreland, and Mary Drouin; summaries in the Houston *Post*, July 19, October 20, 1953; and Ebey, "Address to City Club," manuscript of a speech delivered in Portland, Oregon, August 28, 1953, Ebey Papers, HMRC.

4. All physical descriptions are based on photographs in the Ebey Papers and the O'Leary Papers, HMRC. For Barnett's and Drouin's charges, see Norma Louise Barnett to William E. Moreland, August 19, 1952, and Andre and Mary Drouin to William E. Moreland, August 7, 1952, Ebey Papers, HMRC. For more on H. L. Kilpatrick's problems, see David Hulburd, *It Happened in Pasadena* (New York, 1951), 53.

5. Interview with George Ebey; Ebey to Leonor Ebey, August 20, 1952, Ebey Papers, HMRC; quote in last paragraph from Thomas C. Reeves, *Freedom and the Foundation: The Fund for the Republic in the Era of McCarthyism* (New York, 1969), 25.

6. Caute, *The Great Fear*. For more on Joseph R. McCarthy, see Reeves, *The Life and Times of Joe McCarthy*, and David Oshinsky, *A Conspiracy So Immense* (New York, 1983).

7. For the international and national events related to the Red Scare atmosphere, see the essay on sources.

ONE: A NERVOUS NEW CIVILIZATION

1. Thomas Thompson, *Blood and Money* (New York, 1976), 31; Larry McMurtry, "The Southwest as the Cradle of the Novelist," in Robert W. Walts (ed.), *The American Southwest: Cradle of Literary Art* (San Marcos, Tex., 1981), 38.

2. McComb, *Houston: A History*, 9–15; Don E. Carleton and Thomas H. Kreneck, *Houston: Back Where We Started* (Houston, 1979), 1–3; WPA, *Houston*, 52–87.

3. For the Jacksonian era and "liberated capitalism," see Richard Hofstadter, "Andrew Jackson and the Rise of Liberal Capitalism," in *The American Political Tradition* (New York, 1973), 56–85; Carleton and Kreneck, *Houston*, 1.

4. McComb, *Houston*, 16–37.

5. Ibid., 65; Harold L. Platt, "Houston at the Crossroads: The Emergence of the Urban Center of the Southwest," *Journal of the West* (Spring 1971): 51–61.

6. Interview with Bernard M. Sakowitz; Walter Prescott Webb (ed.), *The Handbook of Texas* (Austin, 1952), vol. 1, 665; George Fuermann, *Houston: The Feast Years* (Houston, 1962), 45; McComb, *Houston*, 76–81.

7. Marilyn McAdams Sibley, *The Port of Houston: A History* (Austin, 1968); U.S. Bureau of the Census, *Twelfth Census of the United States, 1900* and *Fourteenth Census of the United States, 1920* (Harris County, Tex.), Houston schedules.

8. McComb, *Houston*, 93, 99, 101; Charles N. Glaab and A. Theodore Brown, *A History of Urban America* (New York, 1967), 97; Harold L. Platt, "City Building and Progressive Reform: The Modernization of an Urban Polity, Houston, 1892–1905," in Michael Ebner and Eugene Tobin (eds.), *The Age of Urban Reform* (New York, 1977), 28–42.

9. McComb, *Houston*, 97; Howard Barnstone, *The Architecture of John F. Staub: Houston and the South* (Austin, 1979), 5–12.

10. Bruce J. Weber, "Will Hogg and the Business of Reform" (Ph.D. dissertation, University of Houston, 1979); John O. King, *Joseph Stephen Cullinan* (Nashville, 1970), 82–111; Timmons, *Jesse H. Jones.*

11. Timmons, *Jesse H. Jones*, 118; McComb, *Houston*, 97.

12. Timmons, *Jesse H. Jones*, 136–145; McComb, *Houston*, 84; Arthur M. Schlesinger, *The Age of Roosevelt: The Coming of the New Deal* (Boston, 1959), 426; newspaper clippings file in the Melvina Passmore McDonald Collection, HMRC.

13. William P. Hobby, "How a City Began," in Michael Cadoret and Sibylle de L'Epine (eds.), *Houston* (Manero, 1949), 25; William Goyen, "While You Were Away (Houston Seen and Unseen, 1923–1978)," *Houston Review* 1 (Fall 1979): 84–85.

14. Charles C. Alexander, *Crusade for Conformity: The Ku Klux Klan in Texas, 1920–1930* (Houston, 1962), 3, 9. For a discussion on the post–World War I Red Scare, see Stanley Coben, "Study in Nativism: The American Red Scare of 1919–1920," *Political Science Quarterly* 89 (March 1964): 52–75.

15. Kenneth T. Jackson, *The Ku Klux Klan in the City, 1915–1930* (New York, 1967), 37; Lipset and Raab, *The Politics of Unreason*, 123; see also Charles C. Alexander, *The Ku Klux Klan in the Southwest* (Lexington, Ky., 1966), 29.

16. Alexander, *Crusade for Conformity*, 5, 13.

17. Alexander, *The Ku Klux Klan in the Southwest*, 76, 92.

18. For Holcombe and the Klan, see Alexander, *Crusade for Conformity*, 10–13. For the hostility of elites, see McComb, *Houston*, 113 and Timmons, *Jesse H. Jones*, 121. Bruce Weber's Ph.D. dissertation on Will C. Hogg details Hogg's opposition to the Klan.

19. Alexander, *The Ku Klux Klan in the Southwest*, 233–256.

20. McComb, *Houston*, 116; Hobby, "How a City Began," 26; WPA, *Houston*, 119; U.S. Bureau of the Census, *Fourteenth, Fifteenth, and Sixteenth*

Censuses of the United States, 1920, 1930, and 1940 (Harris County, Tex.), Houston schedules; Timmons, *Jesse H. Jones*, 153–161.

21. WPA, *Houston*, 121, 4.

22. U.S. Bureau of the Census, *Sixteenth Census of the United States, 1940* (Harris County, Tex.), Houston schedules; Fuermann, *The Reluctant Empire*, 20. For a particularly perceptive discussion of Houston's power elite, see Harry Hurt III, "The Most Powerful Texans," *Texas Monthly* 4 (April 1976): 73–123; Alexander Callow (ed.), *American Urban History* (New York, 1973), 483; WPA, *Houston*, 164.

23. Richard Polenberg, *War and Society: The United States; 1941–1945* (Philadelphia, 1972), 4; Kenneth E. Gray, *A Report on the Politics of Houston* (Cambridge, Mass., 1960), vol. 1, 20. See also George B. Tindall, *The Emergence of the New South, 1913–1945* (Louisiana, 1967), and Edward F. Haas, "The Southern Metropolis, 1940–1976," in Blaine Brownell and David R. Goldfield (eds.), *The City in Southern History: The Growth of Urban Civilization in the South* (Port Washington, N.Y., 1977), 159–191. For discussions of the war's impact on the social, political, and economic life of the South, see Robert J. Havinghurst and H. Gerthon Morgan, *The Social History of a War-Boom Community* (New York, 1951).

24. Fuermann, *Houston*, 17; George Fuermann, *The Face of Houston* (Houston, 1963), 21.

25. John A. Lewis, *The Emergence and Growth of the Gulf Coast and the Southwest Texas State Planning Regions* (Houston, 1971), 35; *Houston* 20 (October 1949): 32; Houston *Post*, December 31, 1949.

26. Lewis, *Emergence and Growth*, 35; *Houston* 20 (October 1949): 32; Houston *Post*, March 29, December 31, 1949; "Booming Houston," *Life*, October 21, 1946, 108–117. For a more detailed discussion of Houston's economic growth during this era, see Leah Brooke Tucker, "The Houston Business Community, 1945–1965" (Ph.D. dissertation, University of Texas at Austin, 1979), especially 15–73; John Gunther quote in *Inside U.S.A.* (New York, 1947), 828.

27. Houston *Post*, March 30, April 1–3, 1948; "Houston Leads Nation in Per Capita Building," *Houston* 20 (April 1949): 8.

28. Houston *Post*, March 30, April 1–3, 1948; Houston *Chronicle*, March 28, 1948; Fuermann, *Houston*, 28.

29. Marguerite Johnston, "From New Eyes," in Cadoret and de L'Epine (eds.), *Houston*, 131.

30. Fuermann, *The Reluctant Empire*, 125; White, "Texas," 10.

31. Houston Chamber of Commerce, *Statistical Abstract* (1977), 7.

32. For an insightful discussion of Texans' perception of outsiders, see Fuermann, *The Reluctant Empire*, 223–238; Houston *Post*, March 28, 1948.

33. "Harvest in Houston," *Time*, March 30, 1953, 68.

34. McComb, *Houston*, 184; Fuermann, *Houston*, 25; John De Menil, "A Provincial Town," in Cadoret and de L'Epine (eds.), *Houston*, 127.

35. McComb, *Houston*, 135–136; Edna Ferber, *Giant* (New York, 1952);

Thompson, *Blood and Money*, 33–34; Houston *Post*, March 17–18, 1949; "Big Time in Houston: Opening of the Shamrock Hotel," *Fortune* 39 (May 1949): 80–82; "Shamrock Opens with a Bang," *Newsweek*, March 28, 1949, 64–66; "$21 Million Hotel Opens: Shamrock," *Life*, March 28, 1949, 27–31.

36. McComb, *Houston*, 135–136; New York *Times*, February 14, 1954; Glenn McCarthy, "Why the Shamrock Hotel Was Built," *Houston* 20 (March 1949): 8; Johnston, "From New Eyes," 133; Wallace Davis, *Corduroy Road: The Story of Glenn McCarthy* (Houston, 1951), 235–259.

37. George Fuermann, *Houston: Land of the Big Rich* (Garden City, N.Y., 1951), 70, 77; Thompson, *Blood and Money*, 33; interview with George Carmack.

38. "Texas: King of the Wildcatters," *Time*, February 13, 1950, 18; Fuermann, *Land of the Big Rich*, 70–76.

39. Eric Hoffer, *The Ordeal of Change* (New York, 1963), 131.

40. George Fuermann, *The Face of Houston* (Houston, 1963), 5; White, "Texas," 10; Johnston, "From New Eyes," 131; Thompson, *Blood and Money*, 31–32.

41. Johnston, "From New Eyes," 135; Houston *Post*, January 1, 1950.

42. Chester E. Eisinger (ed.), *The 1940's: Profile of a Nation in Crisis* (New York, 1969), xv–xxiv.

43. Daniel Bell (ed.), *The Radical Right* (New York, 1963); Hofstadter, *The Paranoid Style*. For a critique of Bell and Hofstadter, see Athan Theoharis, "The Politics of Scholarship: Liberals, Anti-Communism, and McCarthyism," in Griffith and Theoharis (eds.), *The Specter*, 264–280.

44. Theodore H. White, *America in Search of Itself* (New York, 1982), 59; Houston *Post*, July 27, 1953.

45. Polenberg, *War and Society*, 244.

TWO: VOICES FROM THE LEFT

1. Interview with Adria Allen.

2. David Oshinsky, "Labor's Cold War: The CIO and the Communists," in Griffith and Theoharis (eds.), *The Specter*, 120–121; Shannon, *The Decline of American Communism*, 102; Klehr, *The Heyday of American Communism*, 223–225; interviews with Herman Wright, James ("Blackie") Merrill, and Emma Tenayuca.

3. Interviews with Herman Wright, James ("Blackie") Merrill, Chris Dixie, and Emma Tenayuca; "Arthur J. Mandell," House Committee on Un-American Activities Report, October 25, 1955, *Texas* vs. *NAACP* Records, BTHC. For Mandell's political views, see also Vance Trimble, "Summary of Interview," [1950], 12–13, unpublished manuscript, Houston *Press* Records, HMRC.

4. Interviews with Herman Wright, James ("Blackie") Merrill, Emma Tenayuca, Chris Dixie, and John Barnhart. Interview with William Arthur Combs, Oral History Collection (OHC), HMRC. For biographical information

on Mandell, see "Arthur Josephus Mandell" in Ellis Arthur Davis (ed.), *The Historical Encyclopedia of Texas*, 2 vols. (Dallas, 1939), 481.

5. Interviews with John Barnhart, Chris Dixie, Herman Wright, and James ("Blackie") Merrill.

6. Ibid.; interview with Gilbert Mers, OHC, HMRC. For the relationship between the Communist party and the CIO, see Cochran, *Labor and Communism*. For the "Popular Front," see Norman Markowitz, "A View from the Left: From the Popular Front to Cold War Liberalism," in Griffith and Theoharis (eds.), *The Specter*, 92–115.

7. Interview with W. A. Combs; W. A. Combs, "History of W. A. Combs and His Various Partnerships" (June 6, 1978), typescript in Combs Papers, HMRC.

8. John Kenneth Galbraith, *A Life in Our Times* (New York, 1981), 24.

9. Ronnie Dugger, *Our Invaded Universities* (New York, 1974), 10, 39, 41 (quotes); "Robert H. Montgomery," Biographical Vertical Files, BTHC; interviews with Chris Dixie and Herman Wright; interview with Creekmore Fath.

10. *The Daily Texan*, March 7, 1948 (first quote); Galbraith, *A Life in Our Times*, 24.

11. Interviews with Combs, Dixie, Wright, and Fath.

12. Ibid.; interview with John Barnhart.

13. Interviews with Wright, Combs, and Dixie.

14. Houston *Chronicle*, August 31, 1937; Galveston *Daily News*, July 26, 28–29, 1938.

15. Interviews with Dixie and Wright.

16. "National Maritime Union" file, Labor Movement in Texas Collection, BTHC; interview with James ("Blackie") Merrill; Houston *Post*, May 10, 15, 1939; Houston *Chronicle*, April 24, 1939.

17. Interview with Dixie.

18. Cochran, *Labor and Communism*, 61; Houston *Chronicle*, May 15, 1939.

19. Interview with James ("Blackie") Merrill; Houston *Chronicle*, May 15, 1939; Houston *Press*, May 23, 1939.

20. Houston *Chronicle*, May 21, 1939.

21. Houston *Post*, June 6, 1939.

22. "Sewall Myer," Biographical Files, HMRC; interviews with Dixie, Wright, Tenayuca, and Merrill.

23. James R. Green, *Grass-Roots Socialism: Radical Movements in the Southwest, 1895–1943* (Baton Rouge, 1978), 6, 64, 248.

24. Caute, *The Great Fear*, 185; Cochran, *Labor and Communism*, 46; interview with Tenayuca.

25. Interviews with Emma Tenayuca and Herman Wright; Earl Browder, "The American Communist Party in the Thirties," in Rita James Simon (ed.), *As We Saw the Thirties: Essays on Social and Political Movements of a Decade* (Urbana, Ill., 1976), 216–253.

26. "Texas Labor in the Thirties: Gilbert Mers and the Corpus Christi Waterfront Strikes," *Houston Review* 3 (Fall 1981): 317; untitled circular,

October 22, 1935, Labor Movement in Texas Collection, BTHC; Houston *Post*, June 20, 1948.

27. Shannon, *Decline of American Communism*, 73–76, 95; Klehr, *Heyday of American Communism*, 275, 380; interviews with Tenayuca, Wright, and Merrill; Houston *Chronicle*, January 31, 1939. See Tindall, *Emergence of the New South*, 377–386, for the CPUSA in the South.

28. The CPUSA platform is stated in one of the Texas party's circulars, dated 1940, in author's possession; interview with Tenayuca.

29. "La Pasionaria de Texas," *Time*, February 28, 1938, clipping in BTHC Vertical Files; "Pecan Shellers Strike" file, Labor Movement in Texas Collection, BTHC; interview with Tenayuca; Selden C. Menefee and Orin C. Cassmore, *The Pecan Shellers of San Antonio* (Washington, 1940).

30. "Homer Brooks" file, Houston *Press* Records, HMRC; interview with Emma Tenayuca; Houston *Chronicle*, November 7, 1938; Houston *Post*, August 10, 1938.

31. Interviews with Tenayuca, Merrill, Wright, and Fath; "Homer Brooks" file, Houston *Press* Records, HMRC; *Bartchy* vs. *United States of America*, number 762, Opinion of the Court in Certiorari to the Circuit Court of Appeals for the Fifth Circuit, in Ernest Knaebel (reporter), *United States Reports* (Washington, D.C., 1943), vol. 319, 484–491; Klehr, *Heyday of American Communism*, 273.

32. Houston *Post*, August 10, 1938.

33. All information about Benson is from the Houston *Chronicle*, January 13, 15, 1939, and an interview with Emma Tenayuca.

34. For Combs' confrontation with Holcomb and for Combs' speech to Houston clergy, see Houston *Chronicle*, June 8, 10, 1939, and Houston *Post*, June 9, 17, 1939.

35. Houston *Chronicle*, June 15, 1939. For Browder's statement, see Markowitz, "A View from the Left," 98.

36. Houston *Chronicle*, June 16, 1939; Houston *Post*, June 17, 1939.

37. Houston *Post*, July 13, 1939.

38. Richard Henderson, *Maury Maverick* (Austin, 1971), 214–216; "Communist Riot in San Antonio," clipping scrapbook, BTHC; San Antonio *Express*, August 25–26, 1939; Houston *Post*, August 17, 1939; *New York Times*, September 3, 1939. For CPUSA use of the national anthem, see Markowitz, "A View from the Left," 98.

39. Houston *Chronicle* and Houston *Post*, August 28, 1939.

40. Interview with Combs, OHC, HMRC. See interviews with Wright, Dixie, and Barnhart for views contrary to Combs' for the reason for the Mandell-Combs split. Otto Mullinax also left Mandell and eventually formed a law firm in Dallas in 1947 that specialized in labor cases. Ronnie Dugger, "A Free and Active Mind," *Texas Observer*, November 17, 1961, 1, 8.

41. Arthur Mandell to Miss Ima Hogg, April 13, 1943, Hogg Papers, BTHC.

42. For the CPUSA policy shifts of 1939 and 1941, see Cochran, *Labor and Communism*, 156–195. See interview with Emma Tenayuca for impact on Texas' CPUSA.

43. The March 5, 1941, incident is based on information in Trimble, "Summary of Interview"; interview with Herman Wright.

44. Cochran, *Labor and Communism*, 14, 230 (Browder quote), 212 (last quote); Shannon, *Decline of American Communism*, 6-7.

45. The Brooks draft evasion incident is based on information in "Homer Brooks" file, Houston *Press* Records, HMRC; *Bartchy* vs. *United States*, 486-490; Houston *Press*, April 18, 1942, June 7, 1943; interviews with Chris Dixie and Emma Tenayuca. Information on his expulsion from the CPUSA and his later life and death is from Emma Tenayuca.

46. Interviews with Wright and Dixie; Mandell to Hogg, April 13, 1943, Hogg Papers, BTHC.

47. "Ima Hogg," Biographical Vertical Files, BTHC; interview with Ray K. Daily; Mandell to Hogg, April 13, 1943, Hogg Papers, BTHC (quote).

48. Cochran, *Labor and Communism*, 231. For the CPUSA's status in the 1942-1945 period, see Shannon, *Decline of American Communism*, 3.

49. Oshinsky, "Labor's Cold War," 122-128; Cochran, *Labor and Communism*, 284-331.

50. Gary M. Fink, *Labor Unions* (Westport, Conn., 1977), 214; Charles P. Larrowe, *Harry Bridges; The Rise and Fall of Radical Labor in the United States* (New York, 1972), 288-290; Cochran, *Labor and Communism*, 269; Shannon, *Decline of American Communism*, 214-218.

51. Larrowe, *Harry Bridges*, 288-290.

52. Interview with John Crossland, August 17, 1971, Labor Archives Oral History Collection, University of Texas at Arlington (first quote); "Communists" file, Houston *Press* Records, HMRC; Houston *Chronicle*, April 30, 1947.

53. "Communists" file (quote); Trimble, "Summary of Interview," 5.

54. AFL-CIO Records, Series 16, Box 8, Labor Archives, University of Texas at Arlington.

55. For a discussion of the link between waterfront conditions and radicalism, see Cochran, *Labor and Communism*, 58-61. The discussion on Houston-Galveston NMU members and the CPUSA is based on information in "Communists" file, Houston *Press* Records, HMRC, and interviews with James ("Blackie") Merrill and Emma Tenayuca. Mers' quote is in "Texas Labor in the Thirties," 318.

56. "Communists" file, Houston *Press* Records, HMRC; interview with Morris Bogdanow; Houston *Post*, June 20, 1948; Houston *Press*, December 20-22, 1949, July 19, 1950; interview with John Crossland; Austin *American*, February 19, 1947; *Texas Spur*, March, April 1947, Newspaper Collection, BTHC.

57. Texas State Committee, CPUSA, *What the People of Texas Need: The Communist Program for the Lone Star State* (Houston, 1946), in author's possession; interviews with Eleanor Ball and Ray K. Daily; Houston *Post*, April 25, 1947.

58. For Henry Wallace's 1948 campaign, see Norman A. Markowitz, *The Rise and Fall of the People's Century: Henry A. Wallace and American Liberalism,*

1941-1948 (New York, 1973), and Curtis D. MacDougall, *Gideon's Army*, 3 vols. (New York, 1968); interview with Moses Leroy, October 30, 1974, OHC, HMRC.

59. Interview with Herman Wright. See Caute, *The Great Fear*, 178, for the CRC.

60. Program, Houston NAACP Branch Founders Month Observance, February 14, 1947, Gillette Collection, BTHC; Michael Gillette interview with Ben Ramey, July 28, 1973, tape recording in Michael Gillette's possession, Austin, Texas.

61. Caute, *The Great Fear*, 31 (first quote); Markowitz, "A View from the Left," 95–96, 97 (second quote), 98–100; Shannon, *Decline of American Communism*, 141.

62. For a full discussion on the CPUSA-Wallace connection, see Shannon, *Decline of American Communism*, 141.

63. Houston *Press*, December 30, 1947 (quote); Houston *Chronicle*, January 4, 1948.

64. Interviews with Bogdanow and Wright; Oshinsky, "Labor's Cold War," 148 (quote); Caute, *The Great Fear*, 235–236, 352; Cochran, *Labor and Communism*, 323–324; Shannon, *Decline of American Communism*, 155.

65. "Communists" file, Houston *Press* Records, HMRC; Houston *Press*, March 13, 1948.

66. Mona Schacht, "Wallace for President Committee," March 8, 1948, circular, Gillette Collection, BTHC; interview with Bogdanow; Shannon, *Decline of American Communism*, 102; Cochran, *Labor and Communism*, 331.

67. Pat Lunsford, "The Committee to Get Wallace on the Ballot in Texas," March 11, 1948, circular; idem, "Keynote Address," March 21, 1948, Austin, Texas, mimeographed document; J. Frank Dobie, "Message to the Committee to Get Wallace on the Ballot in Texas," March 21, 1948, Austin, Texas; and Pearl Fox, "Minutes of the Committee to Get Wallace on the Ballot in Texas," March 21, 1948, Austin, Texas, all in the Gillette Collection, BTHC; interviews with Herman Wright and John Henry Faulk; Houston *Post*, March 22, 1948; MacDougall, *Gideon's Army*, vol. 2, 741.

68. Houston *Post*, March 28, 1948; Houston *Press*, March 28, 1948.

69. Minutes, Executive Board, Texas State Industrial Union Council, April 3, 1948, Series 16, Box 2, Folder 2, Texas State CIO Council Records, Labor Archives, University of Texas at Arlington; interview with Herman Wright.

70. The Progressive Party of Texas, "Minutes of the Founding Convention," April 25, 1948, Houston, Texas, Gillette Collection, BTHC; MacDougall, *Gideon's Army*, vol. 2, 740; Houston *Post*, April 26, 29, 1948; Houston *Press*, April 26, 1948; interviews with John Henry Faulk, Herman Wright, and Morris Bogdanow.

71. The Galveston NMU power struggle episode is based on information in R. J. Savage, "Patterns for Peace" (Galveston, Tex., n.d.), typescript of a news broadcast; author unknown, typescripts of news broadcasts, Radio Station KGBC, Galveston, Texas, June 3, 17, 18, 21, 22, 1948; and reporter's

notes, all in "Communists" file, Houston *Press* Records, HMRC; Ronnie Dugger, "Seamen Facing Legal Showdown," *Texas Observer*, August 25, 1961 (Tex George quotes), 1–2; interview with Herman Wright; Houston *Post*, June 19, 1948.

72. Houston *Post*, April 30, 1948; interviews with Herman Wright and Morris Bogdanow; Ben Ramey interview, in possession of Michael Gillette, Austin, Texas; MacDougall, *Gideon's Army*, vol. 2, 741.

73. Houston *Post*, September 1, 1948.

74. Henry Wallace's Houston appearance is based on accounts in the Houston *Press*, Houston *Post*, and Houston *Chronicle*, September 28–30, 1948; MacDougall, *Gideon's Army*, vol. 2, 740; Shannon, *Decline of American Communism*, 177, 179–180; and interviews with Herman Wright and Morris Bogdanow.

75. Caute, *The Great Fear*, 34; Seth McKay, *Texas and the Fair Deal, 1945–1952* (San Antonio, 1954), 274; J. Frank Dobie to Herman Wright, January 11, 1949, J. Frank Dobie Papers, Humanities Research Center, University of Texas at Austin; Lon Tinkle, *An American Original: The Life of J. Frank Dobie* (Austin, 1983), 211.

76. Interview with Chris Dixie (first quote); *The Pilot*, n.d., clipping in "Communists" file, Houston *Press* Records, HMRC (second quote); interview with Herman Wright (third quote); Combs, "History," 3; Fink, *Labor Unions*, 214.

77. For the CPUSA's problems after 1948, see Shannon, *Decline of American Communism*, 155, 185–226, and Starobin, *American Communism in Crisis*, 220–223; Oshinsky, "Labor's Cold War," 127–128; Cochran, *Labor and Communism*, 11; Harvey Klehr, "The Party's Over," *The New York Review of Books*, November 18, 1982.

78. Houston *Press*, January 16, 1949.

79. For the Smith Act, see Michael R. Belknap, *Cold War Political Justice: The Smith Act, the Communist Party, and American Civil Liberties* (Westport, Conn., 1977). For a discussion of the legal aspects of federal deportation policy during this period, see Milton R. Konvitz, *Civil Rights in Immigration* (Ithaca, N.Y., 1953), 93–131; Houston *Post*, December 16, 1949; Caute, *The Great Fear*, 229, 231 (Maverick quote).

80. The Wittenburg-Green episode is based on coverage in the Houston *Post*, December 16 (Green quote), 17, 19, 21, 23, 24, 1949, and Houston *Press*, December 21, 1949 (King quotes); interviews with Morris Bogdanow and Herman Wright; United States Court of Appeals for the Fifth Circuit, Numbers 13069, 13112, *Estes* vs. *Potter*, August 25, 1950; Caute, *The Great Fear* 233–234. Emanuel Bloch would later be defense attorney for Ethel and Julius Rosenberg (Shannon, *Decline of American Communism*, 220). Carol King soon pushed the issue of INS deportation hearings to the United States Supreme Court. The court ruled that INS agents could not conduct hearings such as those in the Wittenburg-Green incident (*New York Times*, February 22, 1950).

81. Shannon, *Decline of American Communism*, 204–205; Caute, *The Great Fear*, 176; Houston *Press*, July 10, 1950; "Communists" file, Houston *Press* Records, HMRC; interview with Morris Bogdanow.

82. Houston *Press*, July 10, 1950; interview with Bogdanow.

83. Houston *Post*, July 16, 1950; interview with Bogdanow; "Communists" file, Houston *Press* Records, HMRC.

84. Houston *Chronicle*, July 17, 19, 1950; Houston *Post*, July 16, 1950; Houston *Press*, July 18, 19, 1950; interviews with Bogdanow and Wright; "Communists" file, Houston *Press* Records, HMRC.

85. Caute, *The Great Fear*, 187 (quote); Starobin, *American Communism in Crisis*, 220–223; interviews with Bogdanow, Wright, and Tenayuca.

THREE: FEAR AND MONEY

1. Marvin Henry to Jesse Jones, July 5, 1950, Jones Papers, BTHC (first quote); John Gunther, *Inside U.S.A.* (New York, 1947), 827 (second quote); White, *America in Search of Itself*, 61 (third quote).

2. Ralph S. O'Leary to Mavis McIntosh, January 15, 1954, O'Leary Papers, HMRC. For more on the role played by political and elite rhetoric in sanctioning the Red Scare nationally, see Griffith, *The Politics of Fear*, and Athan Theoharis, *Seeds of Repression: Harry S. Truman and the Origins of McCarthyism* (Chicago, 1971).

3. White, "Texas," 31–32.

4. James Presley, *A Saga of Wealth: An Anecdotal History of the Texas Oilmen* (Austin, 1983), 191 (quote). For more on "Silver Dollar" Jim West, see Fuermann, *Land of the Big Rich*.

5. For a discussion of the problem of determining power structures in American society, see Hammack, "Problems in the Historical Study of Power," 323–349, and Pessen, "Who Rules America?," 5–26.

6. This list is drawn from a variety of sources, but most helpful were Fuermann, *Land of the Big Rich*; Timmons, *Jesse H. Jones*; Griffin Smith, Jr., "Empires of Paper," *Texas Monthly* (November 1973): 53–109; and Hurt "The Most Powerful Texans," 73–123. Also helpful were interviews with George Fuermann, Leon Jaworski, William Ballew, Jr., Leopold Meyer, Bernard Sakowitz, Glenn McCarthy, George Carmack, George A. Butler, and Jubal R. Parten.

7. For "Jesus H. Jones," see Bert Cochran, *Harry S. Truman and the Crisis Presidency* (New York, 1973), 116; Merle Miller, *Plain Speaking: An Oral Biography of Harry S. Truman* (New York, 1973), 196; and Arthur M. Schlesinger, Jr., *The Coming of the New Deal* (Boston, 1959), 426.

8. Timmons, *Jesse H. Jones*, especially 282; interview with George A. Butler, OHC, HMRC.

9. Timmons, *Jesse H. Jones*, 117, 119, 154–155.

10. Fuermann, *Land of the Big Rich*, 127–128; Hurt, "The Most Powerful Texans," 73–74; "James A. Elkins," *Texas Scrapbooks: Biography*, vol. 36,

HMRC; Smith, "Empires of Paper," 57; interviews with Leopold Meyer, William Ballew, George Carmack, George A. Butler, and Jubal R. Parten.

11. Information for the Browns is from news clippings in the Biographical Vertical Files, BTHC; Robert Caro, *The Years of Lyndon Johnson: The Path to Power* (New York, 1982), 369-373, 469-473; Fuermann, *Land of the Big Rich*, 119-123; James Conway, *The Texans* (New York, 1976), 90-116; Hart Stilwell, "Will He Boss Texas?," *The Nation*, November 10, 1951, 398-400; Green, *The Establishment in Texas Politics*, 106-107.

12. "Gus Wortham," *Texas Scrapbooks: Biography*, vol. 60 and *Houston Scrapbooks: Biography*, vol. 17, HMRC; Lila Humphreys Gordon, "Portrait of an Optimist," *Houston Town and Country* (December 1975): 18-21; Gus Wortham to Lyndon B. Johnson, November 10, 1950, and Lyndon B. Johnson to Gus Wortham, November 3, 1950, Box 445, County Correspondence, Senate Files, Johnson Papers, LBJ Library.

13. Fuermann, *Land of the Big Rich*, 129-130; "Hobbys" file, Houston *Press* Collection, HMRC; *Dallas Morning News*, March 13, 1953; interviews with George Carmack and Jubal R. Parten.

14. Kilman and Wright, *Hugh Roy Cullen*, interviews with George Fuermann, William Ballew, Jr., and Gould Beech.

15. Fuermann, *Land of the Big Rich*, 99-110; "Oscar Holcombe," *Houston Scrapbooks: Biography*, vol. 2, HMRC.

16. Interviews with Fuermann, Ballew, Parten, and Carmack; interviews with Leopold Meyer and George A. Butler, OHC, HMRC.

17. For more on these interrelationships, see Conway, *The Texans*, 101-103, and Hurt, "The Most Powerful Texans," 73-74; Smith, "Empires of Paper," 57; "James A. Elkins," *Texas Scrapbooks: Biography*, vol. 36, HMRC; interview with George A. Butler, OHC, HMRC.

18. "Gus Wortham," *Texas Scrapbooks: Biography*, vol. 60, HMRC; Gordon. "Portrait of an Optimist," 19; Houston *Post*, April 25, 1951; Timmons, *Jesse H. Jones*, 160-161; Jesse Jones to Mark Ethridge, July 20, 1950, Jones Papers, BTHC.

19. Conway, *The Texans*, 101-103; Hurt, "The Most Powerful Texans," 73 (first quote); Green, *The Establishment in Texas Politics*, 17 (second quote); interviews with Leopold Meyer, William Ballew, Jr., and Jubal R. Parten.

20. The Hofheinz-Holcombe story is from Ray, *The Grand Huckster*, 175, 234-235; Tucker, "Houston Business Community," 181; Conway, *The Texans*, 101; interview with Glenn McCarthy.

21. Interviews with Leopold Meyer, A. J. Tucker, and Jubal R. Parten; Herman Brown to "Those Concerned," January 19, 1952 (quote), and Robert W. Henderson to W. Alvis Parish et al., April 20, 1951, Parish Papers, HMRC; interview with George A. Butler.

22. For the zoning issue in Houston, see Barry A. Kaplan, "Urban Development, Economic Growth, and Personal Liberty: The Rhetoric of the Houston Anti-Zoning Movements, 1947-1962," *Southwestern Historical Quarterly* 84 (October 1980): 133-168.

23. Hugh Roy Cullen to Jesse H. Jones, December 23, 1946, Jones Papers,

BTHC (first quote); Fuermann, *Land of the Big Rich*, 115 (second quote).

24. The unmailed letter of Cullen and several drafts are in the Cullen file, December 2, 1955, Jones Papers, BTHC. Cullen summarized his conflicts with Jones in a letter to James A. Linen, October 5, 1953, copy in Eisenhower Papers, Official File, Box 1275, DDE Library.

25. Conway, *The Texans*, 96. For the Red Scare's anti-labor roots, see David M. Oshinsky, *Senator Joseph McCarthy and the American Labor Movement* (Columbia, Miss., 1976).

26. Caro, *Path to Power*, 469; W. A. Parish to Beauford Jester, January 18, 1949, Parish Papers, HMRC.

27. White, "Texas," 10 (first quote); Charles J. V. Murphy, "Texas Business and McCarthy," *Fortune* 49 (May 1954): 100 (second quote); Gunther, *Inside USA*, 827 (third quote).

28. Jesse Jones' nephew-in-law and lawyer, George A. Butler, later recalled, "I don't suppose [Elkins and Jones] ever disagreed" about political issues (interview with George A. Butler, OHC, HMRC). For more on McCarthyism as an expression of the American political culture, see Griffith and Theoharis (eds.), *The Specter*; interviews with Jubal R. Parten and William Ballew.

29. Houston *Chronicle*, April 29, 1953. For the U.S. Chamber of Commerce and the Red Scare, see Peter H. Irons, "American Business and the Origins of McCarthyism: The Cold War Crusade of the United States Chamber of Commerce," in Griffith and Theoharis (eds.), *The Specter*, 72–89; Caute, *The Great Fear*, 349–350; Chamber of Commerce of the U.S.A., *A Program for Community Anti-Communist Action* (Washington, D.C., 1948); Minute Women of the U.S.A., Inc., *Newsletter*, O'Leary Papers, HMRC.

30. "Has America's Campaign for Tolerance Backfired?," *Houston* 19 (January 1947): 34.

31. "Shadow Boxing with Communism," *Houston* 21 (January 1948): 17; "What Can Americans Do to Stop the Spread of ISMS?," *Houston* 20 (June 1949): 20.

32. Caute, *The Great Fear*, 350; Lipset and Raab, *The Politics of Unreason*, 210; Oshinsky, *McCarthy and the American Labor Movement*, 169–172. For an analysis of the theoretical correlation between small businessmen's antilabor perceptions and their support of McCarthyism, see Martin Trow, "Small Business, Political Intolerance, and Support of McCarthy," *The American Journal of Sociology* 64 (November 1958): 270–281.

33. Caute, *The Great Fear*, 446, 447, 79; Richard Rovere, *Senator Joe McCarthy* (New York, 1959), 137–140, 162–169; Alan Barth, *The Loyalty of Free Men* (New York, 1959), 9–10; Dozier C. Cade, "Witch-Hunting, 1952: The Role of the Press," *Journalism Quarterly* 29 (Fall 1952): 396–407; Jean Franklin Deaver, "A Study of Joseph R. McCarthy and 'McCarthyism' as Influences upon the News Media and the Evolution of Reportorial Method" (Ph.D. dissertation, University of Texas at Austin, 1969), 236–243; Bayley, *Joe McCarthy and the Press*, 218–219. See also Aronson, *The Press and the Cold War*, especially 64–102.

34. Erickson, *Wayward Puritans*, 10–22.

35. For the Houston Open Forum incident, see undated Houston *Chronicle* clipping in the Ideson Papers, HMRC.

36. For the role played by the rhetoric of elites in creating the Red Scare of the 1950s, see Theoharis, *Seeds of Repression*.

37. Jesse H. Jones, *Fifty Billion Dollars* (New York, 1951), 280; Timmons, *Jesse H. Jones*, 351–361; Caro, *Path to Power*, 597–598, 667–668. For the Texas Regulars episode, see Green, *The Establishment in Texas Politics*, 46–57. See Markowitz, *Rise and Fall*, 68–73, 130–132 for the Jones-Wallace feud.

38. Gunther, *Inside USA*, 828.

39. Jones, *Fifty Billion Dollars*, 290; Margaret Truman, *Harry S. Truman* (New York, 1974), 160; Jones-Truman correspondence in Box 32, Jones Papers, LC.

40. Timmons, *Jesse H. Jones*, 382; Jesse H. Jones to Dwight D. Eisenhower, June 18, 1952, Jones Papers, LC.

41. Timmons, *Jesse H. Jones*, 365; interview with George A. Butler; James F. Byrnes' correspondence with Jesse H. Jones, Jones Papers, BTHC.

42. Houston *Chronicle*, September 17, 1948; George E. Sokolsky to Jesse H. Jones, September 11, 1948, Jones Papers, LC.

43. Jesse H. Jones to George E. Sokolsky, September 23, 1948, Jones Papers, LC.

44. Theoharis, *Seeds of Repression*; Earl Latham, *The Communist Controversy in Washington: From the New Deal to McCarthy* (Cambridge, Mass., 1966), 417; Griffith, *Politics of Fear*; Reeves, *The Life and Times of Joe McCarthy*, 213.

45. Timmons, *Jesse H. Jones*, 109; Schlesinger, *Coming of the New Deal*, 426.

46. Dwight R. G. Palmer to Jesse H. Jones, October 30, 1952; Jesse H. Jones to Stephen Mitchell, October 22, 1952; and Jesse H. Jones to Cordell Hull, October 2, 1952, all in Jones Papers, BTHC.

47. Jesse H. Jones to Dwight D. Eisenhower, November 10, 1950, and Jesse H. Jones to J. W. Butler, May 2, 1950, Jones Papers, LC.

48. "M. E. Walter," Biographical Vertical Files, BTHC; interviews with George Carmack and Mary Lasswell; Ray, *Grand Huckster*, 89, 175, 276.

49. Interviews with George Carmack and Mary Lasswell; Houston *Chronicle*, January 13, 1966 (quotes); Sam Low to Lyndon B. Johnson, July 8, 1954, Box 25, Selected Names ("Sam Low"), Johnson Papers, LBJ Library.

50. Office memorandum to M. E. Walter, March 1, 1952 (quote). Jones and Walter's communications, scribbled on Jones' mail, are scattered throughout the Jones Papers and are filed according to the correspondent's last name (for example, see Folder 1, Box 3M441 or "C" file, Box 3M436, all in Jones Papers, BTHC).

51. Timmons, *Jesse H. Jones*, 376–379, 386; Fuermann, *The Reluctant Empire*, 145.

52. Jesse H. Jones to Lyndon B. Johnson, June 7, 1952, Jones Papers, BTHC; Jesse H. Jones to Dwight D. Eisenhower, July 17, 1952, Jones Papers, LC.

53. Murphy, "Texas Business and McCarthy," 101.

54. For more on Sokolsky, see Warren I. Cohen, *The Chinese Connection: Roger S. Greene, Thomas W. Lamont, George E. Sokolsky and American–East Asian Relations* (New York, 1978).

55. Houston *Chronicle*, November 7, 13, 1950.

56. Houston *Chronicle*, October 24, 1950, July 11, 1951.

57. J. Edgar Hoover to Jesse H. Jones, February 15, 1950, Jones Papers, BTHC.

58. H. L. Hunt to Jesse H. Jones, December 19, 1951; notes and memoranda, Jesse H. Jones to/from M. E. Walter, n.d.; Jesse H. Jones to H. L. Hunt, April 20, 1954; and Jesse H. Jones to Zell Howard, July 20, 1954, all in Jones Papers, BTHC. For the H. L. Hunt–Sears connection, see "McCarthy, Hunt, and Facts Forum," *The Reporter*, February 16, 1954, 26–27.

59. Interviews with Marguerite Johnston and Mrs. Ralph S. O'Leary; "Ed Kilman," Vertical File Collection, BTHC.

60. For Kilman's views, see his collection of columns and writings and the transcription of his interview with Cullen in the Kilman Papers, HMRC.

61. *The Daily Texan*, December 4, 1947; Eugenie R. Voss to T. S. Painter, January 9, 1947, and T. S. Painter to E. M. Biggers, January 26, 1948, "Communism," OPR, BTHC.

62. Houston *Post*, December 24, 1947.

63. E. M. Biggers to T. S. Painter, January 1, 1948, and others, in "Communism," OPR, BTHC.

64. Voss to Painter, January 9, 1947, and Dudley K. Woodward to E. M. Biggers, January 7, 1947, in "Communism," OPR, BTHC.

65. Houston *Post*, July 31, 1950.

66. Oveta Culp Hobby, "A Free Press Demands Excellence and Continuous, Conscientious Performance," *The Alabama Publisher* (January–March 1950): 3–4, 13.

67. Interview with Marguerite Johnston.

68. Houston *Post*, April 10, 1951.

69. Houston *Post*, April 8, June 6, 22, July 9, 1951; McCarran editorial in Houston *Post*, August 22, 1951.

70. Interviews with George Carmack and Ben Kaplan. The charge of sensationalism to attract readers is a judgment of my own.

71. Houston *Press*, September 9, 1953. For other examples of *Press* Red Scare editorials, see April 6–7, June 6, July 14, August 11, 1951, Houston *Press*; Bayley, *McCarthy and the Press*, 174.

72. Bayley, *McCarthy and the Press*, 48, 219; Homer P. Rainey, *The Tower and the Dome: A Free University vs. Political Control* (Boulder, 1971), 5; White, "Texas," 34–35. Interviews with several persons involved in Red Scare pressure groups emphasized that they were mobilized not only by the knowledge of international and national events, but by developments in the community as reported by the local press.

73. For more on Cullen and his worldview, see Kilman and Wright, *Hugh Roy Cullen*.

74. Ibid., 248–250; Ray, *The Grand Huckster*, 125; *New York Times*, February 14, 1954; McComb, *Houston*, 175.

75. Kilman and Wright, *Hugh Roy Cullen*, 248–250; McComb, *Houston*, 176–177.

76. Kilman and Wright, *Hugh Roy Cullen*, 30–31; "H. R. Cullen, Philanthropist," *The Texas Spectator*, July 14, 1947, 9.

77. Reference to Dulles is from a tape-recorded interview with Hugh Roy Cullen, n.d., Kilman Papers, HMRC; Kilman and Wright, *Hugh Roy Cullen*, 169–170, 212–215, 265–266; Murphy, "Texas Business and McCarthy," 212; Fuermann, *The Reluctant Empire*, 65; Hugh Roy Cullen to Dwight D. Eisenhower, October 11, 1954, Eisenhower Papers, DDE Library (quote regarding UN).

78. Hugh Roy Cullen to Dwight Eisenhower, October 11, 1954, Eisenhower Papers, DDE Library.

79. Kilman and Wright, *Hugh Roy Cullen*, 226; Hugh Roy Cullen, "Patriots Must Rally to Save Our Nation from Socialism!," reprint of a speech delivered on June 12, 1950, in Houston, Texas, in author's possession; Houston *Post*, July 3, 1950.

80. Green, *The Establishment in Texas Politics*, 48–57, 109–110, 112, 148; Hugh Roy Cullen to Dwight D. Eisenhower, October 27, 1953, Eisenhower Papers, DDE Library.

81. For more on the Cullen-McCarthy relationship, see Reeves, *The Life and Times of Joe McCarthy*, 319, 419; Kilman and Wright, *Hugh Roy Cullen*, 284; Murphy, "Texas Business and McCarthy," 101; Oshinsky, *A Conspiracy So Immense*, 169; Houston *Post*, April 4, 1954 (first quote); tape-recorded interview with Hugh Roy Cullen, Kilman Papers, HMRC (second quote).

82. Richard M. Fried, "Electoral Politics and McCarthyism: The 1950 Campaign," in Griffith and Theoharis (eds.), *The Specter*, 220; Kilman and Wright, *Hugh Roy Cullen*, 270–271; Fuermann, *The Reluctant Empire*, 64.

83. Tape-recorded interview with Hugh Roy Cullen, Kilman Papers, HMRC; Paul Husserl, "Texas Oil on Troubled Air Waves," *The Nation*, November 3, 1951, 370–371; Ronnie Dugger, "The Old Scotchman's Bankruptcy," *The Texas Observer*, April 17, 1964, 7–8.

84. "H. R. Cullen, Philanthropist," 9.

85. Murphy, "Texas Business and McCarthy," 180, 211; Green, *The Establishment in Texas Politics*, 9; Reeves, *The Life and Times of Joe McCarthy*, 319, 337, 540.

86. Murphy, "Texas Business and McCarthy," 212 (first quote); "McCarthy, Hunt, and Facts Forum," 19–20; Reeves, *The Life and Times of Joe McCarthy*, 319, 337; Hurt, *Texas Rich*, 157–159, 161, 163.

87. Walter Goodman, *The Committee: The Extraordinary Career of the House Committee on Un-American Activities* (New York, 1968), 3–174; Green, *The Establishment in Texas Politics*, 69–76; interview with J. R. Parten.

88. "Martin Dies," Biographical Vertical Files, BTHC.

89. *Dallas Morning News*, March 29, 1959; "Dies" file, BTHC; Martin Dies to

Hugh Roy Cullen, May 10, 1954, Official Files, Box 1275, Eisenhower Papers, DDE Library.

90. Houston *Post*, March 21, 1947; *Houston* 22 (September 1948): 51; Houston *Chronicle*, September 28, 1949.

91. Houston *Chronicle*, July 17, 1950; Houston *Post*, July 3, 1950; "Marshall Bell," Biographical Vertical Files, BTHC; *Dallas Morning News*, January 16, 1948.

92. *Dallas Morning News*, January 2, 1949; Austin *American*, January 9, 1949; Houston *Chronicle*, January 2, 1949.

93. State of Texas, *House Journal*, 51st Legislature, Regular Session (Austin, 1949), 125, 664, 1036, 1445, 2108, 2143, 2383, 2432; State of Texas, *Senate Journal*, 51st Legislature, Regular Session (Austin, 1949), 152, 340, 754, 935, 1635, 1681. For the May 2, 1949, resolution, see *House Journal*, 51st Legislature, Regular Session, 1457–1459, 2038.

94. *Dallas Morning News*, September 30, 1950 (first quote); Vernon's Annotated Texas Statutes, art. 6889-3, 363–366; State of Texas, *House Journal*, 52nd Legislature, Regular Session (Austin, 1951), 553–555; *The Daily Texan*, February 14, 1951 (Garrison quote).

95. State of Texas, *House Journal*, 52nd Legislature, Regular Session (Austin, 1951), 216–217; interviews with John Barnhart and Maury Maverick, Jr.; Caute, *The Great Fear*, 72.

96. House and Senate Resolution 136, copy in Woodward Papers, BTHC; *Dallas Morning News*, March 18, 1951; Austin *American*, April 7, March 18, 1951; *The Daily Texan*, March 20, 1951; interviews with Barnhart and Maverick; Claude W. Voyles, James P. Hart, and Theophilus S. Painter to Reuben E. Senterfitt, undated enclosure in Dudley K. Woodward, Jr., to Reuben E. Senterfitt, March 30, 1951, Woodward Papers, BTHC.

97. Dudley K. Woodward, Jr., to James P. Hart, June 19, 1951, Woodward Papers, BTHC; interview with Maury Maverick, Jr.

98. Houston *Post*, March 4, 9, April 15, 1951; Houston *Chronicle*, February 28, 1951; *The Daily Texan*, April 26, 1951.

99. Houston *Post*, March 4, April 15, 1951; Houston *Chronicle*, March 17, 1951; Caute, *The Great Fear*, 73.

100. White, "Texas," 32.

101. Quoted in Murphy, "Texas Business and McCarthy," 214.

FOUR: RED SCARE ACTIVISTS ORGANIZE

1. Davis, *Fear of Conspiracy*, xv; interview with W. Kenneth Pope, January 7, 1983.

2. Houston *Post*, April 26, 1951.

3. Robert Griffith, "American Politics and the Origins of McCarthyism," in Griffith and Theoharis, *The Specter*, 11; Caute, *The Great Fear*, 350–351.

4. Caute, *The Great Fear*, 351 (quote); Loren D. Stark to Rogers Kelly, August 31, 1955, in Americanism Committee, The American Legion, 8th

District, Department of Texas, *Analysis of the Ray Murphy Committee Report* (Houston, 1955), 2.

5. Houston *Post*, March 14, 28, June 20, 1948.

6. McComb, *Houston*, 50; Spellman, *Growing a Soul*, 128.

7. *Time*, September 17, 1951, 96–97; "Radicals Retain Reins in Methodist Federation," *The Christian*, September 19, 1951, 1068.

8. Roy, *Communism and the Churches*, 292–294; idem, *Apostles*, 317.

9. Elizabeth Dilling, *The Red Network* (Chicago, 1934), 190–192; Roy, *Apostles*, 308–311; Ralph Lord Roy, "Methodism's Malcontents," *The Pastor* (November 1952): 7–8, 25; Goodman, *The Committee*, 73–75.

10. Interviews with W. Kenneth Pope and Grady Hardin; Roy, *Apostles*, 311.

11. Bayley, *McCarthy and the Press*, 174; Houston *Press*, December 26, 28, 30, 1947; Roy, *Apostles*, 311–312; Spellman, *Growing a Soul*, 360–361.

12. Spellman, *Growing a Soul*, 361–363.

13. Roy, *Communism and the Churches*, 291; idem, *Apostles*, 314; Spellman, *Growing a Soul*, 365; The House Committee on Un-American Activities, *100 Things You Should Know about Communism and Religion* (Washington, D.C., 1948); Caute, *The Great Fear*, 101.

14. Roy, *Communism and the Churches*, 230–231; Ronald Radosh, *Prophets on the Right: Profiles of Conservative Critics of American Globalism* (New York, 1975), 232; interviews with W. Kenneth Pope and R. A. Childers.

15. Stanley High, "Methodism's Pink Fringe," *Reader's Digest* (February 1950): 134–138.

16. For a critique of High's article, see Roy, *Apostles*, 313–314; interviews with R. A. Childers, W. Kenneth Pope, and Grady Hardin; Spellman, *Growing a Soul*, 366–367.

17. Spellman, *Growing a Soul*, 369; Michael Paul Rogin, *The Intellectuals and McCarthy: The Radical Specter* (Cambridge, Mass., 1967).

18. Interview with Grady Hardin.

19. Spellman, *Growing a Soul*, 367.

20. *Is There a Pink Fringe in the Methodist Church? A Report to Methodists from the Committee for the Preservation of Methodism* (Houston, April 1951), 2–3.

21. Spellman, *Growing a Soul*, 368; *Is There a Pink Fringe*; Roy, *Apostles*, 327; interviews with R. A. Childers and Grady Hardin.

22. *Is There a Pink Fringe*.

23. Ibid.

24. Roy, *Apostles*, 327; *The Methodist Challenge* 20 (December 1951), clipping in Box 7, O'Leary Papers, HMRC; "Which Way Methodists?," *The Christian Century*, April 23, 1952, 4.

25. Harry and Bonaro Overstreet, *The Strange Tactics of Extremism* (New York, 1964), 157–169; Roy, *Apostles*, 322–327; "Another Church Social Action Body under Fire," *The Christian Century*, March 26, 1952, 357; "Methodists Take Cautious Course," *The Christian Century*, May 21, 1952, 630.

26. Herbert A. Philbrick, "The Communists Are After Your Church!," reprint from *Christian Herald* (April 1953) and an untitled mimeographed

circular, n.d., Box 7, O'Leary Papers, HMRC; interview with R. A. Childers.

27. Spellman, *Growing a Soul*, 368 (quote).

28. William Bradford Huie, "Minute Women to the Rescue," *American Mercury* 74 (April 1952): 126–127; Gordon D. Hall, *The Hate Campaign against the U.N.: One World under Attack* (Boston, 1953), 26–27; Houston *Post*, October 11, 1953.

29. Stevenson's views are based on her writing in the Minute Women of the U.S.A.'s national newsletters; several issues are in the O'Leary Papers, HMRC; Carol Felsenthal, *The Sweetheart of the Silent Majority: The Biography of Phyllis Schlafly* (New York, 1981); the "awakened feminism" view is from an interview with Dallas Dyer McGregor, OHC, HMRC; Warren Leslie, *Dallas Public and Private* (New York, 1964), 107–110.

30. Suzanne Stevenson, "Circular of Principles," undated mimeographed material in the O'Leary Papers, HMRC.

31. Minute Women of the U.S.A., Inc., *Newsletter* (several issues, but especially February 1951), O'Leary Papers, HMRC; interviews with Adria Allen, Virginia Biggers, and Dallas Dyer McGregor.

32. Minute Women of the U.S.A., Inc., *Newsletter* (February 1951) (quote), O'Leary Papers, HMRC.

33. This and most of the following information about the Minute Women of the U.S.A., Inc., is based on the research of Ralph S. O'Leary as it appears in a series of articles in the Houston *Post*, October 11–28, 1953, and in reporter's notes in the O'Leary Papers, HMRC.

34. Huie, "Minute Women," 27; Houston *Post*, October 14, 1953.

35. George Peck, "Servitude without Pay," in A. G. Heinsohn, Jr. (ed.), *Anthology of Conservative Writing in the United States, 1932–1960* (Chicago, 1962), 359–361; Houston *Post*, February 29, 1952; Lamar Fleming to Jesse H. Jones, October 8, 1951, Box 3M439, Jones Papers, BTHC; *New York Times*, April 12, 1950.

36. Huie, "Minute Women," 27; Houston *Post*, November 19, 1953.

37. H. and B. Overstreet, *Strange Tactics of Extremism*, 214; Caute, *The Great Fear*, 526, 532; Houston *Post*, October 11, 1953.

38. Houston *Post*, October 23, 1953; The Anti-Defamation League of B'Nai B'Rith, "Minute Women of the U.S.A., Inc.," *The Facts* 7 (June–July 1952): 1, copy in O'Leary Papers, HMRC; Hall, *Hate Campaign*, 26.

39. John Bainbridge, "Danger's Ahead in the Public Schools," *McCalls* 79 (October 1952): 89; reporter's notes, O'Leary Papers, HMRC; interviews with Dallas Dyer McGregor and Virginia Biggers; Hall, *Hate Campaign*, 27.

40. Ronald Lora, "A View from the Right: Conservative Intellectuals, the Cold War, and McCarthy," in Griffith and Theoharis (eds.), *The Specter*, 55; Reeves, *The Life and Times of Joe McCarthy*, 220–221; Radosh, *Prophets on the Right*, 249.

41. Richard M. Fried, "Electoral Politics and McCarthyism: The 1950 Campaign," in Griffith and Theoharis (eds.), *The Specter*, 220; Radosh, *Prophets on the Right*, 232.

42. John Flynn, *While You Slept: Our Tragedy in Asia and Who Made It* (New York, 1951); interviews with Margaret Bleil and A. J. Tucker.

43. Reeves, *The Life and Times of Joe McCarthy*, 467; Radosh, *Prophets on the Right*, 232; Minute Women of the U.S.A., Inc., *Newsletter* (January 1953), O'Leary Papers, HMRC.

44. T. Harry Williams, *Huey Long* (New York, 1970), 699–700; Lipset and Raab, *The Politics of Unreason*, 244; Benjamin R. Epstein and Arnold Foster, *The Radical Right: Report on the John Birch Society and Its Allies* (New York, 1967), 131, 134; Reeves, *The Life and Times of Joe McCarthy*, 358–362.

45. Epstein and Foster, *The Radical Right*, 136; Roy, *Apostles*, 228; Caute, *The Great Fear*, 369; Margaret Hartley, "The Subliterature of Hate in America," *Southwest Review* 37 (Summer 1952): 187; Herbert S. Parmet, *Eisenhower and the American Crusades* (New York, 1972), 60.

46. John O. Beaty, *The Iron Curtain over America* (Dallas, 1952), 58–59, 194; Roy, *Apostles*, 88–89; Spellman, *Growing a Soul*, 333–337; *The Reporter*, February 16, 1954, 20–21; B'Nai B'Rith, "Minute Women," 3.

47. John Bainbridge, "Save Our Schools," *McCalls* 79 (September 1953): 84; James Rorty, "What Price McCarthy Now?," *Commentary* 19 (January 1955): 33; interview with Adria Allen; Hartley, "Subliterature of Hate," 186; Hulburd, *It Happened in Pasadena*, 87–90.

48. Minute Women of the U.S.A., Inc., *Newsletter* (October 1957), O'Leary Papers, HMRC; interview with Virginia Biggers.

49. Hurt, *Texas Rich*, 155–156, 159–160, 193.

50. Interviews with Mary Drouin, Virginia Biggers, and Adria Allen; O'Leary, reporter's notes, O'Leary Papers, HMRC; Houston *Post*, October 11–28, 1953; Hall, *Hate Campaign*, 28.

51. *New York Times*, December 8, 1950, November 12, 19, 1953; Saul Carson, "On the Air: Trial by Sponsor," *New Republic*, September 11, 1950, 22–23; Caute, *The Great Fear*, 527, 530–531.

52. *New York Times*, November 19, 1953; Ralph McGill, "Houston and the Minute Women," Atlanta *Constitution*, October 31, 1953; St. Louis *Post-Dispatch*, November 7, 1953.

53. Gordon D. Hall, "Hucksters of Hate," *The Progressive* 17 (August 1953): 7; Houston *Post*, October 11, 1953; *New York Times*, February 2, 1952.

54. Houston *Post*, October 12, 1953; Minute Women of the U.S.A., Inc., *Newsletter* (February and March 1951), O'Leary Papers, HMRC.

55. Interviews with Adria Allen and Virginia Biggers; Houston *Post*, April 19, 1951.

56. Houston *Press*, July 27, 1954; O'Leary, reporter's notes, O'Leary Papers, HMRC; interview with Dallas Dyer McGregor; Houston *Post*, October 11, 12, 1953.

57. Houston *Post*, October 12, 1953; interview with Virginia Biggers; Leslie, *Dallas Public and Private*, 116–117; Mrs. W. G. Dodge to Martin Dies, September 24, 1951, Dies Papers, SHRC; *San Antonio Express*, February 28, 1952.

58. Houston *Post*, October 12, 1953; interviews with Virginia Biggers and Adria Allen.

59. Minute Women of the U.S.A., Inc., *Newsletter* (October 1951), O'Leary Papers, HMRC; Houston *Post*, October 12, 1953.

60. This and the following information about Minute Women members is largely based on material gathered by Ralph O'Leary in his research for the Houston *Post*'s series, October 11–28, 1953. I have supplemented O'Leary's material with Morrison and Fourmy's Houston city directories for the years 1949–1954, interviews with former Minute Women, and the correspondence of Minute Women with public figures and newspapers.

61. Testimony given to the Better Business Bureau of Houston by Mrs. J. H. Woods concerning her conversation with Mrs. Alfred Wells, O'Leary Papers, HMRC; interview with Mary Drouin.

62. Mrs. Andre (Mary) Drouin to Lyndon B. Johnson, May 25, 1951, Box 454, Senate Files, Johnson Papers, LBJ Library; interviews with Mary Drouin and Virginia Biggers.

63. Interviews with Mary Drouin, Adria Allen, Virginia Biggers, Dallas Dyer McGregor, Eleanor Ball, A. J. Tucker, Kate Bell, George W. Ebey, William Moreland, and Ida Darden; O'Leary, reporter's notes, O'Leary Papers, HMRC; Houston *Post*, October 11–28, 1953.

64. Virginia Biggers, Minute Women of the U.S.A., Inc. (Houston Chapter) *Newsletter* (October 1952), O'Leary Papers, HMRC; Green, *The Establishment in Texas Politics*, 53; Houston *Press*, July 5, 1939; Houston *Post*, October 16, 1953; interview with Virginia Biggers.

65. Interviews with Virginia Biggers, Mary Drouin, Adria Allen, and Eleanor Ball; O'Leary, reporter's notes, O'Leary Papers, HMRC; American Legion, *Analysis of Ray Murphy Report*, 2; Virginia Hedrick to Jesse Jones, February 10, May 4, June 13, 1955, Jones Papers, BTHC; Houston *Chronicle*, May 6, 1955; Houston *Post*, October 18, 1953; Virginia Hedrick to Lyndon B. Johnson, January 27, 1953, Senate Files, Johnson Papers, LBJ Library.

66. Minute Women of the U.S.A., Inc., *Newsletter* (February 1951), O'Leary Papers, HMRC; interviews with Virginia Biggers, Adria Allen, and Mary Drouin; Houston *Post*, October 12, 1953; Eleanor Watt to M. E. Walter, June 6, 1954, Jones Papers, BTHC.

67. Houston *Post*, October 12, 21, 1953; Faye Weitinger to the Editor, Houston *Chronicle*, June 5, 1954, Jones Papers, BTHC; Mr. and Mrs. J. C. Weitinger to Governor Allan Shivers, February 17, 1954, Shivers Papers, Texas State Archives; Mrs. J. C. Weitinger to Senator Price Daniel, August 16, 1953, Daniel Papers, SHRC; interviews with Virginia Biggers, Adria Allen, Mary Drouin, and Dallas Dyer McGregor.

68. Interviews with Ida Darden, Mary Drouin, Virginia Biggers, Dallas Dyer McGregor, and Adria Allen; O'Leary, reporter's notes, O'Leary Papers, HMRC. For an example of Helen Thomas' work, see Helen Thomas to Price Daniel, November 4, 1954, Daniel Papers, SHRC.

69. Caute, *The Great Fear*, 101–102, 572.

70. Interviews with Ida Darden, Adria Allen, Mary Drouin, and Virginia Biggers; Houston *Post*, October 16, 1953; Helen D. Thomas, "Individuals from Texas Reported as Having Been Affiliated with Communist or Communist-Front Organizations—As Compiled from Official Government Reports, 1934–1954" (Houston, 1956), in *Texas* vs. *NAACP* Records, BTHC.

71. Caute, *The Great Fear*, 572; Reeves, *The Life and Times of Joe McCarthy*, 208.

72. Interviews with Ida Darden, Adria Allen, A. J. Tucker, and Eleanor Ball; Houston *Post*, October 17, 1953; O'Leary, reporter's notes, O'Leary Papers, HMRC; Helen Thomas to Martin Dies, April 24, 1953, June 21, 1954, and June 27, 1954, Martin Dies to Helen Thomas, April 29, 1953, and June 28, 1954, all in Dies Papers, SHRC.

73. A nearly complete run of *The Southern Conservative* is in the Darden Collection, HMRC. Example is from *The Southern Conservative* (September 1951); interview with Ida Darden.

74. Houston *Post*, October 11, 1953; *The Southern Conservative* (March 1953).

75. Houston *Post*, October 11, 1953; Green, *The Establishment in Texas Politics*, 58–60; Ida Darden, "Devotion to Constitutional Government Seemed to Sort of Run in the Family," *The Southern Conservative* (March 1951); interview with Ida Darden.

76. Elsie Daniel to M. E. Walter, June 5, 1954, Jones Papers, BTHC; interview with Eleanor Ball; Anne Harrison to Lyndon B. Johnson, March 24, April 25, May 19, 31, July 2, 1952, and Elsie Daniel to Stuart Symington, June 19, 1954, William Knowland, July 29, 1954, and Lyndon B. Johnson, January 24, 1952, all in Senate Files, Johnson Papers, LBJ Library; Mrs. E. M. Harrison to Price Daniel, June 26, 1953, Daniel Papers, SHRC.

77. Mrs. J. D. Mabry to Lyndon B. Johnson, May 14, 1951, September 19, 1951, Senate Files, Johnson Papers, LBJ Library; Mrs. J. D. Mabry to the Editor, Houston *Chronicle*, June 3, 1954, Jones Papers, BTHC.

78. Interviews with Dallas Dyer McGregor, Eleanor Ball, and A. J. Tucker; Houston *Post*, October 14, 21, 1953.

79. Interviews with Dallas Dyer McGregor, Virginia Biggers, Mary Drouin, Adria Allen, Eleanor Ball, A. J. Tucker, and George W. Ebey; Houston *Post*, October 21, 1953; Houston *Press*, August 14, 1953, July 3, 1960.

80. Houston *Post*, October 14, 1953.

FIVE: THE RED SCARE BEGINS

1. Erickson, *Wayward Puritans*, 22; Pope, *A Pope at Roam*, 95.

2. Barry J. Kaplan, "Urban Development, Economic Growth, and Personal Liberty: The Rhetoric of the Houston Anti-Zoning Movements, 1947–1962," *Southwestern Historical Quarterly* 84 (October 1980): 154–157; McComb, *Houston*, 157–158.

3. Reeves, *The Life and Times of Joe McCarthy*, 224, 304–305.

4. Ibid., 319; Houston *Post*, September 18–19, 1950.

5. Reeves, *The Life and Times of Joe McCarthy*, 7–9; Houston *Post*, September 19, 1950.

6. Houston *Post*, September 19, 1950.

7. Eric Goldman, *The Crucial Decade and After: America, 1945–1960* (New York, 1960), 214.

8. Houston *Post*, February 25, 1951; *New York Times*, February 25, 1951.

9. Olcutt Sanders to the Houston *Post*, undated news clipping, Bell Papers, HMRC; Houston *Post*, October 16, 1953; O'Leary, reporter's notes, O'Leary Papers, HMRC.

10. Houston *Post*, October 11–16, 1953; interviews with Virginia Biggers, Mary Drouin, Adria Allen, Eleanor Ball, and A. J. Tucker.

11. Interviews with Adria Allen (quote) and Mary Drouin; Adria Allen to Lyndon B. Johnson, February 15, 1951, Senate Files, Johnson Papers, LBJ Library.

12. Houston *Post*, September 21, 25, 26, 1951, October 17, 1953; Hulburd, *It Happened in Pasadena*.

13. Houston *Press*, September 25, 1951.

14. Houston *Post*, September 26, 1951, October 17, 1953; William H. Dalton, "Members of Communist Fronts to Address Teachers" (November 1951), circular in O'Leary Papers, HMRC.

15. Houston *Post*, September 26, 1951.

16. "This Actually Did Happen!! United Nations Seizes, Rules, American Cities" (December 1951), circular in O'Leary Papers, HMRC; Houston *Post*, October 19, 1953.

17. Ida Darden, "Why Should a Public Library Promote the Works of Subversive Writers?," *The Southern Conservative* (January 1952); Houston Public Library Board, *Minutes*, February 1, 1952, July 21, 1953, HMRC; Fuermann, *Reluctant Empire*, 128, 134–136; Maury Maverick, "San Antonio— More Fighters than Fire," *New Republic*, June 19, 1953, 12–13.

18. Interviews with W. Kenneth Pope, Grady Hardin, and R. A. Childers; R. A. Childers to Holger Jeppeson, March 22, 1952, O'Leary Papers, HMRC.

19. J. O. Webb, "Must a Church Select a Speaker with Communist-Front Record?" and "Whom It May Concern," February 7, 1952, in Childers to Jeppeson, March 22, 1952, O'Leary Papers, HMRC; interview with R. A. Childers; Houston *Post*, October 18, 1953.

20. Interviews with Mary Drouin, Mrs. Loren Stark, and R. A. Childers; Houston *Chronicle*, February 9, 1952; Houston *Post*, October 18, 1953.

21. Jesse Jones to Rufus Clement, February 5, 1951, Jones Papers, BTHC.

22. Interview with W. Kenneth Pope, January 7, 1983; Pope, *A Pope at Roam*, 97–98.

23. Interviews with W. Kenneth Pope and R. A. Childers; Pope, *A Pope at Roam*, 97–99. The Tuttle telegram is quoted in Childers to Jeppeson, O'Leary Papers, HMRC; Houston *Chronicle*, February 11, 1952; Houston *Post*, February 11, 1952, October 18, 1953; "Victory for the People," *Time*, May 25, 1953, 96.

24. Interviews with R. A. Childers, Grady Hardin, and William E. Moreland; Childers to Jeppeson, March 22, 1952, O'Leary Papers, HMRC; Houston *Post*, October 18, 1953; H. W. Bishop to Holger Jeppeson, April 7, 1952, General Correspondence, Board of Education, Houston Independent School District (hereafter cited as HISD).

25. Interviews with Grady Hardin, W. Kenneth Pope, and R. A. Childers.

26. Helen Thomas to Martin Dies, April 24, 1953; Martin Dies to Helen Thomas, April 29, 1953; Helen Thomas to Martin Dies, June 21, 1954 (quote); Helen Thomas to Martin Dies, June 27, 1954; Martin Dies to Helen Thomas, June 28, 1954; Mrs. J. C. Weitinger to Martin Dies, no date; Martin Dies to the Coordinator of Information, House of Representatives, June 3, 1954; Mrs. J. C. Weitinger to Martin Dies, February 15, 1954; all in Dies Papers, SHRC.

27. Mrs. E. M. Harrison to Price Daniel, February 2, 1953; Price Daniel to Mrs. E. M. Harrison, March 17, 1953; Bertie Maughmer to Price Daniel, June 10, 1953; Price Daniel to Bertie Maughmer, June 17, 1953; E. M. Biggers to Price Daniel, December 28, 1954; Price Daniel to E. M. Biggers, January 4, 1955, all in Daniel Papers, SHRC.

28. Interviews with Mary Drouin and Virginia Biggers; Houston *Chronicle*, February 6, 1952; unsigned (anonymous HISD teacher) to William E. Moreland, February 5, 1952, O'Leary Papers, HMRC; H. and B. Overstreet, *Strange Tactics of Extremism*, 170–171; Caute, *The Great Fear*, 372; Roy, *Apostles*, 234.

29. Louise Tennent to Ralph O'Leary, undated and unsigned to Moreland, February 5, 1952, both in O'Leary Papers, HMRC; interview with William E. Moreland.

30. Houston *Chronicle*, February 6, 1952.

31. Unsigned to Moreland, February 5, 1952, O'Leary Papers, HMRC; interview with William E. Moreland.

32. Patrick J. Nicholson, *In Time: An Anecdotal History of the First Fifty Years of the University of Houston* (Houston, 1977).

33. Houston *Post*, March 11, 12, 14, 1952, October 18, 1953; Houston *Chronicle*, March 11–14, 1952; interview with Louis J. Kestenberg.

34. Doctors for Freedom, untitled circular, March 16, 1952, and Daniel Jackson, M.D., to Henry A. Peterson, M.D., May 1, 1952, both in O'Leary Papers, HMRC; W. M. Wallis, M.D., to Jesse Jones, October 7, 1952, Jones Papers, BTHC; *Medical Record and Annals of the Harris County Medical Society* 46 (April 1952): 944.

35. Houston *Post*, October 19, 1953; Louise Tennent to Ralph O'Leary, n.d. and "Summary of J. H. Woods' Testimony to Better Business Bureau Concerning the Minute Women," both in O'Leary Papers, HMRC; Mrs. Charles C. Whitney to Margaret Bleil, November 1, 1953, Ebey Papers, HMRC.

36. Spellman, *Growing a Soul*, 369.

37. Pope, *A Pope at Roam*, 96; interviews with W. Kenneth Pope, Grady Hardin, and R. A. Childers.

38. Pope, *A Pope at Roam*, 100; interview with Pope.

39. Interviews with Pope and Hardin.

40. Houston *Post*, October 16–17, December 3, 1953; "Are the American 'Friends' Our Enemies?," undated circular in O'Leary Papers, HMRC; interview with Grady Hardin; Pope, *A Pope at Roam*, 95.

SIX: THE RED SCARE AND THE SCHOOLS

1. E. L. Doctorow, *The Book of Daniel* (New York, 1972), 132–133; Fuermann, *Reluctant Empire*, 61.

2. Caute, *The Great Fear*, 403, 405–406, 445.

3. Ibid., 294, 595. Dondero's remarks are in *Appendix to the Congressional Record, Proceedings and Debates of the Seventy-Ninth Congress, Second Session*, vol. 92, part 2 (Washington, D.C., 1946), A3516–A3518.

4. Interviews with Ida Darden, George Ebey, Margaret Bleil, and A. J. Tucker; E. M. Biggers to Price Daniel, August 14, 1953, Daniel Papers, SHRC.

5. Edmund E. Reutter, *The School Administrator and Subversive Activities* (New York, 1951), 8, 19; Revised Civil Statutes of Texas (1949 Supplement), section 2908b.

6. J. W. Edgar to City and County Superintendents (Texas), April 28, 1950, in author's possession; State of Texas, *House Journal*, 51st Legislature, 1st Called Session (February 23, 1950), 200–201.

7. Bascom Hayes, "To the Superintendent Addressed," May 9, 1955, and J. W. Edgar, "To All Superintendents," April 10, 1953, both in author's possession; *Vernon's Annotated Revised Civil Statutes of the State of Texas*, art. 6252-7, 447–450.

8. Rainey, *The Tower and the Dome*, 6–9; Green, *The Establishment in Texas Politics*, 84. See Dugger, *Invaded Universities*, for more on this thesis.

9. Rainey, *The Tower and the Dome*, 6.

10. Fuermann, *The Reluctant Empire*, 142–147; National Commission for the Defense of Democracy through Education of the National Education Association, *Report of an Investigation, Houston, Texas: A Study of Factors Related to Educational Unrest in a Large School System* (Washington, D.C., 1954), 18 (hereafter cited as NEA, *Report*); interviews with William E. Moreland and George W. Ebey.

11. Arthur Bestor, *Educational Wastelands: The Retreat from Learning in Our Public Schools* (Urbana, 1953), 43–47; Ronnie Dugger, "Training the Gifted," *The Texas Observer*, March 21, 1958, 8.

12. The Committee for Sound American Education, "Your Children Are Threatened" (Fall 1954), pamphlet in O'Leary Papers, HMRC.

13. Ibid.

14. S. A. Embry to the Houston *Post*, n.d., Ebey Papers, HMRC.

15. Interviews with Dallas Dyer McGregor, William E. Moreland, and Margaret Bleil.

16. Fuermann, *The Reluctant Empire*, 144–145; interview with A. J. Tucker.

17. Clippings from Houston *Post* and Houston *Chronicle*, October 1953, in Bell Papers, HMRC; Fuermann, *The Reluctant Empire*, 142, 144–145; interview with William E. Moreland.

18. Clipping from Houston *Post*, n.d., Bell Papers, HMRC; interview with William E. Moreland; "John Birch Society, Inc." (1962), brochure in Texas AFL-CIO Records, Series 25, Box 2, Labor Archives, University of Texas at Arlington.

19. Mrs. Earl Maughmer, Jr., to Senator William E. Jenner, April 30, 1953, Dies Papers, SHRC.

20. The Forum of Public Education, *A Handbook of Facts about the Houston Independent School District* (Houston, 1951), 8; NEA, *Report*, 15; Houston *Chronicle*, July 3, 1970; Houston *Post*, May 9, 1957; Ewing Werlein to Georgiana Williams, May 11, 1943, Hogg Papers, BTHC; H. L. Mills to Martin Dies, October 7, 1954, Dies Papers, SHRC.

21. Fuermann, *The Reluctant Empire*, 142.

22. Murphy, "Texas Business and McCarthy," 101.

23. Houston *Post*, November 28, 1975; interviews with W. Kenneth Pope and Grady Hardin.

24. Sue Brandt, "Russia Is Wiping Out 7 Sins for Bright Future," *The Daily Texan*, February 25, 1943, 2; Ewing Werlein to Homer P. Rainey, March 5, 1943, OPR, BTHC.

25. Ewing Werlein to Lyndon B. Johnson, January 24, 1952, Senate Files, Johnson Papers, LBJ Library; Ewing Werlein to William E. Moreland, January 29, 1952, General Correspondence Files, HISD; interview with William E. Moreland.

26. McComb, *Houston*, 164–165; Ewing Werlein, "To All Friends of the Public Schools of Houston," September 27, 1948, circular in Hogg Papers, BTHC; Houston *Post*, October 11, 1949; Green, *Establishment in Texas Politics*, 123.

27. O'Leary, reporter's notes, O'Leary Papers, HMRC; interview with Virginia Biggers.

28. McComb, *Houston*, 164; Houston *Press*, October 10, 25, 1949; Frank A. Magruder, *American Government* (Boston, 1947), 36.

29. Houston *Press*, October 25, November 15, 1949; interviews with William E. Moreland and Ray K. Daily.

30. Houston *Press*, October 26, 1949; interviews with William E. Moreland and Ray K. Daily.

31. Ronnie Dugger, "Houston's Textbook Woes," *The Texas Observer*, April 11, 1958, 5.

32. Carl Victor Little column, Houston *Press*, undated clipping, O'Leary Papers, HMRC.

33. Houston *Post*, October 19, 1953; John Wood, "The Greatest Subversive Plot in History—Report to the American People on UNESCO," *Congressional Record*, 82nd Congress, 1st Session (October 1951); interviews with Virginia Biggers, Louis J. Kestenberg, and Adria Allen.

34. Houston *Post*, October 19, 1953, and undated clipping in O'Leary

Papers, HMRC; Houston *Chronicle*, December 8, 1952; Ministers, Christian Churches of Harris County to Holger Jeppeson, March 30, 1952, General Correspondence Files, HISD; interviews with William E. Moreland, Louis J. Kestenberg, and Ray K. Daily.

35. Houston *Chronicle*, December 8, 1952.

36. Houston *Post*, October 21, 1953.

37. Houston *Post*, October 14, 21, 1953; interviews with Dallas Dyer McGregor, Virginia Biggers, and Ray K. Daily.

38. Houston *Chronicle*, October 31, 1952; O'Leary, reporter's notes, O'Leary Papers, HMRC.

39. Biographical file, Daily Papers, HMRC; interview with Ray K. Daily; Ray K. Daily to Ima Hogg, February 16, 1943, Hogg Papers, BTHC.

40. Interviews with A. J. Tucker, James Hippard, and Ray K. Daily.

41. Houston *Post*, October 15, 1952.

42. Committee for Sound American Education, campaign circular, October 29, 1952, O'Leary Papers, HMRC.

43. Houston *Press*, October 29, 1952; Houston *Post*, October 29, 1952.

44. William P. Hobby's speech in transcript form is in Box 3M443, Jones Papers, BTHC; Jesse Jones to A. Jennette Jones, December 8, 1952, Jones Papers, BTHC.

45. Houston *Post*, October 15, 1953.

46. Houston *Press*, October 29, 1952.

47. Houston *Post*, October 29, 1952; interview with Ray K. Daily.

48. Houston *Chronicle*, October 28, 1952; interview with Dallas Dyer McGregor.

49. Houston *Post*, October 21, 1953; O'Leary, reporter's notes, O'Leary Papers, HMRC; interview with Ray K. Daily. Both Daily and Rogers had been seriously Red-baited for over one year prior to the 1952 campaign. R. G. Schneider to Ray K. Daily, April 25, 1951, Daily Papers, HMRC.

50. Interview with James Hippard.

51. Houston *Post*, October 17, 1952; interviews with William E. Moreland and Dallas Dyer McGregor.

52. Houston *Post*, October 6, 9, 1952.

53. Houston *Post*, October 29, 1952; O'Leary, reporter's notes, O'Leary Papers, HMRC.

54. Carl Victor Little column, Houston *Press*, undated clipping, O'Leary Papers, HMRC.

55. Houston *Post*, November 6, 1952; interviews with Dallas Dyer McGregor and Ray K. Daily.

56. Interviews with A. J. Tucker, Dallas Dyer McGregor, James J. Hippard, Eleanor Ball, and Ray K. Daily.

57. Don E. Carleton, "McCarthyism in Local Elections: The Houston School Board Election of 1952," *The Houston Review* 3 (Winter 1981): 168–177.

58. Interview with Chris Dixie; James Delmar campaign brochure, May 1951, and Committee for Sound American Education, campaign brochure, November 1954, both in O'Leary Papers, HMRC.

59. NEA, *Report*, 14; Fuermann, *The Reluctant Empire*, 143; interviews with William E. Moreland, Eleanor Ball, and R. A. Childers.

60. Houston *Post*, July 8, 1971; interview with A. J. Tucker.

61. Houston *Post*, May 15, 1971; interviews with Eleanor Ball, Ray K. Daily, William E. Moreland, and Chris Dixie.

62. Houston *Post*, April 21, 1953, September 23, 1954; interviews with Eleanor Ball, Ray K. Daily, and A. J. Tucker.

63. Carter Wesley column, *The Informer*, undated clipping, Bell Papers, HMRC.

SEVEN: THE VICTIM IS A SYMBOL: THE GEORGE W. EBEY AFFAIR

1. In Irwin Shaw, *The Troubled Air* (New York, 1951), 252.

2. Houston *Post*, July 19, 1953 (quote); interviews with William E. Moreland and Ray K. Daily.

3. Interviews with Grady Hardin, W. Kenneth Pope, R. A. Childers, Eleanor Ball, George W. Ebey, and Ray K. Daily.

4. Interview with William E. Moreland; Houston *Post*, July 19, 1953.

5. Houston *Post*, July 10, 1953; interview with William E. Moreland.

6. William E. Moreland, "Statement on Members of the Board of Education, Houston Independent School District," July 15, 1953, Ebey Papers, HMRC; interview with Moreland.

7. Moreland, "Statement"; George W. Ebey to Jennie L. Davis, February 3, 1955; William E. Moreland to George W. Ebey, July 30, 1952, all in Ebey Papers, HMRC.

8. Ebey to Davis, February 3, 1955, Ebey Papers, HMRC; Houston *Post*, July 26, August 9, 1952.

9. Interviews with Moreland and Ebey; Ebey to Davis, February 3, 1955; Ebey to Moreland, February 11, 1953, all in Ebey Papers, HMRC.

10. Interview with Ebey.

11. George W. Ebey, "Personal File Form for Columbia University," June 8, 1953, and General Research Company, *George William Ebey*, 2 vols. (Houston, 1953), vol. 1, 2, all in Ebey Papers, HMRC.

12. Hugh Thomas, *The Spanish Civil War* (New York, 1961), 392 fn.; General Research Company, *Ebey*, vol. 2, 345–346; George W. Ebey to the Editor, *Honolulu Advertiser*, April 23, 1936, Ebey Papers, HMRC; Reutter, *The School Administrator*, 7.

13. Interview with Ebey; J. B. Matthews, "Communism and the Colleges," *American Mercury* 76 (May 1953): 111–115.

14. General Research Company, *Ebey*, vol. 1, 29–38.

15. Ebey, "Personal File Form"; Lauris Norstad to Commanding General, Army Air Forces, Personnel Services Division, Awards Branch, December 15, 1946, all in Ebey Papers, HMRC.

16. General Research Company, *Ebey*, vol. 1, 53–79; interview with Ebey.

17. Interview with Ebey; Joseph C. Goulden, *The Best Years, 1945–1950*

(New York, 1976), 52–65; Charles G. Bolte, "The New Veteran," *Life*, December 10, 1945, 57–58, 60, 63–64, 66.

18. Ebey to Davis, February 3, 1955, Ebey Papers, HMRC; "AVC Regrets," *Fortnight*, September 12, 1947, 16; George W. Ebey, "The Social Responsibility of the Veteran in a Democracy," *The Social Service Review* 21 (September 1947): 345–362.

19. Interview with Ebey; Goulden, *The Best Years*, 65; American Veterans Committee, "Statement Regarding Ineligibility of Communists for Membership in the AVC," Ebey Papers, HMRC.

20. General Research Company, *Ebey*, vol. 2, 341–344; interview with Ebey.

21. Interviews with Ebey and Moreland.

22. George W. Ebey, "Front Line Observations on Curriculum Improvement," *North Central Association Quarterly* 27 (January 1953): 21.

23. Houston *Post*, July 19, October 20, 1953.

24. Paul Rehmus to George W. Ebey, February 5, 1953, Ebey Papers, HMRC; interview with Ebey; General Research Company, *Ebey*, vol. 1, 125.

25. George Ebey to Leonor Ebey, August 20, 1952, Ebey Papers, HMRC; Houston *Press*, August 18, 1952; Houston *Post*, August 18, 1952.

26. Ebey to Moreland, February 11, 1953, Ebey to Davis, February 3, 1955, Ebey Papers, HMRC; interviews with Ebey and Moreland; Houston *Post*, July 22, 1953.

27. Interviews with Virginia Biggers, Adria Allen, Mary Drouin, A. J. Tucker, Ray K. Daily, Eleanor Ball, Margaret Bleil, William E. Moreland, and George W. Ebey; Andre and Mary Drouin to William Moreland, August 7, 1952, Ebey Papers, HMRC.

28. Interviews with Mary Drouin and Adria Allen; Houston *Post*, July 19, October 20, 1953.

29. Houston *Post*, July 19, 1953; James Delmar to Woodrow Seals, August 18, 1952; William Moreland to Norma Louise Barnett, August 26, 1952; W. Kenneth Pope to George Ebey, September 19, 1952, all in Ebey Papers, HMRC.

30. Paul A. Rehmus to George W. Ebey, September 3, 1952; clipping, *Portland Oregonian*, August 26, 1952; clipping, *The Oregon Daily Journal*, August 26, 1952, all in Ebey Papers, HMRC; Houston *Post*, July 19, 1953.

31. Rehmus to Ebey, September 3, 1952, Ebey Papers, HMRC.

32. Mrs. W. N. (Adria) Allen to Board of Education, HISD, September 22, 1952, General Correspondence Files, HISD; interview with Adria Allen.

33. George Ebey, untitled manuscripts of speeches, including September 23 (quote) and October 22, 1952, Ebey Papers, HMRC.

34. Houston *Post*, July 19, 1953; interview with George Ebey.

35. Houston *Post*, July 19, 1953; George W. Ebey, "Address to City Club," speech typescript, n.d., Ebey Papers, HMRC.

36. Mrs. W. J. Edwards, untitled brochure, January 1953, O'Leary Papers, HMRC; Ebey, "Address to City Club," Ebey Papers, HMRC; Edward L. Barrett, Jr., *The Tenney Committee* (Ithaca, N.Y., 1951).

37. George W. Ebey, "Reply to Mrs. W. J. Edwards," February 1953, typescript, and Bishop Donald Tippett to James Delmar, June 25, 1953, Ebey Papers, HMRC; Ingrid W. Scobie, "Jack B. Tenney and the 'Parasitic Menace': Anti-Communist Legislation in California, 1940–1949," *Pacific Historical Review* 43 (May 1974): 188–211; Caute, *The Great Fear*, 77–78.

38. Ebey, "Reply," Ebey Papers, HMRC; interview with George Ebey.

39. Ebey, "Address to City Club," and Ebey to Moreland, February 11, 1953, Ebey Papers, HMRC; interviews with Ebey and Moreland; Houston *Post*, July 29, 1953; Houston *Chronicle*, February 7, 1953.

40. Interview with George and Leonor Ebey; Paul Rehmus to George Ebey, December 19, 1952, Ebey Papers, HMRC.

41. George W. Ebey, "Partial Account of John Rogge's Activities," undated mimeographed material; John P. Rogge to W. W. Kemmerer and Hugh Roy Cullen, February 10, 1953; Ebey to Rehmus, February 17, 1953, all in Ebey Papers, HMRC; interviews with Virginia Biggers, Adria Allen, and George Ebey.

42. Spellman, *Growing a Soul*, 370–371, 379–380; interviews with W. Kenneth Pope and Grady Hardin.

43. Nicholson, *In Time*, 301; interviews with Louis J. Kestenberg and George W. Ebey.

44. S. A. Embry to Ralph S. O'Leary, n.d., Ebey Papers, HMRC (quote); interviews with Virginia Biggers, Adria Allen, Mary Drouin, and Louis J. Kestenberg.

45. Nicholson, *In Time*, 301–304; Houston *Post*, April 21–24, October 21, 1953; "Communist Party," Vertical File Collection, BTHC; interviews with Virginia Biggers, Adria Allen, Mary Drouin, Louis J. Kestenberg, A. J. Tucker, George Ebey, and Mrs. Ralph S. O'Leary. Mrs. O'Leary stated that her husband interviewed several University of Houston faculty members who insisted on anonymity. Some of the information from these interviews is in his reporter's notes, O'Leary Papers, HMRC.

46. Houston *Post*, April 3, 1953; Texas Legislature, *House Journal*, 53rd Legislature, Regular Session, 346.

47. *Dallas Morning News*, February 13, 1953; *House Journal*, 53rd Legislature, Regular Session, 3099–3100; *Gilmore* vs. *James* (Washington, D.C., 1967), 274 F. Supp. 75; Greg Olds, "Student Loyalty Oath Buried—Fourteen Years after Its Death," *The Texas Observer*, February 17, 1967, 8–9.

48. *Dallas Morning News*, February 13, 1953; interview with Maury Maverick, Jr.; *House Journal*, 53rd Legislature, Regular Session, 347–349.

49. *House Journal*, 53rd Legislature, Regular Session, 3176; Fort Worth *Star-Telegram*, March 11, April 20, 1953.

50. *Dallas Morning News*, May 3, 1953; Houston *Post*, April 10, 1953.

51. *Dallas Morning News*, April 28, 1953; *El Paso Times*, April 28, 1953; *House Journal*, 53rd Legislature, Regular Session, 1590–1591, 1672–1681; *Senate Journal*, 53rd Legislature, Regular Session, 177, 511; interview with Maury Maverick, Jr.

52. Houston *Post*, October 20, 1953. Ralph O'Leary of the *Post* learned about this meeting from several women who claimed to have participated in it. They refused to allow O'Leary to reveal their identity and they remain anonymous. Interview with Mrs. Ralph S. O'Leary.

53. Houston *Post*, October 20, 1953; Houston *Press*, May 13, 1953; interviews with Moreland and Ebey.

54. Houston *Post*, May 12, July 19, 1953; Board of Education, HISD, *Minutes* 40, 15–16; interviews with George Ebey, William E. Moreland, and A. J. Tucker.

55. Houston *Post*, July 19, 1953.

56. Interviews with George Ebey and A. J. Tucker; Houston *Post*, July 19, 1953.

57. Interview with Ebey; Houston *Press*, May 19, 1953; Houston *Post*, May 13, 1953.

58. Ebey, "Address to City Club," Ebey Papers, HMRC; Houston *Press*, May 20, 1953; interview with Ebey.

59. Jack Harwell to T. Otto Nall, June 9, 1953, and Bernard Nolting to Ralph S. O'Leary, n.d., O'Leary Papers, HMRC; interviews with W. Kenneth Pope and Grady Hardin.

60. Roy, "Methodism's Malcontents"; Goodman, *The Committee*, 352; Ralph Winnett and William R. Bectel, "The Protestant Church under Fire," *New Republic*, July 27, 1953, 10; interview with W. Kenneth Pope.

61. Houston *Chronicle*, May 27, 1953, and Jack Harwell to T. Otto Nall, June 9, 1953, O'Leary Papers, HMRC; Spellman, *Growing a Soul*, 230–231, 366, 370; interviews with R. A. Childers, W. Kenneth Pope, and Grady Hardin.

62. Interview with Grady Hardin; Spellman, *Growing a Soul*, 371–372; *Journal of the Fifteenth Annual Session of the Texas Annual Conference of the Methodist Church, June 1–5, 1953*, 110–111.

63. Margaret Bleil to James Delmar, May 21, 1953, Ebey Papers, HMRC; Houston *Post*, July 19, 1953.

64. Mrs. J. Edward Jones to the Editor, Houston *Chronicle*, June 4, 1953.

65. Houston *Press*, May 26, June 3, 1953; Houston *Chronicle*, May 25, 1953.

66. Houston *Chronicle*, May 20, 1953.

67. Houston *Chronicle*, May 26, 1953.

68. J. B. Adoue to Members, Property Owners Association of Houston, Inc., June 29, 1953, Ebey Papers, HMRC.

69. J. H. Stewart, "To All Houston Barbers," mimeographed circular, July 7, 1953, Ebey Papers, HMRC.

70. Harvey Schechter to Thomas Friedman, June 5, 1953; Eddie Dyer to George Ebey, May 19, 1953; Kenneth Fellows to William E. Moreland, May 19, 1953, all in Ebey Papers, HMRC; interview with Ebey.

71. Allan Rhinehart to Stone Wells, May 13, 1953; Helen Farrens to James Delmar, May 18, 1953; Miner T. Patton to the Editor, Houston *Press*, May 21, 1953, all in Ebey Papers, HMRC.

72. Harold Fey to Gladys Kinsler, June 4, 1953, Ebey Papers, HMRC.

73. Houston *Chronicle*, June 16, 1953.

74. Houston *Press*, July 9, 1953; interview with Ebey.

75. General Research Company, *Ebey*, Ebey Papers, HMRC; Ebey, "Address to City Club," Ebey Papers, HMRC; interview with Ebey.

76. General Research Company, *Ebey*, vol. 2, 174–335, Ebey Papers, HMRC.

77. Norman K. Hamilton to the Board of Education, HISD, August 5, 1953; Joy Gibser to James Delmar, August 10, 1953, Ebey Papers, HMRC.

78. Ebey, "Address to City Club," Ebey Papers, HMRC; Houston *Post*, November 30, 1972; Green, *The Establishment in Texas Politics*, 163; George Ebey to Don E. Carleton, April 12, 1972, letter in author's possession.

79. Houston *Post*, July 14, 1953.

80. Board of Education, HISD, *Minutes* 40, 287–290; Houston *Press*, July 14, 1953; Houston *Post*, July 14, 1953.

81. Houston *Post*, July 15, 16, 1953; interview with Eleanor Ball.

82. George Ebey to Jennie Davis, February 3, 1955, Ebey Papers, HMRC; interview with Ebey.

83. Houston *Post*, July 16, 1953; Jack Binion, "Brief in Behalf of Dr. George W. Ebey," typescript, July 15, 1953, Ebey Papers, HMRC.

84. George W. Ebey, "Statement to the Board of Education," July 15, 1953, typescript in Ebey Papers, HMRC.

85. Houston *Press*, July 16, 1953.

86. Board of Education, HISD, *Minutes* 40, 294–300.

87. Houston *Press*, July 16, 1953; Houston *Post*, July 16, 1953.

88. Houston *Post*, July 16, 1953.

89. Houston *Chronicle*, July 16, 1953; Houston *Post*, July 16, 1953.

90. "Houston: That Word," *Time*, July 27, 1953, 51; "Ebey Story," *Nation*, September 26, 1953, 242; "School Man Fired as Controversial," *The Christian Century*, August 17, 1953, 885; John K. Norton to George W. Ebey, August 7, 1953, and Bishop Tippet to George W. Ebey, August 18, 1953, Ebey Papers, HMRC.

91. Urban League of Portland, "The Tragedy of Dr. Ebey," mimeographed circular, 1954, Ebey Papers, HMRC; *The Oregonian*, July 17, 1953; *Oregon Daily Journal*, July 18, 1953.

92. Richard Barss, "The Ebey Affair," *The Education Digest* 19 (November 1953): 1–3.

93. George W. Ebey to Wilma Morrison, July 16, 1953, Ebey Papers, HMRC.

94. John Crossland to James Carey, July 16, 1953, Ebey Papers, HMRC; *Jewish Herald-Voice* (Houston), July 30, 1953, clipping in O'Leary Papers, HMRC.

95. Houston *Post*, July–August, 1953; Houston *Chronicle*, July–August, 1953; Houston *Press*, July 18, 1953.

96. Houston *Press*, July 21, 1953.

97. George Ebey to Jennie L. Davis, February 3, 1955, Ebey Papers, HMRC.

98. Houston *Post*, July 9, 1953.

99. Hulburd, *It Happened in Pasadena*, 162; Caute, *The Great Fear*, 403–445.

100. Hulburd, *It Happened in Pasadena*, ix.

101. Ebey to Davis, February 3, 1955, Ebey Papers, HMRC; interview with Ebey.

EIGHT: "OVETA DOESN'T BROOK BACK-TALK"

1. Maverick, "San Antonio," 12–13.

2. Harvey Schechter to Dr. Robert Skaife, June 5, 1953, Ebey Papers, HMRC; Houston *Press*, June 22, 1953.

3. Houston *Press*, May 29, 1953.

4. Harvey Schechter to Dr. Robert Skaife, June 5, 1953, Ebey Papers, HMRC; O'Leary, reporter's notes taken from an unpublished investigation by the Houston *Post* on Joe Worthy, no date [1953?], O'Leary Papers, HMRC.

5. NEA, *Report*, 18; Houston *Press*, May 20, 1953.

6. "Joe Worthy Speaks Out," tape recording of radio program, May 20, 1953, Houston, Texas, Ebey Papers, HMRC; interview with Ebey.

7. Houston *Press*, May 25, 1953.

8. NEA, *Report*, 47–48.

9. O'Leary, reporter's notes, O'Leary Papers, HMRC; interviews with Kate Bell, Margaret Bleil, and Eleanor Ball.

10. Interviews with Louis J. Kestenberg and Mrs. Ralph O'Leary; O'Leary, reporter's notes, O'Leary Papers, HMRC; Houston *Post*, October 21, 1953; Nicholson, *In Time*, 301–304.

11. Reeves, *The Life and Times of Joe McCarthy*, 512; Murphy, "Texas Business and McCarthy," 49; *Fortune* (May 1954): 100; Art Shields, "The Man Who Gave Joe a Cadillac," *The Daily Worker*, October 22, 1953.

12. Houston *Press*, October 22, 1953; Houston *Post*, October 22, 1953; *Dallas Morning News*, September 30, October 1, 1953; Reeves, *The Life and Times of Joe McCarthy*, 512–513, 759.

13. Curtis Quarles to W. P. Hobby, July 29, 1953, Ebey Papers, HMRC.

14. Houston *Post*, May 5, 1950.

15. Interviews with Joe Ingraham and Jack Porter, November 9, December 16, 1972, May 21, 1973, Oral History Collection, DDE Library; Mary Drouin to Price Daniel, December 15, 1952, Daniel Papers, SHRC.

16. Parmet, *Eisenhower*, 76–77, 91.

17. Interviews with Virginia Biggers and Mary Drouin.

18. Fuermann, *The Reluctant Empire*, 145; Parmet, *Eisenhower*, 76; James A. Clark and Weldon Hart, *The Tactful Texan: A Biography of Governor Will Hobby* (New York, 1958), 194–196.

19. Sherman Adams, *First Hand Report* (New York, 1961), 62, 306; Dwight D. Eisenhower, *Mandate for Change, 1953–1956* (New York, 1963), 129.

20. Clark and Hart, *The Tactful Texan*, 197; Doctors for Freedom, mimeographed circular, March 16, 1953, O'Leary Papers (first quote). For the right-wing attack on Hobby and HEW, see Houston *Post*, October 31, 1953,

and letters and telegrams in the Eisenhower Papers, General File 182, Box
1286, including Virginia Biggers to DDE, March 12, 1953; Elsie Daniel to
DDE, March 12, 1953; Mrs. J. D. Mabry to DDE, March 13, 1953; and Dr.
R. L. Royce to DDE, March 13, 1953 (second quote). See also Mrs. J. D.
Mabry to Martin Dies, January 10, 1953, Dies Papers, SHRC (third quote) and
Mrs. John W. Daniel to Price Daniel, March 12, 1953, Daniel Papers, SHRC
(fourth quote).

21. Caute, *The Great Fear*, 293, 472; interview with Virginia Biggers.

22. William S. White, "Joe McCarthy, the Man with Power," *Look*, June 16,
1953, 29–33.

23. Reeves, *The Life and Times of Joe McCarthy*, 498–503.

24. Ibid., 141–143; H. R. Cullen to DDE, October 31, 1953, Central Files,
Eisenhower Papers, DDE Library (first quote); interview with Eleanor Ball
(second quote).

25. Interviews with Marguerite Johnston and Mrs. Ralph S. O'Leary.

26. Interviews with George Carmack, George Fuermann, and Mrs. Ralph
O'Leary.

27. Caute, *The Great Fear*, 503–504, 516–517; Les K. Adler, "The Politics of
Culture: Hollywood and the Cold War," in Griffith and Theoharis (eds.), *The
Specter*, 242–260.

28. Houston *Press*, March 9, 20, 1953; Houston *Post*, July 6, 9, 1953.

29. Interviews with Mrs. Ralph O'Leary and George Carmack; Ralph S.
O'Leary to the Broun Award Committee, American Newspaper Guild,
January 15, 1954, O'Leary Papers, HMRC.

30. Biographical notes in O'Leary Papers, HMRC.

31. O'Leary's informant remains unidentified. The following discussion of
O'Leary's research is based on his own version as revealed in his letter to the
Broun Award Committee, January 15, 1954, O'Leary Papers, HMRC, and an
interview with Mrs. O'Leary.

32. Houston *Post*, October 11, 1953.

33. Houston *Post*, October 11, 21, 1953; George Schnitzer, Sr., to the
Houston *Post*, April 15, 1954, OPR, BTHC; interview with Mrs. Ralph
O'Leary.

34. Arthur Laro to Bill Collyns, November 27, 1953; Gordon Hall to Ralph
O'Leary, February 14, 1954, all in O'Leary Papers, HMRC; Ann Wurzbach to
John McCully, November 4, 1953, and McCully to Wurzbach, November 10,
1953, Box 8, Series 25, AFL-CIO Records, University of Texas at Arlington;
Atlanta *Constitution*, October 31, 1953; St. Louis *Post-Dispatch*, November 7,
1953; "Houston Scare," *Time*, November 2, 1953, 50; Ralph S. O'Leary,
"Daughters of Vigilantism," *Nation*, January 9, 1954, 26–28.

35. Cullinan's letter is in the Houston *Post*, October 21, 1953; William P.
Hobby, Jr., to Ralph O'Leary, November 1, 1953.

36. Interview with J. R. Parten. For the Shivers-Parten feud, see Houston
Post, July 16, 1952; Reeves, *Freedom and the Foundation*, 34.

37. J. R. Parten to David Freeman, October 21, 1953; Parten to Robert
Hutchins, October 27, 1953; Parten to Clifford Case, November 30, 1953; and

Case to Parten, December 3, 1953, all in Parten Papers, J.R. Parten Oil Company, Houston, Texas; Paul Lazerfeld and Wagner Thielens, Jr., *The Academic Mind: Social Scientists in a Time of Crisis* (Chicago, 1958).

38. Herold C. Hunt to Clifford Case, January 18, 1954, Parten Papers.

39. Clifford Case to the Members of the Board of the Fund for the Republic, memorandum, January 22, 1954, Parten Papers; Reeves, *Freedom and the Foundation*, 84; Caute, *The Great Fear*, 429.

40. Claude Franklin to Ralph O'Leary, March 11, 1954, O'Leary Papers, HMRC; Houston *Post*, November 13, 1963.

41. Interview with Mrs. Ralph O'Leary.

42. Houston *Post*, October 19, 1953.

43. Houston *Post*, October 31, 1953.

44. Timmons, *Jesse H. Jones*, 389–390.

45. Houston *Chronicle*, December 1, 1953.

46. Houston *Post*, October 23, 1953; J. C. Weitinger, Ross Biggers, and Willard O. Hedrick to the Houston *Post*, October 22, 1953, O'Leary Papers, HMRC.

47. Houston *Post*, October 24, 1953.

48. Houston *Post*, undated clipping, O'Leary Papers, HMRC.

49. Houston *Post*, December 3, 1953; Faye Weitinger to Allan Shivers, February 17, 1954, Box 180, Shivers Papers, Texas State Archives; Clark and Hart, *The Tactful Texan*, 198.

50. Dies, December ?, 1953; Martin Dies to Mrs. J. C. Weitinger, December 8, 1953; Mrs. J. C. Weitinger to Martin Dies, February 15, 1954; Martin Dies to Mrs. J.C. Weitinger, March 2, 1954, all in Dies Papers, SHRC.

51. NEA, *Report*, 2.

52. Richard Barss to Robert Skaife, July 17, 1953, Ebey Papers, HMRC; Houston *Post*, July 30, 1953; interview with Margaret Bleil.

53. Houston *Post*, October 6, 1953; interview with Margaret Bleil; Houston *Chronicle*, October 6, 7, 1953.

54. Margaret Bleil to Richard Kennan, November 18, 1953, Ebey Papers, HMRC; Charles H. Tennyson to Richard B. Kennan, December 8, 1953, Bell Papers, HMRC.

55. Houston *Post*, July 21, 1953; Houston *Chronicle*, undated clipping, Bell Papers, HMRC; Houston *Press*, July 30, 1953.

56. Houston *Chronicle*, undated clipping, Bell Papers, HMRC; Houston *Press*, July 23, 1953; Houston *Chronicle*, August 20, 1953; interview with William E. Moreland.

57. Houston *Chronicle*, August 20, December 1, 1953.

58. Houston *Chronicle*, January 21–27, 1954.

59. Houston *Chronicle*, January 10, 12, 1954.

60. Houston *Press*, undated clipping, Bell Papers, HMRC; interview with William E. Moreland.

61. NEA, *Report*, 11–12; Houston *Chronicle*, January 24, 1954.

62. NEA, *Report*, 11–12; interview with Margaret Bleil, Kate Bell, A. J. Tucker, and Mrs. Ralph O'Leary.

63. Houston *Post*, January 31, 1954; interview with A. J. Tucker.

64. NEA, *Report*, 12; Houston *Chronicle*, February 4, 1954.

65. The Jaeger-Gilmore episode is based on accounts in the Houston *Post*, March 11, 1954; Houston *Press*, March 9, 1954; and Ronnie Dugger, "Ordeal by Righteousness," *The Texas Observer*, March 7, 1958, 1, 4; Charles Gallenkamp, "D. H. Lawrence and Subversion," *New Republic*, April 19, 1954, 22.

66. Houston *Post*, May 24, 1954; George Ebey to Jennie L. Davis, February 3, 1955, Ebey Papers, HMRC.

67. Interviews with Margaret Bleil, Dallas Dyer McGregor, A. J. Tucker, R. A. Childers, Kate Bell, and William Moreland.

NINE: DEMAGOGUES IN AUSTIN: McCARTHY AT SAN JACINTO

1. D. B. Hardeman, "Shivers of Texas: A Tragedy in Three Acts," *Harper's Magazine* (November 1956): 54; E. M. Biggers to Price Daniel, August 14, 1953, Daniel Papers, SHRC.

2. Caute, *The Great Fear*, 49.

3. Virginia Hedrick to Jesse Jones, February 10, May 14, June 13, 1955, Jones Papers, BTHC.

4. George E. Reedy, Jr., to Lyndon B. Johnson, January 21, 1954, Box 374, Senate Files, Johnson Papers, LBJ Library.

5. Sam Low to Lyndon B. Johnson, January 22, 1954, Box 25, Select Names, Senate Files, Johnson Papers, LBJ Library.

6. *New York Times*, February 22, 26, 1954; Houston *Post*, undated clipping, Clipping Files, Texas AFL-CIO Records, University of Texas at Arlington; interview with Virginia Biggers.

7. Houston *Post*, undated clipping, Clipping Files, Texas AFL-CIO Records, University of Texas at Arlington; interview with Virginia Biggers; Merle Miller, *Lyndon: An Oral Biography* (New York, 1980), 157–159.

8. For more on Schultz, see Reeves, *The Life and Times of Joe McCarthy*, 642, 658, and Caute, *The Great Fear*, 444, 522, 573; Houston *Post*, February 1, 3, 1954.

9. For a detailed analysis of the Shivers-Yarborough contest, see Green, *The Establishment in Texas Politics*, 135–170, as well as idem, "McCarthyism in Texas: The 1954 Campaign," *The Southern Quarterly* 16 (April 1978): 255–276; Sam Kinch and Stuart Long, *Allan Shivers: The Pied Piper of Texas Politics* (Austin, 1973), 147–150; Clark and Hart, *The Tactful Texan*, 198; Allan Shivers, "To the People of Texas," *Department of Public Safety Guide to Safe Driving*, Box 1977/81, 115, Shivers Papers, Texas State Archives.

10. Green, "McCarthyism in Texas," 259; Houston *Post*, October 11, 1953. For Minute Women reaction to Shivers' charges, see Letters to the Editor sections, Houston *Chronicle*, Houston *Post*, and Houston *Press*, December 1953, January 1954.

11. "Press Memorandum," Office of the Governor, November 27, 1953, and

"Report," State Industrial Commission, December 7, 1953, both in Shivers Papers, Texas State Archives.

12. Green, "McCarthyism in Texas," 261; Houston *Post*, March 10, 1954; unidentified clipping of a United Press International story, January 28, 1954, in Clipping Files, Texas AFL-CIO Records, University of Texas at Arlington; Austin *American*, February 14, 1954.

13. Fort Worth *Star-Telegram*, February 16, 1954; Green, "McCarthyism in Texas," 260; Caute, *The Great Fear*, 62, 70–72; Walter Gellhorn, *The States and Subversion* (Ithaca, New York, 1952).

14. L. E. Page, "Statement to Meeting of the Post Commanders and Adjutants," January 16, 1954, Shivers Papers, Texas State Archives; Green, "McCarthyism in Texas," 259, 261; Houston *Post*, March 10, 1954.

15. Houston *Post*, March 10, 1954; *Dallas Morning News*, April 2, 1954.

16. *Dallas Morning News*, March 11, 1954; San Antonio *Express*, March 10, 1954.

17. Miller, *Lyndon*, 162; unidentified clippings of a United Press International story, March 14, 1954, and an Associated Press story, March 12, 1954, Clipping Files, Texas AFL-CIO Records, University of Texas at Arlington; *Dallas Morning News*, March 17, 1954; *House Journal*, 53rd Legislature, 1st Called Session, 35–37, 51; Caute, *The Great Fear*, 72.

18. Green, "McCarthyism in Texas," 260; Corpus Christi *Times*, April 1, 1954.

19. *Dallas Morning News*, April 1, 1954; Corpus Christi *Times*, April 1, 1954.

20. *House Journal*, 53rd Legislature, 1st Called Session, 368–371; interview with Maury Maverick, Jr.; Corpus Christi *Caller*, April 9, 1954.

21. *House Journal*, 53rd Legislature, 1st Called Session, 368–371; interview with Maury Maverick, Jr.

22. *House Journal*, 53rd Legislature, 1st Called Session, 361–363; interview with Maury Maverick, Jr.

23. Green, "McCarthyism in Texas," 260–261; Corpus Christi *Caller*, April 9, 1954; Houston *Post*, April 17, 1954; *Vernon's Annotated Statutes*, art. 6889-3A, 367–370.

24. *New York Times*, July 4, 1954; Tom Curtis, "Intelligence in Houston," *The Texas Observer*, March 28, 1975, 6–7.

25. Ronnie Dugger, "John Stanford's Books and Papers," *The Texas Observer*, February 7, 1964, 8–10, and "What the Officers Saw Fit to Seize," *The Texas Observer*, February 5, 1965, 11–12; *Stanford* vs. *Texas* 379 US 476, January 18, 1965; Maury Maverick, Jr., to the author, November 1, 1983.

26. Caute, *The Great Fear*, 107.

27. Ibid., 107, 541; Reeves, *The Life and Times of Joe McCarthy*, 553; Griffith, *Politics of Fear*, 243–269.

28. Fort Worth *Star-Telegram*, March 28, 1954; Houston *Post*, April 4, 7, 1954; Roderick J. Watts to Price Daniel, November 6, 1954, Daniel Papers, SHRC.

29. Reeves, *The Life and Times of Joe McCarthy*, 583; Houston *Post*, April 4, 7,

1954; *The Daily Texan*, March 30, 31, April 1, 6, 7, 1954; James Presley, *A Saga of Wealth: The Rise of the Texas Oilman* (New York, 1978), 322.

30. *House Journal*, 53rd Legislature, 1st Called Session, 197–198, 260; unidentified clipping of an Associated Press story, April 6, 1954, clipping of an Associated Press story, April 6, 1954, Clipping Files, AFL-CIO Records, University of Texas at Arlington; interview with Maury Maverick, Jr.

31. Reeves, *The Life and Times of Joe McCarthy*, 579, 590; interviews with Adria Allen and Virginia Biggers.

32. See Reeves, *The Life and Times of Joe McCarthy*, 579–596, for the deep controversy swirling about the McCarthy hearings; transcript of a telephone conversation, Hugh Roy Cullen to Lyndon B. Johnson, April 8, 1954, Box 117, "LBJ-A" Subject Files, Johnson Papers, LBJ Library; Houston *Post*, April 10, 1954.

33. Cullen to LBJ, telephone transcript, April 8, 1954, Johnson Papers, LBJ Library.

34. Unidentified clippings of UPI and AP stories, April 15–17, 1954, Clipping Files, Texas AFL-CIO Records, University of Texas at Arlington.

35. Fuermann, *The Reluctant Empire*, 93; Reeves, *The Life and Times of Joe McCarthy*, 594; Houston *Post*, April 22, 1954.

36. Ray, *The Grand Huckster*, 202–203.

37. *The Daily Texan*, April 22, 1954.

38. Reeves, *The Life and Times of Joe McCarthy*, 619.

39. Caute, *The Great Fear*, 541.

40. Murphy, "Texas Business and McCarthy," 100–101, 208, 211–212, 214, 216; Reeves, *The Life and Times of Joe McCarthy*, 604.

41. Interviews with Jack Porter and Joe Ingraham, Oral History Collection, DDE Library; Houston *Post*, undated clipping, Clipping Files, AFL-CIO Records, University of Texas at Arlington; Houston *Press*, July 27, 1954; Mrs. J. C. Weitinger to Senator Price Daniel, August 16, 1953, Daniel Papers, SHRC.

42. Bayley, *Joe McCarthy and the Press*, 174–175.

43. Houston *Chronicle*, June 2, 1954. For the Lustron affair, see Reeves, *The Life and Times of Joe McCarthy*, 152–158.

44. Letters quoted were sent to the *Chronicle* by Eleanor Watt (June 6, 1954), Faye Weitinger (June 5, 1954), Lucille Ray (June 2, 1954), Mrs. M. A. Lamkin (June 2, 1954), Mrs. J. D. Mabry (June 3, 1954), and Elsie Daniel (June 5, 1954), all in Folder 4, Box 3M445, Jones Papers, BTHC.

45. See George Green's "McCarthyism in Texas" in the *Southern Quarterly* for a full discussion of the Shivers-Yarborough campaign of 1954. The Shivers quotation is from page 262. For Minute Women activity in support of Shivers, see Mrs. J. D. Mabry to Martin Dies, September 7, 1954, Dies Papers, SHRC.

46. Houston *Post*, undated clipping, O'Leary Papers, HMRC.

47. Kinch and Long, *Allan Shivers*, 158; Green, "McCarthyism in Texas," 265.

48. Green, *Establishment in Texas Politics*, 155–156, 158–159. See also Donald

Parker, "The Texas Gubernatorial Campaign of 1954" (M.A. thesis, Texas Christian University, 1975).

49. Interviews with Grady Hardin, Kenneth Pope, Louis Kestenberg, Eleanor Ball, R. A. Childers, A. J. Tucker, and Ray K. Daily; Houston *Post*, November 1, 1954.

50. Houston *Post*, October 5, 1954; interviews with A. J. Tucker, R. A. Childers, and Eleanor Ball.

51. Houston *Post*, November 2, 1954.

52. Houston *Post*, November 1–2, 1954.

53. Ibid.; Houston *Chronicle*, August 29, 1965.

54. Houston *Chronicle*, undated clipping, O'Leary Papers, HMRC; interviews with A. J. Tucker, Margaret Bleil, and Eleanor Ball.

55. Houston *Post*, November 2–3, 1954; interviews with A. J. Tucker, William Moreland, and R. A. Childers; Jesse Jones to R. A. Childers, November 5, 1954, Jones Papers, BTHC.

56. Reeves, *The Life and Times of Joe McCarthy*, 662, 665, 671. The pro-McCarthy mail is in the Senate Files, Johnson Papers, LBJ Library and similar files in the Dies and Daniel Papers, SHRC. *Dallas Morning News*, December 3, 1954.

57. NEA, *Report*, 12–13, 60–61.

58. Ibid., 18, 43–44.

59. Ibid., 31–32.

60. Houston *Chronicle*, December 30, 1954.

61. *New York Times*, December 30, 1954; "Teachers and Houston," *Newsweek*, February 15, 1954, 64; Houston *Chronicle*, December 30, 1954; Houston *Press*, December 29, 1954.

62. Houston *Chronicle*, April 27, 1955; Houston *Post*, April 26, 1955; "Houston Letter," *The Texas Observer*, September 21, 1955, 5; interview with William Moreland.

TEN: BERTIE AND THE BOARD

1. Mrs. Earl Maughmer to Senator William E. Jenner, April 30, 1953, Dies Papers, SHRC.

2. Virginia Biggers to the Houston Bar Association, September 9, 1955, Box 3M444, Jones Papers, BTHC; interviews with Virginia Biggers and Adria Allen; Citizens League for School Home Rule, "To All Who Believe in Home Rule," undated [ca. 1955] mimeographed circular, Bell Papers, HMRC; Ronnie Dugger, "150,000 Young Minds," *The Texas Observer*, February 21, 1958, 8; "Dr. Kerr's Plan," *The Texas Observer*, January 31, 1958, 5.

3. McComb, *Houston*, 166; Houston *Post*, February 19, 28, May 1, 1956; interviews with William Moreland and A. J. Tucker.

4. Green, *The Establishment in Texas Politics*, 171–176.

5. Interview with Dallas Dyer McGregor; Houston *Press*, August 14, 1953, September 7, 1955, August 11, 1956.

6. Interview with Dallas Dyer McGregor; "Bertie and the Board," *Time*, August 15, 1960, 60; Houston *Press*, August 11, 1956.

7. Houston *Post*, October 17, 1956.

8. Houston *Post*, October 24, 1956; "Bertie and the Board," 60; Dugger, "150,000 Young Minds," 8.

9. Ronnie Dugger, "Houston's Textbook Woes," *The Texas Observer*, April 11, 1958, 5; "Houston School Board Conservatives Elected," *The Texas Observer*, November 4, 1956, 7.

10. "Bertie and the Board," 60; Houston *Post*, November 7, 1956.

11. Dugger, "150,000 Young Minds," 8; "A Houston Teacher," *The Texas Observer*, March 7, 1958, 7.

12. Board of Education, HISD, *Minutes*, November 12, 1956, 26, December 10, 1956, 82–83, October 28, 1957, 332; Houston *Post*, October 29, 1957; Houston *Press*, November 14, 1956; Ronnie Dugger, "Education in Orthodoxy," *The Texas Observer*, March 14, 1958, 8.

13. Dugger, "150,000 Young Minds," 8, and "Houston's Textbook Woes," 5, 8; HISD, *Minutes*, March 25, 1957, 371; "Bertie and the Board," 60.

14. HISD, *Minutes*, March 25, 1957, 260, 362–363; Houston *Press*, March 22, 1957; "Pro-UN Books Fought," *The Texas Observer*, April 2, 1957, 8; Dugger, "Houston's Textbook Woes," 5, 8; Houston *Post*, March 26, 1957; *New York Times*, March 27, 1957, vol. 25, 7; "Bertie and the Board," 60; interview with William E. Moreland.

15. Interview with William E. Moreland; HISD, *Minutes*, April 8, 1957, 63, April 10, 1957, 71; "The Last Brake?," *Time*, April 22, 1957, 54; Houston *Post*, April 9, 1957; Dugger, "Education in Orthodoxy," 1.

16. "Houston Schools Embroiled," *The Texas Observer*, April 16, 1957, 6; HISD, *Minutes*, April 10, 1957, 66, 68; Houston *Post*, April 11, 1957; Dugger, "Education in Orthodoxy," 1.

17. "Cotton Curtain," *Time*, August 5, 1957, 42; Ronnie Dugger, "Board Purges Social Courses," *The Texas Observer*, March 28, 1958, 1, 8.

18. Arden MacNab, "Houston Teacher Tells of Pressures," *The Texas Observer*, November 22, 1957, 6; interviews with Margaret Bleil, Kate Bell, and three HISD classroom teachers who have asked to remain anonymous.

19. Houston *Press*, May 10, 1956.

20. Houston *Post*, July 1, 1957.

21. Mike Dorfman to Richard [?], typescript memorandum, June 17, 1958, and Neil McNeil to Mike Dorfman, August 1, 1957, both in "Arthur Mandell," Clipping Files, Houston *Press* Records, HMRC.

22. Houston *Press*, October 17, 1958.

23. Houston *Post*, February 14, 25, 1958.

24. Houston *Post*, February 24, 1959; interview with Dallas Dyer McGregor.

25. Houston *Press*, January 14, June 28, October 9, 17, 1958; Houston *Post*, June 24, 1958; interview with Dallas Dyer McGregor.

26. Houston *Press*, October 9, 17, 1958; interviews with Eleanor Ball and R. A. Childers; "The Houston Schools," *The Texas Observer*, October 31, 1958,

27. Houston *Press*, October 9, 17, 1958; interview with Dallas Dyer McGregor; McComb, *Houston*, 167.

28. HISD, *Minutes*, February 23, 1959, 308–309; Houston *Post*, February 24, 1959.

29. Interview with Dallas Dyer McGregor.

30. Houston *Post*, July 4, 13, 1960; Houston *Press*, July 13, 1960; "Bertie and the Board," 60.

31. Houston *Press*, August 11, 1960; HISD, *Minutes*, August 30, 1960, 164–166.

ELEVEN: CONCLUSION: BEYOND THE RED SCARE

1. In Arthur Miller, *The Crucible* (New York, 1968), act 2, 69.

2. Interview with Adria Allen.

3. For more on the Radical Right, see Davis (ed.), *The Fear of Conspiracy*, 315–348; Lipset and Raab, *The Politics of Unreason*, 248–337; and Bell, *The Radical Right*.

4. "Houston Board Feels Its Muscles," *The Texas Observer*, July 1, 1961, 6; McComb, *Houston*, 167.

5. Houston *Chronicle*, May 7, 1961; "Houston's Economic Course," *The Texas Observer*, May 20, 1961, 7; "Controversial Lectures Set," *The Texas Observer*, April 15, 1961, 5; "Strube Directs High School's Weekly Series," *The Texas Observer*, April 29, 1961, 1; interviews with HISD teachers who prefer to remain anonymous.

6. Houston *Post*, April 9, 11, 1961; "Roberts Controversy Rages," *The Texas Observer*, April 29, 1961, 3.

7. *The Texas Observer*, May 20, 1961, 8; Willie Morris, "Houston's Superpatriots," *Harper's Magazine* (October 1961): 54.

8. "A Houston Travesty," *The Texas Observer*, June 17, 1961, 4; "Houston Board Feels Its Muscles," 6; interview with Margaret Bleil.

9. Houston *Chronicle*, May 7, 1961; Epstein and Forster, *The Radical Right*, 74–76; Morris, "Houston's Superpatriots," 52–53.

10. Lipset and Raab, *The Politics of Unreason*, 248–257; Davis (ed.), *The Fear of Conspiracy*, 35–42, 327–336.

11. Lipset and Raab, *The Politics of Unreason*, 269; Houston *Post*, April 8, 1961; Morris, "Houston's Superpatriots," 49.

12. Houston *Post*, April 8, 1961, October 3, 1965; Morris, "Houston's Superpatriots," 49, and "Tormented Atmosphere of Houston," *The Texas Observer*, June 17, 1961, 1.

13. *The Texas Observer*, July 15, 1961, 7; Morris, "Tormented Atmosphere of Houston," 6.

14. Barry Kaplan, "Urban Development, Economic Growth, and Personal Liberty: The Rhetoric of the Houston Anti-Zoning Movements, 1947–1962," *Southwestern Historical Quarterly* 84 (October 1980): 161.

15. Willie Morris, "Tormented Atmosphere of Houston," *The Texas Observer*, July 8, 1961, "Houston's Superpatriots," 48, and *North toward Home* (New York, 1967), 266.

16. Houston *Chronicle*, May 7, 1961; Morris, "Houston's Superpatriots," 52-53.

17. Lipset and Raab, *The Politics of Unreason*, 251; Frances Fitzgerald, "The Triumphs of the New Right," *New York Review of Books*, November 19, 1981, 23.

18. Epstein and Forster, *The Radical Right*, 199; Alan Crawford, *Thunder on the Right: The "New" Right and the Politics of Resentment* (New York, 1980), 4-5.

19. McComb, *Houston*, 142; interview with J. R. Parten; Houston *Post*, December 31, 1961, November 3, 1966, June 9, 1969; interview with Marguerite Johnston.

20. For popular perceptions about the connection between the Radical Right's activities and Kennedy's assassination, see Leslie, *Dallas Public and Private* and Arthur M. Schlesinger, Jr., *A Thousand Days: John F. Kennedy in the White House* (New York, 1983), 1024-1025; Lipset and Raab, *The Politics of Unreason*, 270.

21. Lipset and Raab, *The Politics of Unreason*, 352-353; Crawford, *Thunder on the Right*, 123-125.

22. Fitzgerald, "The Triumphs of the New Right," 19-26; Richard Sennett, "Power to the People," *New York Review of Books*, September 25, 1980, 24-26. For more on Reagan's use of McCarthyism, see Ronnie Dugger, *On Reagan: The Man and His Presidency* (New York, 1983), 268-284.

23. Dugger, "150,000 Young Minds," 8; interviews with several HISD teachers who prefer to remain anonymous.

24. These observations are based on the author's experience as a student teacher in the HISD during the 1968-1969 school year and interviews with various HISD teachers (1969-1972) and students. The persistence of political pressure and teacher fears in the early 1970s was vividly revealed by the fact that teachers still refused to allow their names to be used in this study. The Galambos quote is from his article, "New Ideas and Extremism in Schools," *The Texas Observer*, May 1, 1964, 10-11.

25. "Man Named Magruder, the DAR, and a Quiet Textbook Controversy," *The Texas Observer*, June 13, 1955, 6.

26. *Austin American-Statesman*, November 12, 1982; Crawford, *Thunder on the Right*, 37, 157; Houston *Chronicle*, October 28, 1981.

27. "George Garver," Vertical File Collection, HMRC.

28. McComb, *Houston*, 168; Houston *Chronicle*, July 31, 1975.

29. Talcott Parsons, "Social Strains in America," in Daniel Bell (ed.), *The Radical Right* (New York, 1964), 217-218.

30. White, "Texas," 34.

31. Lipset and Raab, *The Politics of Unreason*, 7, 215.

32. For the Red Scare in Dallas, see "Red Art Onslaught Hot," *The Texas*

Observer, February 15, 1956, 6, and Leslie, *Dallas Public and Private*, 116. For San Antonio, see *New York Times*, June 7, 1953, and Maverick, "San Antonio," 12–13.

33. *The Daily Texan*, October 26, 1983.

34. *New York Times*, December 14, 1983.

INDEX

—